BRITISH WAR AIMS
AND PEACE DIPLOMACY
1914-1918

BRITISH WAR AIMS
AND PEACE DIPLOMACY
1914-1918

V. H. ROTHWELL

CLARENDON PRESS · OXFORD
1971

Oxford University Press, Ely House, London W.1

GLASGOW   NEW YORK   TORONTO   MELBOURNE   WELLINGTON
CAPE TOWN   SALISBURY   IBADAN   NAIROBI   DAR ES SALAAM   LUSAKA   ADDIS ABABA
BOMBAY   CALCUTTA   MADRAS   KARACHI   LAHORE   DACCA
KUALA LUMPUR   SINGAPORE   HONG KONG   TOKYO

PRINTED IN GREAT BRITAIN
BY THE UNIVERSITY PRESS
ABERDEEN

PREFACE

I wish to express my thanks to Professor John Grenville for suggesting the subject of this book to me and for giving me unstinting help throughout the process of research and writing. I must also thank two of my contemporaries as researchers into British history during the First World War, Dr. Michael Ekstein Frankl and Dr. John Stone. I think that our many conversations were mutually beneficial; they were certainly so for me. Professor Douglas Dakin and the staff of the Clarendon Press made a number of useful suggestions for improvement. However, I am solely responsible for the contents of this book.

I have to thank the following for permission to inspect and to quote documents in which they hold the copyright: the Trustees of the British Museum; Lord Robertson of Oakridge and the Trustees of the Centre for Military Archives, King's College, University of London; the Warden and Fellows of New College, Oxford; Mr. A. J. P. Taylor and the First Beaverbrook Foundation; *The Spectator*; Professor A. K. Lambton and Mr. F. Noel Baker; the Honourable Godfrey Samuel and the Clerk of the House of Lords Record Office; Mr. L. P. Scott; and Lord Ponsonby of Shulbrede Priory. Unpublished Crown-copyright material in the Public Record Office has been reproduced by permission of the Controller of H.M. Stationery Office. Finally, I am grateful to Messrs. Putnam and Co. for permission to quote a passage from *An Ambassador in Bonds* by Sir Lancelot Oliphant.

Edinburgh,
September 1970.   V. H. ROTHWELL

116116

CONTENTS

viii   *Contents*

NOTE ON REFERENCES

THE abbreviations CAB, FO, WO, ADM, BT and CO in the footnotes refer to the Cabinet, Foreign Office, War Office, Admiralty, Board of Trade and Colonial Office papers in the Public Records Office. The location of a collection of documents may in all cases be ascertained by reference to the Bibliography. Where, as is frequently the case except in parliamentary debates, the text of a public speech has been taken from *The Times* of the following day no source is given in the footnote reference.

INTRODUCTION

THIS work is a history of British official thinking on war aims in the First World War and of the British part in the attempts which were made to end the war by negotiation. These attempts concerned Germany less than they concerned her smaller allies—Austria–Hungary, Turkey and Bulgaria.

It would be well to make clear the subjects with which the work does not treat and does not purport to treat. It largely neglects internal pressures from unofficial sources on the formulation of war aims, partly because much has been written on this,[1] and partly because the author has come to believe that these pressures were less important than the preconceptions of the leaders and their response to the military situation and to the policies of their allies. It is interesting to note that Professor Renouvin has recently expressed a similar conclusion.[2] Where internal pressures are vital as in understanding Lloyd George's war aims speech of 5 January 1918, they are discussed.

Secondly, there is no attempt at a major reassessment of relations between the British government and the Arab nationalist and Zionist movements though the author has written elsewhere on an associated subject.[3] British policy toward the German colonies is not dealt with in detail owing directly to the appearance of a scholarly monograph on the subject.[4] Finally, there is no comparative assessment of the war aims of the different belligerents in these pages. Readers will agree that such a synthesis would warrant a full work in itself. In essence, this study discusses *why* the British leadership—ministers, civil servants, generals and admirals—thought that the defeat of Germany was necessary and justified, and *how* they sought to make peace with her smaller allies. The two subjects cannot really be treated apart. What the British wanted

[1] See the works by H. Hanak, L. Martin, A. J. Mayer, H. M. Pelling, A. J. P. Taylor (*The Troublemakers*) and H. R. Winkler cited in the Bibliography.

[2] P. Renouvin, 'L'Opinion Publique et la Guerre en 1917' in *Revue d'Histoire Moderne et Contemporaine*, xv (1968), 4 ff., especially p. 22.

[3] V. H. Rothwell, 'Mesopotamia in British War Aims 1914–1918', *Historical Journal*, xiii (1970), 273–94.

[4] W. R. Louis, *Great Britain and Germany's Lost Colonies 1914–1919* (1967).

above all in the Great War was the defeat of Germany and there was much feeling—as strong in the General Staff as anywhere—that a separate peace with at least one of her allies was essential for such victory. Likewise, the War Cabinet debates and episodes in diplomacy which are the main concern of the work cannot be understood without reference to the military history of the war. It is hoped that readers will feel that this necessary background has been adequately sketched.

During the first two years of the war the British government under Asquith were unwilling to formulate any war aims other than the defeat of Germany and the restoration of Belgium. Accordingly, this history begins in detail only in the middle months of 1916 when attempts began in earnest to define more detailed objectives.

These attempts left open the question of what precisely constituted a war aim. Even senior professional officials in the British Foreign Office were not sure. This is illustrated by a debate which took place within the office in the autumn of 1917 when a Polish National Council of nationalist exiles requested the British government for recognition with the obvious ultimate aim of securing an undertaking that Britain would be prepared to prolong the war, if necessary, in order to achieve Polish independence.

J. D. Gregory, the Poland specialist at the Foreign Office, wrote that the allies would probably find it physically impossible to defeat Germany to the point where she was prepared to cede the Polish-speaking parts of Germany to a Polish state and, in any case,

It is clear that not one of the allies would be willing to prolong the war by a day in order to do so.

We can hardly, therefore, declare it to be 'one of the essential objects of the war', as in that case we should be bound to go on until we had achieved it.

A war aim is something which we intend or hope to attain either by fighting or by negotiation and it is inconceivable that Polish unity can be solved by the latter method.

Gregory concluded that the wisdom of declaring Polish independence to be among allied war aims was doubtful since any declaration could only be 'a pious aspiration'. George Russell Clerk, one of Gregory's seniors, demurred from this analysis:

I think that what the Poles, be they the Polish National Council or Poles in general, want is a definite statement from the allies that they consider the creation of a free and united Poland, with access to the sea, desirable and just in itself and that to the best of their power they will aid the Poles in achieving this object. This does not seem to me to commit the allies to fighting until Germany is so utterly defeated as to admit of the creation of such a Poland, but it does mean that the sympathies of the allies are with the Poles in their efforts to attain this result. I do not see that there is any ground for a charge of bad faith in enunciating such an aspiration, though its realization may at the moment seem hardly within the bounds of possibility, while on the other hand it is important to let the Poles realize that in struggling for their independence they are, in the opinion of the allies, fighting in a just cause and in the interests of permanent peace in Europe. A Polish army fighting in France helps to weaken Germany and thereby not only helps the allies as a whole but also helps Poland. Nobody can expect the war to continue until all the allies have attained all their war aims, but that need not prevent them from setting those aims before their eyes and doing their utmost towards attaining them.

The Permanent Under-Secretary, Lord Hardinge, uttered the last word: 'So long as it is only a pious aspiration it does not much matter what is said'.[5]

The debate ended at this rather inconclusive point. However, behind Clerk's glosses and Hardinge's bluntness, the presupposition was clearly that any British commitments to the Poles and, un-doubtedly, to other peoples whose future was at stake in the Great War, were moves in the struggle against Germany and did not bind Britain to anything. This was certainly the opinion of almost all ministers of the Crown in Britain during the war and of the large majority of their leading advisers. Their supreme war aim was to inflict defeat on a nation, Germany, which they considered guilty of aggression and to teach it that aggression was profitless. As William Robertson put it in 1917: 'Our aim is, as I understand it, to deal German despotism such a blow as will for generations to come prevent a recurrence of the horrors of the last two and a half years.[6] The parallel with the policy of the United States in its more recent war in Vietnam is so obvious that one hesitates to state it.

This attitude and the associated questions of British relations with the United States and policy toward the League of Nations are discussed at length in the body of this work. Here it must be emphasized that the British leaders had no doubt that their cause

[5] Minutes by Gregory and Clerk, 3 Oct. 1917, and Hardinge, no date, FO 371/3001, no. 189230.   [6] Speech by Robertson to munitions workers, 4 Apr. 1917.

was righteous. This stemmed to a large extent from a belief that Britain was the innocent and Germany the guilty party in the outbreak of war. When after the armistice of 1918, the German government suggested that an international committee should be set up to examine responsibility for the outbreak of the war, Eric Drummond wrote: 'It is good to think that we have nothing to fear from full publication' (of relevant documents).[7] The existence of this attitude is essential to an understanding of British policy toward Germany between 1914 and 1918. It helps to account for Lord Hardinge's apparently childish remark that he had known the Kaiser for thirty years and, 'I used to rather like him in some ways but I can only regard him as an arch-fiend at present.'[8]

British leaders were prepared to pay a very large price for the defeat of Germany in terms of international power politics. In 1917, brooding over the world situation after his departure from the Foreign Office, Edward Grey perceived the passing of the European age in world history: 'After this war, even the Great Powers of Europe will be too weakened in comparison with the United States and Japan to dominate the world.'[9]

Under the Asquith government the structure of control in Britain's international relations was relatively simple. Foreign policy was controlled by Edward Grey as Foreign Secretary working on friendly if slightly distant terms with the Prime Minister. Grey exercised his power within limits. He could not go as far as he would have liked in seeking good relations with the United States owing to the attitude of his colleagues; and he did not feel able to contradict the government's military and naval advisers when they said that complete allied victory was certain provided that the nation made the necessary efforts, even though he did not think that this was a sound assumption on which to base policy. However, Grey's was the guiding hand in foreign policy. He certainly was not a puppet in the hands of professional advisers. Indeed, during most of his war-time tenure of the Foreign Secretaryship before Hardinge's return as Permanent Under-Secretary in June 1916 he did not have a really close adviser among the senior staff of the office except possibly Eric Drummond.

[7] Minute by Drummond, *c.* 5 Dec. 1918, FO 371/3451, no. 199873.
[8] Hardinge to Lord Crewe, 8 Oct. 1914, Hardinge MSS. CXX, part II, no. 51.
[9] Grey to J. St. Loe Strachey, 30 Oct. 1917, Strachey MSS.

The Lloyd George government which took office in December 1916 ushered in a more complex regime. The government itself consisted of a War Cabinet of only four members in addition to the Prime Minister: Andrew Bonar Law, the leader of the Conservative party, Arthur Henderson, the most outstanding of those Labour politicians who had clearly identified themselves with support for the war, and two Conservative elder statesmen, Lord Curzon and Lord Milner. The Foreign Secretary, Arthur James Balfour, was a member in all but name. The original War Cabinet underwent two losses—those of Henderson who resigned in August 1917 and of Milner when he became Secretary of State for War in April 1918. Also there were four additions—those of General Smuts (June 1917), Edward Carson (a member from July 1917 to January 1918), George Barnes who succeeded Henderson as Labour representative, and Austen Chamberlain who took Milner's place in 1918. Two other men who figure prominently in these pages, General Robertson and Lord Robert Cecil, treated themselves as full members whenever they thought that it was in the public interest that they should do so.

Lloyd George's position in this government was very much that of *primus inter pares*. Its Conservative members represented perhaps half the British nation whereas Lloyd George had the support of only a fraction of his own Liberal party and only a very uncertain and limited measure of Labour support. This obviously gave great power to the Conservatives. Several times between 1917 and 1919 at conferences abroad Lloyd George said to Balfour's secretary, Ian Malcolm, that he could not have carried on if he had not had full confidence in Bonar Law's power and will to manage the House of Commons while he was away.[10] In addition, the Prime Minister dreamed of a 'National Party' whose members would probably be mostly Conservatives but which would serve as a means for him to retain the premiership after the war.[11] Lloyd George could take no major decisions without the assent of at least some of his colleagues.[12]

[10] Ian Malcolm, *Vacant Thrones* (1931), pp. 64–5.
[11] Trevor Wilson, *The Downfall of the Liberal Party* (1966), pp. 120–7.
[12] I cannot agree with the view put forward by Dr. Kenneth O. Morgan that 'at the level of central decision-making . . . Lloyd George's wartime supremacy was generally beyond challenge.' Dr. Morgan goes on to concede that Lloyd George was always acutely aware that he lacked a solid party base and to write: 'It is, however, by the peacetime premiership of 1918–22 that the claim . . . that Lloyd George inaugurated a new era of prime ministerial government must be tested.' Kenneth O. Morgan, 'Lloyd George's Premiership: A Study in Prime Ministerial Government', *Historical Journal*, xiii (1970), pp. 130–57, especially pp. 138, 141–2, 156–7.

He had also to keep a wary eye on the Liberals outside the government, led by Asquith, who courted the support of the General Staff and who twice refused offers to join the War Cabinet.[13]

Twice, in March and April 1917 and in the summer of 1918, the War Cabinet was expanded into an Imperial War Cabinet which included prime ministers and leading ministers from the Dominions (Canada, Australia, South Africa, New Zealand and Newfoundland) and certain dignitaries who were held to represent the non-self-governing Empire of India. In view of the immense contribution which the 'Empire' as it then was still usually called was making to the war effort, its leaders had the moral and political right to make their influence felt wherever they chose. They were always concerned that the German colonies, especially those occupied by South Africa, Australia and New Zealand, should remain in allied hands. In this way they betrayed, to Lloyd George's mind, a narrow and mistaken conception of war aims. In 1918, most of them, especially the Canadians, added their voices to those which called for the abandonment of the western strategy, a development highly relevant to war aims.[14]

Beneath this structure, there were several sources of power including the government's advisers in the Admiralty and the War Office. The admirals did not make their influence appreciably felt until the possibility of an armistice with Germany was imminent. They then struggled mightily to ensure that the government would insist upon terms which would cripple German naval power forever.[15]

Pressure from the high command of the army was much more frequent and when one speaks of the army, it is almost possible to refer solely to the chief of the Imperial General Staff—from the end of 1915 to February 1918 General William Robertson. Appointed to that office on terms which made him the sole source of professional military advice to the government and which practically usurped the functions of the secretary of state for war, Robertson took a broad view of his powers. He rejected the view of his office according to which he should simply give advice and then leave it to ministers to accept or reject that advice. He argued strongly for the acceptance of his views and was in effect a senior member of the War Cabinet.[16]

[13] Wilson, op. cit. pp. 122–4.   [14] See Chapter V: 2 below.
[15] See Chapter VI: 2 below.
[16] W. R. Robertson, *From Private to Field Marshal* (1921), p. 255.

It was inevitable that Robertson should have clashed with a Prime Minister who held totally opposed views on strategy. Robertson supported and championed the views of the General Staff and the British High Command in France that the war could only be won on the Western Front, that all the British Empire's military resources should be concentrated there except such as were essential to defend such imperial interests as the Suez Canal, and that the strategy of attrition, wearing down the Germans with constant attacks which did not produce dramatic results was, no matter how costly, necessary to demoralize and weaken the enemy and make final victory possible. This was the western school of strategy. Its opponents, of whom the most eminent was Lloyd George, believed that it was doubtful whether victory could be attained on the Western Front, that it was in any case certain that victory there would be prohibitively costly in human lives, and that a decision should be sought through the elimination of Germany's allies. A Germany demoralized and economically weakened by their loss would then probably acknowledge defeat. Even if this did not happen, large amounts of territory would be occupied and preserved from German domination after the war.

The westerners rejected this 'eastern' case, arguing that allied victories against Austria and Turkey and in the Balkans would not affect Germany seriously and that she would very probably be able to prevent them by moving in troops from her superior logistic position in the heart of Europe.[17] Lloyd George was always reluctant to impose his strategical views. Partly this was the result of the difficulty of finding alternative military leaders and of fear of the reaction from his colleagues and from public opinion if he attempted to enforce changes. He sometimes expressed surprise that his government had lasted as long as it had.[18] It is also possible that he lacked complete confidence in his own judgement despite the fervent terms in which he advocated the eastern strategy.[19]

Even today it is difficult for the historian not to feel involved in these debates on which depended the lives of many thousands of men and the defeat of what is now generally recognized as a German attempt to become the strongest power in the world. Fortunately, perhaps, this strategic debate is not of direct relevance to the present

[17] See Victor Bonham-Carter, *Soldier True* (1963), pp. 107–9 for a moderate and persuasive statement of the western case.   [18] Lord Riddell, *War Diary* (1933), p. 330.
[19] Cf. J. M. Kenworthy, *Soldiers, Sailors and Others* (1933), pp. 76, 81.

work. However, its outline is essential to an understanding of the strange paradox that in 1917–18 many civilian ministers wished to eliminate the lesser enemy states by combined military and diplomatic action while the General Staff were insistent that this desirable result must be achieved by diplomatic pressure only.

Setting aside the strategic debate, it was still more important that Robertson, though he wavered slightly in the terrible winter of 1917–18, was adamant that military victory over Germany was essential for the British Empire and that any suggestion to the contrary was treason. The leaders of the British Army were held in enormous popular prestige during the First World War and if they had appealed to the country against a hint from the government that they were prepared to consider a negotiated peace, it is impossible to calculate what the results would have been. Robertson certainly did not rule out military intervention in politics as unthinkable. As early as March 1916, he observed to General Murray, the commander in Egypt, 'Practically anything may happen to our boasted British Constitution before this war ends and the great asset is the army—whose value will be fixed largely by the extent to which we at the top stick together and stand firm.'[20] The knowledge that Robertson and almost all other senior officers favoured a *guerre à l'outrance* undoubtedly had a restraining influence on ministers who otherwise might have been more ready to consider a negotiated settlement with Germany. The years 1916 and 1917 in British history were in a real sense the age of Robertson.

If war-time conditions gave the chief of the General Staff extraordinary control over national policy, Lloyd George had the assistance of others whose advice and help he found infinitely more congenial. There is a legend that under Lloyd George Britain was governed by two men, the Prime Minister and whoever had spoken to him most recently. The author of this jibe was responsible for a very perceptive half-truth. Lloyd George had little inclination and less time to formulate policies in his own mind. No doubt recognizing this, he was ready to listen to advice from anyone, from Maurice Hankey, the Secretary of the War Cabinet, downwards, who could gain access to him. The most celebrated of his war-time

[20] Robertson to Murray, 8 Mar. 1916 in *Egypt 1916–1917: Private Letters between General Sir Archibald Murray and General Sir William Robertson* (privately printed, 1932), B. M. Add. MS. 52463, p. 47.

initiatives, the institution of convoy in 1917, would in all probability not have been achieved but for the prodding and tactical advice of Hankey and a number of naval officers.[21]

The existence of Lloyd George's 'Garden Suburb' or personal secretariat of advisers is well-known. One of its most notable members, Leo Amery, realized that under the new Prime Minister he would have a heyday. In 1917, he wrote to his political teacher, Lord Milner, 'I think that our Round Table friends are not really abreast of the times in the exaggerated stress they lay on "influence not being government". In the complications of modern affairs a thought out policy is so important that whoever controls the thinking department and supplies the ideas eventually controls the administration.'[22]

The preference for advice from such quarters had many aspects. The great hope of most 'Garden Suburb' members was that the war might be used to foster the unity of Britain and her overseas dominions and this encouraged an attitude of indifference to the peace settlement on the continent of Europe—especially east-central Europe—always excluding Belgium. In the actual conduct of foreign policy, Lloyd George preferred to do business either by dealing directly with foreign statesmen at the almost innumerable inter-allied conferences held during the war or by sending ministers like Smuts and Milner and senior advisers like Philip Kerr on missions. Sometimes he chose to deal personally with foreigners such as the Bourbon prince, Sixte, and the Greek armaments manufacturer, Basil Zaharoff. Indeed, Lloyd George was prepared to conduct foreign policy through almost any channel except the Foreign Office. He disliked diplomats on the whole and thought that their methods were time-consuming and ineffective. 'I want no diplomats', he told Sixte, 'diplomats were invented simply to waste time.'[23] Hence it must be understood that after Lloyd George's advent to power, Britain had two foreign policies, those of the Prime Minister and of the Foreign Office.

The lack of regard for the Prime Minister in the Foreign Office becomes fully intelligible in this context. One of its mildest mani-festations was the frequent practice of referring to him as 'the little

[21] Cf. Captain Roskill's letter to *The Times*, 16 Nov. 1968. Captain Roskill has since discussed this point in considerable detail in *Hankey: Man of Secrets: Vol. I 1877–1918* (1970), pp. 355–8, 379–84, 389–90.

[22] Amery to Milner, 10 July 1917, CAB 17/190.

[23] G. De Manteyer, *Austria's Peace Offer* (1921), p. 168.

man' in which even Arthur Balfour indulged.[24] Whatever may be thought of this incivility, it is difficult not to feel that the office had a legitimate grievance that, as one of its members once said, it was possible for someone to 'have a diplomatic position without the Foreign Office knowing anything about it'.[25]

Sometimes the twain met as when Lord Reading was appointed High Commissioner to the United States. He had the confidence of Lloyd George but he worked with and through the Foreign Office. Often, however, it did not and the office was left with a disheartening feeling that it was working to no purpose. It is small wonder that Lord Eustace Percy, one of the most able of its relatively junior members, was to characterize the Lloyd George government as 'a driverless team of horses'.[26]

Within the Foreign Office itself the power structure under Balfour was equally intricate. In discussing the policies of this legendary man, it is not always easy to avoid treating him as, in the words of Lord Bertie, a 'philosophic idler'[27] who was content to leave real power in the hands of nominal subordinates. Balfour did, truly, lead a wonderful social life. In the words of his war-time parliamentary private secretary and devoted admirer, Sir Ian Malcolm, 'He was the great social ornament of a London that admired brains and appreciated wit, elegance and charm.'[28] Yet this did not make him a dilettante. He worked relentlessly hard as Foreign Secretary, invariably observed a six-day week,[29] and would brook no attempts to reverse those aspects of foreign policy to which he attached real importance. In addition, his personally good relations with Lloyd George and the constant availability of Maurice Hankey as a channel of communication and co-ordination with the Prime Minister prevented the emergence of a public schism between Lloyd George and the Foreign Office even when they were pursuing parallel but separate foreign policies.

Balfour's main concerns in foreign policy were, briefly, that it was essential, unless physically impossible, to defeat Germany in the

[24] B. E. C. Dugdale, *Arthur James Balfour* (1936), ii. 182.

[25] Ronald Graham to Lord Bertie, 10 Jan. 1918, FO 800/175.

[26] E. Percy, *Some Memories* (1958), pp. 54–5.

[27] Lady Algernon Gordon Lennox, ed., *The Diary of Lord Bertie of Thame* (1924), ii. 99, entry for 30 Dec. 1916.

[28] Ian Malcolm, *Lord Balfour: A Memory* (1930), p. 33.

[29] Ibid. pp. 38–9.

interests of the future security of the British Empire, and that the best if not the only prospects for future peace in the world lay in a permanent Anglo-American alliance. A large number of subsidiary policies could be added; one, which is of particular relevance to this book, was that the price of weaning away Germany's allies would be too high if it involved incurring the hostility of Britain's present allies. The place of Anglo-American relations in Balfour's thinking was so central that it cannot be overemphasized. A little after the armistice in 1918 he responded to a suggestion from the French ambassador that Britain and France should settle the terms of peace before the peace conference so as to exclude the United States from effective participation by saying that it was 'little short of insanity' and that the maximum degree of American participation in world affairs was wholly desirable.[30]

Under both Grey and Balfour, the professional staff at the Foreign Office could control policy only in small matters. There was an instance in February 1916 when Grey informed a leading member of his staff, Lancelot Oliphant, that the government had decided to hand the whole of the German colony of Cameroon, which had been conquered by British and French forces, over to French administration as a means of raising France's morale. Oliphant was asked to inform Picot, a French diplomat who was in London to discuss the future of the Ottoman Empire with Mark Sykes, accordingly. Oliphant later recalled:

Whether owing to my ancestry, my time in oriental bazaars or sheer cussedness I can't say, but this idea did not appeal to me. I said, therefore, that while I would, of course, carry out his instructions yet I would ask permission to be allowed to give M. Picot only as much of the Kamerun as he might wish. The Secretary of State approved my doing this provided I made no attempt to haggle. I readily agreed. I then invited M. Picot to come and see me and in the meantime asked Mr. Strachie of the Colonial Office to bring over some maps of the Kamerun. On M. Picot's arrival I laid out the maps and said I would be grateful if he would show us exactly what part of the Kamerun the French would like, supposing I were in a position to meet their wishes.

Now M. Picot was a good patriot: but even so it never dawned on him to ask for the whole of the Kamerun. He therefore traced on the map an enormous area of about 143,000 square miles or four-fifths of that

[30] Balfour to Lloyd George, 29 Nov. 1918, FO 800/199.

country. I then said I was happy to be able to agree then and there to this proposal and asked him to inform his government accordingly. He went away entirely satisfied and left me no less content. A strip of land had been saved for the Empire amounting to over 34,000 square miles (bigger that is than Scotland or twice as big as Denmark or Switzerland) marching with the whole eastern frontier of Nigeria.[31]

In this way a member of the Foreign Service brought it about that for the next forty-five years some hundreds of thousands of Africans would be ruled by Britain and not by France. (Oliphant's work did not prove permanent; in 1960–1 French Cameroon and most of British Cameroon were reunited in a single independent state.) In larger matters most members of the office were actually happy to have chiefs who led. Hardinge was clear where his duty lay. While still Viceroy he wrote: 'There should be only one policy i.e. the policy of the Secretary of State, to be carried out by the Permanent Under-Secretary after full discussion with his chief.'[32] His reaction to Balfour's appointment as Foreign Secretary was that since he was old and in poor health it would probably fall to Hardinge himself to 'run most of the business as I am now doing. I am careful, however, to leave to him the final decision on all questions of policy.'[33] Some eighteen months later, he reaffirmed: 'All decisions in questions of high policy have in the end to be submitted to the approval of the Secretary of State.'[34]

However, the burden of work at the office increased enormously during the war. Between 1914 and 1916 the number of staff rose from 150 to 500 and the number of telegrams received to 300 daily.[35] The result was that much of importance could not be referred to the

---

[31] L. Oliphant, *An Ambassador in Bonds* (1947), pp. 34–5. Corroborative evidence for the above account of this episode is to be found in a minute by Oliphant, 25 June 1918, FO 371/3128, no. 112912, which gives an account similar to the one above. See also War Committee, 22 Feb. 1916, CAB 42/9/3, for the decision to accede to French claims in Cameroon. Oliphant may have exaggerated his role in this matter; the line of only offering the French as much of the Cameroon as they requested was agreed upon at an inter-departmental meeting of officials before Oliphant met Picot. It was recognized that this was a departure from the War Committee decision. Record of this meeting in a memorandum by A. J. Harding of the Colonial Office, 11 Jan. 1917, FO 371/2859 no. 161193. There is an account of the transfer of most of Cameroon to France in Louis, op. cit. pp. 60–2, but this is incomplete and makes no reference to the aspects of the episode discussed above.

[32] Hardinge to G. B. Allen, 28 Apr. 1915, Hardinge MSS. XCIII, part II, no. 328.

[33] Hardinge to V. Chirol, 4 Jan. 1917, Hardinge MSS. XXIX.

[34] Hardinge to R. Wingate, 25 July 1918, Hardinge MSS. XXXVIII.

[35] Lord Hardinge, *Old Diplomacy* (1947), p. 197.

Foreign Secretary and had to be dealt with by the staff and by Lord Robert Cecil as Balfour's assistant on the basis of what was known in general about the attitudes of the War Cabinet and the Foreign Secretary. Cecil minuted the draft answer to a parliamentary question in November 1918: 'Mr. Balfour *must* see this answer before it is given.'[36] The inference can clearly be drawn that answers to parliamentary questions on foreign policy were sometimes drawn up and given without Balfour having seen them.

Throughout the two years and more with which this book is chiefly concerned the atmosphere within the office was made less pleasant than it would have been by a clash of personalities between the Foreign Secretary's two chief assistants, Hardinge, and Lord Robert Cecil who had entered the office as Grey's parliamentary under-secretary in May 1915. Cecil was Minister of Blockade from February 1916 to July 1918 and was then appointed Assistant Secretary of State, ranking directly after Balfour. Despite the importance of his blockade duties, he took a hand in most aspects of foreign policy from the time of his entry into the office and especially after his uncle, Balfour, became Foreign Secretary. Whatever the original reasons for their hostility—perhaps nothing more than a feeling of jealousy on Hardinge's part that he was exercising less power than during his earlier tenure as Permanent Under-Secretary from 1906 to 1910—it became serious in the summer of 1918 when both appealed to Balfour, then on holiday at his country residence in Scotland, for different nominees to be appointed chief civil servant in a new Middle East Department within the Foreign Office of which Cecil was to be head. Cecil himself favoured Eyre Crowe whereas Hardinge wanted the post to go to Ronald Graham.[37]

Cecil had his way and Hardinge's criticisms of him became outspoken. He was, 'An able man, but all the Cecils are in my opinion cranks and very few of them know what it is to be straight. Even the great Lord Salisbury, for whom I had the very greatest respect, was an unblushing liar when it suited his purpose.'[38] It seems possible that Cecil had given a promise at some time in the past that Graham should have the Middle East job and had then broken it. Robert Cecil was an outstanding public servant who never acted out of mean

[36] Minute by Cecil, *c.* 5 Nov. 1918, FO 371/3449, no. 185754.
[37] Cf. Hardinge to Cecil, 20 Aug. 1918, and Balfour to Drummond and Hardinge, 28 Aug. 1918, Balfour MSS., B.M. Add. 49745; Cecil to Balfour, 21, 23 and 31 Aug. 1918, B.M. Add. 49738.
[38] Hardinge to Wingate, 28 Nov. 1918, Hardinge MSS. XXXIX.

or petty motives but he did not feel bound by the rules of strict honesty when there was a question of preferring an individual whom he considered to be mediocre or of carrying out a policy which he considered to be detrimental to the interests of the State.

Another powerful man who was, however, in the fortunate position that he enjoyed the respect and goodwill of almost everyone was Eric Drummond, successively private secretary to Asquith, Grey and then Balfour. The Balfour papers in the Public Record Office[39] show Drummond giving advice to the Foreign Secretary on countless occasions and usually having it accepted. How far Drummond initiated policy and how far he merely advised in the sense of translating what he knew to be in Balfour's mind into a practical suggestion for dealing with a given situation can often not be ascertained, but it is doubtful whether any British Foreign Secretary has ever had a more competent or loyal aide than Eric Drummond.

Other senior Foreign Office men who were much concerned in aspects of foreign policy which are discussed in these pages included George Russell Clerk, Lancelot Oliphant, Ronald Graham, Maurice De Bunsen, Louis Mallet and, rather less senior than these, J. D. Gregory. On a lesser level, certain young men—Harold Nicolson, Lord Drogheda, Howard Smith and Laurence Collier—who enjoyed the confidence of their superiors were at various times employed to carry out the rather tedious work of drafting letters and telegrams and collating information on matters of current interest. However, they were far too junior to have a voice in policy. Most of these men worked in the War Department of the Foreign Office which was set up in 1914 to handle political relations, as opposed to matters connected with the economic blockade, with most countries in the world.

Two men who had once been powers in the Foreign Office, William Tyrrell and Eyre Crowe, made a come-back during the last three years of the war. Without discussing the reasons—essentially lapses of character[40]—for their temporary eclipse, it may be pointed out that as early as 1916 Tyrrell, who had been one of Grey's closest advisers,[41] was carrying out highly secret work on the formulation

---

[39] FO 800/199 ff.

[40] There was no question of Crowe losing favour because his wife and mother were German. Grey, at a time when he was not well-disposed toward Crowe for quite other reasons, deplored the campaign against him on these grounds by some newspapers and demagogic orators; cf. Grey's minute, *c.* 19 Nov. 1915, FO 800/243.

[41] Cf. Zara Steiner, 'Grey, Hardinge and the Foreign Office 1906–10' in *Historical Journal*, x (1967), 415–40.

of war aims. Crowe made a slower recovery but a sure one owing to the favour with which Cecil regarded him at the Ministry of Blockade. By the beginning of 1918 he had returned to the political work which was his only true interest. He was a member of the Phillimore committee on the league of nations, assumed important responsibilities in Middle East policy and played a role in the armistice negotiations.

Finally, mention must be made of the innovation of the Political Intelligence Department[42] and the work of Mark Sykes. A negotiator of the Sykes-Picot agreement of 1916 and later the Lloyd George government's chief adviser on Middle East policy, Sykes was employed in the War Cabinet Secretariat (not to be confused with the 'Garden Suburb'). He worked in co-operation with the Foreign Office and was *persona grata* there even if his judgement was not always trusted. He was chiefly concerned with matters outside the scope of this work—relations with Arab nationalists and Zionists—and figures here chiefly as an opponent of a negotiated peace with Turkey.

On British diplomats overseas, less need be said. Sir Francis (later Lord) Bertie, ambassador in Paris, was as senior as anyone in the Foreign Office hierarchy and liked to make his influence felt. He was known as 'the Bull' to his subordinates owing to his habit of storming into a room with masculine vigour almost oozing from his person.[43] In 1916 he intrigued with Asquith against Grey,[44] but his influence waned under Lloyd George. It was characteristic of that Prime Minister's attitude toward diplomacy that he regarded the Paris embassy as a convenient dumping-ground for an unwanted cabinet minister. He put it to this use in April 1918 when Lord Derby was sent there to make way for an abler man, Milner, at the War Office.

George Buchanan in Petrograd was a central figure in British foreign policy during the first two years of the war but by the middle of 1916 he was receding in importance owing to the decline of Russian power. Rennell Rodd in Rome lost much of his authority owing to his unfashionable sympathy with Italian war aims. The sad story of Sir Cecil Spring-Rice's failure to 'get on' with President Wilson is well-known.[45] In these pages little new is said either about

---

[42] See Chapter V: 2 below for a full discussion.
[43] Cf. David Kelly, *The Ruling Few* (1952), p. 182.   [44] See below, p. 41.
[45] See Spring-Rice's own testimony in S. Gwynne, ed., *The Letters and Friendships of Sir Cecil Spring-Rice* (1929), ii. 313–14, 366–8, 372.

that or about Britain's more successful attempts to establish real contact with the United States Administration after America entered the war. Lord Reading as High Commissioner and Ambassador and the British agent, William Wiseman, won the esteem of Woodrow Wilson and his confidant, Colonel Edward M. House—which was no mean feat—and were able to talk to them man-to-man, though Reading was disappointed that Wilson and House did not take him completely into their confidence so that he was substantially dependent on Wiseman.[46]

Less important than Reading but perhaps more important than any ambassador in 1917 or 1918 was the minister in Berne, Horace Rumbold. He was sent there in 1916, in place of an indifferent predecessor, to collect information about the enemy states and to report upon and deal with peace feelers from them, the majority of which throughout the war were put forward in Switzerland. Rumbold did his delicate work well. His superiors in the Foreign Office had no criticism to make of him.

Personalities were, of course, important in the conduct of foreign policy. Lord Robert Cecil and Lord Hardinge came from similar social backgrounds, generally saw eye-to-eye on policy and were both very able—which did not prevent them from disliking one another. Likewise, Hardinge's undoubted wish that Ronald Graham should eventually become Permanent Under-Secretary sprang not only from a high estimate of Graham's own qualities but also from Hardinge's admiration—entirely platonic and honourable—for Graham's wife, Sybil. What makes it possible to speak of a composite Foreign Office view on most questions is the authority actually exercised by Balfour as Foreign Secretary together with a genuine unanimity of views on most matters. Where opinion within the office was divided as over relations with the United States and a separate peace with Turkey there is in these pages, it is hoped, as much discussion as the evidence allows.

On what principles was foreign policy based? Perhaps the only real one was that it existed solely to further the interests, above all the security, of the British Empire. In the case of ministers, simple geographical ignorance meant that this could hardly be otherwise.

[46] H. M. Hyde, *Lord Reading: the Life of Rufus Isaacs, First Marquess of Reading* (1967), pp. 284–6; the (second) Marquess of Reading, *Rufus Isaacs: First Marquess of Reading 1914–1935* (1945), p. 119.

Smuts appalled Henry Wickham Steed by confessing that he did not know whether Moravia was Austrian or Hungarian.[47] In the same way, at the Versailles peace conference, Cecil shocked Lewis Namier by revealing ignorance that Austrian Galicia was in fact Austrian and not Hungarian. 'What a funny shape Austria must be', he mused.[48] It is entertaining to record that several months before this Cecil had replied to a parliamentary question whether the government would take steps to inform the British people of the 'heroism' of the Czechs and Yugoslavs and of their 'general position in Austria' by saying: 'I should have thought everyone knew where Bohemia was and where the territories inhabited by the Jugo-Slavs are situated.'[49]

The professional staff of the Foreign Office were not at all ignorant of the lands with which their work concerned them. Also, they were normal human beings who felt sympathy for the sufferings of the Armenians, and for the Czechs who were very far from being faced with the prospect of extermination but whose leaders always presented their case well and made a good impression on British politicians and diplomats. However, they too saw their work in terms of safeguarding British interests. The setting up of the Political Intelligence Department was a real innovation. It meant that for the first time a British government was receiving advice on foreign policy from men who were *parti pris* on issues which were not of obvious or direct concern to the British Empire, ranging from the break-up of Austria–Hungary to the alleged inefficiency of the colonial administration of some of Britain's allies. Even so, this development had little significance in the long term or even at the time. With this exception, anyone who studies the records of the British Foreign Office in the First World War is likely to be left with feelings either of distaste or admiration for its members depending on the view which one takes of what foreign policy is about.

[47] H. Wickham Steed, *Through Thirty Years* (1924), ii. 156.
[48] A. J. Toynbee, *Acquaintances* (1967), pp. 65–6.
[49] *Commons Debates*, 5th series, CVI, col. 2022, 11 June 1918.

I

WAR AIMS, AUGUST 1914–DECEMBER 1916

I. WAR AIMS DURING THE FIRST TWO YEARS OF THE WAR, AUGUST 1914–AUGUST 1916

IN August 1914 Britain went to war with Germany in protest against her invasion of Belgium and for nearly two and a half years official explanations of war aims were to centre on this fact. Yet Belgium was from the first only a symbol of wider issues as Edward Grey made clear in a famous speech on 3 August 1914 when he said that failure to uphold the treaty of 1839 on Belgian neutrality would 'lose us all respect' and would make possible 'the whole of the western Europe opposite to us . . . falling under the domination of a single power.'[1] However, the restoration—itself a not altogether unambiguous term—of Belgium remained for long the one essential and declared British war aim behind a great deal of verbiage about the need to 'crush Prussian militarism'.

The lack of definition in British aims except on Belgium is clear in Asquith's speeches during the first few weeks of war. In London on 4 September he remarked that refusal to respect the independence of small nations was 'the one capital offence in the code of those who have made force their supreme divinity.'[2] At Dublin on 25 September he declared that there were two reasons why Britain was at war with Germany: she had violated Belgium and had miscalculated that Britain would be indifferent to this.[3] British war aims were the repudiation of militarism and guarantees for small nations.[4] All this was adorned with outbursts against 'hordes who leave behind them at every stage of their progress a dismal trail of savagery, of devastation and desecration worthy of the blackest annals in the history of

---

[1] Text of this speech in Viscount Grey of Fallodon, *Twenty-Five Years 1892–1916*, undated edition, iii, 296–320.

[2] H. H. Asquith, *'The Justice of our Cause' and 'The Duty of Everyman'* (1914), p. 5.

[3] Ibid. pp. 21–2.   [4] Ibid. p. 23.

barbarism.'[5] During these early weeks the Prime Minister made two other pronouncements: the British Empire had no desire to expand[6] and Britain had gone to war not only because of the invasion of Belgium but also because Germany had refused to guarantee the French colonial empire.[7] A speech at the Guildhall on 9 November 1914, which was to be Asquith's last substantial exposition of war aims for fifteen months, was of a piece with what had been said before. Britain demanded the restoration of Belgium, French security against aggression, adequate guarantees of the independence of small states and the destruction of Prussian militarism.[8]

For nearly three years British leaders asked the nation to accept these speeches as a satisfactory explanation of why the country was at war and why hundreds of thousands of its young men must die in battle. Asquith seemed to regard the text of his speeches as sacrosanct. When in February 1915 Lloyd George said roundly to an American journalist that Britain would not have gone to war but for the German invasion of Belgium the Prime Minister was irritated. He answered a member of Parliament who asked him whether this was the government view:

I must refer the honourable Member to the speech which I made in this House on 6 August which explained fully the policy of the government and the reasons which led up to the war.[9]

Other questions on war aims during the first two years of the war met with a similar response from ministers.[10]

There was good reason for Asquith's irritation against Lloyd George for he had implied what the French would interpret as British indifference to German aggression against them. Asquith pointed this out when asking Lord Robert Cecil to withdraw a similar question to the one above, a request with which Cecil complied.[11] Apart from the accumulation of 'secret treaties'—the Straits

---

[5] Ibid. p. 30. Speech at Cardiff, 2 Oct. 1914.
[6] Ibid. p. 28. Cardiff speech.
[7] H. H. Asquith, *Speeches* (1927), pp. 192–201. Speech on the vote of credit, 7 Aug. 1914.   [8] Ibid. p. 224.
[9] *Commons Debates*, 5th series, lxx, col. 1132, 8 Mar. 1915.
[10] Kent Forster, *The Failures of Peace* (Washington, 1941), pp. 18–19, 31–3.
[11] Asquith to Cecil and Cecil to Asquith, 2 Mar. 1915, Cecil MSS., B.M. Add. 51073. I am grateful to Mr. D. C. Holland, the Librarian of the House of Commons, for furnishing me with a copy of Cecil's withdrawn question. Without this the correspondence cited above would not be intelligible. Mr. D. C. Holland to the author, 20 Nov. 1967.

agreement with Russia, the treaty of London with Italy, the Sykes-Picot agreement and others—whose texts the government were pledged not to reveal, there was a constant danger that any attempt to proclaim war aims in detail would imperil relations with allies who felt that their aims had not been given sufficient support.

Another obstacle was continuing party mistrust. When the Liberal Colonial Secretary, Harcourt, asked the Conservative leaders, Bonar Law and Lansdowne, for their opinion of a memorandum which he had written on 'Spoils', they refused point-blank to tell him.[12] The reason for this was, at least in part, a belief that when the war ended the Liberal party would split over peace terms with one section supporting far more generous peace terms for Germany than the Conservatives could possibly accept.[13] Silence on war aims was thus necessary so long as the Conservatives' role was that of a loyal opposition in war-time, soon to be transformed into that of junior partner in a coalition government.

Party differences as an impediment to the elaboration of war aims were to become less formidable as the struggle wore on and party spirit seemed less and less important. A further early difficulty was that the leaders thought that any declarations on war aims which went beyond the fiery rhetoric of Asquith's early speeches would weaken the war-spirit of the masses. During 1917 this was to be transformed into a conviction that detailed war aims were essential to retain the loyalty of the working classes, but the prevalent attitude during the early part of the war was summed up by Curzon in a speech to an audience of public schoolboys in October 1914: 'It will be time to discuss the terms of peace when peace can be obtained with honour; but it is premature, it is impertinent even in the pulpit [a reference to a preacher who had announced war aims as the subject of his next sermon] to talk about peace now.'[14]

Most important of all, there was a firm conviction in official quarters by the end of 1914 at the latest, that the war would be long-drawn out. In December 1914, Sir Arthur Nicolson, Permanent Under-Secretary of State at the Foreign Office, wrote:

It is no use whatever our thinking of peace until we are in a position to dictate its terms and we shall not be in that position until the Germans

---

[12] Lansdowne to Bonar Law and Bonar Law to Harcourt, both 1 Apr. 1915, Bonar Law MSS. 37/1/1 and 37/5/14.

[13] Bonar Law to Walter Faber, 15 Dec. 1914, Bonar Law MSS. 37/4/36.

[14] G. N. Curzon, *The War: A Speech delivered in Harrow Speech Room 14 October 1914* (The Victoria League, London, n.d.).

have been far more heavily defeated and more weakened than has hitherto been the case. I myself look forward to a prolonged struggle and one can do so without any misgiving as every month that passes strengthens our position very considerably.[15]

Nine months later, he admitted that the war was likely to last at least a year longer before the essential task of inflicting salutary military defeat on Germany had been accomplished.[16] According to Austen Chamberlain, 'All our plans are being made on the assumption that the war will continue throughout 1916'.[17]

In these circumstances, a tendency for war aims to be allowed to fall into the background was natural on the part of leaders who were besieged with innumerable urgent problems. This leaves the historian with the obligation to reconstruct the thinking of the nation's leaders on this subject from more scattered and less full sources than the rich records available from the late summer of 1916.

For Grey unwillingness to draw up a comprehensive programme of war aims reflected no lack of concern with the problem of the peace settlement. Such a course of action would have meant lengthy negotiations with France and Russia and a risk of serious quarrels. He felt that allied action should await definite German peace overtures when the Entente could draw up their terms on the basis of their estimate of their strength *vis-à-vis* the enemy. At such a time Britain would certainly insist upon 'the restoration of Belgium and a peace that would be free from the menace of Prussian militarism under which Europe has been for so long'. Russia and France would put forward conditions of their own which Britain would probably have to accept as essential conditions of peace.[18]

The meaning eventually to be attached to the phrase about ending the menace of Prussian militarism would depend upon the policy of the United States. Any quarrel between Britain and America would be a 'crowning calamity' and would be 'probably fatal to our chances of success.'[19] If the United States entered the war or even merely agreed to play an active part in post-war international security arrangements, Britain could safely consent to a peace based very

[15] Nicolson to Lord Hardinge, 1 Dec. 1914, Hardinge MSS. XCIII, pt. I, no. 323.
[16] Nicolson to Hardinge, 1 Sept. 1915, Hardinge MSS. XCIV, part I, no. 98a.
[17] Chamberlain to Hardinge, 17 Aug. 1915, Hardinge MSS. CXXI, part I, no. 47.
[18] Grey to Buchanan, 29 Jan. 1915, FO 800/75.
[19] Grey to Spring-Rice, 3 Sept. 1914, FO 800/84; quoted in G. M. Trevelyan, *Grey of Fallodon* (1937), p. 314.

largely on the territorial *status quo*.[20] On the other hand, as Grey noted in a moment of pessimism about Anglo-American relations, if the Americans were not prepared to join such arrangements, the only way in which peace could be made durable would be by fighting on until Germany was completely broken.[21]

Grey's views on the importance of relations with the United States were not shared by the majority of his staff at the Foreign Office or by Cecil Spring-Rice in Washington who once apologized for discussing Anglo-American relations at length: 'This is a long letter about a subject which, after all, is very secondary.'[22] Spring-Rice had been embittered by his experiences in Washington but the comparative unimportance which British diplomats attached to the United States had deeper roots. They had not yet learned to take America altogether seriously. Hardinge while Permanent Under-Secretary, once referred to the 'American "nation" ' with 'nation' in inverted commas.[23] The implication seemed to be that the United States was a ramshackle state like Austria-Hungary rather than truly a great power. On such an assumption it is not surprising that Hardinge thought that it would be a great misfortune if the United States entered the war on the allied side. No help whatever could be expected from such a nation in the actual prosecution of the war and yet belligerency would give her a voice in the peace negotiations, 'And that is the very last thing we ought to desire since her influence is certain to be on the side of Germany and for obtaining easy terms.'[24]

Nicolson, Hardinge and probably most other senior Foreign Office men (with the notable exception of Grey's secretary, Eric Drummond) looked to a permanent Anglo-Russian alliance to guarantee peace. Providing that Germany was defeated, Hardinge

[20] Memorandum on Grey's views as expressed by Eric Drummond to Howard Taylor, 6 Sept. 1915, FO 800/85.

[21] Grey to Spring-Rice, 2 Jan. 1915, FO 800/85. Shortly before this Grey had spoken of the democratization of Germany by the spontaneous action of the German people as an acceptable alternative to United States involvement in the peace settlement. Grey to Spring-Rice, 22 Dec. 1914, FO 800/84.

[22] Spring-Rice to Hardinge, 11 Aug. 1916, Hardinge MSS. XXIV.

[23] Hardinge to Bertie, 2 Feb. 1917, Hardinge MSS. XXIX.

[24] Hardinge to R. H. Benson, 23 June 1915, Hardinge MSS. XCIV, part II, no. 36. According to Lord Crewe most members of the Cabinet favoured American entry into the war. Crewe to Spring-Rice, 18 June 1915, FO 800/85. The very clear difference in attitude to the United States between British diplomats and politicians is discussed in Ernest R. May, *The World War and American Isolation 1914–1917* (Cambridge, Mass., 1959), pp. 375–6.

could see no obstacle to this except for the settlement of remaining Anglo-Russian problems in Asia[25] which could surely be achieved, making the whole of that continent with the exception of Japan and its position in China, a satrapy of the British and Russian empires.[26]

Nicolson had a blind faith in 'my beloved Russians'.[27] Yet during the first two years of the war it did seem more likely that Britain would have to concentrate her hopes for world peace on Russia rather than on the United States. Grey was aware of this despite his personal inclinations. During the negotiations which preceded the treaty of London, he argued that Italy's aspirations in Dalmatia deserved sympathy despite their lack of an ethnographic basis because: 'It must be remembered that in some, perhaps in a few years there may be one great Slav power in which Serbia and Montenegro are merged and which will be more powerful to Italy than Austria has been.'[28] Later in the same telegram he spoke about 'a great Slav Power such as will exist in the future'. What he had in mind was presumably the expansion of Russia into the Balkans since a united Yugoslav state could hardly be described as more powerful than Austria–Hungary. He would have deplored such a development, but if it came about, Britain, having cast in her lot with Russia against Germany, could have done nothing to prevent it.

Grey's thinking on foreign policy was sophisticated and realistic. He was prepared to curtail British naval rights by conceding the

---

[25] *Note on Persia.* Persia was central in Foreign Office thinking on Anglo-Russian relations in Asia and indeed generally. The prevalent idea in the Office was that Persian independence should be liquidated in such a way that Russia would feel that her ambitions had been satisfied while Britain would be left with a sufficiently strong position in the southern and eastern parts of the country to use them for the defence of India if despite all the efforts of British diplomacy there was finally a break between Russia and England. In January 1917, Oliphant, the Foreign Office's Persia specialist, wrote that partition would be 'inopportune at present' but was 'probable some day'. Memorandum, *c.* 27 Jan. 1917, FO 371/2981. The Russian Revolutions of 1917 brought a reprieve for the cause of Persian independence since the British had no desire to end it except as an act of policy in relations with a Russia which had insistent aspirations there. Yet there was regret that the work of many years to eliminate Persia as a subject of contention between British and Russian imperialism had become irrelevant. Commenting on the probable need to move British troops into north-west Persia to block a Turkish advance, Hardinge must have sighed as he wrote: 'If anybody had said ten years ago that in this year of grace a move of British troops to Northern Persia would be under contemplation I would have set him down as a lunatic.' Hardinge to Bertie, 5 Mar. 1918, FO 800/178.

[26] Hardinge to Grey, 3 Mar. 1915, and to Nicolson, 8 Apr. 1915, Hardinge MSS. XCIII, part. II, nos. 302 and 318.

[27] Nicolson to Buchanan, 15 Mar. 1915, FO 800/377.

[28] Grey to Buchanan, 27 Mar. 1915, FO 371/2507, no. 35975.

American demand for Freedom of the Seas (i.e. immunity of merchant ships from destruction or capture in wartime), ostensibly and in part genuinely, in return for the entry of the United States into a 'great League of Peace' but commented: 'I believe also that in view of the future development of the submarine and our excessive dependence on overseas commerce it will be to our interest that the sea should be free in time of war.'[29] Such a man had little to learn about *Realpolitik*.

Evidence about the thinking of Grey's colleagues on the long-term implications of the war is fragmentary. It is probable that for most of them the main concern was simply to inflict on Germany such a defeat that she would never again be tempted to use force to achieve aggressive objects (this, of course, is to employ the terms in which they themselves saw the war). Recognition by Germany that aggression had failed emerges as Asquith's main concern from a minute which he wrote in September 1914. According to this Germany must set aside all hope of making a separate peace with any member of the Entente, must evacuate all occupied territory in France, Belgium, Russia and Serbia and must possibly also surrender all her warships on the high seas and agree to pay compensation to the Entente as *preliminaries* to a full peace settlement in which the allies would impose such additional demands as they thought necessary.[30]

Detailed formulation of war aims only came when an existing ally put forward insistent demands (Russia and Japan) or when attempts were being made to win over new allies (Italy, Rumania and the Sherif of Mecca). Considerations of permanent policy were not absent from this diplomacy. Professor C. Jay Smith has argued in a brilliant article[31] that, during the winter of 1914–15, Grey strongly encouraged Russia to lay claim to Constantinople as a means of preserving the balance of power in Europe by deflecting Russian ambitions away from German and Austrian territory. This argument has its limitations. Probably a desire on the part of the British to give Russia a good reason for not making a separate peace was as im-

---

[29] Draft copy of telegram to Spring-Rice with minute by Grey, 7 June 1915, FO 800/95. The telegram was not sent owing to direct instructions from Asquith. Cf. Mark Bonham-Carter to Eric Drummond, 10 June 1915, FO 800/100. On this question see also Charles Seymour, *The Intimate Papers of Colonel House* (1926–8), i. 376–7, 428–9.   [30] Asquith's minute on Spring-Rice to Grey, 20 Sept. 1914, FO 800/84.
[31] C. Jay Smith, 'Great Britain and the 1914–15 Straits Agreement: the British Promise of November 1914', *American Historical Review*, lxx (1965), 1015–34.

portant as anything. Also, Grey wanted to serve a specifically British interest: the deflection of Russian ambitions from Persia, in whose future Britain had a vital stake, to the Straits, whose opening would not, the pre-war discussions of the Committee of Imperial Defence had decided, endanger the security of the British Empire. Finally, in considering the possibility of a compromise peace, Grey thought that it would be much easier to negotiate if Russia's territorial claims centred on Constantinople and left Austria alone, presumably on the grounds that Germany would be much readier to desert Turkey than Austria.[32] The remarks quoted above which Grey made during the negotiations with Italy suggest that he realized that if Russia did march into eastern Europe there was little that the western states could do to limit her power. In addition to Russian ambitions, a policy, if such it can be called, of preserving a balance of power in Europe was threatened by another aspect of British diplomacy: the attempts which were made between 1914 and 1916 to induce Bulgaria and Rumania to enter the war. The former was offered Serbian territory for which the Serbs would clearly have to be given compensation from the Dual Monarchy. Rumania was offered Hungarian territory directly. All this was tending toward the adoption of a policy of favouring the break up of Austria–Hungary. In July 1915, Nicolson recorded that allied offers to Rumania 'comprised practically one half of Hungary.'[33]

The idea that Turkey would have to pay the penalty for her entry into the war had become a commonplace even before the actual declaration in November 1914. On 20 October Asquith had informed the King that the Cabinet considered that in future, 'Great Britain must finally abandon the formula of "Ottoman Integrity" whether in Europe or Asia'.[34] In his notable Guildhall speech on 9 November he repeated publicly almost the same words: 'It is the Ottoman Empire and not we who have rung the death-knell of Ottoman dominion, not only in Europe but in Asia.'[35]

In early March 1915, the War Council (the Cabinet committee entrusted with the higher direction of the war) began debating the

[32] Michael G. Ekstein Frankl, 'The Development of British War Aims, August 1914–March 1915' (University of London, Ph.D. thesis, 1969), Chapter V.

[33] Nicolson to Hardinge, 21 July 1915, Hardinge MSS. XCIV, part I, no. 65a. There is a much fuller account of British policy toward Austria–Hungary in 1914–16 in Chapter II: 3 below.

[34] J. A. Spender and Cyril Asquith, *Life of Earl Oxford and Asquith* (1932), ii. 129

[35] Reference as in note 8 above.

future of Constantinople in earnest, and, after Russia made her formal demand for the city a few days later, they accepted a formula put forward by Grey that it should be acceded to in view of the likelihood that otherwise Russia would make a separate peace with Germany. In return Russia must accept British desiderata in Asiatic Turkey and Persia. The only demands actually agreed upon were that Russia must give Britain a free hand in Arabia and the neutral zone of Persia as defined under the Anglo–Russian pact of 1907, though the right to make further demands at a later date was reserved. At this meeting and at another one nine days later[36] ministers discussed what Britain wanted in Turkey. There was general agreement that Britain must assume permanent control of Basra vilayet at the head of the Persian Gulf and also, directly or indirectly, of Baghdad vilayet to the north. The question whether the defence requirements of the new Mesopotamian dependency included a corridor to Alexandretta on the Mediterranean as strongly urged by Kitchener, was left undecided. The debate was characterized by a spirit of misgiving and *ennui* at the prospect of further accessions to the already vast British Empire. Although Lloyd George spoke excitedly in favour of acquiring Palestine, Grey expressed a more general attitude when he wrote on the same day at the second of these debates, 'Palestine might be given to Belgium, Christian, Liberal and now noble Belgium'.[37]

The same spirit is breathed by the report of a committee which Asquith set up under the chairmanship of Maurice De Bunsen, ambassador at Vienna in 1914, to consider war aims in Asiatic Turkey.[38] The aim of 'straightening out ragged edges' and 'consolidating' the existing Empire was avowed, and the preservation of Turkey as an independent, federal state except for Constantinople and Basra was recommended as preferable to partition, to maintenance of the existing regime or to division of the country into spheres of influence. As in the War Council debates in March and in the attempts which had been made by the Foreign Office and the India Office at the end of 1914 to induce Persia to cede or lease certain islands off her south-western coast,[39] the need to maintain and

---

[36] War Council, 10 and 19 Mar. 1915, CAB 42/2/5 and 14.

[37] Minute by Grey, 19 Mar. 1915, FO 800/88.

[38] Committee of Imperial Defence: Report of a Committee, 30 June 1915, CAB 27/1 which also contains very extensive minutes and memoranda used by this committee.

[39] India Office Library: Political and Secret special subject files, vol. 85 (1913), file 3615, part II *passim*.

strengthen British paramountcy in the Persian Gulf was the committee's main concern. If Turkey was partitioned despite their recommendations, vast new commitments (a naval base at Haifa and military duties in Mesopotamia and Persia where it was expected that Russia would annex her zone outright) would be warranted by the need to keep the Gulf British. Even under the federal solution Turkey was to lose Basra vilayet and to recognize the complete independence of the east Arabian states of Kuwait and Nejd bordering the Gulf. Turkey would have to grant full autonomy to the Hejaz in order to fulfil the requirement that the Moslem Holy Places should be under an independent Moslem regime which would not be hostile to Britain, but there she might keep a purely nominal authority which it was considered necessary to deny her in east Arabia. The attraction of the recommendations for the Arabian peninsula was that they involved virtually no new military or financial commitments. As Arthur Hirtzel, secretary of the Political and Secret Department in the India Office, put it, 'The "protectorate over Arabia" therefore amounts to nothing more than Arabia for the Arabs under the aegis of Great Britain'.[40] The establishment of such a regime in the Arabian peninsula as being vital to the security of the Indian Empire was to remain a fundamental British aim throughout the war though it was one of which the ordinary British citizen was scarcely aware.

It is regrettable that no minutes were taken of the meeting at which the De Bunsen committee decided its order of priorities for the future of Turkey as a whole excluding Arabia.[41] However, it is clear that the preference for federation was chiefly dictated by a desire not to increase imperial responsibilities in addition to important other considerations: the difficulties of arranging partition with Russia and France which appalled Nicolson for one[42]; the possibility of tempting Turkey into an early peace; and a conviction that if Turkey was partitioned or divided into spheres, British trade would be squeezed out of the French and Russian areas.

The report of the De Bunsen committee is interesting on one more count. It strongly favoured British control in Basra, but added that unless the Government of India recommended annexation as absolutely essential, the vilayet might become part of a federal Turkey if the inhabitants 'preferred' this to British rule. This faintly

---

[40] A. Hirtzel, 'Future Settlement of Eastern Turkey in Asia and Arabia', 14 Mar. 1915, CAB 42/3/15.

[41] Secretary's note on 13th meeting of committee, 28 May 1915, CAB 271/1.

[42] Nicolson to Hardinge, 11 Mar. 1915, Hardinge MSS. XCIII, part I, no. 364.

foreshadows a problem which was later to bedevil foreign policy and war aims, that of the self-determination of peoples.

The Anglo–French–Russian negotiations which led to the Sykes–Picot agreement and the Anglo–Arab diplomacy which preceded the Hejaz revolt of June 1916 must now be traced in brief outline since, like the War Council's decision on Constantinople and the work of the De Bunsen committee, they are relevant to two of the main themes of this book, the general discussion of war aims, and the attempts to bring about a compromise peace with Turkey.

War-time contact between the British and Sherif Hussein of Hejaz began at the end of October 1914 when Kitchener wrote to the Sherif holding out the prospect not only of an independent Hejaz but also of the transference of the Islamic Caliphate to his family.[43] The correspondence was then continued on the British side by Sir Henry MacMahon as Kitchener's successor in the British residency at Cairo. Perhaps the most important of the letters which they exchanged was that of 24 October 1915 in which MacMahon promised the Sherif what the latter's agent in Cairo had declared to be the Arabs' minimum terms including their rule in an area to the east of and comprising Homs, Hama, Aleppo and Damascus. This left the status of Palestine unclear and, in addition, both parties reserved complete freedom of action in Mesopotamia in the course of negotiations about the future of that country during the next three months. However, in a letter of 13 December 1915, MacMahon promised the Sherif that if he 'spared no effort' to attract all Arabs to the allied cause: 'You may rest assured that Great Britain has no intention of concluding any peace in terms of which the freedom of the Arab peoples from German and Turkish domination does not form an essential condition.' A later official commentary suggested that this promise had been invoked at the outbreak of the revolt on 4 June 1916.[44]

The zeal with which negotiations were pursued in the autumn of 1915 sprang in large part from the British military reverses at Gallipoli and in Mesopotamia. There was a fear that Germany would seek to exploit these by reinforcing the Turks and threatening the entire British position in the east.[45] MacMahon was consequently

---

[43] E. Kedourie, *England and the Middle East: the Destruction of the Ottoman Empire 1914–1921* (1956), p. 52.

[44] Political Intelligence Department/Foreign Office: Memorandum on Commitments to Sherif Hussein, Nov. 1918, G.T. 6185, CAB 24/68.

[45] Cf. minute by Nicolson, 20 Dec. 1915, FO 800/95.

ordered to pursue negotiations more vigorously.[46] As distinct from the need for help wherever it could be obtained, the prospects for the success of the experiment of Arab independence were considered poor by most British officials. To Nicolson the very idea of an Arab state was a 'fantastic dream'.[47] MacMahon himself thought that where the Arabs were independent they would always be divided into petty, warring states.[48] Even so, from June 1916, Britain was committed to a policy of liberation from Turkish rule in the Arab east.

The negotiations which led up to the Sykes–Picot agreement[49] began in October 1915 when it became obvious that the Arabs would not enter the war unless promised an independent state or confederation, thus making necessary negotiations with France owing to her interests in Syria.[50] After initial deadlock, the Foreign Office entrusted negotiations to Mark Sykes. He negotiated an agreement with the Quai D'Orsay official, Picot, which, in outline, provided for non-interference in the affairs of Arabia, French rule in a 'Blue' area on the Syrian coast and in Cilicia, British rule in southern Mesopotamia, an international regime in Palestine except for Haifa and Acre which would go to Britain, and an Arab state or confederation in the inland areas between the French Blue and the British Red. The new state would be divided into Area A where France would have exclusive rights of providing advisers and developing the country economically, and Area B to the south-east and east where Britain would hold a similar position. One special feature was that at the insistence of Kitchener, who according to his biographer supervised every detail of these negotiations,[51] Mosul was assigned to France so as to interpose a barrier between British and Russian territory. (It may be added that the French themselves very much wanted the vilayet.)[52]

[46] E. Kedourie, 'Cairo and Khartoum on the Arab Question 1915–18' in *Historical Journal*, vii (1964), 281.

[47] Nicolson to Hardinge, 11 Nov. 1915, Hardinge MSS. XCIV, part I, no. 167a.

[48] MacMahon to Hardinge, 4 Dec. 1915, no. 180 in ibid.

[49] For a good general account based on published documents and Sykes's papers see L. Stein, *The Balfour Declaration* (1961), pp. 249–66. Other references follow. The text of the actual agreement is in *Documents on British Foreign Policy*, 1st series, iv. 245–7.

[50] Cf. memorandum by Hankey on British relations with the Arabs, 20 Mar. 1916, CAB 42/11/6.

[51] P. Magnus, *Kitchener: Portrait of an Imperialist* (Grey Arrow ed.), p. 301.

[52] Hardinge to Wingate, 28 Dec. 1915, Hardinge MSS. XCIV, part II, no. 157 and Holderness to Hardinge, 25 Nov. 1915, Hardinge MSS. CXXI, part I, no. 68.

The agreement was endorsed by Crewe, Kitchener, Bonar Law, Grey, Nicolson, Hirtzel and Holderness on 4 February 1916,[53] and the way was thus clear for Sykes and Picot to go to Petrograd to seek Russian endorsement and to discuss any Russian claims in Asiatic Turkey. Sazonov, the Tsar's Foreign Minister, claimed a zone in north-east Turkey. He also insisted after Paléologue, the French ambassador, had accused Sykes to his face of trying to use France as a buffer between Britain and Russia,[54] that the Blue area should be moved bodily to the north-west so as to bring the British and Russian spheres more nearly into contact. Despite the misgivings of Balfour and Kitchener, the agreement as thus changed was endorsed by the War Committee, the successor to the War Council, on 23 March 1916.[55] By the spring of 1916, Britain had a policy framework for the future of the Middle East which was added to occasionally, as when Grey wrote to Bertie in May 1916 that Britain would insist upon the abolition of the capitulations in Egypt in the terms of peace.[56]

The negotiations with Italy which led to the treaty of London and to her entry into the war, at first against Austria only, are remarkable in two respects.[57] Firstly, the territorial pledges to Italy that she should receive Trentino, Trieste, Istria and large specified territories in Dalmatia were of a uniquely binding sort. According to the treaty, Italy 'will receive' the stated gains. This contrasts with the other secret treaties in which the territorial provisions were made contingent on the outcome of the war. This was to give Foreign Minister Sonnino a formidable weapon in seeking to thwart Anglo–French efforts in 1917–18 to bring about a separate peace with Austria on the basis of only minimal territorial losses to the Monarchy.

Secondly, the records of the negotiations reveal much enthusiasm among the senior staff of the Foreign Office for the principle of nationality, though to Grey this may have been less important than the preservation of a semblance of the balance of power in eastern Europe after the Entente had won the war. G. R. Clerk thought that the Italian claim to Dalmatia was 'unjustified in itself' because of the national factor and 'would drive Dalmatia and the Slav countries behind it into the arms of Austria'. Nicolson held at first that the

[53] Record of this meeting in CAB 37/142/10.
[54] Buchanan to FO, 10 and 12 Mar. 1916, CAB 17/176.
[55] War Committee, 23 Mar. 1916, CAB 42/11/9.
[56] Grey to Bertie, 19 May 1916, CAB 37/148/17.
[57] For a detailed account of the making of the treaty of London see W. W. Gottlieb, *Studies in Secret Diplomacy in the First World War* (1957), pp. 312 ff.

Italian claim to Dalmatia 'cannot be conceded' as it 'would be storing up trouble for us in the future'.[58]

What was seen as the imperative military necessity of inducing Italy to enter the war caused these scruples to be abandoned. Clerk, in a sort of epilogue to the London negotiations, observed that Serbian as opposed to Yugoslav national claims, had been 'fully safeguarded' but that the idea of not making pledges to Italy which would stand in the way of Yugoslav unity had had to be abandoned.[59] All these issues—concern for the post-war balance, the nationality issue and the problem of whether, and if so what, long-term sacrifices should be made for the immediate purpose of winning the war—were to be constants in British east European policy throughout the war.

Likewise, in the Far East and the Pacific much was done to clarify the post-war settlement owing to the uncertainty of the alliance with Japan and the need to win increased help from her or at least to deter her from making a separate peace with Germany of which there were occasional rumours. Thus in May 1916, Grey reported to his colleagues that the Japanese ambassador had told him that Japan was receiving offers through its Stockholm legation of the German colonies occupied by Japan in return for making a separate peace and for inducing Russia to do the same—a broad hint that Britain should acquiesce to Japanese wishes on these territories.[60] There was indeed a growing realization that Japan could not be denied Kiaochou and the German north Pacific islands and this led to a formal commitment in February 1917.[61] Even before this, in August 1916, Grey had promised Japan that her assent would be necessary in any new general formula that the allies adopted on the war and that Britain would carefully consult with Japan on anything east of Asia Minor.[62]

When external prodding to agree upon peace objectives was less pressing, there was unwillingness to formulate war aims. Probably most ministers would have agreed vaguely with Lloyd George's call for a peace in Europe 'predicated first of all on new geographical

[58] Minutes by Clerk and Nicolson, 6–7 Mar. 1915, FO 371/2507, no. 28275; Nicolson to Grey, 22 Mar. 1915, no. 34055 in ibid.
[59] Minute by Clerk, 2 May 1915, FO 371/2508, no. 53085.
[60] Memorandum by Grey, 4 May 1916, CAB 37/147/10. Cf. F. W. Ikle, 'Japanese-German Peace Negotiations during World War I' in *American Historical Review*, lxxi (1965), 62–76.
[61] W. R. Louis, *Great Britain and Germany's Lost Colonies 1914–1919* (1967), pp. 39 ff., 70–1, 78–80. But see also Chapter II: 2 below.
[62] Grey to Greene (ambassador in Tokyo), 11 Aug. 1916, CAB 37/153/35.

boundaries based on national lines, on the will of the respective peoples'.[63] Probably also most of them would have supported such changes for the same particular reason that Winston Churchill advanced in January 1915: 'I think the case for settling generally on ethnological principles is a strong one and a hard rule for Austria and Germany.'[64]

Indecision was also the hallmark of a desultory discussion on the German colonies during the War Council debate on Constantinople in March 1915. This trailed off into a discussion of what should be done with the German fleet. Churchill called for its destruction and for the neutralization of the Kiel Canal while opposing the loss to Germany of East Africa. Bonar Law agreed that the first condition of peace was the elimination of the German fleet. The First Sea Lord, Fisher, argued that if, after the war, Germany began building a new fleet it should be instantly annihilated. Kitchener, a little more moderate on naval matters as befitted a soldier, thought that a heavy indemnity spread over many years would make it impossible for the Germans to rebuild their navy.[65] It is curious that after this consideration of the future of the German fleet largely ceased and that it was not until after the armistice that the Admiralty drew up the precise terms which it wished to impose upon Germany (see Chapter VI below).

One reason for the comparative lack of discussion of the future of the German colonies and fleet was that the leaders realized that military victory could not be guaranteed. The one thing which no minister, even in the darkest moments of the war, ever imagined was a settlement in which Belgium did not recover complete independence. Grey's speeches were at one with those of Asquith in that they began by calling for the restoration and indemnification of Belgium and then, going on from the particular to the general endorsed 'the right of independent sovereignty for the different nations; the right to pursue national existence, not in the shadow of Prussian hegemony or supremacy but in the light of equal liberty'.[66] If necessary, it could be argued that the restoration of Belgium signified the attainment of these worthy objectives. Even the public

[63] Lloyd George's remarks to an American journalist in *Pearson's Magazine*, xxxix (March 1915), 267.
[64] Churchill to Kitchener, 21 Jan. 1915, Robertson MSS. I/13/3.
[65] War Council, 10 Mar. 1915, CAB 42/2/5.
[66] Speech by Grey in London, 22 Mar. 1915.

demand that Belgium should be indemnified might be negotiable as Eric Drummond, speaking on Grey's behalf, informed an American who was known to have contacts with the German government through the United States embassy in Berlin. (Drummond authorized the man in question to convey this to Bethmann-Hollweg if he wished to do so.)[67]

However, British ministers never felt so desperate as to consider initiating peace overtures to Germany. That would have been an admission both of defeat and of being the aggressor as Asquith remarked in an important speech in April 1916.[68] In addition, throughout the first two years of the war the leaders continued to hope that they would be able to achieve much more than a settlement based on the *status quo*. In February 1915 Nicolson was convinced that Germany would 'doubtless like a *status quo ante*' peace and rejected such an idea out of hand.[69]

Given this will to victory the British were faced with a great problem in their relations with the United States. President Woodrow Wilson was known to favour a negotiated end to the war, preferably through his own mediation. If the British government made it clear that they were wholly unsympathetic to this the President might endanger the allied war effort by denouncing their blockade measures against the Central Powers and by taking measures against their trade with the United States. The danger of this happening was lessened by Grey's diplomacy which aimed at making as many concessions as possible to the Americans while still allowing an effective blockade of Germany, and still more by America's explicit intention during the early stages of the war to profit through increased war trade.[70]

A considerate response to Washington's peace proposals was nevertheless accepted as necessary by British ministers. However, it was difficult for even Grey to take them seriously owing to America's unwillingness, made clear by Wilson's confidant, Colonel House, when he visited London early in 1915, to participate in the peace conference or to promise that she would become a member of any post-war league.[71] Wilson and House continued to hope that

[67] Memorandum cited in note 20 above.
[68] Speech by Asquith, 11 Apr. 1916.
[69] Minutes by Nicolson, 26 Feb. 1915, FO 371/2505, no. 22617, and 27 Mar. 1915, FO 371/2509, no. 25218.
[70] E. R. May, op. cit. 18 ff.
[71] Seymour, op. cit. pp. 370, 375, 384, 388.

despite this their mediation would be acceptable and Grey kept this
hope alive with certain letters which he wrote to House during 1915
and which particularly emphasized that the United States must be a
member of a league of nations for any peace settlement to be stable.[72]
The Colonel's basic sympathies in the war were entirely with the
British and the French, and he gradually became convinced that
German policies on submarine warfare would sooner or later make
America's entry inevitable. Together with his correspondence with
Grey, these considerations led House to ask Wilson in late 1915 to
allow him to go to Europe again. The British were unwilling to invite
him while the President would only let him go on the clearest under-
standing that the United States was only prepared to use 'moral
force' to bring about peace negotiations.[73]

The famous House–Grey memorandum of 22 February 1916
sprang from these unlikely origins. House offered United States
mediation in London and Paris on the most favourable terms: it
would not be proposed if the Entente were winning but only if they
were losing or if there was a stalemate. The proposed peace terms—
the restoration of Belgium, the cession of Alsace-Lorraine to France
and of Constantinople to Russia and the handing over to Germany
of additional colonies—were highly favourable to the allies. If
Germany rejected them, the United States would enter the war on
the side of the Entente. In his diary House recorded that all the
leaders with whom he talked (Asquith, Balfour and Lloyd George
as well as Grey) professed the greatest possible enthusiasm for the
scheme, pleading only that the time for its implementation was not
yet.[74]

Professor Link is surely right in thinking that the British leadership were so anxious to 'humour' House that they deliberately gave
him a false impression that they favoured a negotiated peace.[75] Even
the theory that they were insuring against military defeat holds little
water. Early in 1916 none of the British political leaders, not even

---

[72] Seymour, ii. 54–5, 87–9.

[73] Arthur S. Link, *Wilson: Confusions and Crises 1915–1916* (Princeton, 1964),
pp. 110, 112–13. This work is henceforward referred to as Link, *1915–1916*.

[74] See the extracts from House's diary in H. Montgomery Hyde, *Lord Reading: the
Life of Rufus Isaacs, First Marquess of Reading* (1967), pp. 196–9. The extracts in Seymour, ii. 179–85, 193–6, while not giving a distorted picture of what the diary says,
exclude some of the passages in which British ministers other than Grey are recorded as
expressing fervent support for the memorandum. It may be that it was thought that the
publication of these passages in full would make House look foolish.

[75] Link, *1915–1916*, p. 130.

Lloyd George, had lost all faith in the General Staff or the High Command or were pessimistic about the military prospects. At the War Committee on 22 February Grey formally presented the document which he had drawn up with House. This recorded the purported American mediation offer as presented by the Colonel but contained no commitment on the part of the British government except that the offer would be discussed. It was stated that Britain could not act on the matter even if she wanted to do so without the support of her allies. Asquith commented that even if the United States were really willing to enter the war it was doubtful whether it was desirable that they should do so since they favoured a draw which the Entente would look upon as a defeat.[76] Ministers were happy to fall back on the argument that the attitude of France made it idle to discuss American mediation further. Grey wrote some nine months later: 'The War Committee were informed of what had passed with Colonel House and we were unanimously of opinion that the time had not come to discuss peace and such communication as there has been with Colonel House since then has been on that basis.'[77]

From almost every point of view this was not the moment for American mediation. The Anglo–American cold war over blockade regulations and what was considered to be American passivity in the face of such outrages as the sinking of the *Lusitania* had aroused feelings of contempt for the United States in Britain among both leaders and led. A furious denunciation of the idea of entrusting British security after the war even in part to a league of nations, which Hankey wrote in May 1916, was tinged with anti-American sentiment. It was idle to expect the United States to play a serious role in a league of which they might nominally be a member: 'They are so cosmopolitan and so wedded to the almighty dollar that they cannot be judged even by the comparatively low standards of other nations in regard to matters of national honour.'[78]

Grey never fell victim to the anti-American contagion, but, whatever might have been his personal views, he had little alternative but to take the line of his colleagues that military victory was preferable to the enlistment of American help to end the war by diplomacy. The best face which he could now put upon things was to say:

[76] War Committee, 22 Feb. 1916, CAB 42/9/3.
[77] Memorandum, 9 Dec. 1916, FO 800/96.
[78] Hankey to Balfour, 25 May 1916, Balfour MSS., B.M. Add. 49704.

As long as the military and naval authorities of the Allies say they can beat the Germans there need be no talk of mediation: but if the war gets to a stalemate the question to be asked will not be whether mediation is good electioneering for President Wilson but whether it will secure better terms for the Allies than can be secured without it.[79]

This attitude, combined with the previous dishonesty to House, involved a high price in terms of Anglo–American relations. Wilson was so excited by British assent to the House–Grey memorandum—for House presented the results of his mission in such a way that British policy seemed far nearer the President's own than he had thought possible—that he reversed his policy and endorsed the agreement fully. He inserted the word 'probably' to qualify his readiness to lead the nation into war only in recognition of the constitutional principle that it was not possible for the president alone to do that.[80] In May he approached Grey with a view to putting the memorandum into operation, and publicly announced (in a major change of policy) America's readiness to join a league of nations. He was met with an outright refusal.[81] Never assigning a pivotal role to Anglo–American relations in his thinking on international relations, Wilson became thoroughly disillusioned with the British and abandoned all idea of basing his war diplomacy on particularly close relations with them. By the time of his re-election to the presidency in November he was contemplating entry into the war on the German side in the event of Germany welcoming his overtures and the Entente rejecting them.[82] The next stage in American diplomacy was to be one which the British could not manipulate through genial dinner party conversations with the President's Anglophile assistant.

Lloyd George's future position as Prime Minister warrants a special effort to trace his attitude toward war aims and the negotiated peace question during the first two years of the war. This is no easy task since it is doubtful whether he had fixed views except on the desirability of partitioning Turkey (on which see Chapter III: 3 below). As to Germany, Lloyd George was probably never wholly convinced that she posed a mortal threat to the British Empire or that the war was not the result of a tragic misunderstanding. His

[79] Copy of letter from Grey to Bertie, 5 May 1916, Hardinge MSS. XXIII.
[80] Link, *1915–1916*, pp. 136–8.
[81] Arthur S. Link, *Wilson: Campaigns for Progressivisim and Peace 1916–1917* (Princeton, 1965), pp. 16–20, 34–8.
[82] E. R. May, op. cit. pp. 361–2.

Mansion House speech at the time of the Agadir crisis in 1911, warning Germany that he supported the use of force to uphold vital national interests, is well known, and Lord Loreburn, one of the Liberal ministers who resigned in 1914, once told C. P. Scott that Lloyd George said 'I'm very sorry' when a telegram was received at the time of Agadir, announcing that the Germans were giving way.[83] His secretary and mistress has recently stated that his mood was one of relief when Britain went to war in August 1914.[84] Yet, looking 'terribly worn and tired', he told C. P. Scott on 3 August that he would have resigned if Britain had declared war on a Germany which had respected Belgian neutrality or had marched across only its south-eastern corner.[85] It is small wonder that during the crisis which led to war Lloyd George's attitude was an enigma to his Cabinet colleagues.[86]

After the outbreak of war Lloyd George remained ready to consider a negotiated peace. It has been pointed out that it was not until six weeks after the outbreak of war that he could bring himself to make a speech supporting British participation.[87] About the new year 1915–16 he told Scott that he favoured a compromise peace settlement imposed on the exhausted belligerents by the United States though Scott found it impossible to judge whether or not he was serious.[88] He repeated this line of argument to Colonel House in terms too flattering to the American Administration for the historian to find them wholly sincere.[89]

Soon, however, Lloyd George was to begin travelling along the road which was to lead him to give the 'knock out blow' interview to the American correspondent Roy Howard in September 1916. On a visit to London in April, Lord Bertie was gratified to find that, though Lloyd George was pessimistic about an early peace, he was determined to fight on: 'No lame peace for him. It would, he considers, be better to lose a great part of our population than to submit to Germany.'[90] A month later, he was anxious that the American

---

[83] C. P. Scott, Journals, 9 Oct. 1914, B.M. Add. 50901. Henceforward this work will be cited as Journals followed by the date and the number of the B.M. additional document.   [84] Frances Lloyd George, *The Years That Are Passed* (1967), pp. 73–4.

[85] Journals, 3 Aug. 1914, 50901.

[86] Viscount Samuel, *Memoirs* (1945), pp. 103–4.

[87] A. J. P. Taylor in the *Sunday Express*, 20 Jan. 1963.

[88] Journals, 11–15 Dec. 1915 and 27–29 Jan. 1916, 50902.

[89] Hyde, op. cit. 194–6.

[90] Memorandum by Bertie on conversations with Balfour and Lloyd George, 14 Apr. 1916, FO 800/175.

public should be in no doubt that Britain was not prepared to discuss peace at the moment.[91] The possible reasons for this hardening of attitude—a more profound realization of the German menace, a conviction that the British people were determined upon victory, or a bid for national leadership by putting himself forward as the man to win the war—are not mutually exclusive and must remain conjectural. It required supreme office to dissipate some of the ardour which Lloyd George felt for the *guerre à l'outrance* during 1916.

2. ATTEMPTS AT CLOSER FORMULATION OF WAR AIMS, AUGUST–NOVEMBER 1916

THE main reason for the debate on war aims which took place in British government circles during the second half of 1916 was a feeling, after eighteen months of warfare marked by unexampled losses in both lives and wealth, that it was hardly conceivable that the war could continue much longer. This attitude was tinged with irrationality but was perhaps natural in leaders to whom total war was a completely novel experience. In January 1916 Grey wrote:

I do not believe that a satisfactory peace can be secured only by the policy of exhausting Germany. I think that Germany will be exhausted before another year is over and that the same is true of others; and if things remain as they are, I think that there will be a sort of general collapse and inconclusive peace before next winter. I believe that the only chance of victory is to hammer the Germans hard in the first eight months of this year. If this is impossible we had better make up our minds to an inconclusive peace.[92]

Such arguments were reinforced by the pleadings of the military leadership for more men. At the same time that Grey was composing the remarks quoted above, Robertson, in the course of an appeal for the army to be given as many men as possible wrote that 'If we do not exert our maximum effort this year with the object of gaining decisive victory and so dictate our own terms of peace, we shall probably have to conclude later an unsatisfactory peace, making our subsequent existence intolerable and having to maintain a large and ruinous army in readiness for the next struggle'.[93]

[91] Cf. Guy Locok of the Foreign Office to J. T. Davies, Lloyd George's secretary, answering a query from Lloyd George on British propaganda in the United States. Lloyd George MSS. D/16/17/9. Locok to Davies, 11 May 1916.
[92] Memorandum by Grey, 14 Jan. 1916, CAB 42/7/8.
[93] Robertson to Clive Wigram, 12 Jan. 1916, Robertson MSS. I/12/30.

If peace was likely in the near future, the wisdom of having a definite programme of war aims was obvious. Yet it was not until August that a committee under the chairmanship of Sir Louis Mallet of the Foreign Office, was set up with a brief to consider British policy toward the German colonies and the possibility of territorial exchanges among the colonial possessions of the allies.[94]

Progress in setting up such a body as the Mallet committee was slow. It might never have been set up at all but for Lord Hardinge's return as Permanent Under-Secretary in June 1916. Arthur Nicolson, his predecessor, was on his own admission a very poor administrator and not the sort of man to press strongly for the setting up of committees. In addition his relations with Grey were bad. Paul Cambon recorded that when he went to the Permanent Under-Secretary's room after Hardinge's return he was usually absent, consulting with Grey, and that this was a complete contrast with the situation under Nicolson.[95]

Besides having good relations with his chief and being a competent executive, Hardinge was very anxious that work should be done on war aims and complained of Grey's laxity on this point.[96] Hardinge was mildly obsessed with the notion that the French had a comprehensive programme of war aims and that British diplomatists would be at a serious disadvantage in peace negotiations unless they were similarly equipped. More important, he believed, while the Somme offensive was taking place in July, August and September, that it was probable that it would inflict such damage that Germany would have to sue for peace on allied terms in the autumn.[97] Early in September Hardinge asked Grey to recall immediately Ronald Graham from Egypt to act as Assistant Under-Secretary and fit himself for 'all the many peace and post-war questions that are likely to arise in the near future'.[98]

[94] Foreign Office to Board of Trade, 8 Aug. 1916, CAB 16/36. This letter informed the Board of Grey's wish to set up a committee under Mallet. Similar letters were doubtless sent to the India, Colonial and War Offices and to the Admiralty since these were also represented on the committee which first met on 4 Sept. 1916.

[95] Paul Cambon, *Correspondance*, ed. Henri Cambon, iii (1946), 116.

[96] Hardinge to V. Chirol, 3 Aug. 1916, Hardinge MSS. XXIV. 'When I got back to England I found that nothing had been done in the way of defining our desiderata when the time comes for peace negotiations.'

[97] There are several letters in the Hardinge MSS. in which he expresses this belief. See also Hardinge to Hamilton Grant, 4 June 1916, India Office Library, EUR MSS. D 660 (Grant papers).

[98] Hardinge to Grey, 9 Sept. 1916, FO 800/96.

Hardinge and the members of the War Committee were undoubtedly influenced by the optimistic reports on the military
situation which they received from Robertson. Toward the end of
July Hardinge wrote: 'Robertson told me only yesterday that complete victory is only a question of time, the superiority in everything
having passed into our hands.'[99] At the same time, Robertson, finding the War Committee 'a little uneasy' that the Somme offensive
seemed likely to inflict 200,000 to 300,000 casualties on the British
army, reassured them that during the past six weeks the German
and Austrian forces had suffered 750,000 casualties on the Western,
Italian and Russian fronts. He felt that this was successful in sooth-
ing ministers and in confining criticism to 'a few outsiders, e.g. F. E.
Smith and Winston.'[100] Robertson may well have exaggerated his
estimate of military prospects as part of his well-known effort to
ensure the maintenance of the western strategy and out of loyalty to
Douglas Haig. His letters to Haig and Murray at this time are
distinctly restrained as to the results that might be expected from
the Somme offensive.[101]

Enthusiasm over western prospects was not the only consideration
which led the Foreign Office to pay close attention to war aims.
Drummond probably echoed a general feeling when he suggested
to Grey that the imminent entry of Rumania into the war might
shorten the conflict by three months.[102] There were also signs of discontent outside the office at the lack of clarity on war aims. In August
Lloyd George told Lord Esher, 'No one in England had any idea of
what our peace objectives should be, apart from vague generalities'.[103]
The inference was no doubt that this was hardly a satisfactory state
of affairs. A few days later Robertson wrote to Lloyd George, then
his departmental chief, expressing great anxiety: '. . . In regard to
our position in the event of negotiations opening for an armistice or
peace. They may arise any day in some form or another though by
no means in a definite form and I fear that we may be caught un-
prepared and find that we have mobilized for Peace as we did for
war—inadequately and subordinate to France.'[104]

[99] Hardinge to Lord Chelmsford, 27 July 1916, Hardinge MSS. XXIII.
[100] Robertson to Haig, 29 July and 1 Aug. 1916, Robertson MSS. I/22/61–62.
[101] Robertson to Haig, 14 Aug. 1916, ibid. I/22/68; *Egypt 1916–17: Private Letters
between General Sir W. R. Robertson and General Sir Archibald Murray* (privately printed,
1932), e.g. pp. 137–8, Robertson to Murray, 1 Aug. 1916, B.M. Add. 52463.
[102] Drummond to Grey, 27 July 1916, FO 800/96.
[103] *The Journals and Letters of Reginald, Viscount Esher*, ed. Oliver, Viscount Esher,
iv (1938), 48.   [104] Robertson to Lloyd George, 17 Aug. 1916, WO 106/1510, no. 17.

To complicate the belated interest in war aims of the Foreign Office and of such powerful figures as Robertson, there was a conflict between Grey and some of his senior officials. Hardinge favoured work on war aims simply because he thought that Germany would probably soon acknowledge defeat. He was utterly opposed to anything which smacked of a compromise peace as this, 'I really believe would result in the eventual destruction of our country'.[105] Grey was less sanguine than many of his colleagues that the Somme offensive might result in military victory but felt that combined military and economic pressure might, by the autumn, force a Germany which was still undefeated to seek American mediation to end the war. He was convinced that the Entente must treat this seriously rather than run the risk of permanently alienating the sympathies of the United States.[106] In alarm at hearing this, Bertie turned to Asquith with the suggestion that if the Americans did propose mediation, the allies should refuse it by saying that if Germany desired peace she must approach the allies as a whole directly with her terms.[107] Assuming that the Prime Minister was aware of Grey's views, he thus came to realize that the Foreign Office were divided on the peace issue. This may well have convinced him that the problem needed a thorough airing. He was also aware that many of his colleagues were dissatisfied with the vagueness of the country's war aims programme,[108] and that, in the case of the Foreign Office, as one official put it, 'Pressure is being put on from all sides for discussion of this question'.[109] At all events, at the end of August he asked the members of the War Committee to consider generally problems in peace negotiations as between the enemy and Britain and Britain and her allies. This was, he declared, 'not merely a Foreign Office question, it affected also the naval, military and Board of Trade departments'.[110]

By the time that Asquith issued his call, the Foreign Office had made some progress on war aims on the theoretical level as well as

[105] Hardinge to Rodd, 5 July 1916, Hardinge MSS. XXIII.
[106] Cf. memorandum by Bertie on conversations with Grey and Hardinge, 11 Aug. 1916, FO 800/171.
[107] Bertie to Asquith, 17 Aug. 1916, FO 800/190.
[108] Cf. memorandum by E. S. Montague, 29 Aug. 1916, CAB 29/1.
[109] Theo Russell to William Tyrrell, 26 Aug. 1916, FO 800/96.
[110] War Committee, 30 Aug. 1916, CAB 42/18/8. An examination of the Asquith MSS. in the Bodleian has revealed nothing on the Prime Minister's attitude on war aims during 1916.

in ascertaining French and Russian desiderata. On 24 August Grey had an interview with Paul Cambon in which the French ambassador hinted that his country might have territorial aspirations in western Germany additional to the recovery of Alsace-Lorraine and agreed that Britain and France ought to try to discover Russian war aims in Europe and to draw up a joint approach on American mediation and the conditions on which an armistice could be granted.[111]

Grey was pursuing a definite design. If the United States did offer mediation, he wanted France to act as spokesman for the Entente, partly to help ensure her loyalty to the alliance and partly because France was America's traditional friend whereas to many Americans Britain was still the traditional enemy.[112] However, the preliminary enquiries which were made in late August and early September were discouraging. Both France and Russia professed to be too uncertain about their aims, especially on the frontiers of Germany, for discussion to be useful.[113] In the middle of September, the Foreign Office definitely abandoned its attempts to elicit Russia's European aims.

It was easier to make progress when laying down what was desirable in theory. Early in August the office produced a 'Suggested Basis for a Territorial Settlement in Europe' written by William Tyrrell and Ralph Paget.[114] This paper gave as its recipe for European peace the implementation of the national principle in making peace arrangements, and rejected the imposition of any crippling economic disadvantages on any state after the war. It was recognized that the nationality principle would have to be modified by certain pledges to and claims of the allies, especially Italy, by the need 'not (to) push the principle of nationality so far as unduly to strengthen any state which is likely to be a cause of danger to European peace in the future' as well as by the demands of Russia, geographical factors and the military situation.

The authors felt that they had learned from the past and had found in the national principle a key to future peace which had been denied to earlier statesmen:

[111] Cf. Grey to Bertie, 24 Aug. 1916, FO 371/2804, no. 170012.
[112] Cf. Grey to Spring-Rice, 29 July 1916, FO 800/86.
[113] Bertie to Hardinge, 4 and 20 Sept. 1916, FO 800/168; Hardinge to Bertie, 15 Sept. 1916, copies in Hardinge MSS. XXV and FO 800/178.
[114] Most of this is in D. Lloyd George, *My Memoirs of the Peace Conference* (1939), i. 11–23. The names of the authors are not given but are correctly identified in *The History of The Times*, iv (1952), part I, 319–20. The document in full is in CAB 29/1.

The Congress of Vienna attempted to secure a balance of power against France by the creation of kingdoms which were expected to prove a formidable barrier to any French aggression in the future. But these creations did not fulfil that expectation because they were artificial and did not bring contentment and prosperity to the people who formed part of them. The solution we recommend has this in its favour, that it is based on more solid and lasting foundations than were obtained by the provisions of the treaty of Vienna.

Accordingly, France should receive Alsace-Lorraine but not any German-speaking territory on the west bank of the Rhine; Denmark should receive Schleswig but not Holstein; Poland should become a fully independent state comprising Russian, German and Austrian territory; Austria–Hungary should be broken up completely; and Bulgaria, despite the fact that she was an enemy, should receive the Uncontested Zone of Macedonia because the population was mostly Bulgarian. Of particular interest is the suggestion of a union between Germany and German-speaking Austria. While Prussia was being weakened by the loss of Alsace-Lorraine, Posen and Schleswig, the supposedly peaceful Catholic elements in the south would be strengthened by the addition of German-speaking Austria:

The preparations for this war, the impulse to this war, the aggressive designs connected with this war, are all traceable to Prussian enterprise and it is not extravagant to hope that a defeated Prussia will considerably lose its power for evil and should it further be confronted by a large, wealthy and influential southern federation within its own borders, we shall not be far wrong in expecting to achieve the diminution of its influence, which can only be brought about by the play of political forces within the German federation.

Thus the enemy was not Germany but Prussia. Furthermore, we learn that the war was caused not by the German or Prussian people but by their ruling classes who had deceived their subjects:

We must remember that the leading people in Germany who are mainly responsible for this war never allowed their countrymen to suspect that their designs were aggressive. . . . In practice, their policy which remained carefully concealed from their countrymen, was dominated by ideas of aggression in order to secure expansion of territory and spheres of influence.

It is perhaps unnecessary to say that such an interpretation of the German problem could hardly fail to give rise to an unwarrantably optimistic view of the possibilities of establishing a peaceful European order in which Germany was an integral part. The logic of the view that all that was necessary to make Germany peaceful was the defeat and consequent discredit of the Prussian aristocracy emerges clearly from this reasoning.

Paget and Tyrrell were members of an internal Foreign Office committee on war aims which presented a report shortly before Paget took up an appointment as British minister to Denmark which he received in August. A diligent search through the Foreign Office records of the period has failed to elicit any minutes of the committee, its report or even a membership list. Its origins can probably be traced to a memorandum which the retired Lord Bryce, a former ambassador in Washington and one of the most respected figures in British public life, sent to the Foreign Office early in April 1916, setting out his ideas on 'Settlement in South-East Europe and West Asia' with a request that it should be shown to Asquith. Drummond commented that while policy in Asiatic Turkey had already been decided at least in broad outline, Bryce's remarks on the Balkans constituted: 'The sort of question which could be thrashed out by the Committee I have ventured to propose for considering our desiderata as regards the reconstruction of Europe. Sir R. Paget, Mr. O'Beirne and Sir W. Tyrrell would make a very strong combination especially as regards south-east Europe where the most difficult problems arise.'[115]

The members of the committee did not include Hardinge who, otherwise, would hardly have responded to the Paget–Tyrrell paper by saying that it required 'a good deal of digestion' and that he would withhold judgement on it for a time.[116] It probably included no one senior in the office hierarchy to Paget or Tyrrell[117] and if this is so, it may reasonably be assumed that its recommendations on territorial changes were identical with or little different from those in the paper. Evidence on the thinking of the committee—and also one of the very few direct indications of its existence though not the only one—occurs in a letter written by Paget in October 1916 in the course of an amiable discussion of a proposal by Captain Consett, naval attaché to the British legations in Scandinavia, that Britain should insist in the terms of peace that the Kiel Canal be filled in.

---

[115] Bryce's letter to Grey with his memorandum and minute by Drummond, all 6 Apr. 1916, FO 800/105.   [116] Undated minute by Hardinge, FO 371/2804, no. 180510.
[117] O'Beirne accompanied Kitchener on his voyage to Russia and was drowned.

Paget disagreed only to the extent of thinking that it ought to be blown up with high explosives which 'would be quicker, cheaper and just as effective' and had also been recommended by the Foreign Office's secret committee on war aims. He continued that the committee had recommended military victory as an end in itself: 'We should get into endless difficulties if once we started negotiating and bargaining, and moreover it would mean that the military party in Germany still possessed life and its one thought would be to prepare for a war of revenge. All this has been definitely stated in our report.' Hardinge had been delighted by this recommendation but Grey, alas, had not so far endorsed it.[118]

Germany, then, was suffering from a unique and dangerous political disease. This impression of Foreign Office thinking emerges even more clearly from a paper written in January 1917 by Mallet, Clerk and, again, Tyrrell. Though specifically written to refute General Staff arguments that it was desirable that most of the German colonies should be returned, it puts aside individual territorial problems and gives a fundamental analysis of the reasons why those concerned professionally with Britain's international relations thought that the war was necessary, and what they hoped to gain from it. In view of this and the fact that the paper has never previously been published, it is proposed to deal with it at some length.[119]

The paper begins with a quotation from one of the Kaiser's speeches: 'I look upon the people and nation handed on to me as a responsibility conferred upon me by God; and that it is, as is written in the Bible, my duty to increase this heritage for which one day I shall be called upon to give account; those who try to interfere with my task I shall crush,' and explains how he has faithfully carried out this policy, transforming the satiated *status quo* power that was Bismarckian Germany. 'History bears us out when we assert that until the accession of the present German emperor, our disagreements with Germany were more in the nature of squabbles than of fundamental divergences of views.'

However, after 1890 matters had so far deteriorated that by 1914 the authors felt that German political thought could be expressed in the following synopsis:

[118] Paget to Sir M. Findlay, 2 Oct. 1916, Paget MSS., B.M. Add. 51256.
[119] Memorandum dated 21 Jan. 1917, CAB 16/36.

We are becoming more and more convinced that the needs of our Empire compel us to seek what belongs to others. We quite realize that we came into the world many years too late to obtain what we should call our proper share of the colonial possessions of the world. Our political importance, our industrial prosperity, the needs of our population, are in themselves sufficient justification for us to claim a place in the sun; the colonies we have hitherto obtained have turned out bad investments: what we want are colonies that promise a better prospect of success under our management.

Some people in Britain had been foolish enough to suppose that German ambitions could be satisfied peacefully by limited concessions, but 'No such illusion existed in Germany, who made every preparation to obtain by force what she could not obtain by consent'.

The authors go on to argue that the two chief obstacles to future peace were the impossibility of effectively crushing Germany, and Germany's uniquely aggressive nature. After observing that France had been so heavily defeated in the wars of a century ago that it had ceased to be aggressive, the paper continues:

But can this be said in the present instance? The General Staff are in a far better position than the Foreign Office representatives to know how far Germany is already defeated, but it is our conviction that defeat has not yet gone so far as to induce her to abandon the policy which led to this war and is it altogether improbable that she may revert to her former policy of friendship and alliance with Russia in order to achieve the same objective in another way?

The most promising prospect for such a policy would be secured by a peace the result of a draw which would give a further lease of power to the reactionary parties in both countries. The most efficacious way to defeat such an orientation in German policy would be not to increase but to diminish the power of Germany and *pro tanto* to reduce her value as an ally.

In the light of recent history we should beware of reviving the illusion as to the likelihood of Germany acting as a buffer between us and Russia. On the contrary our best guarantee for future peace and security will be found not in reliance upon Germany but in the cultivation of the closest relations of confidence and friendship with Russia.

Our safety from the recurrence of our present calamities, we believe, will be best secured if we inflict such a defeat as will compel the Germans of their own free will to return to the policy with which they were satisfied until the present emperor came to the throne, and the retention by the allies of the German oversea possessions, which represent to the average

German the tangible results of the Emperor's world policy would be at the same time, the best means of securing this desirable object and one of the most effective blows which the allies could strike at the 'military domination of Prussia'.

There need, in our opinion, be no anxiety lest the measure of chastisement which we may be able to inflict will obliterate the German nation. Prussia survived the disasters of Jena and Tilsit and France recovered from the invasion of her territory and its prolonged occupation twice within sixty years. We are not out to destroy a nation of 70,000,000 people in the centre of Europe and we do not believe that if such were one of the objects of this war we should be able to achieve it.

After arguing that Germany had very few objective grounds (the need for sources of raw materials and for population outlets) for laying claims to a colonial empire, and that in official German policy the chief purpose of the existing colonies was to prepare for aggression against the possessions of others, the report explains that the loss of these colonies would be a precondition of the achievement of another important war aim, the end of German naval power:

It is admitted in German colonial circles which are demanding the return of the German colonies, that colonies and a fleet stand together or fall together, and in a recent lecture the director of the German Colonial Economic Committee went so far as to state that 'Colonies without a navy means suicide but that a navy without colonies was objectless'.

The close connection thus established between the colonial venture and the naval preparations makes it permissible to hope that if we are able to hold the German colonies, the naval policy may fall into disrepute.

The paper next reaches the heart of its analysis when it spells out as the supreme war aim the defeat of Germany's bid to become a world power, obliging her to restrict her energies to the continent of Europe:

It is a question whether the time has not now come for the adoption of a different attitude towards Germany, based upon the German assumption that there is not room in the world for two world dominions and accepting, however reluctantly, the burden of which the German Emperor is so anxious to relieve us.

The fact is that we cannot allow any nation to share our supremacy at sea: our geographical position alone obliges us to claim this monopoly. As our population increases it becomes more and more dependent on overseas trade; for food we are entirely dependent upon it, while Germany is so situated on the Continent that apart from her own agricultural resources she can freely and abundantly draw upon the granaries of her eastern neighbours: for Great Britain therefore a supreme navy is a vital necessity; for Germany a luxury. . . . It is our conviction that it will ultimately be in the interests of both Germany and England that Germany should confine her energies to exploiting the position which she achieved for herself in 1870 and that Great Britain should be allowed to continue her existence as an overseas empire which has no continental ambitions. It is only if this position be accepted that it will ever become possible for the two countries to develop side by side without coming into conflict with each other. It is only on such a condition that an identity of interests can arise between the two countries and in our opinion it should be the aim and object of this country to recreate a condition of things on the continent which will give expression to the above policy. The surest guarantee of peace is a unity of interests. The surest balance of power rests on such a unity of interests.

After subscribing to the view that this task was less formidable than it might sound because the German people were basically peace-loving and would lose faith in their masters in the event of military defeats and the loss of the colonies, the writers give their definition of an acceptable 'peace on terms' if complete victory proved impossible:

In order to obtain a true meaning of this expression, we should clear our minds as to what a 'peace on terms' really amounts. If we do so we shall be forced to the conclusion that the only peace on terms which we can contemplate is a draw in our favour: a draw in our favour which would enable us to keep the German colonies, and also to insist that the European settlement should be a genuine and not a shop-window dressing. In other words the only peace we can accept is one which would enable us to insist that the restoration and restitution of Belgium is one that leaves Belgium completely independent and unfettered. If on the other hand, we are confronted by a situation which would amount to a draw in favour of Germany, we shall strive in vain for such a settlement. We do not think that we can insist too strongly on this point.

The paper concludes that a straight exchange such as that suggested by the Staff (Belgium for the German colonies) would be impossible since the colonies and direct or indirect control of Belgium were both essential German war aims. There was no alternative but to fight on until Germany acknowledged the loss of both.

If the proposals in both the Paget–Tyrrell and Mallet–Clerk–Tyrrell papers had been implemented and if the war had ended with

Russia one of the victorious Great Powers—an outcome still hoped for at the beginning of 1917—Germany would have been left with precious little scope for a great power role even in Europe. At most she could hope for a measure of economic predominance in the markets of the new nation states in eastern Europe. Hence the fervour with which it was desired that military defeat would 'cure' the Germans of their relish for a role as a great world power.

Robertson was keenly interested in war aims. He defined the ultimate objectives of the war in terms of achieving them, explaining shortly after he became chief of the General Staff that his policy was to achieve a decisive military result to the war and: 'A "decisive result" means such a result as will eventually enable the Government to dictate terms of peace.'[120] Yet his views on the changes which it would be possible or desirable to bring about as a result of the war were rather perverse by contemporary British standards, whether popular or official. While he favoured the suppression of Germany's bid to become a major naval power and subscribed to the current myth that the Germans of south Germany and Austria were inherently less aggressive than those of Prussia, his main fear was of the Slav or Latin nations trying to upset the European balance, thus repeating what Germany was trying to do in the present war. He regarded a strong Germany as an essential British interest to counter this. He therefore rejected the argument that Germany was uniquely aggressive, and, despite the sacrifices which he was constantly exhorting ministers to demand from the nation to achieve victories on the west front, he evidently did not think that anything approaching total military defeat could be inflicted upon Germany: 'It is hard to believe that Germany will ever be so crushed as to consent to the transfer of Posen to Poland.'[121]

Robertson's views were widespread in the General Staff. Its evidence to the Mallet committee argued the need for a strong

[120] Memorandum by Robertson, 20 Jan. 1916, copy in Balfour MSS., B.M. Add. 49726.

[121] Memorandum, 30 Aug. 1916, CAB 29/1; also in D. Lloyd George, *War Memoirs*, n.d. but 1938, i. 497–503. This famous memorandum is Robertson's most substantial pronouncement on war aims. A few weeks after writing it Robertson complained that the War Committee were not prepared to pay much attention to his views on war aims and that in any case he had little time to think about the subject (*The Journals and Letters of Reginald, Viscount Esher*, iv. 54). According to Lloyd George, Robertson later withdrew the memorandium and stated formally that it was not to be regarded as an exposition of his views (D. Lloyd George, *War Memoirs*, i. 467).

Germany and questioned the wisdom of depriving Germany of any of her colonies except those occupied by Japan and the Dominions which, it was conceded, those powers were determined to retain.[122] In the face of furious protests from the Foreign, Colonial and India Offices and the Admiralty, the General Staff was forced to moderate its stand and to refrain from making provocative statements about the sterling value of a strong Germany, though it continued, un-repentant, to argue that Germany should receive back her larger colonies (German East Africa, and the Cameroons), and also Togo.[123]

The views of the General Staff on the fate of the colonies were most unlikely to be adopted if the allies won the war. More significant was their conviction that war aims against the smaller enemy powers should be reduced to a minimum to induce them to end their alliance with Germany. As a concomitant of this, Britain should assume full military and political control of the Entente. In one of the first of his pronouncements along these lines, Robertson argued that Britain, from such a position of leadership, ought to oblige Russia to abandon its claim on Constantinople in the hope of inducing Turkey to come to terms. Likewise, Bulgaria should be offered vast new territories, mostly at the expense of Greece. Grey's rejoinder denied the feasibility of a British take-over of the Entente and dismissed Robertson's proposal to cede Salonika to Bulgaria as 'absolutely impossible' and 'most treacherous'.[124] Apart from the political extravagance of Robertson's proposals, they were nullified by his insistence that Turkey and Bulgaria and, later, Austria, must be induced to break with Germany by diplomatic concessions alone, unsupported by military pressure. In this way Robertson's hopes of ending the war with Germany's partners were made to fit neatly into the western strategy but only at the cost of making it virtually certain that they would not be fulfilled: it is unlikely that Austria, Turkey or Bulgaria would ever have been ready to make a separate peace unless the catalyst of military defeat were added to even the most attractive territorial and financial baits. Lloyd George was aware of this and was consistently and fervently in favour of military opera-tions against these states—the props as he called them. If they collapsed or made peace on terms, the allies would be able to concentrate all resources against a Germany demoralized and

[122] General Staff memorandum, 7 Sept. 1916, CAB 16/36.
[123] General Staff memoranda, 22 Sept. and 21 Dec. 1916 in ibid.
[124] Memoranda by Robertson, 12 Feb. 1916, and Grey, 18 Feb. 1916; also War Committee, 22 Feb. 1916, all in CAB 42/9/3.

economically weakened by the loss of her allies. Even if this did not happen territory could be occupied for use as 'bargaining counters' at the eventual peace conference.[125]

An interesting sign of increased sophistication on Robertson's part in his approach to political-military problems is apparent in a suggestion made in August 1916 that Bulgaria should be bribed out of the war with the 'Uncontested Zone' of Macedonia. This, he explained, 'is based not on sentimental considerations but solely on the grounds of military expediency'.[126] However, he was now treading on safe ground on account of the general conviction in British ruling circles that Bulgaria was entitled to this area with its largely Bulgarian population not only as a reward for breaking with Germany but also as a contribution to stability in the Balkans. Yet Robertson remains a peculiarly single-minded man. While the war continued all that mattered was the defeat of the German armies on the west front; afterwards, the defence of the balance of power against everyone including Britain's present allies.[127]

Admiralty attitudes make a nice contrast with those of the General Staff. Writing in October 1916, the First Sea Lord, Sir Henry Jackson, was able to show clearly that any outcome to the war other than complete victory and the elimination of German naval power would be practically a defeat from a naval point of view because of the formidable expenditure that would be required for new warships, coastal fortifications and so on.[128] Also, far more than the General Staff the Admiralty leaned to the view that Germany was the sole threat to international peace which was unremarkable in view of the long record of Anglo–German naval rivalry before the war. Admiral of the Fleet, Sir A. K. Wilson, in the course of a rebuttal of War Office views on the future of the German colonies, argued: 'The German colonies were mainly useful as an excuse for a strong navy and to give the ruling powers [*sic*] an opportunity for meddling in world politics'.[129] The aim of reducing Germany to a purely European power is manifest in this.

---

[125] Cf. Lloyd George's remarks in Hankey, *The Supreme Command* (1961), ii. 598–9 and in H. Wickham Steed, *Through Thirty Years* (1924), ii. 245.

[126] Robertson, 'Note on the Position of Bulgaria', 4 Aug. 1916, CAB 42/17/5.

[127] Cf. the attitude of Haig who in August 1917 argued simultaneously against driving Germany to the point of revolution and against a negotiated peace. *The Private Papers of Douglas Haig 1914–1919*, ed. Robert Blake (1952), p. 252.

[128] First Sea Lord, 'Note on the Possible Terms of Peace', 12 Oct. 1916, CAB 29/1.

[129] Memorandum, 15 Sept. 1916, CAB 16/36.

Distrust of Russia lingered on among the sailors as is shown by the favour with which Churchill and Balfour as First Lords and Admiral Jackson regarded the annexation of Lemnos to the British Empire as a counter to the future Russian naval base at the Straits.[130] The Admiralty were also anxious that Britain should occupy or consolidate her hold on the oil-bearing territory in Mesopotamia and near the Persian Gulf, but most of their territorial proposals were designed to curb German naval capabilities: she should lose all her colonies and also Heligoland; the Kiel Canal should be occupied by a joint Anglo–Russian force pending a final decision on its fate; and the Netherlands should cede Cadzand to Belgium to make Antwerp more defensible and should be compensated with German territory.[131]

These territorial proposals were fairly comprehensive but Jackson spoke in uncertain terms about the future of the German fleet. He recognized that it would probably be impossible to end completely Germany's position as a naval power:

The point of view of our allies must necessarily carry weight when considering the terms of peace. These may think the balance of power in Europe better adjusted if Germany is allowed to maintain a moderate-sized fleet, say one appropriate to a second-class power, as some compensation for British supremacy at sea. They would probably have the United States strongly on their side in this and we should be prepared for such a proposal.[132]

Beyond this he did not feel able to go.

The War Committee seems never to have held a debate on war aims despite Asquith's call at the end of August. It is certain that it did not discuss the papers by Paget and Tyrrell or Robertson though these were, of course, circulated to members.[133] The attempt to formulate war aims was marked by an Asquithian muddle. At the same time that he set up the Mallet committee, the Prime Minister ordered that there should be a parallel committee on policy in Persia. In November 1916 Hankey wrote an irate letter to him recalling this

---

[130] Churchill to Grey, 2 Mar. 1915, FO 800/88; memorandum by Bertie on conversation with Balfour, 14 Apr. 1916, FO 800/175; First Sea Lord's memorandum cited above.

[131] Ibid. First Sea Lord's memorandum.   [132] Ibid.

[133] Cf. Lloyd George, *My Memoirs of the Peace Conference*, i. 23; the Earl of Crawford and Balcarres to Robertson, 29 Sept. 1916, WO 106/1510.

instruction and saying that after he had exerted himself to carry out the necessary preparatory work, he had discovered that a committee on Persia had been set up early in the war under Curzon's chairmanship.

Is it not desirable (asked Hankey) that we should be in possession of some information in regard to the constitution, functions and scope of Lord Curzon's committee? There is always a possibility of a danger of a certain amount of overlapping. The question of Persia can hardly be regarded as a thing entirely apart. . . . It is submitted that it is not sound that various sub-committees should prepare for the Government what we might call 'watertight compartment reports'.[134]

Even so, the subject did exercise the attention of ministers and their leading advisers and at the end of October Hankey wrote what he described as a summary of ministerial views, drawing also some conclusions. He began by listing the minimum territorial changes upon which writers of recent papers seemed to be agreed: the restoration of Belgium; German withdrawal from the occupied territories in northern France and the cession of at least the French-speaking areas of Alsace-Lorraine to France; some arrangement on Poland acceptable to Russia; the annexation of Constantinople by Russia if the allies achieved their desiderata in Asiatic Turkey; the achievement by Italy and Rumania of their promised rewards; and the restoration of Serbia. He pointed out that the Mallet committee was still considering the future of the German colonies. Hankey continued that there seemed to be general recognition that there were two other obstacles in the way of peace talks: the need to 'inflict on Germany such humiliation that she will never again repeat the experiment of forcing Europe into war'; and a need for a considerable improvement in the military situation in favour of the allies, in particular the occupation of much of the territory to which they intended to lay claim:

Notwithstanding these [i.e. Entente] moral and potential advantages, it is impossible to contemplate with equanimity the prospect of a discussion of peace terms at any date, however remote, until the balance of advantage has inclined far more decisively than at present to the side of the allies and this makes it absolutely vital that our staying power should be safeguarded.[135]

[134] Hankey to Asquith, 10 Nov. 1916, CAB 17/181.
[135] Hankey, 'General Review of the War', 31 Oct. 1916, CAB 42/22/14.

It is likely that what Hankey wrote commanded general assent. It was certainly acceptable to the two most dynamic men in British government, Lloyd George and Robertson.[136] The debate was less important in clarifying territorial desiderata than in reaffirming the need to defeat Germany as the only hope for future security and in establishing that American or other mediation was unacceptable.

Lloyd George retrospectively justified the Roy Howard interview as intended to counter a definite plot, involving the German government and the United States ambassador in Berlin, Gerard, designed to force President Wilson and the Entente into peace talks with Germany.[137] The implication was clearly that even if Germany wanted peace she could not have it because her chastisement had been insufficient. At a banquet in London in late October, Asquith delighted Bertie by assuring him that the idea of mediation was 'dead'.[138]

When therefore in mid-November Lansdowne, who had the rank of minister without portfolio, made the first of his appeals for peace negotiations,[139] he stood no chance of success, faced as he was by the Robertson–Lloyd George combination and by a Prime Minister whose attitude was basically unsympathetic. Encouraged by Lloyd George not to be 'afraid to let yourself go' in answering Lansdowne,[140] the chief of the General Staff replied with a paper which, now that it is available in full,[141] justifies the conjecture of one student writing in the cold light of after years, that, 'It must be the most bellicose document ever inflicted on a British Cabinet'.[142] Its gist was that it was unpatriotic and unmanly to think of peace or peace terms until Germany had been crushed, a result which could certainly be achieved if only the nation would double its efforts. 'Its chief object', explained Robertson to Haig, 'is to combat the unfounded pessimism which prevails in Government circles.'[143]

---

[136] Cf. Lloyd George, *War Memoirs*, i. 531. 'The Asquith Government examined the whole position with great care and came to the unanimous conclusion that to enter into peace negotiations with Germany before inflicting a complete defeat upon her armies would be disastrous.'

[137] Journals, 20–22 Nov. 1916, 50903.

[138] *The Diary of Lord Bertie of Thame*, ed. Lady Algernon Gordon Lennox (1924), ii. 47. Entry for 26 Oct. 1916.

[139] Text of this memorandum in Earl of Oxford and Asquith, *Memories and Reflexions* (1928), ii. 165–75.

[140] William Robertson, *Soldiers and Statesmen* (1926), i. 280.

[141] Partial text in ibid. i. 281–4; in full in CAB 37/160/15.

[142] Paul Guinn, *British Strategy and Politics 1914–1918* (1965), p. 175.

[143] Robertson to Haig, 27 Nov. 1916, Robertson MSS. I/22/91.

Robertson was at pains to convince Lansdowne that he did not include him among the 'cranks, cowards and philosophers' whom Robertson's memorandum denounced. The paper was designed to repulse pessimism 'as a whole' and was 'not intended to be in particular a reply to yours. In fact I read yours through but once and merely to enable me to understand what was meant by the "knock out blow" to which you referred'.[144] In all probability Robertson exaggerated the extent of the 'pessimism' which he detected in high political quarters. At the same time as he wrote his memorandum, Grey, who was afraid that the submarine offensive might actually give Germany victory within two or three months,[145] appealed for the military situation to be kept under constant review and for the war to be wound up 'through the medium of not unsympathetic mediation' if there appeared to be no chance of victory.[146] This might appear merely a truism but was quite brave in the atmosphere of the time. One of the last acts of the old War Committee was to make military service an obligation to which all men under sixty were liable. A week later the great proponent of the knock out blow became Prime Minister.

Of the 'subject peoples' of eastern Europe, the one with whose fate the Foreign Office felt most concern was the Poles. No doubt this owed something to a belief that the eighteenth-century partition of Poland and the suppression of the nineteenth-century risings were crimes whose results could not endure. However, as the historian of the rebirth of Polish independence has pointed out, there was very little sign of concern over Poland in the west between the last of the risings in 1863 and the outbreak of the World War.[147] More important was a fear, which increased as the Central Powers occupied Russian Poland in 1915, that they would make some dramatic political offer to the Poles which would win their active support against Russia and its tottering war effort.[148]

Russia's defeats convinced many Polish nationalists that she would never be able to implement the manifesto of August 1914

[144] Robertson to Lansdowne, 1 Dec. 1916, Robertson MSS. I/21/47.
[145] Grey to Balfour, n.d. but with insertion that it was written in late Nov. 1916, Balfour MSS., B.M. Add. 49731.
[146] Memorandum, 27 Nov. 1916, CAB 37/160/20; partially cited in G. M. Trevelyan *Grey of Fallodon* (1937), pp. 322–4.
[147] Titus Komarnicki, *The Rebirth of the Polish Republic* (1957), pp. 30–2.
[148] Cf. Grey to Bertie, 24 Aug. 1916, CAB 37/154/18.

with its promise of autonomy for Poland within the Russian Empire. Less prone to turn to Germany or Austria than the British feared, they began looking to the Powers of the western Entente to bring about Polish independence or autonomy. In 1915 Roman Dmowski, perhaps the most important nationalist leader of the time, moved from Petrograd to London. Another leader, Count Horodyski, developed the most intimate contacts with the Foreign Office. In 1916 Eric Drummond, whose Catholic faith helped to account for his friendly attitude to the Poles, asked Horodyski to report on the quality of British representation at the legation in Berne—a delicate task indeed to entrust to a foreigner.[149]

It was thus a source of regret that Russia warned her allies against trying to raise the Polish issue,[150] and that when Paléologue tried to do so he only succeeded in infuriating Sazonov. Drummond, for all his sympathy with the Poles, could understand that the Russians 'regard Poland as a purely Russian question much the same as we do Ireland'. He fell back on the hope that since it was inconceivable that Germany would grant autonomy to the Poles in Prussia, the Russian Poles would be neutral as between the belligerents.[151]

When Russia began pressing for the publication of the Straits agreement in August 1916, she coupled this with an offer to issue a manifesto of political concessions to the Poles.[152] This was most welcome to the Foreign Office though Grey favoured publication of the agreements in any case to counter the influence of the pro-German party at the Russian court and to reassure the Russian public that it was worthwhile to continue the war.[153] The Russians had made it clear that the amount of autonomy which they would be prepared to grant would depend entirely on the frontiers of the restored kingdom, that is on how much Polish-speaking territory belonging to Germany and Austria, Russia would be allowed to annex in return for granting Polish autonomy.[154] Yet the principle was accepted that in return for allied consent to a declaration on Constantinople, Russia must make a public promise of autonomy to the Poles. There was much delay caused by the unwillingness of the French to agree to the publication of the agreements for fear of show-

[149] Drummond to Grey, 16 Aug. 1916, FO 800/96.
[150] A. Nicolson to Grey, 18 Aug. 1915, FO 800/379.
[151] Drummond to Spring-Rice, 25 July 1916, FO 800/86.
[152] Buchanan to Grey, 17 Sept. 1916, CAB 42/20/6.
[153] Draft by Grey of telegram to Bertie, *c.* 19 Sept. 1916, FO 800/59.
[154] Buchanan to Grey, 3 Aug. 1916, FO 371/2750, no. 153149.

ing that their consent to Russian demands had been tardy by comparison with that of the British. Also both the British and the Russians doubted whether publication was wise before the military position on the Russian and Middle Eastern fronts had improved. Finally, a two-sided statement on the acquisition of Constantinople by Russia as an Entente war aim and on autonomy for the Poles was made by the Russian Prime Minister, Trepov, in the Duma early in December.

By this time the British Government were in favour of the internationalization of the Polish problem by means of an Anglo–French endorsement of the Russian promise. In January 1917, the War Cabinet asked Milner to use his discretion in influencing the Russians in this direction during his forthcoming mission to Petrograd.[155] Soon the obstacle posed by the existence of the Tsarist regime to a British hand in the Polish problem was to be removed.

Trepov's announcement that Russia would acquire Constantinople at the end of the war made little impression on Russian opinion. One reason for this was that the Russian government had been unable to give more than a general abstract of the agreement with its allies. This in turn was partly because of a warning from Baron Sonnino that if the full text of the agreement was made known, Italian opinion would demand to know what had been done to satisfy Italian aspirations in Turkey and that the only answer which he could give would lead to his downfall and possibly to Italy leaving the war.[156] Indeed, from the time in May 1916 when Asquith let slip to the Italian ambassador that Britain, France and Russia had comprehensive agreements on the future of Turkey, Sonnino had insistently demanded to know their terms as a preliminary to staking out claims for Italy. After Italy's belated declaration of war on Germany on 28 August 1916, it became impossible to refuse her either the required information or negotiations on any claims which she might make. The latter finally began between the four Entente powers in London in the following January. From the first the Italians made it clear that they would not be content with the small Adalia region in the south-west corner of Asia Minor which had been promised them in principle during the previous set of London negotiations nearly two years before.[157]

[155] War Cabinet, 18 Jan. 1917, CAB 23/1.
[156] Rodd to F.O., 4 Dec. 1916, FO 371/2772, no. 245352.
[157] For this paragraph, cf. C. Jay Smith, *The Russian Struggle for Power* (1956), pp. 423–31.

Italian claims in Asia Minor were troublesome on two counts: they clashed with those of France and they raised for the first time the question whether Turkey would survive the war as an independent state.[158] Even supposing that the allies had the resources for a war of annihilation against Turkey, the prospect of her disappearance from the face of the globe was alarming because of the effect which it was believed that it would have on Indian Moslem opinion. Practical necessities like those of placating Polish nationalism and Italian imperialism were always more likely to shape British policy toward the post-war map of the world than ideal schemes of the sort outlined by Paget and Tyrrell.

[158] Grey to Buchanan, 21 Nov. 1916, CAB 37/160/8.

II

THE PATTERN OF POLICY UNDER
LLOYD GEORGE, DECEMBER 1916–
MAY 1917

1. GERMANY, THE UNITED STATES AND PEACE

WITHIN less than a fortnight of coming to power, the Lloyd George government was faced with two events which had long been anticipated in official circles: what purported to be a German peace offer[1] and an American attempt at mediation. Germany's profession of a readiness for peace, which came in a speech by Bethmann-Hollweg on 12 December, would not have provided British ministers with a great preoccupation had it not been followed by the American note six days later. Robertson noted with pleasure that the War Cabinet's reaction to it was 'solid and sensible' and that the only ground for fear was that if Germany offered to leave Belgium and northern France including Alsace-Lorraine, France might be tempted to leave the war.[2] Likewise, it seemed to Hardinge that the only question as to the German note was how best to reject it in view of the absolute lack of evidence that militarism in Germany— 'I mean the spirit which prepared for and provoked the war'—was broken.[3]

Grey, in a note written on the very day that he vacated the Foreign Secretary's room to Balfour, reaffirmed that the 'defeat of Germany is and will continue to be the only satisfactory end of the war', but went on to argue that if Britain's allies were not prepared to fight on,

---

[1] The terms which the German government decided upon in discussions preceding this 'offer' included the exercise by Germany of 'guarantees' over the whole of Belgium or alternatively the annexation of Liège, the annexation of the Briey-Longwy basin and an indemnity from France and the annexation of the Belgian Congo. H. W. Gatzke, *Germany's Drive to the West : Germany's Western War Aims in the First World War* (1950), pp. 142-4.

[2] Robertson to Haig, 18 Dec. 1916, Robertson MSS. I/22/95. Robertson also said that the government had received nothing from Germany except a note embodying Bethmann's speech.

[3] Hardinge to Buchanan, Dec. 1916 (no precise date), Hardinge MSS. XXVIII.

American mediation should be sought on the basis of the agreement with House of the previous February.[4] Once Germany had made her peace move, Grey saw Britain's role as an educational one: she should supply the allies with information on shipping and finance so that they could make up their own minds whether it was possible to continue the war.[5]

To those who could only see the need to inflict defeat on Germany, Grey, as always, was anxious to make the common-sense point, that it was impossible to banish all thought of a compromise peace. He was supported by a section of opinion within the Foreign Office. Drummond and Cecil agreed that United States mediation would have to be sought if Belgium or France left the war. Drummond put forward a 'domino' theory of possible international doom for Britain: if Belgium or France were bribed out of the war by Germany, Russia and Italy would become helpless while Japan would make peace. Britain's only hope of continuing the struggle would then be to intensify the blockade of the continent of Europe and this would involve her in war with the United States. Britain would be fighting alone against the world.[6]

In fact, the reaction to the German note in the Entente states was uniformly hostile. The problem then became one of framing an answer to Germany which could not be used, for propaganda purposes, to depict the war as one essentially between Germany and England and which would win sympathy for the Entente in the United States. The latter consideration made it essential that France and not Britain should take the lead in making the reply as Balfour and Paul Cambon fully agreed.[7] The War Cabinet resolved that the best answer would be to tell Germany that it was idle of her to talk about peace without mentioning terms, that a major inter-allied conference was undesirable as likely to arouse unwarranted peace hopes among the public and that the question of actually inviting Germany to state her terms was 'more controversial and should be deferred pending Briand's visit'.[8] Even in the unlikely event of

[4] However, the Foreign Office did not know whether President Wilson still supported the House-Grey memorandum. Cf. Drummond to Cecil, 21 Dec. 1916, FO 800/197.

[5] Memorandum by Grey, 9 Dec. 1916, and Grey to Drummond, 12 Dec. 1916, FO 800/96.

[6] Drummond to Cecil, 13 Dec. 1916, with minute by Cecil, FO 800/197. The letter is also minuted as having been seen by Balfour.

[7] Balfour to Bertie, 15 Dec. 1916, FO 371/2805, no. 254951.

[8] War Cabinet, 18 Dec. 1916, CAB 23/1.

Germany stating her war aims in terms which were not obviously unacceptable, the British were not sure that they wanted to listen.

Had it not been for fear of the American reaction to an intemperate rejection, the German move would have been dealt with even more summarily. An enquiry into British economic and financial dependence on the United States in October had shown that the degree of dependence was great if not total.[9] Before the peace notes were received, little doubt was felt in the Foreign Office that if the allies appeared to be intransigent on the peace question Wilson would administer suitable punishment by exerting pressure on American businessmen and finance-houses to end or reduce their dealings with the allies.[10] Such fears were justified. In September 1916 Congress had given the President power to curb or end all financial and economic relations with the belligerents. He never did actually openly threaten to use these powers, but by November he was moving toward denial of loans to the British in response to their unbending attitude on the peace question.[11] Cecil pleaded with the non-Foreign Office ministers not to forget that Wilson could, if he wished, make the allied war effort impossible.[12]

The interpretation to be placed upon the President's move was a baffling problem. This is well shown by the conflicting reports which reached Lloyd George: that there had been German–American collaboration on the German peace move of 12 December[13]; that Wilson was determined to cajole the allies into peace negotiations on the supposition that once talks had started they could never be broken off[14]; that he was making a last desperate effort to bring about peace before Germany extended her submarine campaign and confronted the United States with a very grave new threat to her interests[15]; that he was pro-allied and was preparing the American

[9] Departmental memoranada on dependence on United States, Oct.–Nov. 1916, CAB 42/23/7; Treasury memorandum by R. H. Beard, Oct. 1916, Balfour MSS., B.M. Add. 49745.

[10] Cf. L. Collier's minute on despatch from Spring-Rice, 1 Dec. 1916, FO 371/2803, no. 250109.

[11] E. R. May, op. cit. pp. 330–5; L. W. Martin, *Peace Without Victory : Woodrow Wilson and the British Liberals* (1958), pp. 112–13.

[12] Memorandum by Cecil, 15 Dec. 1916, appendix to War Cabinet minutes, 18 Dec. 1916, CAB 23/1.

[13] Hardinge to Lloyd George, 14 Dec. 1916, Lloyd George MSS. F/3/2/1; Robertson to Lloyd George, 14 Dec. 1916, ibid. F/44/3/3.

[14] Guy Locock to Hankey, 16 Dec. 1916, ibid. F/60/2/2/.

[15] Copy of telegram Spring-Rice to FO, 15 Dec. 1916, ibid. F/3/2/3; C. P. Scott to Lloyd George, 24 Dec. 1916, ibid. F/45/2/2.

people for war.[16] The Prime Minister's own judgement was that Wilson was fulfilling an electoral pledge to 'pro-German Jews' who had supplied him with funds in the recent electoral campaign in return for a promise that if re-elected he would try to negotiate peace. As with the 'knock out blow' interview, 'the government had positive evidence of this.'[17]

It is now known that although Wilson had been sounding out Germany on peace the German note of 12 December was not produced in collaboration with him and at first disappointed him.[18] British leaders could not know this; their Washington embassy did not receive even the faintest indication that an American peace move was in the offing until Wilson's note of 18 December was made public property.[19] Also, they felt genuine indignation at Wilson's well-known statement that the war aims of the two sides were, as stated, identical. The mild-mannered Herbert Samuel thought that this was 'monstrous'.[20]

Another enquiry into allied dependence on the United States was ordered,[21] and the War Cabinet began discussing the sort of war aims which they could specify in their reply to Wilson.[22] Cecil suggested that they should specify the cession of Alsace-Lorraine to France as also strategic frontiers, and that there should be a 'final settlement of the Turkish question'. In this way the British government were forced toward something which they had always opposed: public statements of war aims while Germany remained undefeated.

Professor Arthur S. Link has argued that Wilson's peace mediation attempts were deliberately sabotaged by his own Secretary of State, Lansing, in conferences with the French ambassador, Jusserand, on 20 December and with Spring-Rice two days later in which he said that the President was pro-allied and wanted the United States to enter the war. To help him in this objective, the

---

[16] Northcliffe to Lloyd George quoting Roy Howard, 27 Dec. 1916, ibid. F/41/7/2; C. Delmé Radcliffe to Lloyd George quoting an American diplomat, 24 Dec. 1916, ibid. F/56/1/2.

[17] Journals, 26–30 Jan. 1917, 50903. Cf. Bone (London representative of *Manchester Guardian*) to C. P. Scott, 21 Dec. 1916: 'Have seen G. He says Wilson's note is a German move and that we will not declare terms.' Scott MSS., B.M. Add. 50909.

[18] A. S. Link, *Wilson: Campaigns for Progressivism and Peace 1916–1917* (1965), p. 214.

[19] Cf. Spring-Rice to FO, 22 Dec. 1916, FO 371/3075, no. 582.

[20] Samuel to his Mother, 24 Dec. 1916, Samuel MSS. A 156.

[21] War Cabinet, 23 Dec. 1916, CAB 23/1.

[22] Cf. note 17 above for Lloyd's George's alleged preference for a refusal to state terms to the Americans.

Entente should proclaim maximum war aims which Germany would reject out of hand.[23] The implication is that if only Lansing had been loyal, the Entente, driven to despair by knowledge of their dependence on the United States, might have agreed to enter into peace talks and so, owing to Wilson, the war might have ended in the winter of 1916–17.

This argument would seem to draw support from certain established facts: Lansing had done his utmost to discourage the President from issuing the peace note of 18 December and found it deplorable that his attitude was not wholly pro-ally[24]; and on 21 December the Secretary of State gave a public press conference in which he stated that the United States were on the verge of war.[25] No doubt this did have a reassuring effect on official opinion in the allied countries though it was at least partly cancelled out by the retraction of the statement which Wilson promptly compelled Lansing to make. In any event, Professor Link's conjectures obviously merit the closest attention, and with this in mind, the Foreign Office records on the United States peace move have been examined. No evidence has been found to support the assertion of Wilson's biographer. Spring-Rice did indeed report an interview with Lansing on 22 December but its contents were unspectacular: the Secretary of State is merely recorded as saying that the peace note was a genuinely neutral action prompted by the President's wish to know the terms of both sides. Spring-Rice sent his report not in a telegram but in a letter which did not reach the Foreign Office until ten days later. He also reported an interview between Lansing and Jusserand the previous day in which, far from the former reassuring the ambassador about the administration's intentions, the two men violently quarrelled.[26]

At first Spring-Rice interpreted Wilson's note as the work of 'court Jews' and pro-Germans like the former Secretary of State, Bryan, who were using Wilson as their unconscious tool. Their objective was to force the allies into declaring their terms.[27] The President himself was truly neutral in attitude and his only interest

[23] Link, *1916–1917*, pp. 223–5.
[24] Daniel M. Smith, *Robert Lansing and American Neutrality 1914–1917* (University of California Publications in History, LIX, 1958), pp. 146–9.
[25] Ibid. pp. 150–1.
[26] Spring-Rice despatch, 22 Dec. 1916, FO 371/3075, no. 583; report on Lansing-Jusserand interview in ibid. no. 586.
[27] Spring-Rice to FO, 23 Dec. 1916, FO 371/2806, no. 260913.

was peace irrespective of terms.[28] A few days later Spring-Rice changed his interpretation: Wilson was really afraid that submarine outrages might force him to break off diplomatic relations with Germany and he wanted to convince the American people that he had done everything that he could to prevent this.[29] At this time Cecil was still complaining to the United States ambassador, Walter Page, that American policy appeared to be pro-German[30] while Harold Nicolson was writing about 'the German character of Mr. Wilson's demands.'[31]

In short, there is no doubt that the British government, in framing their reply to Wilson, were under no illusion that he secretly supported them. The replies to both Germany and the United States were drawn up at an Anglo–French conference in London on 26–28 December. The note to Germany was brief. It was only specific on the need to restore Belgium, otherwise denouncing the German move as an impertinent fraud.[32] The French would have preferred a brief reply to the United States, while going into detail, if at all, only to Germany, for they felt that there were some allied war aims, especially those concerning Turkey, which would be as unpalatable to the United States as to Germany and that it would thus be best to say them to the enemy.[33] Therefore it was a British decision to make a detailed reply to the United States. The final note to Wilson was based mainly on drafts by Balfour and Cecil which, according to the former, were 'worked up by the French draftsmen, and then subjected to some hours' hammering at the hands of a joint committee of which I was one of the unfortunate members'. The resulting document was sent to the various allied capitals for scrutiny and possible modification.[34]

The reply, as delivered to the United States on 10 January 1917,[35] demanded the restoration of Belgium and Serbia and the evacuation of the occupied territory in France, Russia and Rumania together with the payment of indemnities. There was also a demand for a

[28] Spring-Rice to FO, 24 Dec. 1916, ibid. no. 260933.
[29] Spring-Rice to FO, 27 Dec. 1916, ibid. no. 263332.
[30] Cf. Cecil to Spring-Rice, 26 Dec. 1916, ibid. no. 263429.
[31] Minute, 29 Dec. 1916, ibid. no. 263816.
[32] James Brown Scott (ed.), *Official Statements of War Aims and Peace Proposals December 1916–November 1918* (1921), pp. 26–8.
[33] Berthelot's remarks at Anglo–French conference, CAB 28/2 I.C. 13.
[34] Cf. Balfour to Lord Sanderson, 4 Jan. 1917, Balfour MSS., B.M. Add. 49739; also Hankey to B. E. C. Dugdale, 29 May 1927, ibid. B.M. Add. 49833.
[35] Scott, op. cit. pp. 35–8.

stable regime in Europe based upon the principle of nationality and upon guarantees for the independence of small nations which was held to involve the liberation of the subject races of Austria–Hungary and territorial changes designed to create strategically defensible frontiers. The note concluded with the need for 'the setting free of the populations subject to the bloody tyranny of the Turks, and the turning out of Europe of the Ottoman Empire as decidedly foreign to western civilisation'.

The note reflected one genuine element in British official thinking about the post-war world which was, as Balfour put it, that 'It is in the interests of future peace that territorial arrangements after the war should take account of the principle of nationality'.[36] However, all reference to the freedom of Poland had to be slurred over in deference to Russian wishes. It did not reflect an even more important characteristic, the hope that a defeated Germany would become democratic and would lose its appetite for expansion and its hopes for world-power status. Yet pains were taken in drafting the note to restrict the calls for restoration to Europe and to provide no grounds for the restoration of the German colonies. No doubt an argument which Drummond had put to Lloyd George—that it was idle to call for a change of spirit in Germany while she was manifestly undefeated and that such an appeal could only weaken the opponents of militarism—commanded wide assent.[37] However, Balfour, who was always anxious to be as frank as possible in his dealings with American leaders, on his own initiative and without submitting the text to his colleagues, drafted a supplementary note in which he discussed the need for complete allied victory in order to discredit aggression and for 'some form of international sanction' to enforce international law and treaties.[38]

The American peace note was a most unwelcome development to the British but they managed to restrain themselves by venting their spleen against the smaller neutral powers which followed it with moves of their own or seemed likely to do so. When the Scandinavian nations presented a peace note Balfour crossed out the word 'polite' from a minute by one of his officials, 'It has been decided by the

---

[36] Balfour to Buchanan, 3 Jan. 1917, FO 371/3075, no. 2031.
[37] Drummond to Lloyd George, 15 Dec. 1916, FO 800/197.
[38] Scott, pp. 45–9. For Balfour's sole authorship see his *Chapters in Autobiography* (1930), p. 236. He did obtain the permission of the Anglo-French conference to write such a paper. Link, op. cit. p. 238.

Secretary of State to return a polite ackt'.[39] The British minister in Bangkok was praised for warning the Siamese government in the strongest terms not to give any support to Wilson.[40] The United States was never addressed in this way and the Entente leaders were largely successful in making it clear that they were most unwilling to negotiate with Germany without worsening their already strained relations with Washington. They were aided by Germany's folly in replying to Wilson on 27 December that the war ought to be ended by direct negotiations between the belligerents with no neutral mediation and by her subsequent moves toward unrestricted submarine warfare. Wilson still had ambitions as a peacemaker as he showed in his 'peace without victory' address on 22 January but his final efforts in this direction were futile.

This is shown by an event during the mission of Sir Francis Hopwood to Copenhagen in February 1917 to probe Austrian intentions on a separate peace (see Section 3 below). Andersen, a friend of the King of Denmark who had numerous contacts with the Foreign Office and the German and Russian governments, told him that during a recent visit to Berlin, Bethmann-Hollweg had announced German readiness to enter into peace talks with Britain in the strictest confidence. The reaction in London came in no uncertain manner. Lloyd George suggested to Balfour that the government surely did not want 'even informal conversations with Germany at this stage'[41] and Balfour vetoed the idea absolutely: 'We have no desire to negotiate with Germany.'[42] The following month the King of Denmark offered himself as peace mediator and met with an official refusal from Britain whose terms, when presented by Ralph Paget, were supplemented by a rebuke (actually administered to Andersen) for obtuseness in not realizing: 'That one could not treat with the Germans on the same footing as one would another enemy. They had placed themselves beyond the pale and could only be treated as criminals.'[43]

Such were British attitudes when President Wilson, convinced that German policies on naval warfare left him with no alternative, reluctantly led the United States into the World War.

---

[39] Minute by Oliphant with correction by Balfour, 1 Jan. 1917, FO 371/3075, no. 421.
[40] Hardinge's minute on a telegram from H. Dering, Bangkok, 29 Dec. 1916, FO 371/3076, no. 35353.   [41] Lloyd George to Balfour, 17 Feb. 1917, FO 800/199.
[42] Balfour to Paget (for Hopwood), 17 Feb. 1917, Paget MSS., B.M. Add. 51252.
[43] Paget to F.O., 27 Mar. 1917 and Balfour to Paget, 29 Mar. 1917, ibid.; Paget to Hardinge, 30 Mar. 1917, B.M. Add. 51253.

2. DISCUSSION OF WAR AIMS

If the members of the new War Cabinet desired advice on the nation's war aims, they were soon to be presented with an *embarras de richesses*. The Mallet committee published four reports between January and July 1917. They first recommended that the German islands in the Pacific south of the equator should be retained by Australia and New Zealand while those north of the line, together with Kiaochou, should remain in Japanese hands, the Admiralty having testified that they were of limited strategic importance. The second a month later set up a scale of priorities for the German African colonies with Togo as the most expendable and with South West Africa, whose return, it was thought, would lead with absolute certainty to the withdrawal of South Africa from the Empire, at the opposite extreme.[44]

In view of Lloyd George's refusal to accept as binding the report of the much more authoritative committee on territorial war aims set up by the Imperial War Cabinet in April 1917, it must be assumed that he regarded the Mallet reports as the merest guides even supposing that he took any serious notice of them at all. In February, Amery suggested to Hankey a more detailed fact-finding approach to the formulation of war aims with a view to allowing British negotiators at the peace conference to ascertain exactly what they wanted and to bring forward arguments to justify their claims. At the same time, Hankey received a similar proposal from Professors Zimmern and Toynbee which suggested that the Admiralty Intelligence Department should be expanded into a Peace Terms Intelligence Section. Hankey himself favoured the setting up of a sub-committee of the War Cabinet to follow up the work of the Mallet committee.[45] These proposals were realistic. There was very

---

[44] The two remaining reports dealt with possible exchanges of colonial territory among the allies and with economic aspects of the colonial peace settlement. The reports of this committee, though not its numerous memoranda in CAB 16/36, were used by W. R. Louis, op. cit. pp. 70–4, making detailed discussion here superfluous. Apart from the special claims of the Dominions mentioned above two points are worth noting in parenthesis: that the committee recommended keeping the colonies for precisely the reasons put forward in public debate—that they would be used to furnish black armies to attack neighbours and naval bases to threaten imperial communications, that Germany grossly ill-treated the 'natives' and that their return would damage British prestige in the existing British colonies. Secondly, that a public campaign was conducted in France for depriving Germany of colonies on exactly the same grounds. Cf. C. Fidel, *La Paix Coloniale Française* (1918), pp. v–vii, xiii–xv, 29–38, 40–1, 57–60 and map at end.

[45] Amery to Hankey, 7 Feb. 1917; memoranda by Zimmern and Toynbee, n.d. and 13 Feb. 1917; minute by Hankey, 31 Jan. 1917, all in CAB 21/62.

little prospect of an early end to the war and the new Prime Minister was temperamentally utterly averse to having his hands tied by a firm programme of commitments. In fact, in the spring of 1917, the Foreign Office began work of the detailed kind favoured by Amery.[46]

The Lloyd George government was obliged to pay far more attention than its predecessor to the views of the Dominions on war aims. This could hardly be otherwise given the new government's early decision to summon an Imperial War Cabinet to co-ordinate the help which the Dominions were giving and to ask them to do more.[47]

As early as 22 December 1916, the War Cabinet agreed on the necessity of consulting the Dominions on peace terms: 'There was a fear on their part that they might be asked to make sacrifices of their interests in order to make it easier for His Majesty's Government to fulfil its pledges to Belgium and France.' Underlying this was the fear, never wholly absent, of an inconclusive end to the war in which a choice had to be made between European and Imperial aims.[48]

One problem was disposed of early in February with the decision to support Japanese claims to Kiaochou and the north Pacific islands. The weakness of the British when confronted with demands of this sort from their allies is shown by the War Cabinet's decision to narrow down the *quid pro quo* demanded from Japan from support for all British war aims to support only for British claims to the German islands south of the equator, a decision from which Curzon insisted on recording his dissent.[49]

Nevertheless, the Foreign Office did hope to obtain long-term political capital out of this concession to the Japanese by posing as

---

[46] H. Nicolson, *Peacemaking 1919* (University Paperbacks ed., 1964), pp. 26–7, 29. Both Amery and Hardinge have claimed the credit for initiating work on the Peace Handbooks mentioned by Nicolson. Cf. L. S. Amery, *My Political Life*, ii (1953), 103; and Hardinge to Wingate, 28 Nov. 1918, Hardinge MSS. XXXIX. In compiling these famous handbooks the Foreign Office worked closely with both the General Staff and Admiralty Intelligence. L. E. Gelfand, *The Inquiry : American Preparations for Peace* (1963), pp. 121–4. In Oct. 1917, the Foreign Office was declared by Bonar Law to be the department chiefly responsible for work on drawing up peace terms. Cf. *Commons Debates*, 5th series, XCVIII, col. 1186, 29 Oct. 1917.

[47] Cf. Lloyd George to Walter Long, 26 Dec. 1916 in *War Memoirs*, i. 1026: 'We want more men from them . . .' Of course, this and not a desire to discuss war aims was the reason for summoning the Imperial War Cabinet.

[48] War Cabinet, 22 Dec. 1917, CAB 23/1.

[49] Louis, op. cit. pp. 78–80; War Cabinet, 14 Feb. 1917, CAB 23/1.

honest broker between Japan and the United States in any future conflicts over Pacific problems. In a speech on 27 April 1917 to the Imperial War Conference, which, under the chairmanship of the Colonial Secretary, Walter Long, ran parallel to the Imperial War Cabinet, De Bunsen, after mentioning the recent agreement with Japan on the north Pacific islands, continued:

This, of course, is an important act of policy which will be something to guide us when peace comes. I think it is very much felt that there must be considerable friction and conflict even, between Japan and the United States with regard to Pacific questions. I think it is hoped that we shall be very much in the position of friends of both parties—we can say that even more today than we could before, owing to the recent action of the United States—and of holding the balance between their aspirations in the Pacific and when the conflict appears imminent we hope to be able to step in and avert it by giving friendly advice to both sides. I think that is very much to be hoped of the future.

He concluded that the recent War Cabinet decision meant that Britain had a Pacific policy whose other ingredient was a determination to do her utmost to satisfy Australian and New Zealand aspirations and that the Japanese had ambitions in the Netherlands East Indies 'but it is hoped that they may be restrained by the lessons of the present war'.[50]

The Dominions fared rather less well than the Japanese whose loyalty, it was thought, could only be guaranteed by being bought. Long, who from the moment he became Colonial Secretary made himself an untiring advocate of Dominion war aims, made a public speech on 31 January 1917 in which he called for the German colonies never to be returned. He incurred much criticism from his colleagues as he himself was to point out.[51] In addition, despite prodding from Long that the War Cabinet should endorse his stand, in which he was supported by a formal request from the Governor-General of South Africa, Lord Buxton, that he should be allowed to make a speech similar to the Colonial Secretary's,[52] ministers decided that Buxton's request must be refused, 'having regard to the general arrangements with our allies that no definite decisions should

---

[50] Minutes in CAB 32/1/1. For the perplexity of British ministers before the problem of doing nothing which would endanger friendship with either Japan or the United States while at the same time doing everything possible to win the war see War Cabinet minutes, 22 May 1917, CAB 23/2 and 19 June 1917, CAB 23/3.

[51] W. Long, *Memories* (1923), p. 240.

[52] Long to Lloyd George, 7 Feb. 1917, Lloyd George MSS. F/32/4/35.

be taken in regard to rearrangement of territory until the question could be treated as a whole at the peace conference at the conclusion of peace'.[53]

When the Dominion leaders, excluding Hughes of Australia who was kept at home by a political crisis, assembled in London the following month it was, naturally enough, more difficult to turn them down when they pressed their demands in person. The Imperial War Cabinet opened on 20 March with an address by Lloyd George.[54] When he came to war aims, he began by enumerating such evidently desirable objectives as strengthening imperial bonds and teaching aggressors that aggression did not pay. On the German colonies, his remarks were ultra-cautious in contrast to those on Turkey and he left no doubt that it might be necessary to return some of them in order to realize the more important aims of the European allies.[55]

Two days later Balfour spoke on war aims in Europe and Turkey. All this was not good enough for the Dominion leaders who could hardly be expected to take a keen interest in the future of Transylvania, one of the subjects upon which Balfour expatiated. After discussing the question of a compromise peace and agreeing that the only thing which might compel Germany to give 'reasonable' terms was 'sheer famine' of which there was as yet little sign and that the Empire must make maximum military efforts in 1917 and if necessary 1918,[56] they began a campaign for the discussion of war aims. On 27 March Smuts and the New Zealand Minister of Finance, Sir Joseph Ward, declared that consideration of war aims was vital because of the need to have a definite policy toward the aims of the other Entente states who would obviously be preoccupied with European issues, and also because public opinion in the Dominions was demanding such consideration. Lloyd George promised to furnish various documents on war aims and to set up a committee if the overseas prime ministers desired after reading them. They did so desire and on 12 April Lloyd George announced that two committees would sit: one under Milner on economic and non-territorial aims and one under Curzon on territory.[57]

Both committees reported within a fortnight and their work was

---

[53] War Cabinet, 8 Feb. 1917, CAB 23/1.
[54] Text in *War Memoirs*, i. 1047–57.   [55] Ibid. pp. 1050, 1052.
[56] Imperial War Cabinet, 23 Mar. 1917, CAB 23/40.
[57] Ibid. 27 Mar. and 12 Apr. 1917.

debated by the full Imperial War Cabinet on 26 April and 1 May.[58]
Neither the reports nor the debates decided anything. The debate
on the Milner committee's report merely served to show the perplexity of the leaders on such subjects as disarmament and the league
of nations.[59] At the end of the debate on the territorial report Lloyd
George succeeded in qualifying its endorsement with the proviso
that it merely gave an 'indication' of the 'relative importance' of
various objectives to be sought at the peace conference and that these
'will require to be correlated with those of the allies'. He thus con-
trived to leave himself with as much freedom as he had claimed in
his opening address on 20 March. Indeed, to Lloyd George and to
most of his colleagues (though not for instance to Curzon) the
obsession of their guests with territorial problems showed a false
understanding of what the war was about. Shortly before the
Imperial Cabinet began the Prime Minister had cited the destruction
of militarism—defined as 'reactionary military government' in Germany and Russia—and the establishment of popular governments as
the basis for international peace and therefore as the true aims of the
war. While he added that the destruction of his *bête noire*, the
Turkish Empire, was essential, it is certain that territorial matters
were decidedly secondary in his view of war aims.[60]

Perhaps the one really solid achievement of the Curzon committee
was to make clear at the highest political level the profound feelings
of the southern Dominions for the retention of the German south
Pacific colonies and of South West Africa. The intense concern of
the Australasian Dominions with security is revealed in the rather
passionate outbursts of the New Zealand representatives, Ward and
Massey (the Prime Minister), at the Imperial War Conference in
which they stated that the Pacific had been grossly neglected in naval
plans for the defence of the Empire and that an imperial navy should be
set up. A resolution was passed that the Admiralty should draw up
a scheme for this despite its protests that nothing could be done
until after the war.[61] Before 1914 most New Zealanders had thought

---

[58] The fullest records of the Milner committee are in CAB 21/71 and there is a
summary of its report in *War Memoirs*, i. 1066–7; there are records of the Curzon committee in CAB 21/77 and CAB 29/1 and its work is analysed in Louis, op. cit. pp. 81–4;
the Imperial War Cabinet debates are in CAB 23/40.

[59] It seems unnecessary to say more since Lloyd George has given a full transcript
in his *War Memoirs*, i. 1037–46; cf. also the notes made by one of the secretaries to the
Milner committee, Thomas Jones, *Whitehall Diary: Volume I 1916–1925*, ed. K.
Middlemas (1969), pp. 30–4.   [60] Journals, 15–17 Mar. 1917, 50903.

[61] Imperial War Conference, 28 and 30 Mar. 1917, CAB 32/1/1.

6

that the main threat to their security came from Germany and had paid little attention to Japan, but after the Japanese occupation of the north Pacific islands there was an upsurge of fear against Japan.[62] Ward was to give eloquent expression to this at the next imperial conference in August 1918 when he declared that the struggle for the Pacific was intensifying so that, 'It is not too much to say that the problem of the future is as to whether the white or yellow races are to predominate in the Pacific'. The numerically insignificant white populations of Australia and New Zealand were appalled at the indifference of Britain to the presence of non-British powers in the Pacific and Indian Oceans.[63] The slightly delirious attitude of the southern Dominions toward the German colonies which they occupied in 1914–15 has recently been described,[64] but considerations such as those put forward by Ward and Massey help to place the matter in its proper perspective, that of the security of Australia and New Zealand.

For the rest, the Curzon report was too idiosyncratic a document to command universal assent. Amery who was its secretary has explained that Hankey instructed his assistant secretaries when compiling minutes to record a decision on every item. This could be difficult, 'But my experience was that if one invented the best decision one could think of, it was rarely queried by those concerned'.[65] In other words, Amery combined his secretarial duties with a political role, doing all he could to ensure that his views as to the need to eliminate Germany as a colonial power and to establish continuity of territory between Egypt and India and Egypt and Rhodesia were accepted[66] while 'putting Europe into proper perspective'. The recommendations of the Curzon committee must be seen in the light of this apologia and of the community of views between Curzon and Amery. The recommendations were that Palestine and Mesopotamia should be annexed outright to the British Empire, entailing the abrogation of the Sykes–Picot provisions on the former, and (of course) that Germany should if

---

[62] B. K. Gordon, *New Zealand Becomes a Pacific Power* (1960), pp. 30–4, 46.

[63] Memorandum by Ward, 'The Pacific Problem', 28 Aug. 1918 in *Western and General Report : British Empire*, no. LXXXIII, CAB 24/151. Despite Ward's pleading the 1918 Imperial War Conference put on one side a report drawn up by the Admiralty in accordance with the instructions of the conference of the previous year and decided to postpone any action until after the war. Cf. memorandum by Admiral Wemyss, 'Naval Defence of the British Empire', 17 May 1918; and conference minutes, 24 July 1918, all in CAB 32/1/2.   [64] Louis, op. cit. passim.

[65] L. S. Amery, op. cit. ii. 94.   [66] Ibid. pp. 102, 106.

possible be deprived of all her colonies. As far as Europe was concerned the committee favoured the restoration of Belgium and
Serbia; a settlement of the Alsace-Lorraine and Polish questions
which 'should correspond as far as possible with the wishes of the
populations concerned and be inherently stable and calculated to
promote a lasting peace'; and the prevention of German expansion
in eastern Europe or the establishment of a French protectorate in
Greece. Even the last two points, it was explained, were dictated
directly by British imperial considerations. The report was infected
with a sense of *ennui* toward the German problem and the complex
problems of central-eastern Europe. This could not be pleasing to
the Foreign Office whose chief had proclaimed at the Anglo–French
conference at the end of December that it was desirable that British
acquisitions as a result of the war should be as few as possible and
who were professionally concerned with European problems.[67] It is
not surprising that in the Imperial War Cabinet debate Cecil should
have supported Lloyd George's line that the report could only be
accepted as a 'guide'.

In-fighting in official circles is also evident in the committee's
firm recommendation that in the event of a compromise peace and
a necessity to restore some German colonies, the Cameroons and
Togo could far more safely be restored than German East Africa
owing to 'the much greater importance to the British Empire of East
Africa and the East African sea and land routes than those of West
Africa'. This was a victory—a very easy one, given the composition
of the committee—for Curzon, Smuts, Chamberlain and Amery,
who had their eyes firmly fixed on the routes to India and Australia,
and a defeat for the Admiralty which, as far as the German colonies
were concerned, attached supreme importance to the acquisition of
Duala in the Cameroons. In his memorandum on war aims in
October 1916, the First Sea Lord, Henry Jackson, had said that
Duala was so fine a harbour that a naval base could be set up there
from which West Africa and the south Atlantic could be dominated,
thus giving it a strategic importance comparable only with that of the
Kiel Canal.[68] This assessment of the port's importance was

---

[67] Cf. minutes of fourth meeting of committee, 29 Apr. 1917, CAB 29/1. The Foreign
Office representative, Clerk, took Austen Chamberlain to task for saying that Belgium
was Britain's only real interest in Europe and expatiated on the dangers of Germany's
Mittel-Europa schemes which, he said, must be firmly blocked 'at Constantinople,
Sofia or even possibly Vienna'.

[68] This memorandum, dated 12 Oct. 1916 and to be found in CAB 29/1, is discussed
in Chapter I, Section 2 above.

reaffirmed before the committee at its second meeting by Admiral Wilson.[69] This was, however, the only meeting to which it was considered necessary to summon an Admiralty representative.[70]

Finally, the committee is notable for the gestation of the self-determination principle as a means of facilitating additions to the British Empire. It recommended a number of exchanges between the colonial possessions of the allies in the interests of administrative efficiency but laid down that the views of the populations concerned should first be obtained. In response to a suggestion from a Canadian minister, Hazen, that the Alaskan Panhandle cutting off the northern part of British Columbia from the Pacific, should be acquired from the United States in return for British Honduras or Guiana, Curzon said: 'It was quite out of the question that these matters could be dealt with like an exchange of pawns on a chessboard without having regard to the feelings and interests of the populations concerned' including the black and Indian peoples of the West Indies as well as the white element there.[71]

This shows that the British leaders were far from being wholly cynical when they expressed in public solicitude for the wishes and interests of 'backward' peoples. But there was a clear and rather smug assumption that these vastly preferred British rule to any other. The minutes of the committee make this clear. Long declared his:

. . . gratitude to the chairman for having laid stress on a matter to which he attached very great importance. Since the war he had had most remarkable testimony from every part of the world in favour of British rule as against that of any other country. Not only in cases of territory already British, but in such cases as those of the Cameroons and Togoland there would be great disappointment among any section of natives who found that they were to be included in the territory of any other power than Great Britain.[72]

Shortly afterwards in the cabinet debate, Smuts announced complete confidence that in a plebiscite the eight million Africans of German East Africa would vote 'unanimously' for British rule. Such fond beliefs were to give British leaders many bright ideas for satisfying their war aims when a clamour against annexations arose following the publication of the secret treaties by the Bolsheviks in

---

[69] Minutes of second meeting, 18 Apr. 1917.
[70] Cf. preamble to copy of report in CAB 29/1.
[71] Minutes of fourth meeting, 29 Apr. 1917.   [72] Ibid.

November 1917 and the growth of support for a Wilsonian peace without acquisitions of new territory based on force.

The first four months of 1917 saw the high-water mark of British attempts to formulate a full programme of war aims. The relative failure of this attempt resulted not only from disagreements about what was theoretically desirable but from a lack of conviction that any full programme could be achieved or that the war should be prolonged to achieve it. A call by Hankey in June 1917 for authority to make secretarial arrangements for the eventual peace conference is remarkable for the assumptions which it makes in passing. The work which had so far been done on war aims stood 'rather as a standard to be aimed at than as a practical policy'; the question of the sacrifices which might have to be made during the process of bargaining deserved equal consideration; thought should also be given to which of the *neutral* capitals would be the best site for the peace conference; the possibility of the victorious allies holding it in one of their own capitals is not even mentioned.[73]

Hankey was far removed from the standpoint represented by Lansdowne and he was writing at a time when the British were considering major new military operations from which it was naturally hoped to achieve much. Yet he took a peace based at least in part on negotiation and not dictation for granted. In the meantime the war must continue not in order to force Germany to concede a list of allied territorial demands on which there could be no compromise but until that intangible objective, the discrediting of militarism among the German people, had been achieved.

3. AUSTRIA–HUNGARY

One of the most perplexing problems facing British leaders during the war was that of policy toward the confederal monarchy of Austria–Hungary. The political and social structure of these two countries was 'oppressive' by modern standards. The German Austrians and the Magyars were in a privileged position, both politically and, particularly in the case of the Magyars, socially and economically by comparison with the other subjects of the Habsburg

[73] Hankey, 'Arrangements for the Eventual Peace Conference', 5 June 1917, G.T. 938, CAB 24/15. The following day the War Cabinet rejected Hankey's request for fear that work on a scheme for merely the technical aspects of the peace conference 'might create a peace atmosphere or give the impression that the government were making preparations for a peace conference'. War Cabinet, 6 June 1917, CAB 23/5.

ruler in Vienna. The these 'subject peoples' included Czechs, Poles, Slovenes, Ukrainians and Italians in Austria, Croats, Serbs, Rumanians, Slovaks, and Ukrainians in Hungary, and Croats and Serbs in Dalmatia and Bosnia–Herzegovina, the former a part of Austria cut off by Hungarian territory, the latter virtually an Austro–Hungarian colony. Their condition varied widely. Some, notably the Poles and Croats, were less underprivileged than the others. Among all of them, it is doubtful whether a majority wanted independence in 1914 and more than doubtful in the case of some such as the Slovenes.

However, politicians from the subject peoples, including the great Masaryk, who escaped to the Entente countries during the early months of the war, set up a powerful agitation there for the reconstitution of east-central Europe on national lines. The activities of these leaders, mostly Czechs and Croats (excluding the Poles whose relations with the British Government are discussed elsewhere in this work) and of their influential coterie of supporters in British public life have been extensively described by themselves and others.[74] Their historian was careful to point out that they were strongly opposed by those who thought that Austria–Hungary was a natural unit by no means irrevocably linked to Germany, whose disruption would be a tragedy, or who regarded the Slavs and Rumanians as barbarians whose national aims were unworthy of satisfaction. Also comparatively few in British ruling circles had really firm views on the future of the Monarchy.[75]

The residue of good will for Austria which survived in Britain to the end of the war contrasted with the fierce hatred of Germany throughout society. The businessman and member of Parliament, sitting on an official committee on economic policy, who remarked in 1917 that he was 'in favour of a high tariff against Germany' after the war to punish her but that 'he would treat Austria differently' epitomized this contrast.[76] The existence of this goodwill owed

[74] H. Hanak, *Great Britain and Austria–Hungary during the First World War : a Study in the Making of Public Opinion* (1962) is the standard work; see also Arthur J. May, *The Passing of the Hapsburg Monarchy* (1966), i. 223–44.

[75] Hanak, op. cit. pp. 1–10, 40, 53–7, 86–8, chapter VI *passim*. See also his 'The Government, the Foreign Office and Austria–Hungary 1914–1918' in *Slavonic and East European Review*, xvii (1969), 161–97. This important article omits much of interest and undoubtedly leaves scope for a further account of British war-time policy toward Austria–Hungary such as is attempted here.

[76] Remarks by Sir C. Henry in minutes of Committee on Commercial and Industrial Policy, 41st meeting, 12 July 1917, B[oard of] T[rade] 55/8.

much to the belief that Germany was almost solely responsible for the outbreak of war. Looking back at that event, Grey thought that Germany had actually forced Austria into war. Austria clearly had no quarrel with Britain or France and if only Germany had left her in peace to settle her quarrel with Russia instead of pressing for war in late July and August 1914 there would assuredly have been no conflict.[77] Arthur Nicolson said farewell to the Austrian ambassador in language which would have been inconceivable if addressed to his German counterpart: 'I am so dreadfully sorry that we shall have to lose you for a time.'[78] This set the keynote. There was never to be any question of a compromise peace with Austria–Hungary being unacceptable on principle. Those like Wickham Steed, Seton-Watson and Namier who favoured such a policy were only to gain partial acceptance for their views in the War Cabinet and the Foreign Office during the last six months of the war when it seemed in any case that all hope of an agreement with the Monarchy had ceased.

During the first two years of the war this question was largely dormant. The aged emperor, Francis Joseph, seems to have had no interest in peace-making and, even if he had, Italy and Russia would have stood decisively in the way of an Austrian approach to the Entente. So anxious were the Foreign Office to reassure Italy that she would receive the territory promised to her in the treaty of London on the east side of the Adriatic that an anodyne British declaration of sympathy with the Czechs was vetoed on the grounds that it would be taken as applying also to the Yugoslavs and so would distress Italy.[79] The same objection applied with equal force to the opposite policy of making peace with Austria and requiring Italy to abandon at least some of her promised territorial rewards. An even more formidable obstacle was Russia, whose pre-war foreign policy had as its dearest wish a desire for expansion at the expense of Austria: *Lâcher l'Autriche et nous lâcherons la France* as Sazonov once indelicately put it to a German diplomat. During the first winter of the war Russia was unresponsive to Anglo–French suggestions that if Austria sued for peace, allowing Russia to annex the Polish and Little Russian areas, the Entente should agree.[80] These suggestions were purely hypothetical and were unprompted

[77] Grey to Spring-Rice, 18 Sept. 1914, FO 800/241; memorandum by Grey on interview with the Spanish ambassador, 6 Jan. 1915, FO 800/95.
[78] Nicolson to Mensdorff, 13 Aug. 1914, FO 800/375.
[79] Minutes by G. R. Clerk and Eric Drummond, 10 Aug. 1916, FO 800/96.
[80] C. Jay Smith, op. cit. pp. 119–24.

by any Austro–Hungarian peace feelers that were regarded in London as coming from official quarters in the Dual Monarchy. When in January 1915, Grey, despite his knowledge of the Russian attitude, was persuaded to sound out the Austrians on the peace question by the French Foreign Minister, Delcassé, who paid a highly secret visit to London for this purpose, the inquiries which were made stopped at a preliminary stage; the British envoy to the Vatican, Howard, who was asked to approach the pro-Austrian clerical circles there, reported that the feeling in those circles was that Austria was not in the mood for peace.[81]

Finally, during the first two years of the war the Foreign Office worked hard for the entry of Rumania, offering her territory in eastern Hungary and the north-eastern corner of Austria. It was generally thought that these offers would alone make a separate peace with the Dual Monarchy or at least with its Hungarian part impossible. When Rumania finally entered the war in August 1916, Clerk commented: 'Our arrangement with Rumania precludes the possibility of terms that Hungary could accept.'[82]

Against this background, the Foreign Office moved spasmodically toward enlisting the support of the subject races. At the end of August 1915, Grey told Supilo, perhaps the most outstanding of the Southern Slav leaders and a man for whom the Foreign Secretary seems to have acquired a liking, that Britain would be prepared to work actively in favour of a union between Serbia and Croatia. Supilo himself demurred owing to a fear that Italy and Russia would respond by exerting themselves against such a union and Grey's promise was altered to read: 'After the war Bosnia, Herzegovina, Southern Dalmatia, Slavonia and Croatia shall be free. They can decide their own fate.'[83] In May 1916 Grey told the moderate conservative Russian politician, Miliukov, who at that time favoured the continued existence of Austria–Hungary, that he would welcome the liberation of the Slavs and also a union between German Austria and Germany 'as it would tend rather to neutralize Prussian influence.'[84]

[81] Ekstein Frankl, op. cit. pp. 182–94.

[82] Minute by Clerk, 31 Aug. 1916, FO 371/2602, no. 171354. On Entente–Rumanian negotiations see Smith, pp. 23–30, 287–309 and A. J. May, I, 217–18.

[83] H. Nicolson, 'Synopsis of our Obligations to our Allies and Others', 6 Feb. 1918, FO 371/3440, no. 31930. For Grey's original offer to Supilo see Drummond to Grey, 31 Mar. 1916, FO 800/196.

[84] Grey to Buchanan, 15 May 1916, CAB 37/147/40.

The Foreign Secretary almost seemed to have written off the Monarchy. Still attracted by the policy with which the Foreign Office had tried to induce Bulgaria not to join the Central Powers in 1914 and 1915, he and his officials favoured the idea of prising her out of the war with offers of Serbian territory with its necessary corollary of extensive additions to Serbia from the Monarchy.[85] In August Paget and Tyrrell put an ideological gloss on this tendency in official thinking in their war aims memorandum with its call for a comprehensive redrawing of European boundaries on nationality lines.

The Foreign Office had already disappointed the hopes of the leaders of the subject peoples once when it largely acquiesced in Italy's claims at the head and on the east shores of the Adriatic despite the fullest presentation of the Southern Slav case by Seton-Watson.[86] It began to retreat from its very mildly pro-Slav stance of 1915–16 at the very time that that stance received its first public endorsement. This was in the allied note to President Wilson of 10 January 1917 and was the result of pressure from the French Foreign Ministry who were impressed by an argument which Benes put to them that it would be logical to include these peoples in what was meant as a comprehensive statement of allied war aims.[87] However, the French made it clear to Benes that there was no possibility of the war being continued simply for the benefit of east European nationalism; while in Britain those newspapers and publicists who favoured the break up of the Monarchy took the realistic line that the inclusion of the Czechs was a mere rhetorical flourish.[88]

By January 1917 there seemed a chance of reaching agreement with Austria. The new emperor, Karl, whose undoubted desire for peace was common knowledge, had recently been crowned, and in

[85] It should be added that the Foreign Office, like the champion of the Yugoslavs, Seton-Watson, were distressed by the enmity between the Croat and Slovene leaders in exile and the Serbian government who wavered between outright opposition to South Slav unity (seeking instead only union with the Serbs in Bosnia–Herzegovina, Dalmatia and Hungary) and a Yugoslav state based on Serbian domination. (Cf. Clerk's minute on record of conversation between Ralph Paget and the Serbian Prime Minister, Pashitch, 20 June 1916, FO 371/2804, no. 117933). For the Foreign Office this was to be a strong reason for doubting the constant refrain of the anti-Monarchy publicists that a Southern Slav state would be a stable bulwark against German schemes of easterly expansion.

[86] A. J. May, 'Seton-Watson and the Treaty of London' in *Journal of Modern History*, xxix (1957), 42–7.

[87] Victor S. Mamatey, *The United States and East-Central Europe 1914–1918* (1957), p. 46.   [88] Hanak, op. cit. pp. 216–18, 226.

the middle of January, the War Cabinet considered a number of telegrams from the British legation in Christiania containing what was represented as an Austrian offer to discuss peace. It agreed to investigate these feelers while informing the allies that they would be consulted before any formal peace talks and demanding from the persons in Christiania better credentials than they had so far produced.[89]

Contact was finally made in Copenhagen. On the British side Sir Francis Hopwood, a leading civil servant then working in the Admiralty, conducted the talks. Plagued by many difficulties including the petty jealousy of the Austrian minister toward the Austrian negotiators who included one of his staff and an industrialist called Westfried, the talks collapsed when it became clear that Germany was aware that they were going on, and when the German chancellor made what appeared to be an attempt to open up conversations with Britain (see Section 1 above). Hopwood drew the conclusion that his mission showed the decisive difficulty of negotiations with unofficial persons and added that since the King of Denmark had informed both Britain and Austria that he was prepared to act as an intermediary in any future peace moves, Austria could have no excuse for using unofficial agents again.[90]

It was now clear that there was a chance, even if only a slight one, of making peace with Austria. This, together with the manifest weakening of Russia, produced much discussion of future arrangements in eastern Europe. At its basis was the security of the British Empire against Germany, a security which Russia was no longer thought to be capable of protecting. At a conference in Rome in the new year 1917, Lloyd George advocated the reinforcement of the Italian army and vigorous offensives on the Italian–Austrian front on the grounds that otherwise the Central Powers would be able to send enough troops to the east to crush Russia.[91] At the same time the Director of Military Intelligence, Macdonagh, was writing that if, as might well be the case, the war had to be continued into 1918 to inflict defeat on Germany, the heavy cost would be justified by the need to exclude German influence for ever from Turkey as the only effective safeguard for the British Empire in Asia.[92]

---

[89] War Cabinet, 18 Jan. 1917, CAB 23/13.
[90] Memorandum by Hopwood, 17 Mar. 1917, FO 800/214.
[91] Hankey, op. cit. ii. 609.
[92] Memorandum by Macdonagh, Jan. 1917, WO 106/1511, no. 72.

Discussion was naturally most extensive in the Foreign Office and was initiated by Drummond. In a paper written in February, he made a passing reference to the Paget–Tyrrell scheme as ideally desirable, and then argued that a separate peace with Austria was essential to shorten the war and should be based on granting the Czechs and Yugoslavs the same degree of autonomy as the Magyars within the Monarchy. All the allied nations on its borders would have to resign themselves to less than they had hoped for: Italy would receive Trentino and possibly Trieste; Serbia, Bosnia-Herzegovina and enough of Dalmatia to give her an adequate coast-line; while Rumania would receive nothing from Austria but would be given Bessarabia by Russia whose reward would be complete freedom to fix her frontiers with Germany and Turkey. Not only would the war thus be shortened, but the ill-will engendered by a break between Germany and Austria would probably lead to a lasting estrangement so that: 'A permanent and powerful barrier against the German *Drang nach Osten* will have been created. This aspect of a separate peace with Austria does not probably need emphasizing.'

Drummond's memorandum was enthusiastically endorsed by Cecil and Hardinge. The latter thought the proposal to make Austria a four-state federation 'practical' and the idea of England, France and Russia continuing the war so that Italy and Rumania could obtain the territories promised them in the secret treaties in full 'absurd'. A separate peace might well not be attainable but it would be a glittering prize if it could be won and 'would mean the crushing of Germany and the destruction of all her hopes'.[93]

The national principle which had been fashionable in the Foreign Office in 1916 when complete victory had been anticipated and when Austria's attitude had seemed to hold out no hopes of an accommodation with her, had been modified and not abandoned: Drummond's federal scheme was a permutation of it and Hardinge argued that Austria would have to defer to it by ceding Bosnia-Herzegovina to Serbia and Galicia to a Polish state and recognized that negotiations might break down on this point. Probably the Foreign Office would have been prepared to retreat from it even further in proportion as Austrian peace approaches became more serious. In April, Hardinge, responding to pressure from a general staff which

[93] Memorandum by Drummond with minutes by Hardinge and Cecil, 12–19 Feb. 1917, FO 800/214.

felt that every day it became clearer that 'the struggle is far more between her [i.e. Britain] and Germany than between the Entente and the Central Powers',[94] virtually promised Robertson that Britain would be prepared to make almost any concession to Austria (or Turkey or Bulgaria) in the interests of a separate peace if only one of the enemy powers would make the first move. Hardinge, who must have reflected that Robertson's grasp of foreign policy was still rather naive, explained that it would be unwise as yet to press for a formal reduction of commitments to Italy since this 'might impose a moral obligation upon the Powers to obtain for Italy her reduced demands'.[95] In other words, if commitments to Italy were reduced now they might not be reduced enough. Nor was this only a matter of expediency in shortening the war. As Eric Drummond remarked, an anti-German Austria would be a greater obstacle to Germany's eastern ambitions than a congeries of weak and probably warring national states.

Drummond's scheme evoked a favourable response but no one supposed that it could be implemented quickly. There was an uneasy suspicion in the Foreign Office that Austria was too dependent on Germany, militarily and otherwise, to break with her even if she wished to do so as indeed, in all probability, was the case.[96] It was also feared that when British and Austrian representatives talked about peace they were speaking at cross purposes. This also was true: the British were only interested in a *separate* peace with Austria whereas Karl and his Foreign Minister, Czernin, were only interested in a *general* peace in which the Monarchy would fulfil a glorious role as intermediary between the Entente and Germany. A further barrier to Anglo–Austrian dealings lay in the cautious mentality of the new Foreign Secretary. Balfour felt no emotional hostility to Austria. On 6 February 1917 he told Maurice De Bunsen's wife 'that although he felt that he could not meet a

[94] Memorandum, 28 Mar. 1917, WO 106/1512, no. 11. This document is unsigned but was almost certainly written by Robertson.

[95] Memorandum by Hardinge, 12 Apr. 1917 answering a memorandum by Robertson, Hardinge MSS. XXXI. There is no copy of Robertson's paper in the Hardinge MSS. but it was clearly a memorandum, 29 Mar. 1917, G.T. 326, CAB 24/9, which repeats the military arguments for seeking peace with the lesser enemy powers in the paper cited in note 94 but omits the political arguments such as the one cited in the text of this chapter. Robertson was indulging in false modesty when he wrote in G.T. 326 that his arguments touched upon 'many complicated questions including the main principles of our policy with respect to Germany' which he did not feel qualified to discuss.

[96] Cf. Mamatey, op. cit. pp. 64–6; May, op. cit. pp. 798, 818.

German again, he would have no objection to meeting Austrians'.[97] In Washington three months later he spoke to House in favour of a reduced Monarchy of three states including Bohemia as an equal constituent.[98] In return for a separate peace, Balfour would almost certainly have been prepared to set aside his preference for the autonomy of Bohemia. What he would not do was to run a serious risk of alienating existing allies—Italy and Rumania—in pursuit of a peace with Austria. He minuted a suggestion from Esher in January 1917 that the allies should work for a separate peace with Austria: 'What does Esher think we can give Austria without letting down our allies?'[99] In March he spoke in favour of fighting on until Rumania had acquired Transylvania though he must have known that it was inconceivable that the Monarchy's Magyar constituent would ever consent to this unless faced with imminent annihilation.[100] It was typical of his greater caution that early in April he rejected a proposal favoured by Cecil and Hardinge for an official disclaimer in the House of Commons of any intention to disrupt the Monarchy. He was only prepared to authorize a colourless statement that the contents of the allies' note to Wilson in January still stood.[101]

The mood in the Foreign Office toward *pourparlers* with Austria was then in the spring of 1917 mixed. An attitude arose which was to persist for a year, that an arrangement was possible and desirable but that the time for it was not yet. Early in March Hardinge wrote that Austria might well be in the mood for peace within two or three months; two months later he repeated himself: Austria was not in the mood for discussions now but she might be after another two months.[102] The persistence of this attitude will be discussed further in this book.

The first major Austrian peace move centred around Prince Sixte of Bourbon and concerned the Foreign Office hardly at all, being handled on the British side by the Prime Minister personally. Sixte's

---

[97] B. E. C. Dugdale, *Sir Maurice De Bunsen : Diplomat and Friend* (1934) quoting Lady De Bunsen's diary, p. 316.

[98] Seymour, op. cit. iii. 46.

[99] Minute by Balfour on a memorandum by Ian Malcolm recording a conversation with Lord Esher, 14 Jan. 1917, FO 800/213.

[100] Imperial War Cabinet, 22 Mar. 1917, CAB 23/43.

[101] See the minutes in FO 371/3076, no. 73859; cf. *Commons Debates*, 5th series, XCII, cols. 1280–81, 4 Apr. 1917.

[102] Hardinge to Findlay, 7 Mar. 1917, and to Lord Bryce, 4 May 1917, Hardinge MSS. XXX and XXXII.

peace efforts are well documented so that an outline only is needed here.[103] While serving as an officer in the Belgian army, Sixte, a claimant to the throne of France and a brother of Karl's wife, the Empress Zita, obtained permission from the French government to sound out his brother-in-law on peace. This led to a meeting between Sixte and the imperial couple in late March 1917 and to a famous letter from Karl to President Poincaré in which he announced his ardent desire for peace. He made it clear that he was thinking of a general peace; his support for France's 'just claims' to Alsace-Lorraine came in the form of a statement that he would use his best endeavours to induce Germany to yield to France. The reaction of the French government, at first favourable, soon became cold and rather hostile. They were angered by a meeting between Karl and the Kaiser early in April and by Austria's action in joining publicly with Germany to offer Russia a separate peace. The Prime Minister, Ribot, imposed the impossible condition that before peace could be concluded with Austria, Italy must give a written promise that she would continue in the war against Germany. Sixte prolonged the life of the peace move by means of a grave deception. While again in Austria early in May, he obtained another note, drafted by Czernin, and altered its text to make it say that Austria was prepared to consider a separate peace whereas the original text spoke of a general peace only. Karl's policy, as he outlined it to Sixte, was to negotiate the broad terms of a general peace in secret with the Entente so that the Monarchy and the Entente powers together could exert pressure on Germany to assent.[104] He may have hinted verbally at a separate peace if Germany refused what he considered reasonable terms,[105] though his Foreign Minister certainly did not do so. Both Czernin and, more hesitantly, Karl were playing a double game. Throughout 1917, they left Berlin in ignorance of their peace moves but they were not disposed to consider a separate peace and urged the Germans to make peace moves of their own.[106]

Britain became involved in Sixte's activities on 11 April when

[103] Sixte's own account in *L'Offre de Paix Separée de l'Autriche* (1920), an inaptly named book; English translation as *Austria's Peace Offer 1916–1917*, ed. G. De Manteyer (1921). See also Kent Forster, *The Failures of Peace* (1941), pp. 95 ff. and an article by James Joll in *The Listener*, 23 June 1966.

[104] Phillipe Amiguet, *La Vie du Prince Sixte de Bourbon* (1934), pp. 119–22, 126.

[105] Amiguet, op. cit. pp. 121, 126; Manteyer, op. cit. p. 142.

[106] P. Renouvin, 'Le Gouvernement Français et les Tentatives de Paix en 1917' in *La Revue des Deux Mondes*, 15 Oct. 1964, pp. 492–513.

Ribot travelled to Folkestone to inform Lloyd George of them.[107] According to Ribot's account of this meeting, which is the only one available,[108] Lloyd George became very excited (*pris feu*) when told what was afoot. He recognized that Italy would pose an obstacle but thought that she would abandon her Adriatic ambitions in return for concessions in Asia Minor. A meeting between Lloyd George, Ribot and Sonnino was due to take place at St. Jean de Maurienne later in the month to deal with this last-named topic. Lloyd George showed his interest in what Ribot had told him by granting interviews to Sixte in Paris both on the journeys to and from the conference which, however, was itself a disappointment. Sonnino was relentless in pressing for sweeping gains in Asia Minor but he was also completely unwilling to support peace talks with Austria. Ribot was by that time almost as hostile though he preferred a passive role, leaving it to Sonnino to dampen the British Prime Minister's ardour.[109]

In fact, Lloyd George's enthusiasm did not decrease. In May, he told his colleagues that, owing to the revolution in Russia, he did not think that there was any chance of winning the war unless Austria could be induced to leave it; otherwise there would have to be a compromise peace with Germany in which she would receive her colonies in return for evacuating Belgium.[110] To Lloyd George this outweighed any obligations to Italy or the risk of alienating that country. The possible long-term dangers of a *status quo* peace in eastern Europe exercised his mind still less. His commitment to a separate peace with Austria if it could possibly be achieved was total.

When, therefore, Sixte returned to France with what he falsely described as an Austrian offer of a separate peace and a report that the King of Italy was trying to negotiate a separate peace with the Central Powers based on the cession only of the Trentino, he was assured of a warm welcome in London once his information was sent there. Ribot, for all his scepticism about what Sixte was doing,

---

[107] This is the generally accepted view. However, Donald McKormick in his biography of Basil Zaharoff states that Zaharoff informed Lloyd George of Sixte's activities in March 1917. No source is given for this assertion. D. G. McKormick, *Pedlar of Death: the Life of Sir Basil Zaharoff* (1965), p. 145.

[108] *Journal de Alexandre Ribot et Correspondances Inedites 1914–1922*, ed. Al. Ribot (1936), p. 67.

[109] Ibid. pp. 65–6, 71–3.

[110] War Cabinet, 9 May 1917, CAB 23/13. A few days later Bonar Law remarked in the Commons that 'no blow would seem so fatal to the Germans as the detachment of one of their allies'. *Commons Debates*, 5th series, XCIII, cols. 1373–4, 14 May 1917.

was prompt in apprising Lloyd George of the prince's message. He also sent him to London and suggested to Lloyd George that a meeting of the Kings of Italy and England and President Poincaré should be arranged to discover the truth about the alleged Italian offer to Vienna and whether Italy would join with Britain and France in the negotiations proposed through Sixte. The idea of a meeting of the three heads of state as a cover for sidestepping Sonnino's opposition appealed to Lloyd George and was approved by the War Cabinet. However, both this and a later British variant proposing a meeting between the three Prime Ministers collapsed when Sonnino said that he had no objections to such meetings but that they must not discuss the question of peace with Austria.[111] The Italian Foreign Minister had finally disposed of Sixte's efforts but, at the same time, Lloyd George, who had been interested in bringing Austria to terms as long ago as December 1914,[112] had acquired a determination to pursue every opportunity for peace with the Monarchy that he was to retain for nearly a year. It was clear that if this came about, Italy would have to accept far fewer gains than she had been promised under the London treaty. Lloyd George came to the conclusion—of a sort which sprang naturally to his mind—that Sonnino's motives in resisting this were purely personal and ignoble: early in 1915, Austria had offered Italy the Trentino in return for neutrality so that if Italy now gained only that area Sonnino's enemies could argue that he had led the country into war to no purpose.[113] Indeed the final Habsburg offer for Italian neutrality had been at least as generous as what Lloyd George in 1917 felt that Italy should be prepared to accept except that the Austrians had never been ready to surrender Trieste. Sonnino's wish that his country should gain much more than this in recompense for her sacrifices was thus neither unintelligible nor unworthy. There was a thoroughgoing conflict of interests in Anglo–Italian relations exacerbated by malice. In May 1915 Lloyd George had described Italy as 'the most contemptible nation'.[114] Under these circumstances, there could be no question of trying sincerely to reach an identity of views with Italy;

---

[111] See War Cabinet, 7 June 1917 as recorded in an undated memorandum by Hankey, 'Proceedings in Regard to a Separate Peace with Austria', Lloyd George MSS., F/160/1/12; cf. Rodd to F.O., 15 June 1917, FO 371/3082, no. 119682.

[112] Ekstein Frankl, op. cit. p. 198.

[113] War Cabinet, 8 June 1917, CAB 23/16. This meeting took a decision that there should be a definite policy of seeking peace with Austria despite the risks involved which were recognized as great.   [114] Ribot, op. cit. p. 243.

the only problem so far as British leaders were concerned was to find suitable tactics to overcome Italian objections to dealings with Austria.

4. THE RABEGH QUESTION: THE POLITICAL–MILITARY PROBLEM IN MICROCOSM

In June 1916 a new belligerent entered the World War when Sherif Hussein of Mecca, ruler of the Hejaz, rose in revolt against Turkey. The military fortunes of his rising were mixed and within four months British ministers were having to debate whether to send troops to the Red Sea port of Rabegh in order to block the route of any Turkish forces advancing from Medina, the second city of the Hejaz which the Turks occupied throughout the war, to Mecca to crush the revolt. This question occupied a grotesquely large amount of the time of the Asquith War Committee during the last three months of its existence and remained to trouble the succeeding government of Lloyd George for several weeks.

A study of this question shows the highly unsympathetic attitude of the General Staff to the use of Britain's immense military might in the First World War for political purposes such as to force a minor enemy state into considering a separate peace; to occupy territory which it was desired to annex or use for bargaining purposes in the peace conference; or simply, as in this case, to preserve existing gains.

During 1916 Robertson virtually dictated British strategic policy to a government which had become supine and he used his influence methodically to bring about the maximum possible concentration of efforts on the Western Front. In February 1916, he obtained War Committee endorsement for a passive military policy in the eastern theatres (Egypt, Mesopotamia and Aden). Where trouble threatened elsewhere, as in Persia, it should be dealt with at the outset 'by timely action with small forces.'[115]

Similar decisions followed. On 7 April 1916, at a time when the British position in the East seemed threatened by the impending fall of Kut, it was decided that in the event of an Afghan invasion of India, a purely defensive posture would have to be adopted.[116] At the same time Robertson gave warning that he would brook no interference in military matters by Mark Sykes whose brain was fertile with military-political plans for the war in the East.[117]

---

[115] Memorandum by Robertson, 25 Feb. 1916, CAB 37/143/25; War Committee, 29 Feb. 1916. CAB 42/9/7.   [116] War Committee, 7 Apr. 1916, CAB 42/12/5.

[117] See memorandum by Sykes, 29 Apr. 1916, and Robertson to Hankey, 9 May 1916, CAB 17/174.

Robertson encountered a first setback in September when the War Committee rejected his plan for a strategic retreat in Mesopotamia and refused to rule out an eventual occupation of Baghdad.[118] It was on this discouraging note that battle was joined on the issue of sending British troops to aid the Sherif's rising.

The De Bunsen and Curzon committees (the latter sitting long after the Rabegh crisis had ended) were agreed that British interests required the expulsion of the Turks from Arabia and the imposition of what the Government of India called a 'Monroe Doctrine'[119] in which the tribal states would be left to settle their own affairs without any interference from outside—except Britain. The success of the Hejaz revolt would surely mean the fulfilment of this policy, its failure might mean disaster. Success might lead also to Arab risings in Syria and Mesopotamia. Above all, British 'prestige' in Asia and Africa was involved, for it was upon prestige, rather than force, that British power in these continents was thought to rest. Lancelot Oliphant, a senior Foreign Office man closely concerned with eastern affairs, wrote that it would be essential to support the revolt to maintain British prestige in the East 'such as it is', a reference to the disasters at the Dardanelles and Kut.[120] Reginald Wingate, governor-general of the Sudan, stated in the same vein that if the revolt succeeded, 'Great Britain will gain enormously in prestige throughout the whole Moslem world. If, on the other hand, it fails, our prestige will proportionately decrease and that of the enemy increase.'[121] The maintenance of prestige was a war aim in itself and was the counterpart of the discrediting of militarism in Europe. It was accepted as an aim even by Robertson and Haig who resorted to the unlikely argument that the tribesmen of Arabia, Persia and Afghanistan had their eyes fixed firmly on the western front and could safely be expected to hold the British in awe and cause them no trouble provided they won victories in France.[122] As always, it is idle to discuss war aims solely in terms of territory.

[118] War Committee, 18 Sept. 1916, CAB 42/20/3.
[119] Letter from Government of India to Mallet committee, 29 Sept. 1916, CAB 16/36.
[120] Oliphant to A. Nicolson, 10 June 1916, FO 371/2773, no. 111398.
[121] Wingate to J. St. Loe Strachey, 26 July 1916, Strachey MSS.
[122] W. R. Robertson, *From Private to Field Marshal* (1921), pp. 272-3; and Haig to Robertson, 8 Oct. 1917, WO 106/1516. Haig thought: 'The leading men in the East . . . have quite sufficient intelligence to understand that the issue will be decided in the theatre where the main German forces are and must be employed.'

It was one thing to want to help the revolt and another to know how to do so. Pitted against the Foreign Office and the British representatives in Egypt, the Sudan and the Hejaz itself, who favoured an active role, were the Government of India (though not the India Office) and the General Staff who opposed help to the Sherif and were frankly unconcerned with his fate. It was for the War Committee to decide between the two conflicting sets of advice in a situation which was complicated by the possibility of French intervention in the Hejaz.

Anyone who has worked through the records of British eastern policy in the First World War cannot fail to have noticed that the Government of India was constantly afraid that Turkey's call for a jehad or Moslem holy war against the British infidel, almost totally ineffective when it was made in 1914, might lead to a revolt among the Indian Moslems. If combined with an invasion of north-west India from the warrior kingdom of Afghanistan, this would mean the creation of a new war front at a time when much of the Indian Army had been sent to fight in the Middle East and France. Almost the entire British bureaucracy in India including the viceroy, Lord Chelmsford, feared that the Hejaz rising might be precisely the catalyst to precipitate such troubles since the Indian Moslems were believed to revere the sultan of Turkey and to despise the Arabs even though they were fellow-Moslems. This fear was aggravated by the weakening in Russia's military position which involved a danger that the Turkish forces in Persia would be able to fight their way through to Afghanistan. In that case, Sir Beauchamp Duff, the commander-in-chief of the Indian Army, was convinced that Afghanistan would enter the World War on the side of Germany and Turkey.[123]

Daily reports on the reaction to the revolt within India were prepared in New Delhi from its outbreak on 4 June until the 10th of the next month and were then replaced by irregular but frequent reports to the end of the month when the Indian Moslems appeared to have become quiescent.[124] Even then the Government of India sought assurances that British aid to the Sherif would be restricted to money, arms and supplies and would be as unobtrusive as possible.[125] The Government of India had ambitions of its own in

---

[123] Duff to Robertson, 21 July 1916, Robertson MSS. I/21/30.
[124] This emerges from the many telegrams in CAB 17/176.
[125] A[rabian] R[eport], XXIIA, Viceroy's telegram, 18 July 1916, CAB 17/176. This was actually the policy favoured in London: cf. minute by Clerk, c. 2 July 1916, FO 371/2773, no. 127886.

the Persian Gulf and Mesopotamia but it was otherwise a restraining influence on the formulation of ambitious war aims in the Middle East. Its most important preoccupation was to ensure the tranquillity of its Moslem subjects, many of whom were noted for their military prowess.

During the last four months of 1916 there was a periodic series of military crises in the Hejaz. During this time the objections to sending troops changed: at first there was general respect in London for the Government of India's views, together with a fear—held as late as October by Sykes[126]—that the presence of foreign troops, even Moslems under British officers, in the Moslem Holy Land would make the Sherif's own followers turn against him; this later gave way to a single-minded determination by Robertson that there should not be the slightest diversion of military resources to the Hejaz regardless of the consequences for British policy in the East.

At the end of August, London was informed that the Turks were in a good position to occupy the port of Rabegh and that the Sherif's son, Feisal, wanted 3,000 trained troops to be sent there to guard the port and with it the route to Mecca.[127] From the first, the proponents of such a step presented it as a once-for-all measure: if only a single brigade were sent to Rabegh there would be no question of further military commitments in the Hejaz. Wingate, the man-on-the-spot responsible for the whole of British military policy toward the revolt and in conjunction with MacMahon—the resident in Cairo whom he was to succeed in November—for political policy, even offered to send Sudanese Moslem troops to Rabegh on condition that they were replaced in the Sudan by white British troops. Owing to the opposition of both the War Office and Sykes, the War Committee decided that British help to the Sherif must still be confined to munitions.[128]

Robertson's response to such requests as those of Wingate was two-fold. First, the consolidation of British influence in such a country as the Hejaz was trivial: 'These various political officers of ours seem to think that now is the most convenient time for putting all our various frontiers in order, quite regardless of the fact that now is about the worst time and forgetting that for years past there

[126] Minute, 9 Oct. 1916, FO 371/2775, no. 199871.
[127] MacMahon to F.O., 30 Aug. 1916, FO 371/2774, no. 172299.
[128] War Committee, 1 Sept. 1916, CAB 42/19/1.

has always been trouble on our different frontiers and I imagine there always will be.'[129]

Secondly, a small force might mushroom; 'One could not forecast what an expedition of this sort might lead up to. Commencement with a brigade might end in many divisions. If the Turks wanted to go [i.e. to Rabegh] they would pile up troops and go.' He went on to cite the Dardanelles, Mesopotamia and Salonika to prove his point.[130]

What made Robertson's attitude particularly distressing was that France was intent on sending the Sherif help in men who, if unaccompanied by British forces, would threaten the policy of excluding any foreign presence from the Hejaz except a British external protectorate. In a choice between French intervention and the collapse of the revolt, however, the British government favoured the former. On 11 September Grey informed Bertie that he had taken note that the French were assembling a Moslem force of technical and artillery units under white officers which they hoped to have ready by mid-October and that Britain intended to send a force to occupy Aqaba at the north-eastern corner of the Red Sea, which was held by only 200 troops, cutting Turkish communications with the Hejaz. This was likely to be the only operation of which the General Staff would approve.[131]

Soon after came reports that the Sherif's forces were losing faith in British good-will and that the threat to Rabegh was still grave. In two meetings in late September the War Committee, at Lloyd George's suggestion, formally instructed Robertson that the success of the revolt was a matter of the highest imperial importance and that he should report on what, if anything, could be done to ensure its success. On the same occasion Grey remarked that this was the first serious clash between ministers and their military advisers that he could recall. Apart from the issues involved, ministers were thoroughly irritated by Robertson's conduct at these meetings which consisted of a parrot-like repetition of the western formula for winning the war, followed by a relapse into complete silence when his

[129] Robertson to Murray, 29 Aug. 1916, Robertson–Murray correspondence, B.M. Add. 52463, p. 153.
[130] War Committee, 18 Sept. 1916, CAB 42/20/3; cf. Robertson's *Soldiers and Statesmen* (1926), ii. 158–60.
[131] Grey to Bertie, 11 Sept. 1916, CAB 42/20/3. It is interesting that the French only decided to send this force, which reached Suez in mid-October, after an internal conflict which paralleled the one in London: the Foreign Ministry pressed for troops to be sent while the War Ministry opposed such a step. Cf. Ed. Brémond, *Le Hedjaz dans la Guerre Mondiale* (1931), pp. 16–3.

listeners were not convinced. When Balfour tried to suggest that
there could never be any question of sending a large force to Rabegh,
he simply refused to reply: 'It was a difficult question to discuss
across the table. His views of the whole business had been expressed
in the paper (a recent memorandum on military policy). He could
not answer Mr. Balfour's queries.'[132]

For a month there was a lull in which Robertson had his way. To
his own representations were added those of the Admiralty who
protested indignantly against the suggestion that the Royal Navy
alone could not defend Rabegh[133]; a report from General Maude in
Mesopotamia that the collapse of the revolt would have no effect on
British prestige there[134]; and a reminder from the Government of
India that it opposed the despatch of even Moslem troops to the
Hejaz. Most important, the Arab forces recovered the initiative.[135]

By the beginning of November, the Turks were again on the
offensive. The War Committee was sufficiently alarmed to decide
that the French should be encouraged to send as many troops as
possible to the Hejaz, and that Wingate should send as many
Sudanese troops as he could muster.[136] Now it was Wingate's turn
to be difficult. He refused to send Sudanese forces unless his original
demand that they should be replaced with British troops from outside the condominium was met.[137] He also rejected a remarkably
generous French offer to replace any Sudanese troops sent to Rabegh
by Senegalese troops from Djibouti.

To those members of the government concerned with eastern
policy—Grey, Curzon and the secretary for India, Austen Chamberlain—by this time, the question was one of preserving the British
Empire. Affirming that the collapse of the revolt would be a 'perfect
disaster'.[138] Chamberlain feared that if no troops were sent to the
Hejaz the Sherif might come to terms with the Turks,[139] enabling

---

[132] War Committee, 18 and 25 Sept. 1916, CAB 42/20/3 and 8.

[133] See War Committee, 28 Sept. 1916, CAB 42/20/9.

[134] See War Committee, 3 Oct. 1916, CAB 42/21/1.

[135] MacMahon to FO, 13 Oct. 1916, A.R., New Series, XIV, 15 Oct. 1916, CAB
17/177.

[136] War Committee, 2 Nov. 1916, CAB 42/23/3. At the same time, Clerk, one of the
senior officials most closely concerned with policy toward the revolt, recorded that 'the
principle of allowing no Christians on Hejaz soil has in fact to go when it is a case of
saving Mecca'. Minute, 4 Nov. 1916, FO 371/2776, no. 221035.

[137] Wingate to FO, 7 Nov. 1916, FO 371/2776, no. 223717.

[138] War Committee, 2 Nov. 1916, CAB 42/23/3.

[139] He actually entered into tentative contacts with them in January 1917: Kedourie,
op. cit. p. 99 n. 4.

them to carry out their old ambition of jehad in India, Afghanistan, Persia, Mesopotamia, Egypt and Aden.[140] To this danger was added that of French pressure for assistance to the Sherif from the two countries which was not only diplomatically embarrassing but also bade fair to end Britain's hopes of primacy in western Arabia. By mid-November the French were seriously considering sending an infantry contingent of their own to reinforce their artillery which was still at Suez, thus assisting the Sherif with French forces alone.[141] Hardinge was alarmed:

I hear privately that the CIGS welcomes this suggestion and would gladly see a French brigade go to Rabegh instead of a British force. To adopt such a proposal would be disastrous since it would imply the reversal of our policy of the last one hundred years which has been aimed at the exclusion of foreign influence on the shores of the Red Sea. The establishment of France at Jibouti has been a thorn in our sides almost from the moment it took place and to allow the French to establish their influence in the Hejaz as predominant over ours will be to abdicate the position that we have always held in the Moslem world.[142]

Sharing these two sets of fears, Grey, Curzon and Chamberlain decided in private conclave that a British brigade of white, Christian troops should go to Rabegh.[143] They had a meeting with Robertson which he records as 'rather unpleasant'[144] and the matter had to be referred to the War Committee. During two lengthy debates it came to no decision and Robertson, with the aid of Bonar Law, succeeded in blocking a compromise suggestion that one brigade of the army in Egypt should be earmarked for *possible* use at Rabegh if the Arabs' military crisis worsened.[145] Under these circumstances, the War Committee felt that it would not be able to object if France demanded that she alone should send troops to support the revolt.[146]

The advent to power of Lloyd George brought no incisive decisions on this problem. In September he had been the first member of the War Committee to take seriously the idea of sending troops to Rabegh. Once Prime Minister, he was hesitant, probably because of pressure from Robertson who wrote to him condemning

---

[140] Memorandum by Chamberlain, 14 Nov. 1916, CAB 42/24/8.
[141] Note from the French embassy, 13 Nov. 1916, FO 371/2776, no. 232712.
[142] Minute, *c.* 18 Nov. 1916, FO 371/2776, no. 235418.
[143] Cf. memorandum by Grey, 11 Nov. 1916, CAB 43/24/8.
[144] Robertson, *Soldiers and Statesmen*, ii. 160.
[145] War Committee, 16 and 20 Nov. 1916, CAB 37/159/45 and CAB 42/24/13.
[146] Hardinge to MacMahon, 22 Nov. 1916, Hardinge MSS. XXVII.

those members of the former government who had been so mistaken as to 'waste brain power over such petty matters as Rabegh, Persia. . . . They lived from telegram to telegram and attached as much importance to a few scallywags in Arabia as I imagine they did to the German attack on Ypres two years ago.'[147] This was intended as a warning to Lloyd George as well as a condemnation of some of his former colleagues: as early as 25 September 1916 Esher had written to Haig that Robertson was 'consumed with suspicion of Lloyd George.'[148]

The new War Cabinet continued the old conflict with Robertson on one side and Curzon and Chamberlain on the other repeating familiar arguments.[149] Finally, after Wingate reported that there was no longer apparently any obstacle to a Turkish advance on Mecca,[150] the Cabinet decided to offer a British brigade and the French contingent at Suez to the Sherif but with the proviso that the British troops would have to be Christians since Wingate reported that no Moslem troops were available in Egypt or the Sudan.[151] They also decided to give the Sherif a political boost by recognizing him as King of the Hejaz—a compromise between addressing him by his original title and recognizing the new one which he had assumed of King of the Arabs.[152]

The man who finally prevented the despatch of British troops to Rabegh was not Robertson—by the second week in January 1917 he was saying that he had washed his hands of that 'comedy'[153]—but the Sherif himself who was unwilling to accept Christian troops and demanded Moslems. After a number of tergiversations in which he sometimes professed readiness to accept Christian troops but never for long enough for any to be sent, Wingate became tired of what even to him had become a farce. With Foreign Office concurrence, he informed the Sherif at the end of January that the offer of troops was permanently withdrawn.[154]

By mid-January 1917 there was no longer any serious possibility that Rabegh or Mecca might be lost to the Turks and the War

---

[147] Robertson to Lloyd George, 8 Dec. 1916, Lloyd George MSS. F/191/3/1.
[148] *The Letters and Journals of Reginald, Viscount Esher*, iv. 55; see also below pp. 121–3.   [149] Cf. War Cabinet, 9 and 11 Dec. 1916, CAB 23/1.
[150] Wingate to FO, 14 Dec. 1916, A.R., New Series, XXII, CAB 17/177.
[151] Cf. War Cabinet, 15 Dec. 1916, CAB 23/1.
[152] See FO 371/2782 *passim*, especially no. 258154, FO to Wingate, 22 Dec. 1916.
[153] Robertson to Murray, 10 Jan. 1917, Robertson–Murray correspondence, B.M. Add. 52463, p. 182.   [154] See telegrams in FO 371/3042, nos. 15877 and 26459.

Cabinet never again had to consider sending troops to the Hejaz. At the same time, the dread prospect of unilateral French intervention ceased. After remaining at Suez for three months while the artillery officers spent an agreeable time learning to ride the camel,[155] the French units were transferred to Djibouti to crush a tribal rising in French Somaliland.[156]

The Rabegh affair was of limited importance in itself. The absence of reaction in India, Egypt and in even the occupied territory in southern Mesopotamia to the evacuation of the Dardanelles and the surrender of the Kut garrison—both direct defeats for British arms —makes it unlikely that a Turkish victory over the Sherif—an in-direct defeat—would really have shaken British prestige in the East to its foundations as both Chamberlain and Lord Islington[157] in the India Office as well as Hardinge and even Grey had feared. The failure of the revolt would have thrown the Sykes–Picot agreement into the melting pot but, in any event, by the time that the war ended, the British had no intention of implementing it. More im-portant is the significance which cabinet ministers, amidst all the preoccupations of the World War, attached to the fortunes of a small ally in the remote Hejaz, and the unmistakable manner in which Robertson indicated how he would treat all future schemes for political-military action against Austria, Turkey and Bulgaria which threatened even momentarily the implementation of the western strategic doctrine.

[155] Brémond, op. cit. p. 66.
[156] Minute by Hardinge on conversation with M. de Fleuriau of the French embassy, 3 or 4 Jan. 1917, FO 371/3042, no. 1189.
[157] Cf. Islington to Lloyd George, 5 Nov. 1916, Lloyd George MSS. E/2/8/1.

III

STRATEGY AND DIPLOMACY, MAY–NOVEMBER 1917

I. RUSSIA, GERMANY AND THE PAPACY

DURING the middle months of 1917, the British government moved toward a reappraisal of war aims. The most salient reason for this was a growing doubt as to whether military victory was possible. During the more sober moments when he was not carrying out Haig's injunctions—advocate an offensive policy on the western front as likely to produce almost marvellous results—Robertson was pessimistic. In February 1917 he warned the War Cabinet, that there was virtually no chance of a successful outcome to the war during the coming year and advised them to impress this upon the country 'in order to prevent such possible disappointment being aroused by a continuance of the war as might end in an unsatisfactory peace'.[1]

The leaders were, however, unable to prevent the rise of such a spirit of war weariness as Robertson feared. As the war wore on many thinking people, including industrial workers and private soldiers, began to doubt whether the sacrifices which were being demanded of them were justified and to seek reassurance in the official enunciation of war aims which they felt able to support. The Union of Democratic Control, founded early in the war to agitate not for a peace-at-any-price but for an immediate negotiated peace on *status quo* lines to be followed by a reform of international relations based on the democratization of foreign policy, attracted more support and for the first time became a force with which the government had to reckon.

This spirit of political uneasiness among large sections of the public fed upon international events: growing war weariness in France and Italy which made British ministers more receptive to such pressures at home and, above all, the entry of the United States into the war and the March Revolution in Russia. President

---

[1] Memorandum on 'Germany's Intentions', 23 Feb. 1917, WO 106/1512.

Wilson's unwillingness to pronounce on war aims after America became a belligerent was frustrating for the radicals in Britain who nevertheless had good reasons for thinking that in him they had a powerful friend. Wilson's peace mediation efforts in the winter of 1916–17 had been inspired in part by a regular stream of material from such luminaries of the Union of Democratic Control as G. Lowes Dickinson, Norman Angell and H. N. Brailsford. This heartened the President not only by its content but also by the impression which he drew from it that the writers represented a vast body of opinion in Britain so that if he made it clear that he shared their views pressure from them upon the government might become irresistible. This was the foremost reason for the 'peace without victory' address in January.[2] Wilson's policy of silence on war aims after America became a belligerent, to be discussed below, made his foreign admirers (though not the British leaders) suspect that his intentions had changed. In fact, he always hoped for a revival of the alliance with radical opinion, especially in Britain, to enforce moderate peace terms once Germany had been defeated. Some of his public pronouncements, most notably the decision to reply in detail to the papal peace note of the summer and the terms of that reply with its call for generosity to a Germany which had become democratic, were designed to counter doubts which had arisen among what Wilson called 'the democratic feeling of the world' as to the purity of his intentions.[3]

In contrast with Wilson's silence, the new Provisional Government in Russia was quickly forced to issue statements calling for a peace settlement without forcible annexations and with changes based solely on self-determination by the socialist factions which had become enormously powerful in Russia with the revolution. These statements certainly did have a great impact in Britain, but with regard to the revision of war aims, Russia's new policy had only a mixed effect. It gave rise not only to demands for the revision of war aims but also for a new political and social order in western Europe. A series of engineering strikes in the early spring had revolutionary overtones and in June some small extremist groups held a conference at Leeds to discuss the extension of the Russian system of Soviets to Britain. To almost everyone in ruling circles the

[2] L. W. Martin, *Peace Without Victory: Woodrow Wilson and the British Liberals* (1958), pp. 114 ff.
[3] Ibid. pp. 133–45; cf. pp. 178–82 of Martin's book.

only really satisfactory answer to such developments seemed to be to press on for victory, thus vindicating their leading position in society. At the height of the Passchendaele offensive Haig suggested to Robertson that an important reason for pressing on for victory was that: 'The chief people to suffer would be the socialists who are trying to rule us all at a time when the right-minded of the Nation are so engaged on the country's battles that they [the socialists] are left free to work mischief.'[4]

In so far, therefore, as the British leadership were driven toward a revision of war aims by the March Revolution, they were more concerned with keeping Russia itself in the war than with appeasing the revolution's admirers among their own citizens. This is well brought out in the affair of the proposed socialist conference at Stockholm. When in May the Petrograd Soviet and the Swedish and Dutch socialist parties began calling for an international socialist conference of parties from all the belligerents and the neutral countries, the War Cabinet were at first inclined to agree in the hope that this would keep Russia in the war. They reversed their decision in late July and early August owing to a gross misconception on their part that the Provisional Government had become strong enough to resist its extremist opponents who wanted to have dealings with the enemy. A quarrel over this issue entailed the resignation of Arthur Henderson from the War Cabinet. His colleagues let him go with few qualms and did not review their decision when the Labour Party conference voted by a large majority in favour of participation in this conference which was actually never to meet.[5] An inter-allied socialist conference in London at the end of August was paralysed by disagreements between supporters of the war and their radical opponents so that its official communiqué had to make the admission, unusual in such documents, that its outcome had been 'wholly disappointing'.[6] The British government had to keep a wary eye on domestic unrest but until a hostile new regime came to power in Russia it felt that it had the situation in the nation under satisfactory control.

While the importance of pressures at home during these middle

---

[4] Haig to Robertson, 13 Aug. 1917, Robertson MSS. I/23/44.

[5] On the Stockholm and Henderson affairs see Arno J. Mayer, *Political Origins of the New Diplomacy 1917–1918* (1959), pp. 191 ff. especially pp. 214–23; and Mary Agnes Hamilton *Arthur Henderson: A Biography* (1938), chapter VII. The relevant War Cabinet minutes in CAB 23/2–3 and CAB 23/13 add little.

[6] Mayer, op. cit. pp. 224–5.

months of 1917, can easily be exaggerated, in the international and military fields, the government was faced by a truly bleak prospect. Russian power was failing, American assistance to the war effort had hardly begun and there were insistent demands from the High Command that it should be given the men and resources to carry out policies in which the politicians increasingly disbelieved. Ministers searched for new formulas. At the end of October Lloyd George tried to give a precise definition of the vague aim of military victory. An allied victory which drove the Germans back to the Meuse would, he thought, mark the defeat of Germany.[7]

Six months earlier, at the same time as Lloyd George was expressing doubt whether the war could be won without a separate peace with Austria, Robert Cecil, one of the hardiest souls in Whitehall, wrote, 'It seems to me increasingly probable that we may have to accept an unsatisfactory peace.'[8] Yet such information as came to hand indicated that Germany would only consent to a peace which left her in effective possession of all her conquests.[9] Lloyd George found German developments unpromising from the point of view of peace. At the end of May, he remarked to Prince Sixte that he was sure that Bethmann-Hollweg favoured an immediate peace on terms that the allies could accept and was completely hostile to the militarists in Germany.[10] Bethmann's fall in July must have made a much greater impression on the Prime Minister than the contemporaneous 'Peace Resolution' which the Reichstag passed.

This was the international background against which ministers sanctioned the Passchendaele offensive. The other pressure working in this direction was the boyish enthusiasm of the General Staff and the High Command in France. Shortly after the war, Haig's former chief of staff, Kiggell, regretted that in 1917 the British and French armies on the Western Front had not had a definite agreement by which the British would always be on the offensive, the French ever on the defensive.[11]

When Britain came under pressure for the first time for the revision of war aims from an ally, she was thus still in a war mood. The ally was the new Provisional Government in Russia. Early in

[7] Journals, 20 Oct. 1917, 50904.
[8] Minute, *c.* 28 April 1917, FO 371/3081, no. 87527.
[9] Cf. Hardinge to Hopwood, n.d. but early July 1917, Hardinge MSS. XXXIII.
[10] Amiguet, op. cit. p. 129.
[11] *Operations on the Western Front 1916–1918* (the so-called 'Haig Memorandum'), B.M. Add. 52460, p. 42.

May it formally presented its allies with a note stating that it wished to consult them on war aims. Cecil drew up the British reply. His original draft offered to 'free' the secret agreements 'from all taint of national aggrandizement' but he toned this down into a simple statement that Britain was ready to 'revise' these treaties.[12] A note rather on the lines of the British reply was published in Petrograd in June after which the Russians began exerting intermittent pressure for an allied conference to revise war aims.

There were a number of reasons why the British government were wary before this pressure. Cecil feared that if the allies promised not to make any territorial changes which did not have the consent of the populations affected, Germany might take cynical advantage of this, for instance by expelling the French inhabitants from some particularly important part of Alsace-Lorraine before a plebiscite. He also thought that the 'more moderate elements in Russia who may be looking to us for guidance and support' would be discouraged if the allies prepared to yield to the 'extremists' on war aims.[13] Balfour's fear was different. He observed to Paul Cambon that inter-allied discussion of war aims 'might somewhat imperil the harmony of their relations and weaken their motives for continued effort'.[14] In other words, the war will of such allies as Rumania and Italy would be shaken by precisely such concessions as Russia would seek. Finally, there was no certainty that revision of war aims or anything else would keep Russia in the war. When Curzon wrote to Cecil condemning 'our wild worship of so-called democracy' and opposing any concessions on war aims to Russia— 'an ally who is really at heart a traitor'—Cecil could only reply that he agreed with Curzon's views.[15]

Under such circumstances, it is not surprising that in July the War Cabinet decided to discourage the Russians from pressing for a conference on war aims.[16] The entire problem ceased to be urgent shortly afterwards when the Kerensky government, under pressure from its own right-wing opposition, the Cadets, abandoned its attempts to revise war aims and only resumed them two months later in the left-wing mood which followed Kornilov's unsuccessful

---

[12] These drafts are in FO 371/3010, no. 90801.

[13] Cecil minute and telegram to Buchanan, 28 May 1917, FO 371/3010, no. 106114; Cecil minute of about the same date, no. 109672 in ibid.

[14] Balfour to Bertie, 21 June 1917, FO 371/3082, no. 125021.

[15] Curzon to Cecil, 1 June 1917 and Cecil to Curzon, 2 June 1917, FO 800/198.

[16] War Cabinet, 16 July 1917, CAB 23/3.

counter-revolution.[17] These renewed efforts also met with opposition from the British who, however, made an important concession by publicly conceding the principle that *eventually* there should be a conference on war aims revision.[18]

Nor did the entry of the United States into the war lead at once to a reappraisal of war aims. Woodrow Wilson had an acute, indeed exaggerated, awareness of the differences between himself and his 'associates' on the objects of the war and hoped to avoid an open split for as long as possible. He also hoped that by the end of the war the Entente powers would be so weakened in comparison with the United States that she would be able to dictate terms. Thus when, during his visit to Washington in the spring of 1917, Balfour tried to acquaint the President with the contents of the secret treaties, he found his host unwilling to listen and it is still one of the mysteries of the World War how far, if at all, Wilson was aware of these texts before Versailles.[19] William Wiseman, the Foreign Office agent who established very close contacts with Wilson and House, looked upon the co-ordination of British and American war aims as one of his most important tasks but even he could achieve little in this direction before the beginning of 1918.[20]

Robert Cecil, always the most articulate of British politicians in discussing international problems, hoped that the war would give rise to a permanent Anglo–American partnership in world affairs. In the course of a plea for the appointment of Grey as British ambassador in Washington, he argued:

Though the American people are very largely foreign both in origin and in modes of thought, their rulers are almost exclusively Anglo-Saxons and share our political ideals. But there seems to me to be more at stake even than cooperation in the terms of peace.

The United States are entering upon an entirely fresh chapter of their history. For the first time they are taking a part in international European affairs; they will soon begin to realize what vast power they have; and unless they are very different from any other nation that has ever existed they will wish to make use of that power. If they make use of it rightly, it may be of incalculable benefit to the human race: and by rightly I mean

---

[17] C. Jay Smith, op. cit. pp. 481, 484.

[18] Cf. Cecil's answer to parliamentary question by Charles Trevelyan, *Commons Debates*, 5th series, XCVIII, cols. 249–50, 18 Oct. 1917.

[19] There are recent discussions of the evidence in Gelfand, op. cit. pp. 11–13, and Laurence Evans, *United States Policy and the Partition of Turkey 1914–1924* (1965), pp. 55–8.   [20] Gelfand, op. cit. pp. 116 ff.

in accordance with our ideas of right and justice. There is undoubtedly a difference between the British and the continental point of view in international matters. I will not attempt to describe the difference, but I know that you will agree in thinking that, where it exists, we are right and the continental nations are, speaking generally, wrong. If America accepts our point of view in these matters, it will mean the dominance of that point of view in all international affairs.[21]

In the context of twentieth-century Anglo–American relations viewed as a whole, Cecil may be seen as an exponent of what Professor Beloff has identified as the 'majority viewpoint' in British official attitudes toward the United States throughout the period. This was 'that America's power should be brought to bear wherever possible in support of British interests'.[22] Under the special conditions of war these interests were, however, of two sorts: long-term political ones such as those with which Cecil was concerned and ones of a more immediate kind connected with the actual prosecution of the war. The non-Foreign Office members of the War Cabinet showed their primary interest in the latter by sending Northcliffe to the United States as special emissary. This great businessman and newspaper proprietor was hardly competent to discuss the league of nations or the future frontiers of Germany but it could be hoped that he would press the Americans into more energetic action in such fields as those of shipping and finance. Indeed, these matters seemed vital. American help in the war effort was so slow in materializing that it evidently supported Robertson's prediction that the United States would be of little use in winning the war.[23]

In short, American and most British leaders were at one in wishing to let the sleeping dogs of war aims lie when the Papacy made a notable attempt to mediate the end of the World War. This was prompted by the Reichstag 'Peace Resolution' of 19 July 1917 calling for a peace of reconciliation and by certain conversations between the German Chancellor, then Bethmann, and Vatican diplomats which gave the Holy See the idea that Germany was prepared to restore Belgium. The effort was misconceived. Bethmann did not

[21] Letter from Cecil to Balfour, 25 Aug. 1917, with covering note by Cecil, 18 Sept. 1917, stating that he is circulating the letter as a Cabinet memorandum, G.T. 2074, CAB 24/26.

[22] Max Beloff, 'The Special Relationship: An Anglo–American Myth' in *A Century of Conflict 1850–1950: Essays for A. J. P. Taylor*, ed. Martin Gilbert (1966), p. 162.

[23] Robertson to Murray, 13 Feb. 1917, Robertson–Murray correspondence, B.M. Add. 52463, p. 197.

inform the High Command, which was soon to demand his de-
position, of his remarks and in any case the entire German leadership were united in having no intention of accepting the 'Peace
Resolution'.[24] The Papal note of 1 August 1917[25] evisaged in essence
a return to the *status quo* with provisions for disarmament and international arbitration. It involved two questions: first, if anything,
should be done to court the good will of the Papacy; and second,
the infinitely larger question of whether the Vatican's move should
be treated as a serious opening to end the war. Both Balfour and
Cecil suspected the Holy See and in particular Pope Benedict XV's
secretary of state, Cardinal Gasparri, of supporting the Central
Powers. Cecil minuted sadly on an intelligence report in February
1917 that the Vatican were trying to dissuade President Wilson from
entering the war: 'The moral failure of the Papacy in this crisis is a
blow to all forms of Christianity.' Balfour consoled him with the
thought that: 'Christianity has survived many bad popes and many
Vatican intrigues. We must hope for the best.'[26] The protestations
of the British minister to the Holy See, De Salis, that it was genuinely
neutral did not carry conviction. Harold Nicolson, who was given
the task of collating all information on the papal note felt that his
sources 'indicate beyond a doubt that the papal move was indirectly,
if not directly, inspired from enemy sources'.[27] In fact, the Vatican
strove to be sincerely neutral and its policy was not anti-Entente
except that it preceded its note by diplomatic probes in the Central
Empires but not in the Entente capitals in most of which it possessed
no official representation.[28]

Whereas the Entente had had to treat Wilson's mediation efforts
with great tenderness owing to the economic and financial strength
of the United States, this need did not arise in the case of the
Vatican not only because of its obvious lack of material resources
but also because of the absence of any feeling of good will toward it.
The note was, therefore, treated as a straightforward means of dis-
covering Germany's intentions. In this respect what is significant is
that there was no longer any talk, as there had been in the previous
winter, of refusing on principle to deal with Germany. On 20

[24] Hans W. Gatzke, *Germany's Drive to the West* (1951), pp. 183–4, 197–202.
[25] Text in Scott, op. cit. pp. 129–31.
[26] Minutes on a letter from Roderick Jones to Cecil, 26 Feb. 1917, Lloyd George
MSS. F/62/3/3.
[27] Memorandum by Harold Nicolson, 23 Aug. 1917, FO 371/3083, no. 165197.
[28] Humphrey Johnson, *Vatican Diplomacy in the World War* (1933), pp. 24–5.

August, the War Cabinet decided its policy: a return to the *status quo* was impossible and the touchstone in deciding whether there could be peace talks with Germany would be her readiness to restore Belgium. The Pope should be informed that it was for the Central Powers to state their war aims, the Entente having done so the previous January. If the enemy showed no desire to reply, Wilson should be encouraged to send a note in idealistic and general terms which the British government would support if they saw fit. The following day they agreed that Belgium should definitely be emphasized in the reply to the Pope.[29]

It is clear that owing to the bleak political and military situation the British leadership were prepared to reconsider their belief that only military defeat could induce the desired 'change of heart' in Germany. They had been edging toward this for some time. In May, when House had suggested to Drummond in Washington that some declaration should be made to encourage the democratic elements in Germany, Drummond produced a draft saying that the sole purpose of the war with Germany was the defeat and overthrow of 'a small military autocracy in Prussia which imposed its wishes even on the German emperor.'[30] Thus, the Kaiser was not beyond redemption. When President Wilson replied to the Pope, the government decided not to associate themselves with him precisely because he raised as the chief objection to a *status quo* peace that it would leave the German people under the rule of their existing 'ruthless masters'.[31] However, the Germany with which the British would be prepared to deal would have to be one which had given evidence of what could genuinely be seen as a revulsion from aggression and it would also have to take the initiative in moving toward peace. De Salis earned a very severe rebuke when he allowed Gasparri to talk him into saying that Britain would welcome any assurances on Belgium that the Papacy could obtain from Germany.[32]

Vatican diplomats explained to Germany the special importance which the British attached to Belgium but the German reply to the

[29] War Cabinet, 20-1 Aug. 1917, CAB 23-3.

[30] Memorandum by Drummond, 23 May 1917, Balfour MSS., B.M. Add. 49687. House assented to this formula. Seymour, op. cit. iii. 60-1.

[31] Cf. FO (drafted by Cecil) to Bertie, 1 Sept. 1917, repeated to Washington, Rome, Petrograd, Tokyo and Le Havre, FO 371/3083, no. 170713.

[32] Cecil to De Salis, 26 Aug. 1917, in 'Correspondence relative to the peace proposals made by His Holiness the Pope to the belligerent powers on 1 August 1917, August–October 1917', *British and Foreign State Papers 1917–1918*, cxi (1921), 575–89, no. 7.

Pope[33] left no scope for the continuation of the Holy See's efforts. Instead of being specific on Belgium or anything else, it merely stated German willingness to make peace 'in harmony with the wishes of His Holiness and with the peace resolution adopted by the Reichstag on 19 July last'.

1917 was a year of peace moves. On the German side this was to a large extent the result of the appointment of a new Foreign Minister, Kühlmann, in August 1917. Already aware of British views on Belgium, the papal note encouraged him to seek authority to make an offer to Britain on Belgium in the hope of making an immediate separate peace with the British. The Kaiser and the military and naval chiefs would only consent to restore Belgian independence under 'guarantees' which would have made it almost fictional and, paralleling the British attitude, they demanded that even this must be preceded by a definite British statement of a wish for peace talks.[34] A German enquiry on this latter point was addressed to London through the Spanish Foreign Ministry in mid-September. It coincided with news from France that a former Premier, Briand, was due to meet a German emissary, Lancken, in Switzerland shortly to discuss peace possibilities. The French government did not know how far Lancken, an official of the occupation government in Brussels, could speak for the rulers of Germany though Ribot, who had recently fallen from Prime Minister to Foreign Minister, had no doubt that the scheme was merely a trap.[35]

The War Cabinet discussed these two sets of moves on 24 and 27 September interrupted by a journey which Lloyd George made to Boulogne to converse with the new French Prime Minister, Painlevé. Ministers were divided as to which peace move they should concentrate on following. Balfour, supported by Milner and Carson, favoured the Spanish move which, as an official German probe, would have meant acting in concert with the allies and which might prove useless since it contained no indication of German terms. Lloyd George, supported by Curzon and apparently Bonar Law, favoured the Lancken–Briand channel which was unofficial and so meant that *pourparlers* could be kept wholly in Anglo–French

[33] No. 10, Enclosure I in ibid.
[34] Fritz Fischer, *Germany's Aims in the First World War* (1967), pp. 410–11, 419 ff.
[35] Ribot, op. cit. pp. 203 ff.

hands. This would have had the advantage of excluding the Americans whose contribution to the war had so far, said Lloyd George, been so small as not to merit taking them into the Entente's confidence. Even more important to the Prime Minister, as he made abundantly clear, he was attracted by the terms which, according to Balfour, Lancken was putting forward—Belgium and Serbia were to be restored while Germany would accept the loss of Alsace-Lorraine and the colonies—terms which were silent as to eastern Europe, implying that Germany would want a free hand in Russia and Rumania. Lloyd George spoke almost with equanimity of Germany annexing Lithuania and Courland and added that in that case 'two great Empires would emerge from the war namely the British Empire and Germany'. He repeatedly argued that the British people would not be prepared to fight for the evacuation of occupied Russian territory 'unless Russia herself fought' as he wrote in pencil in the minutes of the debate. He concluded that if the chief of the General Staff stated that the war could not be won except in the unlikely event of a revival of Russian resistance, the allies would be well-advised to make peace on precisely the terms which Lancken seemed to be offering.

Lloyd George thus brought about a discussion of whether the nation could continue to fight in view of both its own sacrifices and the decline of Russia. The Flanders offensive, still being carried on, had brought huge losses to the British army and few tangible gains while the failure of Kornilov's drive on Petrograd signified the failure of a movement which many ministers had regarded as the last hope of saving Russia.[36] Milner, Balfour and, for what influence his opinion carried, Barnes declared against a compromise peace even in the dark situation which was arising. Bonar Law was ready to continue fighting if there were 'reasonable grounds'. Smuts said that Poland, Lithuania and Courland should be made into buffer states which, if it meant anything at all, was support for Lloyd George.

The debate was at this point broken off to be resumed three days later. It had shown that there was a fundamental split between the Prime Minister and his Foreign Secretary. This was emphasized by an event the day before the second of these two secret debates. Asquith made a speech on war aims at Leeds in which he declared: 'I assume as a matter of course the evacuation by the enemy of the

[36] Cf. War Cabinet minutes, 5, 7, 10, 12 Sept. 1917, CAB 23/4.

occupied territories of France and Russia.'[37] This statement roused Lloyd George to fury since it read like an attempt to veto a compromise peace at the expense of Russia and he was still to be complaining about it bitterly three months later. That, in fact, is exactly what it was. Asquith made his remarks on Russia on the advice of Drummond who had doubtless been informed by Balfour of the drift of Lloyd George's thinking. Drummond was principally moved by a conviction not that a peace at the expense of Russia would be disastrous in itself (though he may have thought this) but that Germany's main war aims lay in western Europe and that she would reveal any overtures from the western allies to herself to Russia which would in disgust leave the war and so give Germany the opportunity to concentrate all her forces in the west for a crushing blow.[38] This was also Balfour's fear as he made clear in a letter to the Prime Minister, begging that Russia should be informed of any British communications with Germany.[39] At the same time, he informed Paul Cambon that Lloyd George was thinking of entering into peace talks with Germany as an insurance against a separate Russo–German peace. The two men agreed that they should do everything that they could to resist this.[40] Lloyd George's anger would have been doubled if he had known that he was being actively opposed not only by Asquith, whose position bore some resemblance to that of leader of an opposition,[41] but also by the Foreign Office.

When the War Cabinet resumed its secret debate on the enemy peace moves on the 27th, the Prime Minister began with a report on his conversations with Painlevé who had told him that the Lancken move was genuine, that Briand had fluctuated in his account of its terms, saying one moment that Germany was *offering* to restore Belgium and Alsace-Lorraine and the next that she was merely willing to *discuss* their future, and that in any case he favoured rejection of the overtures on the grounds that the French people would not fight on if they thought that they could have Belgium and most of Alsace-Lorraine by peaceful means. (Painlevé was not able to tell Lloyd George that on the very day of this meeting the indefatigable Ribot put a stop to plans for a meeting between Lancken and

---

[37] Speech by Asquith at Leeds, 26 Sept. 1917.
[38] Drummond to Balfour, 28 Sept. 1917, FO 800/197.
[39] Balfour to Lloyd George, 24 Sept. 1917, FO 800/214.
[40] Ribot, op. cit. p. 216 n.
[41] Trevor Wilson, *The Downfall of the Liberal Party* (1966), pp. 105-12 for a discussion of the position of the Asquith Liberals under the War Cabinet regime.

Briand by summoning Poincaré to a cabinet meeting at which Briand was censured for sending a telegram to one of his Belgian intermediaries to come to Paris for consultations. The reasoning was that since Briand had consulted the government for permission to meet Lancken, this telegram would give the Germans the impression that a Lancken–Briand meeting had official French approval.)[42]

Lloyd George reported himself as having agreed with everything that Painlevé had said. This is incomprehensible for not only was the French Prime Minister's line of argument directly contradictory to what Lloyd George had told his colleagues before setting out for Boulogne but he now went on to repeat that he was highly attracted by the idea of making peace with Germany on the basis that she would lose in the west and gain in the east. He also denounced Asquith's Leeds speech at length. None of his colleagues is recorded as supporting him. Balfour said that he was opposed to any peace which left Germany stronger than in 1914 while Milner—whose image as the arch-proponent of the appeasement of Germany in the War Cabinet requires revision—opposed a suggestion by Lloyd George that Russia should be informed that unless she resumed participation in the war the allies would cease to fight for her interests; he also said that if Germany was allowed to retain her gains in Russia there would be another war in ten years' time.[43] Churchill told C. P. Scott that even those of Lloyd George's colleagues who had some sympathy with his views on Russia had been astonished by his ardour and had sought to cool it with the obvious counter-arguments: that Russia might still recover; that Germany as a power would be too strong if allowed to dominate eastern Europe; and that a Russia deserted by her allies might, embittered, become Germany's junior partner in future schemes of aggression.[44]

These dramatic debates were followed by an anti-climax which resulted from Balfour's determination not to have any dealings with Germany except in concert with the allies. His immediate response to the Madrid note had been to inform Paul Cambon of its contents and to repeat what he had said many times before, that the allies must maintain a completely united front toward Germany.[45] On 5 October he summoned the five allied representatives (including the

[42] Forster, op. cit. pp. 110–11.
[43] War Cabinet, 24 and 27 Sept. 1917, CAB 23/16 for these debates.
[44] Journals, 26–28 Sept. 1917, 50904.   [45] Ribot, op. cit. pp. 212–13.

Russian chargé) to his room at the Foreign Office and informed them that he was sending a telegram to Germany via Madrid offering to listen to any German communication on peace provided it was understood that the British government would only act in concert with its allies. Once Kühlmann realized that Britain was uninterested in a separate peace, he was precluded by his instructions from sending her further notes.

Even on the assumption that Germany was interested in a general peace, her failure to respond to the British reply was neither unexpected nor unwelcome to Balfour. The Madrid message had prompted him to write a memorandum in which he argued that it would be best if there were no peace talks '*at this moment*'.[46] He said nothing of defeating Germany before peace talks could be considered. The year's warfare, culminating in the battle of Passchendaele in which apparently very meagre results had been purchased at a cost of 300,000–400,000 casualties, had forced a conclusion that the defeat of the German army might be either impossible or prohibitively costly. Indeed, this conclusion was beginning to take root in the General Staff where it mattered little if the blame was attributed to Russia rather than to the inadequacies of British generalship in France. As early as August, while acknowledging the possibility of driving the Germans out of Belgium and northern France, Macdonagh wrote, 'It is difficult to imagine that the allies will be able to cross the Rhine and dictate terms of peace on the enemy's own soil unless some miracle happens on the eastern front.'[47]

The desire for victory was being replaced by the hope that combined military and economic pressure would convince the existing rulers of Germany that their aggressive schemes could not be realized. Abandonment of the aim of military victory did not mean readiness to accept a *status quo* peace or even one along the lines of the House–Grey memorandum of February 1916 which had been highly favourable to the Entente. Balfour was dismayed by a report that the Papacy was trying to induce Germany to offer Alsace-Lorraine to France in return for Madagascar; Germany, he feared, might use Madagascar to establish submarine bases in the Indian Ocean.[48] Likewise the Foreign Office continued to be antipathetic

[46] Text of memorandum in D. Lloyd George, *War Memoirs*, ii. 1237–40. Italics in original.

[47] Memorandum by Macdonagh, undated but Aug. 1917, WO 106/1514.

[48] Des Graz to FO, 5 Oct. 1917, with minute by Balfour, FO 371/3084, no. 196679.

to the 'betrayal' of Russia. In late October it arranged for a member of Parliament to ask a question as to whether the western allies were prepared to make peace at the expense of Russia to which the answer, given by Cecil, was, of course, a resounding negative.[49] The new mood was expressed by Hardinge: 'I am quite convinced that we have only to keep a very stiff upper lip and to rebuff all advances from the Germans until we get the terms that we desire. There must be no wavering whatever.'[50]

To the Foreign Office, then, the hope that Germany would emerge purified and democratized from military defeat had been replaced by the hope that she could be forced to accept such terms as would put some curbs on her power and would, possibly, convince her that it was not worthwhile to seek expansion. Lloyd George's remarks on Russia show that he thought that even this might be too ambitious a goal. Also, a number of ministers (Smuts, Carson, Barnes) said that they had very little idea what British war aims were and hinted that in so far as there was a programme it was unsatisfactory to their way of thinking. George Barnes, the Labour representative, was sure that the British people 'would not be prepared to continue the war in order to win certain islands in the Adriatic for Italy'.[51] With uncertainty as to territorial objectives and whether Germany could be militarily defeated, the way was open for a debate within British ruling circles which was to lead to Lloyd George's great war aims speech of 5 January 1918.

2. AUSTRIA–HUNGARY: THE MILITARY–DIPLOMATIC APPROACH

The peace efforts of Prince Sixte had an important sequel. During his visit to London in the spring of 1917, he spread a report that Austria would be prepared to surrender Trentino as the price of peace but not Trieste.[52] Possession of Trieste was the most important item in Italy's Adriatic ambitions and Lloyd George was impressed by the idea that if only Trieste could be captured,

[49] Minutes in FO 371/3011, no. 197632: cf. *Commons Debates*, 5th series, XCVIII, cols. 1039–40, 25 Oct. 1917.

[50] Hardinge to Townley, 11 Oct. 1917, Hardinge MSS. XXXIV.

[51] War Cabinet, 27 Sept. 1917 as cited in note 43. There is a curious sequel to this. On 13 May 1919 Harold Nicolson wrote in his dairy of the Paris Peace Conference that Barnes had been present at a meeting to discuss Italian claims in Dalmatia and 'is interested in the Adriatic for some odd reason'. *Peacemaking 1919*, p. 332.

[52] Memorandum by Drummond on Prince Sixte, 9 May 1918, FO 800/200.

Austria would resign herself to its permanent loss while Italy would abandon her ambitions farther down the Dalmatian coast. A separate peace with Austria could then be signed or so Lloyd George thought. This belief drew strength from numerous reports that the Austrian public were desperately anxious for peace,[53] and the Prime Minister's ardour was not dampened by reports that Austrian ruling circles were indifferent to the wishes or material sufferings of the masses in deciding whether to continue the struggle.[54]

During the first three months of 1917 Lloyd George had pressed for a concentration of operations in Italy rather than France but his motives were purely military: he wanted to deflect pressure from the Russian front and ensure that the Italian army did not itself suffer disaster. The British and French generals were successful in upholding the western strategy and the offensive proposed by the new French commander, Nivelle, was sanctioned and carried out. While it was going on, the War Cabinet accepted a recommendation from Robertson that no British or French troops should be sent to Italy unless there was clear proof that Austria intended to launch an offensive with substantial German help. Robertson added that even then it was desirable that only French and not British forces should be despatched. British participation in an offensive against Austria was thus ruled out. When the Nivelle offensive was finally abandoned in failure early in May, Lloyd George had so far lost interest in Italy that he did not revive the idea of sending troops there.[55]

Sixte's and other information soon convinced Lloyd George of the need for a combined diplomatic-military approach to Austria whose lynchpin would be the capture of Trieste. However, Douglas Haig was determined to have a major offensive of his own on the western front in the summer and it was evident that this would rule out British help to the Italians. At Milner's suggestion, the War Cabinet set up a Committee on War Policy on 8 June 1917, chiefly to discuss

---

[53] Memorandum for the Prime Minister by Henry Norman, 15 Aug. 1917, Lloyd George MSS. F/160/1/13. Norman, one of Lloyd George's unofficial emissaries, had gone to Switzerland to investigate reported Franco–Austrian peace contacts.

[54] M. P. A. Hankey, 'Proceedings in Regard to a Separate Peace with Austria', n.d. Part I, Appendix III; FO memorandum on conditions in Austria by L. Collier, 7 July 1917, Lloyd George MSS. F/160/1/12. This is henceforward referred to as *Hankey Memorandum*.

[55] W. R. Robertson, 'Despatch of Reinforcements from Western to Italian Front', 17 Mar. 1917, WO 106/1512, no. 4; copy of telegram FO to Rodd, 5 April 1917, no. 19 in ibid.; Hankey, 'The Development of the Military Plans of the Allies in the Principal Theatres of War during 1917', 1 Sept. 1917, G.T. 1925, CAB 24/25.

the merits of Flanders and Italy as sites for a major offensive.[56] On the very same day, Robertson held talks with his French counterpart, Foch, at Abbeville in which they discussed at great length peace prospects with the lesser enemy states. Robertson explained: 'What he proposed to say to his government was that it was essential, from a military point of view, if the Entente was to hold out without Russia until America came in, that one of the minor enemy powers should be detached: and that the Entente Powers should agree to put secondary interests aside and combine diplomatically to detach one of the enemy Powers.'[57]

This closely paralleled what Lloyd George had said to the War Cabinet a month before (see above) though to Robertson it did not matter whether there was peace with Austria, Turkey or Bulgaria whereas the Prime Minister had fixed his sights on Austria. Having already urged Haig to consider the 'general situation', which gave cause for great anxiety, and not merely the situation on the west front,[58] Robertson, on the day following his meeting with Foch, tentatively suggested to Haig that the scheme for a military-diplomatic offensive against Austria had merit. Haig demurred, arguing that the government should send every man, gun and aeroplane that it could muster to the west front to fight the German who 'was now nearly at his last resources'.[59] Thereafter, Robertson suppressed any doubts which he may have had and became Haig's loyal ally in pressing for a Flanders offensive.

In the War Policy Committee, Lloyd George was eloquent in putting forward the case for operations to take Trieste—'the vital necessity of the hour'—but his pleas had no effect on Haig except to convince him that the Prime Minister was anxious 'to show black is white'.[60] More generally, he was faced with a fatal combination of military advice from Haig that German manpower was within six months of total exhaustion if his plans were adopted, and naval advice from Jellicoe, the First Sea Lord, that German submarines were sinking so much shipping that the war could not be continued

---

[56] *Hankey Memorandum*, Part II, p. 1.

[57] Minutes of conference at Abbeville, 8 June 1917, WO 106/1513, no. 5. Foch agreed with this advice and urged the Quai d'Orsay that, in the case of Austria, 'the negotiations must be kept up and allowed to develop'. Geneviève Tabouis, *Jules Cambon: Par l'Un des Siens* (1938), p. 304.

[58] Robertson to Haig, 31 May and 4 June 1917, Robertson MSS. I/23/29 and 31.

[59] Robert Blake, ed., *The Private Papers of Douglas Haig* (1952), p. 236.

[60] Haig to Kiggell, 23 June 1917, Kiggell MSS. II/11/1.

into 1918 unless the Belgian coast were cleared. Denied the un-divided support of his Cabinet colleagues, Lloyd George felt com-pelled to accept military advice. He was to remark with impotent fury on this very point at the time of the critical manpower situation —to a large extent a result of the Passchendaele slaughter—which the British faced a year later.[61] The War Policy Committee gave its consent to a Flanders offensive on 20 July.[62] For a moment Robert-son's victory—for it was his more than Haig's—was total. The War Policy Committee meekly acquiesced in a suggestion that he should not be required to make definite arrangements with the Italians for the possible despatch of artillery to Italy in case the proposed western offensive did not make satisfactory progress. The com-mittee agreed that he should make such arrangements at a time of his own choosing and 'in his own way'.[63]

Lloyd George was undaunted. On the very day that the War Policy Committee decided in favour of a western offensive, Robert-son told Haig that the Prime Minister had talked 'as though he is hoping to switch off to Italy within a day or two after you begin'.[64] At inter-allied conferences in Paris (25–6 July) and London (7–8 August) he renewed passionately his plea for an Italian offensive and the abandonment of all war aims against the Monarchy on its southern and eastern frontiers: 'If we still continued in the expecta-tion of winning Galicia, Bukovina, Banat, Temesvar, Transylvania and all the Serbian claims we really were lacking the courage to face the facts.'[65] He found the French both uninterested and un-sympathetic while Robertson, though he argued very strongly the case for a separate peace with Austria, was hardly helpful since he was adamant that this should be (and presumably in his opinion could be) brought about entirely by diplomatic concessions with no

[61] 'Manpower: Remarks by the Prime Minister...', 28 May 1918, CAB 24/52, G.T. 4679 especially p. 7.

[62] For the work of this committee see *Hankey Memorandum*, Part II and his *Supreme Command*, ii. 675–7, 684; also Lloyd George, *War Memoirs*, ii. 1272–1304; and Blake, op. cit. pp. 240–1.

[63] Memorandum by Robertson, 19 July 1917, copy in Milner MSS. 125, Box AE 1; Interim Report of War Policy Committee, 10 Aug. 1917, p. 44, copy in ibid. Box AE 2. Robertson used the freedom thus given him to return evasive replies to Lloyd George's queries during August when the war front in Flanders was becoming increasingly static as to what contingency plans he was making for operations in Italy. Cf. Lloyd George, *War Memoirs*, ii. 1382.

[64] Robertson to Haig, 21 July 1917, Robertson MSS. I/23/40.

[65] *Hankey Memorandum*, part II, p. 9.

diversion of resources from the west front.[66] This was a most frustrating situation for anyone to whom politics and diplomacy were parts of a single whole and whose attitude was far removed from that of the officers at Haig's headquarters. As Henry Wickham Steed recorded during a visit in September 1916, the officers dismissed the idea of a political-military move against Austria as 'pure politics. . . . They spoke as professionals of a professional undertaking. I spoke of the whole war as one vast politico-military problem. To them it was a game to be won or lost according to the rules. To me it seemed a matter of life and death subject to one rule only—victory.' Their attitude was: 'It would be fatal to mix up politics with strategy and the idea of breaking up Austria was sheer politics.' Haig himself did not deign to join in the discussion.[67]

The London conference agreed only that the allied staffs should consult on the time and place of possible offensive operations against Austria including winter operations and the question of sending British and French guns. Just over two weeks later there were reports of important Italian military victories and this led to a revival of discussion of a political-military offensive, especially as the French General Staff, rather reversing its previous attitude, favoured sending help to the Italian army and Foch went to London on a special mission to persuade the British. Haig was also summoned for a debate which was marked by 'great tension'.[68]

The specific question which had to be settled was the request of the Italian commander, Cadorna, for the British and French to send him two hundred heavy guns. Lloyd George strongly supported him both because he continued to expect that great results would follow from the capture of Trieste and because the results of the Flanders offensive to date justified his worst forebodings. Indeed, the desire to find a means—any means—of saving tens of thousands of young men from what he considered to be a completely useless ritual of slaughter probably outweighed anything else in his mind. Robertson's mental anguish was also considerable. He instructed Maurice, the Director of Military Operations, to draw up plans for operations in Italy while expressing every conceivable doubt on grounds of the unreliability of the Italian troops, the terrain on the Austrian–Italian front and the lateness of the season for military operations

[66] See Robertson's covering note to report of inter-allied conference at Paris, 25–6 July 1917, CAB 28/2, I.C. 24.   [67] Wickham Steed, op. cit. ii. 118.
[68] Hardinge to Balfour, 11 Sept. 1917, FO 800/175.

whether victory was possible.[69] How far his opposition to the idea of using military pressure to bring Austria to terms was a matter of faith rather than reason emerges from a note which Robertson wrote to Maurice from an hotel in Eastbourne where he was resting: 'I am quite convinced, myself, Austria can't cut out and the more DMI can *prove* this the better.'[70]

In the actual debate with ministers, Robertson 'wobbled a little' just as he had done two months before but Haig was vehement that his offensive must go on. The only War Cabinet member who supported him fully was Carson though he also had the backing of Derby and Cecil among non-War Cabinet ministers. Milner and Bonar Law made clear their sympathy with Lloyd George. The underlying tensions among the nation's leaders came to the surface. The Prime Minister threatened to resign and call a general election if he did not have his way while Cecil and Robertson complained bitterly that he treated them with an incivility bordering on open contempt.[71] On 4 September a compromise was reached by which Haig was to consult with the French commander, Pétain, for one hundred guns to be raised along the west front for Italy.[72] Lloyd George had high hopes even of this limited measure of help. When Rodd sent telegrams warning that the Austrians would not come to terms with the Italians—their hereditary enemy—alone, no matter how badly beaten, whereas they could come to terms after being defeated by a joint allied force without feeling dishonoured, the Prime Minister kept a copy of one of them in his papers underlining this passage in red.[73] Then, abruptly and inexplicably, the Italians abandoned their offensive.

So ended the scheme for a political-military blow against Austria. Lloyd George's belief that the Austrians would come to terms after the fall of Trieste rested on as slender a basis of evidence as did Haig's belief that his western offensive would probably produce results

---

[69] Robertson to Maurice, 31 Aug. 1917, Robertson MSS. I/25/4.

[70] Robertson to Maurice, 31 Aug. or 1 Sept. 1917, Robertson MSS. I/25/5. 'Prove' is underlined in the original.

[71] On the debate as to assisting the Italian offensive see the letter cited in note 68 and Hardinge to Rodd, 3 Sept. 1917, Hardinge MSS. XXXIV. Cf. Cecil to Balfour, 29 Aug. and 4 Sept. 1917, Balfour MSS., B.M. Add. 49738. (Balfour was on holiday in Scotland throughout this crisis.) Cf. also Bonar Law to Lloyd George, 18 Sept. 1917, Bonar Law MSS. 84/6/127.   [72] *Hankey Memorandum*, ii. 14–15.

[73] Rodd to FO, 3 Sept. 1917, Lloyd George MSS. F/56/1/49. This is doubtless the communication to which Lloyd George referred in his *War Memoirs*, ii. 1375. It obviously made a great impression on him.

which would be decisive in winning the war. The entire affair showed the difficulty of deciding rationally the main direction of the war effort when the highest political and military leaders had no faith in one another and when both had fixed ideas which they were intent on implementing, paying attention only to evidence which suggested that their schemes were feasible. From a narrower point of view, it showed the folly of denying the Foreign Office a hand in foreign policy.

The Foreign Office as such had played no part either in the Sixte affair or in the succeeding phase of discussions for a political-military offensive. Lloyd George could plead that this was unavoidable for a number of reasons. For instance, Ribot at Folkestone in April and Sixte in Paris a few days later had placed him under a vow of secrecy not to reveal what he was told about Sixte to anyone except the King. But this neglect accorded with his own preferences. Hostile to diplomats as a class, he preferred methods which were at once more devious and private and more direct than those of orthodox diplomacy. A behind-the-scenes intrigue with a shadowy outsider, to be followed by an international conference at which the plans produced by the intrigue would be speedily endorsed was his ideal of how international relations ought to be conducted. The Foreign Office had to accept this with icy reticence. When, in December 1917, Harold Nicolson drew up a memorandum which purported to give a factual survey of Austrian peace approaches to Britain during the past year, he did not even mention Sixte's name![74]

Predominant opinion in the Foreign Office was still that peace with the Monarchy was both possible and desirable but that the time was not ripe. Reports that Austro–German relations were badly-strained were received with scepticism.[75] There was a suspicion that Austria's peace feelers were a German trick[76] and that even if this was not so the Monarchy was still only interested in a general peace, a role which no one in London envisaged as suitable

---

[74] Memorandum by H. Nicolson, 8 Dec. 1917, FO 371/3086, no. 230895. It is interesting to note that Austrian foreign policy was similarly compartmentalized with Karl often pursuing an independent diplomacy from that of Czernin. Cf. A. J. May, i. 489, 491–2.

[75] Townley, to FO, 16 May 1917, FO 371/3076, no. 99324; memorandum by William Tyrrell, 17 May 1917, no. 97879 in ibid.

[76] Minute by Eyre Crowe, 26 Sept. 1917, FO 371/2862, no. 182437.

for it. Vetoing a request by Paget in Copenhagen that he should accept the suggestion of Slatin Pasha, an Austrian Red Cross representative who had worked for the British in the Sudan, that they should meet to discuss peace, Balfour wrote: 'If the Austrian government have anything to say to us which they do not want Germany to hear they can find a better channel; if they have *not* we do not care to know it. We had better get it straight from Germany.'[77] Shortly afterwards Rumbold sent a report from a Czech deputy in the Austrian parliament who claimed to have heard Czernin say, 'There must be talk of a separate peace as this will bring a general peace nearer.'[78]

For several months following Sir Francis Hopwood's mission to Copenhagen, Austria's only serious peace feelers to Britain through diplomatic channels were via the two countries' legations in The Hague and in these Czernin was frank in talking only of a general peace.[79] Finally, Italian susceptibilities continued to be a major preoccupation. Italian war aims were seen as both unjust and unrealistic. Hardinge commented airily on a (false) report that Italy was abandoning her Adriatic ambitions in favour of ones in Asia Minor: 'The Italians having given up their Dalmatian ambitions will in due course have to give up those relating to Asia Minor as being equally unrealizable.'[80] The difficulty lay in saying this while Italy's participation in the war was still needed. The British ambassador in Rome warned that any talk of a separate peace with Austria with its corollary of only meagre territorial gains for Italy 'touches Italy on the quick'.[81] Balfour responded to an appeal from Milner to permit Paget to conduct talks with Slatin by citing 'the delicate position of Italy' as the most formidable of a number of reasons for keeping the Austrians at arm's length.[82]

Yet there was a strong feeling that the time would come for a separate peace with Vienna. In August Hardinge called for the government to work out the 'irreducible' terms which Austria would have to accept in such an eventuality.[83] Perhaps prompted by this

---

[77] Balfour to Paget, 12 Oct. 1917, FO 800/201.

[78] Rumbold to FO, 17 Oct. 1917, copy in Lloyd George MSS. F/59/9/8.

[79] See memorandum by Nicolson cited in note 74; also FO to Townley, 8 Oct. 1917, FO 371/2864, no. 192950.

[80] Minute, *c*. 18 May 1917, FO 371/3087, no. 100042.

[81] Rodd to Balfour, 14 June 1917, FO 800/202.

[82] Balfour to Milner, 12 Oct. 1917, FO 800/200.

[83] Minute, *c*. 23 Aug. 1917, FO 371/2864, no. 164751.

and by a paper which Noel Buxton was circulating to as many public figures as he could reach on the future settlement in eastern Europe,[84] the Foreign Office a month later produced a memorandum on *The Balkans* in which it was argued that for the security of the British Empire in the East, including the new acquisitions in Mesopotamia, it was essential that the Balkan states should be sufficiently contented not to feel tempted to join in German schemes of conquest. A confederal union of Bulgaria and Serbia was recommended, the former absorbing both the Contested and Uncontested Zones of Macedonia from Serbia, South Dobrudja from Rumania and the Greek towns of Serres, Drama and Kavalla, while Serbia took Bosnia–Herzegovina and Montenegro. Rumania would be compensated for the loss of the South Dobrudja with at least part of Bessarabia and preferably also part of Transylvania. Finally, Greece might be offered Cyprus. In this arrangement, Austria–Hungary would be almost totally unimpaired (except for cessions to Italy) or even totally unimpaired since it was stated not to be essential to the success of the scheme that Serbia should receive Bosnia–Herzegovina or Rumania any part of Transylvania.[85]

Nothing could be farther from the dismemberment of the Monarchy than this latest version of a desirable settlement in eastern Europe. Shortly after its appearance, Balfour, in the War Cabinet, made an interesting interpolation in a speech by Lloyd George, surveying the war situation. When the Prime Minister said that Austria seemed very anxious for peace but that her price might be too high, Balfour commented that he thought that but for German pressure Austria would come to terms and that after another winter of war anything might happen.[86]

The arch-foes of the Monarchy remained without a foothold in the Foreign Office until the setting up of the Political Intelligence Department in 1918. Before that they could only influence policy ineffectively from the sidelines. Their influence is apparent in George Russell Clerk's condemnation of the idea of transforming

[84] Cf. Hanak, op. cit. pp. 151–2.

[85] Memorandum, 28 Sept. 1917, copies in FO 800/200 and 214. This document is unsigned but appears to have been written by Tyrrell. A list of contents in Drummond's handwriting in FO 800/214 refers to it as Tyrrell's work. The copy in FO 800/200 is accompanied by commentaries, one of which, dated 9 Oct. 1917, was written by Balfour. This accepts the scheme in principle but dwells on the difficulty of obtaining Serbian, Rumanian and Greek acquiescence.

[86] War Cabinet, 11 Oct. 1917, CAB 23/13.

Austria–Hungary into an anti-Prussian federation in eastern Europe on the grounds that even if the Vienna government showed interest, the project would not be 'either sincere or feasible'.[87] Though the point cannot be documented, it is probable that Clerk's views, which were certainly not conventional in the Foreign Office, were influenced by R. W. Seton-Watson since the two were on good terms. Perhaps, then, Seton-Watson had gained one important convert to his views but one alone was not of much use.

Seton-Watson himself was working in the Intelligence Bureau of the Department of Information, producing reports on Austrian developments. Whatever regard Clerk may have had for him, a more general attitude in the Foreign Office was one of irritation whenever it appeared that the bureau was attempting to influence policy.[88] Also, the office had its quota of fervent admirers of the Monarchy such as Sir Maurice De Findlay, minister to Norway, who once pleaded with Cecil not to pay undue attention to the views on Hungary of Seton-Watson who 'collected Slovaks in rather the same way as I believe one of the Rothschilds collected fleas!'[89] Upon the tendency of government as opposed only to Foreign Office policy, Seton-Watson professed to be sanguine for a time in 1917. Recent speeches by Cecil and Lloyd George, he chuckled in one of his intelligence reports in August, 'will be regarded in Austria as demolishing the whole fabric of speculations and overtures created by the inspired press of Vienna upon the basis of recent British pronouncements'.[90] In fact, Cecil in a speech in the Commons on 24 July[91] had reaffirmed that Britain's only real quarrel was with Germany, while at a luncheon in honour of the Serbian Prime Minister two weeks later, he and Lloyd George promised nothing beyond the restoration of Serbia to its pre-war boundaries though Cecil added some non-committal words about British sympathy with Slav aspirations.[92] As is well known, Professor Seton-Watson was a sincere and disinterested opponent of the entire structure of the Dual Monarchy but, in the summer of 1917, British policy toward it was so far removed from what he wanted that he indulged in what can only be called wishful thinking.

[87] Minute, *c.* 27 Aug. 1917, FO 371/2864, no. 166940.
[88] Cf. minute by Oliphant, 19 May 1917, FO 371/2862, no. 97435; minutes by several Foreign Office members, May 1917, FO 371/3010, no. 105964.
[89] Findlay to Cecil, 4 Jan. 1918, Cecil MSS., B.M. Add. 51091.
[90] Memorandum by Seton-Watson, 11 Aug. 1917, FO 371/2864, no. 158257.
[91] *Commons Debates*, 5th series, XCVI, cols. 1200–3.
[92] Speeches by Cecil and Lloyd George at Serbian luncheon, 8 Aug. 1917.

3. BULGARIA AND TURKEY TO NOVEMBER 1917

Of all the powers in the Quadruple Alliance, Bulgaria was the only one which could, at almost any time after its entry into the war in 1915, have had peace merely by asking for it; a peace, moreover, which satisfied most of her territorial ambitions in return not for belligerency on the side of the allies but merely for neutrality. Bulgaria had emerged badly from the Balkan Wars of 1912–13 with all her neighbours in possession of territory which she considered to be rightfully hers. Her claims were well regarded in Britain by most interested persons, official and unofficial, and not always on their ethnographic merits. There was a background of Bulgarophilism. As Mr. Hanak has said: 'It is hardly an exaggeration to say that all those Englishmen who were interested in the Balkans were pro-Bulgarian and supported Bulgarian claims in Macedonia. . . . These numerous friends were by no means quiescent, even though Bulgaria had in 1915 joined the ranks of the enemy.'[93] The British were apt to attribute that event exclusively to the personal wickedness of the King, Ferdinand. In April 1917, Lloyd George told Prince Sixte that he had 'nothing but sympathy for Bulgaria but not for her King' and went on to use 'some forcible expressions about the King'.[94]

In their discussion of war aims in August 1916, Paget and Tyrrell brushed aside any objections to giving Bulgaria more territory than she had held in 1915 as 'sentimental'. Yet their own recommendation—that Bulgaria should if possible receive the areas which she claimed from Serbia, the so-called Contested and Uncontested Zones in Macedonia, and Turkey-in-Europe except for Constantinople—though avowedly based on the ethnographic principle, had a sentimental Bulgarophil touch and contrasted with the note of moral indignation in their statement that Rumania and Greece had behaved so badly toward the Entente as to deserve no support for their territorial aspirations. However, Bulgaria had been at war with the allies for nearly a year and Rumania was to enter the conflict on the side of the Entente within three weeks of the memorandum being written.

This widespread Bulgarophilism produced an atmosphere in which British leaders could argue in favour of offering her generous

---

[93] Hanak, op. cit. p. 64. H. N. Fieldhouse on 'Noel Buxton and A. J. P. Taylor's *The Troublemakers*' in Gilbert (ed.), op. cit. pp. 175–98 sheds light on British Bulgarophilism. For a defence of Bulgarian claims in Macedonia by a scholar of great integrity see G. C. Logio, *Bulgaria: Problems and Politics* (1919), chapter VII.

[94] Manteyer, op. cit. p. 115.

peace terms with no taint of immorality and little fear of an adverse reaction from public opinion. Early in August 1916 Lloyd George and Robertson pressed for Bulgaria to be offered territorial bribes to leave the war. Grey pleaded against any mention of this subject while negotiations on the entry into the war of Rumania, whose coastal territory on the Black Sea, known as the Dobrudja, was coveted by Bulgaria, were in the balance.[95] Shortly afterwards it became certain that Rumania would at last enter the war. Lloyd George's mind at once turned to the idea of reinforcing the already huge allied force at Salonika and of encouraging Russia to send troops to the Rumanian–Bulgarian front so that the two armies could then strike a devastating blow against Bulgaria from north and south. Russia would be tempted to action with the bait that vast supplies of munitions would be sent her once contact had been established with the British and French forces. Bulgaria, as soon as she announced her readiness for peace, would 'of course' receive all Bulgarian-speaking territory held by the Serbs in 1914. The War Committee authorized Lloyd George to raise this with the French but he found Briand, then Premier, only prepared to urge the Russians to send troops to the Dobrudja if the 'bait' of munitions was not mentioned on the grounds that they might see in this an insulting attempt to bribe them.[96]

Lloyd George's proposal led to a parting of the ways with Robertson and to a crisis which foreshadowed that of the summer of 1917 on whether part of the British military effort should be diverted from the west front to Italy. Robertson was at first uncertain whether to support Lloyd George's scheme for a political-military blow against Bulgaria. He informed the British liaison officer at the headquarters of the Russian army that he would favour the despatch of Russian reinforcements to the Dobrudja and he asked the commander of the British contingent at Salonika, General Milne, about the preparedness of his forces for an offensive, though he was careful, by silence on the subject of reinforcements, to make it clear to Milne that he would have to carry it out with the forces already at his disposal.[97] At the end of September, as the campaigning season in

[95] Grey to Lloyd George, 4 Aug. 1916, FO 800/102. For Robertson's pressure see pp. 50–1 above.

[96] For Lloyd George's actions see War Committee minutes, 10, 22 and 30 Aug. and 3 Sept. 1916, CAB 42/17/5, 42/18/4 and 8, 42/19/3.

[97] Robertson to General Waters, 24 Aug. 1916 and to Milne, 8 Sept. 1916, Robertson MSS. I/14/27 and 31.

Russia drew to a close, Robertson gave a definite opinion that the Russians should reinforce the Rumanians, chiefly to defend Rumania against a winter attack by the Central Powers but to eliminate Bulgaria from the war in the event that such an attack did not materialize.[98]

At precisely this time, the enemy powers launched their variant of the scheme for a double blow in the Balkans. German and Austrian troops from the north-west and Bulgarians from the south attacked Rumania and made rapid strides which were to lead to the occupation of the greater part of her territory by December. The proposal to send reinforcements to Salonika to strengthen the hand of the commander there, Sarrail, in the offensive which he had recently begun thus became one to save Rumania rather than to defeat Bulgaria. When, however, Lloyd George pressed the War Committee for such reinforcements with the addendum that their objectives should include not only the relief of Rumania but also the decisive defeat of Bulgaria, Robertson fell back on an attitude of rigid support for the western doctrine.[99] He had given Lloyd George high praise for unreservedly backing the High Command in France during the Somme offensive when the attitude of many ministers left, to Robertson's mind, much to be desired.[100] He now accused Lloyd George of displaying 'want of confidence in my advice' by raising the question of Salonika reinforcements before the War Committee and hinted at resignation. The Secretary for War replied with an accusation that someone in Robertson's closest confidence had revealed the differences between them on the Salonika problem to the press even before the matter had been mentioned to the War Committee and claimed the right to criticize Robertson without restraint in that body. He concluded with the warning, 'You must not ask me to play the part of a mere dummy. I am not in the least suited for the part.'[101] Although Robertson and Lloyd George were to co-operate against Lansdowne's abortive attempt to raise the issue of a general negotiated peace in November, the stage was now largely set for the regime of complete mistrust which was to characterize their relations throughout Lloyd George's premiership

---

[98] Robertson to Waters, 28 Sept. 1916, ibid. I/14/43.

[99] Cf. Robertson to Colonel Clive (liaison officer at French army headquarters), 9 Oct. 1916, ibid. I/14/44–5.

[100] Robertson to Haig, 1 and 29 Aug. 1916, ibid. I/22/62 and 72.

[101] Robertson to Lloyd George and Lloyd George to Robertson, both 11 Oct. 1916, ibid. I/19/6.

until Robertson's fall in February 1918. The actual quarrel over Salonika policy resulted in an almost complete victory for Robertson. Toward the end of October, the British government decided to send only one additional division there as a moral gesture which, it was recognized, could lead to no practical results and this was the result of pressure from the French rather than a victory for Lloyd George.

British leaders thus differed on the question of what military effort, if any, they were prepared to make to induce Bulgaria to leave the war. They were not divided on the complete desirability of a peace with her. This would strike a severe blow at Germany morally and materially, would enable munitions to be sent to Russia and would provide the basis for peace and stability in the Balkans. Also, 'It would be the end of Turkey.'[102] Superficially, this last proposition was very attractive since some of the major territorial aims of the leading Entente powers were directed against Turkey whereas they wanted nothing from Bulgaria. In any case, the obstacles to a separate peace with Turkey seemed infinitely formidable. The most obvious and seemingly insuperable in itself was Russia's claim to Constantinople. This wrecked the first attempt at peace which was made shortly after Turkey entered the war by Admiral Hall, the chief of Admiralty Intelligence, who, acting entirely on his own initiative and without informing his political superiors, tried to bribe Turkey out of the war. The move collapsed when the Turks demanded a guarantee that they should be allowed to retain Constantinople after the war and when Hall, turning to the Cabinet for this, found that they had just pledged the city to Russia.[103]

Everyone in British official circles believed—rightly or wrongly— that Turkey's one essential war aim was the retention of Constantinople so that there could be no hope of drawing her out of the war without putting pressure on Russia to modify her aims in the Straits area. In November 1915, Grey made an attempt to exert such pressure. Prompted apparently by Robert Cecil,[104] he suggested to Buchanan that in view of the failure of the Gallipoli expedition it was 'worth consideration' whether Russia should abandon her claim to Constantinople in favour of the demilitarization of the Straits and possibly a naval base there. If only Russia would consent to this and

[102] C. Hardinge to A. Hardinge, 23 Aug. 1916, Hardinge MSS. XXIV.
[103] David Woodward in *The Listener*, 9 June 1966, lxxv. 823 ff.
[104] Cecil to Grey, n.d. but apparently early October 1915, FO 800/95.

Turkey made peace Germany's defeat would be practically certain. He added that the idea would only be feasible if Russia were 'really willing' and that Buchanan should not even approach Sazonov unless he thought that there was a chance of a favourable reply. Buchanan answered that there was in fact no chance of this and that any step of the sort proposed by Grey would only serve to produce a 'very bad impression'.[105] If the mere possibility of drawing Turkey out of the war could only be created by weakening, perhaps fatally, Russia's war will, only one course of action was possible. As Grey informed MacMahon who was, possibly as a legacy of his life among the Indian Moslems, strongly in favour of a negotiated peace with Turkey: 'The advantages of peace with Turkey are important and obvious but the disadvantages of drifting into a position of support- ing Turkey against Russia would be still more important and obvious.'[106] As early as January 1915, Grey gave Russia an assurance that Britain would reject all overtures from Turkey for a separate peace between the two countries.[107] Russia's good faith throughout 1915–16 in rejecting all German peace overtures, some of which hinted that she might have Constantinople, made it difficult to entertain even the most tentative Turkish overtures.

Aside from Russia, Britain was formulating extensive aims of her own in Turkey. During the first year of the war, her aims were practically confined to Basra vilayet and even there were not openly avowed.[108] Thereafter, negotiations with Arabs, French and Russians on Asiatic Turkey, though springing from military neces- sity (see above), generated some genuine relish for the break up of Turkey. Arthur Nicolson who in March 1915 had been 'a partisan of the maintenance of Turkish rule with really substantial and serious guarantees and safeguards, in Asia' owing to the 'stupendous' difficulties of arranging partition[109] was writing a year later: 'The more territory Russia incorporates in the districts named [i.e. north- east Turkey] the better it will be and I hope we shall not raise any objections.' He was commenting on another minute by Lancelot

[105] Grey to Buchanan, 16 Nov. 1915, and Buchanan to Grey, 17 Nov.1915, FO 800/75.

[106] Grey to MacMahon, 6 May 1916, FO 371/2768, no. 84855. For MacMahon's views see his telegram to the FO, 4 May 1916 in ibid.

[107] Memorandum on Turkish peace feelers by Lord Drogheda, 20 Nov. 1917, CAB 21/59.

[108] V. H. Rothwell, 'Mesopotamia in British War Aims 1914–1918', *Historical Journal*, xiii (1970). 273–94.

[109] Nicolson to Hardinge, 11 Mar. 1915, Hardinge MSS. XCIII, part I, no 364.

Oliphant, the member of the Foreign Office staff then most closely concerned with the Middle East, which had recorded his, '. . . satisfaction that Russia is determined to acquire a considerable area of the Turkish Empire and that thereby any self-denying ordinance on the part of the allies with a view to bolstering up Turkey is useless.'[110]

Hence when Djemal Pasha, virtually independent viceroy of Syria and Palestine and one of the three men who ruled Turkey in the First World War, approached Russia at the end of 1915 with an offer of peace by which Turkey would surrender Constantinople but would otherwise remain intact with himself as sultan, there was great reluctance in London, as in Petrograd and Paris, to investigate the offer even if, as seemed improbable, it was genuine. Russia asked Britain to probe the matter; Britain asked France; France asked Russia; and Russia responded by again referring the matter to London.[111] While this ludicrous process was taking place, the India Office, supported by Nicolson and Oliphant, argued that the overtures should be rejected since they threatened the success of negotiations with the Sherif and were in any case unacceptable in that they made no mention of allowing Britain to retain Basra.[112] Finally, in mid-January, Nicolson obtained Grey's permission to inform the Russian and French ambassadors that Britain favoured the rejection of Djemal's overtures.[113]

It was difficult for the British to believe that the Turks were interested in peace at a time when their arms were successful in Mesopotamia and the Dardanelles, while the British, for their part, had hope of inflicting such a crushing defeat on Germany that Turkey would be left helpless at the allies' mercy. Russia's increasingly weak military position only appeared to make it more necessary to reaffirm support for her ambitions in the Straits and north-east Turkey in order to preserve her will to continue fighting. During 1916, the Foreign Office enunciated a doctrine that the peace 'offers' which they were constantly receiving from Turkish exiles in Spain and Switzerland should simply be referred without comment to the Russian government.[114] In August, Nicholas II forbade his

[110] Minutes by Nicolson and Oliphant, *c.* 4 Apr. 1916, FO 371/2768, no. 63342.

[111] Cf. Nicolson to Hardinge, 12 Jan. 1916, Hardinge MSS. XCIV, part I, no. 205a.

[112] Letter India Office to FO, 10 Jan. 1916, with minutes by Nicolson and Oliphant, FO 371/2767, no. 5824.

[113] Cf. ibid. nos. 10675 and 13231.

[114] FO to MacMahon, 27 Apr. 1916, FO 371/2768, no. 76954; Hardinge to Alan Johnstone, 27 Sept. 1916, Hardinge MSS. XXV.

minister in Berne from even listening to these emigrés.[115] The question of a separate peace with Turkey seemed closed.

The advent to power of Lloyd George seemed to put the final seal on the matter. He had a consistent loathing and hatred for the Turks based on a definite philosophy of relations between 'civilized' and 'barbarous' peoples (in which latter category he placed the Turks as the prime example). In a remarkable article denouncing the treaty of Lausanne in 1923 he was to write that 'civilized' peoples had the right and duty to intervene in mismanaged territories to 'restore these devastated areas to civilization'. The demands of 'civilized' people became especially strong when they had an ancient historical claim to the lands which they felt called upon to regenerate as was the case with the Greeks and Italians in western Asia Minor. Though Adalia in south-west Asia Minor was 'ethnologically and religiously' Turkish it was very regrettable that Italy had finally decided not to colonize it.[116] Though Lloyd George's words in 1923 owed much of their acerbity to the fact that his government had fallen on policy in Turkey the previous year, there is no doubt that these were his real thoughts. They help to explain his support for Zionism and why the Neville Chamberlain government's pro-Arab policies in Palestine were the one aspect of 'appeasement' which he did not support.

This interpretation is borne out by Lloyd George's statements on Turkey during the first two and a half years of the war. In November 1914, C. P. Scott's impression after meeting Lloyd George was that he was 'not strongly anti-German. He said he should have much greater pleasure in smashing Turkey than in smashing Germany.' He suggested that it would be satisfactory if the war ended with Germany annexing Asia Minor as a *solatium* for losses elsewhere.[117] In March 1915 he would still 'rather crush Turkey than Germany'.[118] Eight months later he confessed 'that personally he should not consider the war as having really succeeded' unless all the non-Turkish portions of the Ottoman Empire were 'liberated'.[119] During the War Committee debate on the House–Grey memorandum in February 1916, he demurred when Kitchener expressed hope that Russia would abandon her claim to Constantinople and make peace

[115] J. Polonsky, *Documents Diplomatiques Secrets Russes 1914–1917* (1928), p. 305.
[116] This article is printed in full in D. Lloyd George, *My Memoirs of the Peace Conference* (1939), ii. 873–80.   [117] Journals, 27 Nov. 1914, 50901.
[118] Ibid. 15 Mar. 1915.   [119] Ibid. 14 Nov. 1915, 50902.

with Turkey. He repeated that he wanted Turkey to be broken up.[120] In his opening address to the first Imperial War Cabinet in March 1917 he declared unequivocally that the destruction of Turkey 'as an Empire' was a British war aim while warning that it might be necessary to restore some of the German colonies.[121] Professor Fischer's comment that Entente war aims in the Great War were 'a characteristic product of the age of imperialism'[122] would certainly be fitting as a description of Lloyd George's attitude toward Turkey. Basic antipathy to the Turks as an inferior people was coupled with a belief that if there had to be a compromise peace it should be one based on the *status quo* except that all the European belligerents should partition Turkey among themselves. For a time in 1917–18, Lloyd George was to cast Russia, another large and in his opinion barbaric nation, in this role.

Most of Lloyd George's colleagues held broadly similar views. In his explanatory addendum to the Entente reply to President Wilson in January 1917, Balfour talked about the iniquity of the Turks and seemed to hint that the destruction of Turkey was the allies' chief war aim. In his address to the Dominion leaders in March he endorsed what the Prime Minister had said by declaring that the reduction of Turkey to a small nation state certainly was an allied war aim.[123] To those ministers and advisers professionally concerned with eastern policy, it was axiomatic that the war against Turkey should be fought to a finish. In a survey of the situation which would arise if Russia left the war, Curzon could see no scope for a separate peace with Turkey.[124] Successive secretaries of state for India, Austen Chamberlain and E. S. Montagu, were opposed to such a policy in principle.[125] The government's chief Middle East adviser, Mark Sykes, never departed from the view which he expounded to the War Committee in June 1916 that unless Turkey was decisively defeated her alliance with Germany would survive to threaten the British Empire in the East after the war.[126] The weekly *Eastern*

---

[120] War Committee, 22 Feb. 1916, CAB 42/2/3.
[121] Text of this address in *War Memoirs*, i. 1047–57.   [122] Fischer, op. cit. p. 320.
[123] Imperial War Cabinet, 22 Mar. 1917, CAB 23/43.
[124] Curzon, Policy in View of Russian Developments', 12 May 1917, G.T. 703, CAB 24/13.
[125] For Chamberlain's views see Imperial War Cabinet minutes as cited in note 123; for Montagu see his memorandum of reflections on the eastern situation, 4 Nov. 1917, G.T. 2837, CAB 24/34.
[126] Sykes, 'The Problem of the East', 20 June 1916 in War Committee minutes, 7 July 1916, CAB 42/16/1.

Reports which he prepared for the War Cabinet are interspersed with warnings against a compromise with Turkey.[127] In the early months of the new government, the only minister who spoke in favour of this was Bonar Law who clashed on the issue with Chamberlain at the Imperial War Cabinet,[128] though it was important that ministers were aware that the Government of India would at any time have been overjoyed if a settlement could be reached with Turkey.

Ideological hostility to Turkey was thus fairly general. In addition, Lloyd George had a firm personal commitment—one so strong that it too could be described as ideological—to seek short-cuts to victory on every war front other than the western. Almost instinctively after becoming Prime Minister, he began pressing Robertson for offensive operations in Palestine.[129] One division was actually withdrawn from Egypt but Murray was ordered to take what aggressive action he could with his forces as was Maude in Mesopotamia. In March Baghdad was captured and it seemed certain that Gaza would fall. This latter development created a mood of almost childish excitement in the War Cabinet which at the end of the month, clearly expecting the early fall of Jerusalem, instructed an unwilling Robertson to order Murray to exploit his 'victory' to the maximum.[130] Immediately after the fall of Baghdad, the British made plans for a permanent structure of British power in Mesopotamia.[131] Similar plans would doubtless have been laid for Palestine if Jerusalem had been occupied. Lloyd George had remarked in private that he was absolutely determined that Palestine should become British and that he would rely upon its conquest by British troops as a means of securing the abrogation of the Sykes–Picot agreement as it related to Palestine.[132] When Mark Sykes set out on a mission to the East at the beginning of April to instigate Arab risings behind the Turkish lines in Syria, the Prime Minister gave him a personal warning not to enter into commitments which would stand in the way of 'securing the addition of Palestine to the British area'.[133]

[127] *Eastern Reports*, XVIII (9 Aug. 1917), CAB 24/144; LVIII (8 Mar. 1918), ibid.; LXVI (2 May 1918), CAB 24/145; LXXXVII (26 Sept. 1918), ibid.; XC (17 Oct. 1918), ibid. On this last date, a fortnight before the armistice with Turkey, Sykes was still writing that she was pro-German and that the idea of ending hostilities with her was not to be thought of.   [128] Imperial War Cabinet; see note 124.
[129] Robertson, op. cit. ii. 164–7.   [130] War Cabinet, 30 Mar. 1917, CAB 23/2.
[131] See note 108; my article on British policy in Mesopotamia.
[132] Journals, 15–17 Mar. 1917, 50903.
[133] Minutes of conference at 10 Downing Street, 3 Apr. 1917, G.T. 372, CAB 24/9; cf. Stein, p. 145.

In fact, the assault on Gaza was repulsed and the advance into Palestine ground to a halt without going beyond Sinai. There were a number of other sobering factors. Within a short time of the March Revolution it became clear that no help against Turkey could be expected from the Russian army in the Caucasus. Owing to the climate, further operations in Palestine or Mesopotamia would be difficult or impossible for many months. The failure at Gaza played into Robertson's hands in his opposition to offensive operations in the East, and Lloyd George, whatever his own views, could not but know that most of his colleagues were highly unwilling to overrule military advice. Curzon, in a paper already cited,[134] was barely able to conceal his joy at the prospect of the conquest of Palestine but added that if the military authorities ruled that the necessary resources could not be provided their opinion would have to be accepted. In these circumstances, even Lloyd George's mind began to turn to the idea of negotiations with the Turks in which Britain would obtain rather less than her maximum aims in the Middle East.

During his visit to Washington in the spring of 1917, Balfour took a less unbending line on Turkey than he had done during the winter. He said to House that if Turkey and Austria were prepared to break with Germany some concessions should be made to them[135] and he helpfully informed Lansing that the Turks were 'nibbling' for peace, a piece of information which was no doubt of use to the President and his secretary of state in deciding to sanction the offer of Henry Morgenthau, a former United States ambassador to the Porte, to conduct a peace mission to the Turks, making use of the fact that Turkey and the United States were not at war (and, in fact, were never to declare war). Balfour gave his assent to this project[136] but it was aborted by Sykes who denounced it to Lloyd George and anyone else who would listen to him in London and by Weizmann who met Morgenthau at Gibraltar and warned him that he was undertaking a forlorn enterprise which could only serve to make him look ridiculous and that the forces of Zionism would be mobilized against him if he persisted.[137]

After the war, Weizmann told an acquaintance that Balfour newly returned from America, had expressed support for his intention of

---

[134] See note 124 above.   [135] Seymour, op. cit. iii. 58.

[136] *Eastern Report*, XVIII (31 May 1918), CAB 24/143 with the inevitable deprecatory comment, given by Sykes's assistant, Ormsby-Gore.

[137] Stein, op. cit. pp. 345 ff.

wrecking the mission.[138] According to Balfour himself, he had originally intended to send Sir Louis Mallet, a former British envoy to Constantinople, to meet Morgenthau and had decided to send Weizmann instead because reports of Morgenthau's plans had appeared in the United States press so that if a former British ambassador met him public opinion would be left with the impression that Britain was begging Turkey for peace.[139] Besides the publicity which he attracted, information reached the Foreign Office that Morgenthau was both pro-Turkish and pro-German[140] and that the President, in return for a separate peace, was prepared to allow the Turks to recover full control in Mesopotamia and Palestine, a policy totally unacceptable to the British.[141] Morgenthau came to be seen as an unsatisfactory mediator because of these complex circumstances and not because British leaders were unwilling in principle to conclude a negotiated peace with Turkey.

In the summer of 1917, there was much more interest in London in peace with Austria than with Turkey. Not only were Austrian feelers more overt than any from Turkey but also to most members of the government, not least the Prime Minister, the idea of a compromise with Vienna was more congenial than that of one with Constantinople. At an Anglo–French dinner at Downing Street on 8 August, attended by Lloyd George, Milner, Curzon, Balfour, Painlevé, Ribot and Albert Thomas, it was agreed that attempts to reach an agreement with Austria must take precedence over Turkey.[142] However, by that time at least one powerful member of the War Cabinet, Milner, was in favour of trying hard to settle peace terms with Turkey. In April 1917, he wrote to a journalist friend that the Turks 'will lose everything east of Cilicia but they might be left with a corner of Europe and all Anatolia'.[143] Milner believed that the Turks might accept these terms, harsh as they were, partly because of general exhaustion and partly, the crux of the matter, because it had become clear by mid-1917 that the Provisional Govern-

[138] William Yale, 'Ambassador Morgenthau's Special Mission of 1917' in *World Politics*, i (1949), 314 ff.

[139] Telegram (drafted by Balfour) for Spring-Rice, 27 June 1917, FO 371/3057, no. 127582.

[140] Spring-Rice to FO, 9 June 1917, ibid. no. 114918.

[141] Spring-Rice to FO, 12 June 1917, ibid. no. 117850.

[142] Ribot, op. cit. pp. 174–5.

[143] Milner to Sidney Low, 8 Apr. 1917, Milner MSS. 144 (VI). For Milner's prodding of the Foreign Office on this question see minute by Cecil addressed to Balfour, *c.* 6 July 1917, FO 371/3057, no. 134859.

ment was either unable or unwilling to maintain Russia's claim to Constantinople. Milner's hopes were shared by Robertson. In April 1917, he wrote to Haig that it was possible that Russia might soon for all practical purposes leave the war which would be a bad blow: 'However, that event would shut out the Constantinople obstacle which has done more than anything to keep the Turks in the field.'[144]

The March Revolution in Russia had a three-fold effect: it removed the initial stumbling block to a peace with Turkey, the Constantinople issue; it weakened the Entente and so made it mandatory for responsible British and French statesmen at least not to ignore any opportunity for a separate peace; and it gave rise to a cry for a peace settlement without annexations and based on self-determination which, though far from welcome in itself, provided a ready-made formula for depriving Turkey of her non-Turkish areas in a manner which she would not find humiliating. To reinforce the attractions of this formula, there was the knowledge that good relations with the United States would be almost impossible if the Entente powers carried out open annexations in the Middle East[145] and there were reports that the Turks were themselves thinking of trying to win over the Arabs including the Sherif of Mecca by offering them autonomy rather on the lines of the Anglo–French proposals in the Sykes–Picot agreement.[146] As early as April the active mind of Mark Sykes suggested the idea that Arab and Armenian communities in Egypt and the western countries including the United States, should be urged to pass resolutions appealing for liberation of their kinsmen from Turkey in order to convince Russian opinion that Anglo–French war aims were not imperialistic.[147]

One consequence of these changes in international conditions was that the negotiations which had begun in London in January 1917 for Italy to be allotted a share in the partition of Turkey were continued in an atmosphere of make-believe. These negotiations involved a triangular contest between the Italians, who laid claim to

[144] Robertson to Haig, 10 Apr. 1917, Robertson MSS. I/23/17.
[145] Cf. Evans, op. cit. pp. 60-1.
[146] Rumbold to FO, 29 Aug. 1917, FO 371/3060, no. 169829 and 25 Oct. 1917, FO 371/3061, no. 205875.
[147] Sykes (in Cairo) to Ronald Graham, 27 Apr. 1917, FO 371/3058, no. 120602.

virtually the entire southern half of Asia Minor, the French, whose Blue zone under Sykes–Picot included territory in Cilicia which Italy coveted, and the British who, strongly supported during the last few weeks of its existence by the Imperial Russian government, were chiefly concerned to deny Italy Smyrna, a port on the Aegean with an important British commercial community 4,000 strong and the Smyrna-Aidin railway, a British-owned enterprise.

At St. Jean de Maurienne in April, Sonnino employed to good effect his expertise in old diplomacy. Lloyd George, anxious to limit Italy's European ambitions, put forward a scheme drafted in the War Office which offered Italy Smyrna. Sonnino accepted and at once produced an earlier Foreign Office plan which denied Italy Smyrna but gave her the Smyrna-Aidin railway and substantial territory in the central part of southern Asia Minor which the British had hoped that Italy, in return for Smyrna, would now leave to the rump Turkish state. He observed that he took it for granted that the new offer was in addition to the old one.[148] Four months of diplomatic negotiations followed in which Sonnino's *coup de théâtre* was transformed into a written agreement. There were two main difficulties. At St. Jean, Lloyd George had demanded that Italy's acquisition of the proposed Asia Minor empire must be conditional on her taking an actual part in the war against Turkey—which she had failed to do despite the fact that she had declared war against Turkey in August 1915. This formula was denounced as 'insulting' by Sonnino and was abandoned by the British with indecent haste at the beginning of June when the Italians offered to send a small contingent to participate in the conquest of Palestine, whose occupation and future government the War Cabinet wished should be exclusively British.[149]

Secondly, the Foreign Office attempted to scale down Italian claims from annexation to a 'sphere of influence'. Cecil observed to the Italian ambassador, Imperiali, that since Russia was pressing for the self-determination of peoples and since it was very unlikely that

---

[148] The official British record of the St. Jean meeting is in CAB 28/2 I.C. 20. The Foreign Office naturally regarded Lloyd George's conduct there as proof of his incompetence as a diplomat and of his folly in usurping their role in diplomacy. Cf. Hardinge to Bertie, 27 Apr. 1917, FO 800/169 and to Rodd, 30 Apr. 1917, Hardinge MSS. XXXI.

[149] War Cabinet, 6 June 1917, CAB 23/3; cf. Robertson to Hardinge, 5 June 1917, and a Foreign Office memorandum on Italy and Asia Minor, 9 June 1917, G.T. 989 and 990, CAB 24/15.

any of the inhabitants in the territory assigned to Italy wished to become her subjects: 'I thought it quite possible that the whole of the Asia Minor agreements would have to be recast in the direction of converting what were to be annexations into spheres of influence or something of that sort.' This was a line of argument which left the ambassador 'very much disturbed'.[150] At the inter-allied conference in London in early August the British proposed a formula under which not only the St. Jean but the Sykes–Picot agreements were merely to divide Turkey into spheres of influence if, as seemed almost certain by that time, Russia renounced her claim to Constantinople. France and Italy rejected this out of hand.[151]

In form, the British now yielded to the Italians. The three western Entente powers exchanged notes which provided for almost the whole of southern Asia Minor to become an Italian dependency with, for good measure, a small sphere of influence to the north-west. In contrast with the promises made to Italy in the treaty of London the new agreement specifically warned that the war might end in circumstances in which Italy would not be able to realize all her aspirations in the Turkish Empire. Also, the notes were made conditional on Russian ratification and not only was the Provisional Government never approached at any time before its overthrow by the Bolsheviks but, as Cecil was to observe triumphantly in November 1918, this condition was included in the knowledge that it was most unlikely that Russia would assent and with the deliberate intention of making the agreement legally null and void at the end of the war.[152] The British and the Italians were both intent on tricking one another and British inability to treat Italy as a serious great power was never better revealed.

The Italians themselves were never sanguine about their Asia Minor prospects except perhaps in the small Adalia region opposite Rhodes. Even before the March Revolution, Sonnino told Milner: 'It was likely . . . that none of our aspirations as regards Asia Minor could in fact be realized in full. It was more or less an ideal programme but even in such a programme Italy ought to have her fair share.'[153] Victor Emmanuel III professed similar views.[154] The near-absurdity of these Asia Minor negotiations no doubt helps to explain

---

[150] Cecil to Rodd, 14, 19 and 22 May 1917, FO 371/3044, nos. 98498, 102248, 104336.
[151] Memorandum by Cecil, 11 Aug. 1917, ibid. no. 158442.
[152] Minute by Cecil, c. 16 Nov. 1918, FO 371/4368, no. 551.
[153] Memorandum by Milner on conversation with Sonnino, 8 Jan. 1917, FO 371/3043, no. 15150.   [154] Rodd to Balfour, 19 Jan. 1917, FO 800/202.

why Italy was so tenacious in upholding her 'realistic' aims in the Adriatic. The entire affair was richly comical—at least by comparison with the grim events around it—and neither its course nor its outcome left British leaders with any feeling that the country's war aims commitments had genuinely increased.

Several weeks before the St. Jean agreement was formally accepted by Britain, the Foreign Office had begun work on drawing up the sort of terms that could be offered to Turkey in a separate peace. At the end of May it had been approached by a man who might be described as an adventurer if it is understood that there was nothing dishonourable or self-seeking about his love of adventure. Aubrey Herbert was typical of a type of Englishman who flourished before 1914. Possessed of a very ample private income, he travelled widely in the remoter parts of the globe and acquired pronounced feelings either of antipathy or sympathy for the peoples whom he met. Herbert's especial favourites were the Albanians but he was also fond of the Turks and had a poor opinion of the Arabs. He had good contacts with the Foreign Office. For instance, he addressed G. R. Clerk by his Christian name in an age when it was unusual for men to do this unless they were close friends.[155] When, therefore, describing himself without any false modesty as one of the only three Englishmen to whom the Committee of Union and Progress, the rulers of Turkey, attached any importance, he volunteered to go to Switzerland to sound out the Turks on peace,[156] the offer was accepted.

A debate then began in the Foreign Office in which a clear line of demarcation emerged between those members who had little first-hand experience of the East and who favoured a separate peace and those who knew the Middle East and whose attitude was at best lukewarm.

Andrew Ryan, a seasoned veteran of the Levant Consular Service and the Constantinople embassy, did not think that the Turks were interested in peace and opposed negotiations in any case on the grounds that only crushing military defeat could extirpate their Pan-

---

[155] Herbert to 'Dear George' (i.e. G. R. Clerk), 21 Aug. 1917, FO 371/3059, no. 164242. On Herbert see Desmond MacCarthy's introduction to Herbert's *Mons, Anzac and Kut*, 1930 ed.; see also Amery, op. cit. ii. 60 and A. T. Wilson, *Loyalties: Mesopotamia 1914–1917* (1930), p. 154.

[156] Herbert to Cecil, 29 May 1917, FO 800/210.

Islamic ambitions[157]—a recognizable variant of the 'crushing of Prussian militarism' theme. Louis Mallet, ambassador to Turkey in 1914, argued that that country should still be treated as 'a military problem' but that contingency plans should be made for a separate peace in case the military position of the allies became desperate.[158] Sykes produced a paper which was turgid even for him and in which he argued that all supporters of an arrangement with Turkey were 'evil, corrupt and hostile' and included such unpleasant-sounding people as 'the Semitic anti-Zionists who are undisguised pro-Turco-Germans'.[159] Ronald Graham, who had spent much of his career in Egypt, opposed a separate peace on the grounds that it would store up 'endless trouble' for the British in Asia.[160]

These men were junior by comparison with the supporters of a negotiated settlement. Drummond felt that it might be possible to conclude a peace based on the fulfilment of allied pledges to the Arabs, autonomy for Armenia, a 'compromise' between Britain and Turkey in Mesopotamia and possibly some sort of Jewish autonomy in Palestine. There need be no question of implementing Sykes–Picot in full and the demise of the Constantinople agreement was taken for granted. A peace with Turkey would mean, 'The complete defeat of Germany's near and middle eastern aspirations and would undoubtedly cause the gravest concern and possible disturbance in Germany itself'.[161]

Clerk agreed and thought that Britain could grant Turkey peace on the basis of British rule in Basra vilayet, 'independence' for Arabia and Baghdad vilayet, 'real autonomy' for Syria and Armenia with the allies exercising such external supervision as might be set up, and a 'special position' for Palestine. French and Italian consent would be essential yet difficult to obtain and the entire idea might seem 'difficult and even visionary' but the British should do everything that they could to bring it about 'at the present time'. After observing that 'the course of the war is not such as to warrant the hope of imposing our terms upon the enemy', he went on to say that local successes against Turkey could not compensate for the absence of victories against Germany and the progress of a financial and economic exhaustion which might end in a general *status quo* peace.

[157] Memorandum by A. Ryan, 13 July 1917, FO 800/205.
[158] Memorandum by Mallet, 14 July 1917 in ibid.
[159] Memorandum by Sykes, 29 July 1917 in ibid.
[160] Minute by Graham, 1 Aug. 1917, FO 371/3057, no. 14896.
[161] Minute by Drummond, 7 July 1917, FO 800/205.

But peace with Turkey frees us from a heavy military, naval and financial drain and gives us fresh resources with which to press home our attack upon Germany. And we can well afford to be generous in our terms to Turkey if we thereby are enabled definitely to defeat Germany. A peace of exhaustion leaves Germany and Turkey free to carry out a *Mittel Europa* policy to a logical conclusion which means that we have lost the war.[162]

In truth, there was nothing 'generous' about the terms which the British were prepared to grant. In essence, the Turks would be left only with a nation-state in Asia Minor and the Constantinople area and British policy had been firmly in favour of Turkish independence in Asia Minor even in the heyday of the Sykes–Picot partition negotiations.[163] What was new was that many men in official London were fired with enthusiasm for such a policy. Cecil, forthright as ever, suggested to Balfour that it would be 'madness' to refuse peace with the Turks if, as a War Office agent in Switzerland had reported, they were prepared to consent to 'changes of rule' in Armenia, Syria and Mesopotamia.[164]

Toward the end of July Herbert returned from his mission after holding conversations with Noureddin Bey, reputedly a close friend of the Turkish Grand Vizier or Prime Minister, Talaat Pasha; with Hakki Halil Bey, former master of the Turkish mint; and with another Turk whose name he could not reveal but who was stated to be very important and very trustworthy. He reported that if only the Entente would abandon the idea of direct annexations and support a policy of 'autonomy' for the Arab and Armenian areas under Turkish suzerainty they could obtain the substance of the power position which they sought in those areas and put Talaat in a strong enough position to depose the incorrigibly pro-German War Minister, Enver, and make peace.[165] 'If we get the luggage it does not very much matter if the Turks get the labels. When Lord Kitchener was all powerful in Egypt his secretary was wearing a

---

[162] Minute by Clerk, 31 July 1917 in ibid.

[163] Cf. minute by Oliphant, 23 Apr. 1916, FO 371/2768, no. 76954. It is most interesting that Oliphant remarked that if there was a revolution in Turkey and an anti-German government came to power, there would be no objection to the conversion of Sykes–Picot from direct partition into a delimitation of spheres of influence *and that the agreement had actually been drawn up in such a way as to allow for this eventuality.*

[164] Copy of War Office telegram from Berne, 22 July 1917, with minute by Cecil, FO 371/3057, no. 144806.

[165] Memorandum by Herbert, 26 July 1917, FO 371/3057, no. 148986 and Rumbold to FO, 24 July 1917, ibid. no. 146009.

fezz. Mesopotamia and Palestine are worth a fezz',[166] argued Herbert plausibly.

The assertion that it would be possible to end the war in the east with no further military effort and minimal political concessions evoked great enthusiasm in the War Office[167] while the Foreign Office were prepared to try to implement it as a policy as was shown by the abortive attempt at the London conference in August to transform the partition agreements into delimitations of spheres (see above). The attempt failed and for several months little was heard from the Turkish politicians in Switzerland or other neutral centres. They and the leaders whom they represented (assuming that they really did represent persons other than themselves) were evidently unable to decide whether to seek a separate peace.

The policy of being prepared to make symbolic concessions to the Turks, partly to win them over to a negotiated peace and partly to satisfy liberal opinion at home and in the United States had, however, taken firm root. A Foreign Office memorandum of October 1917, which appears to have been written by Tyrrell as part of his continuing work on war aims,[168] summarized the thinking of most senior staff in the office by recommending independence and therefore the complete elimination of any Turkish role in Arabia and Mesopotamia where the British felt that their main Middle East interests lay. In Mesopotamia, owing to centuries of political and economic stagnation, British rule would, Tyrrell thought, have to be total in everything but name and was greatly to be welcomed in view of Britain's economic and strategic interests in the territory. But in Armenia, Syria and Palestine, where the enemy were still in occupation and where British interests were smaller, he was content that the Turks should be allowed to retain nominal suzerainty over autonomous native regimes. Except in Armenia, these regimes would, in their turn, be under a new form of external control, French in Syria, British, if it could possibly be arranged, in Palestine. Tyrrell anticipated strong opposition from the French but expected that Italy would give her consent in return for little more than the right to trade in the reconstituted Turkish Empire.

---

[166] Memorandum by Herbert, 29 July 1917, G.T. 1574, CAB 24/21.
[167] Macdonagh to Robertson, 1 Aug. 1917, WO 106/1514.
[168] Memorandum on 'Turkey in Europe and Asia', 22 Oct. 1917, FO 800/214. This is unsigned but the list of contents to part III of this volume of documents, which is in Drummond's hand, describes it as 'Tyrrell's memorandum on peace with Turkey'.

He added a further proposal: that the United States should assume a protectorate over Constantinople to ensure complete freedom of navigation through the Straits both in peace and war while leaving the actual government of the city to Turkey. Tyrrell pointed out that the recent Foreign Office scheme—evidently also his work (see above)—for blocking Germany's eastern ambitions with a Balkan bloc whose most important members would be an Austria and a Bulgaria which had been won away from Germany with generous peace terms, might not be feasible. In that case, an American presence in Constantinople became 'the best means available of breaking the political and military line of Germany's advance to the east and thereby of securing a fair prospect of the maintenance of such new political conditions as may be established in the east as a result of the war'. As in all discussion of political proposals to bring victory in the war nearer, Tyrrell held out the hope that his ideas would be in the long-term interests of the British Empire.

No account of British policy toward Turkey would be complete if it omitted the genuine repugnance felt by most British leaders toward the Turks on account of their (largely successful) attempt to exterminate the Armenian population in the north-east and their ill-treatment of prisoners. These crimes were well-known and when Herbert, a Turcophil but a humane and civilized gentleman, asked permission to send a letter to Talaat appealing for better treatment of British prisoners, the Foreign Office refused to allow it to pass. Clerk remarked that if Talaat could be caught he 'should be tried and hanged for his Armenian massacres'. Cecil minuted, 'If Captain Herbert had heard the account given to me by Mr. Jackson, late United States consul at Aleppo, of the Armenian massacres he would not desire to send this letter—anyhow we can have nothing to do with it'.[169]

Yet Talaat was the man with whom the British had hopes of negotiating the end of Turkish belligerency! Disgust at the idea of allowing the Turks to continue as a ruling race and the development of very definite British ambitions in Palestine and Mesopotamia had to be set against the consideration that neither Turkey nor Germany had been defeated and that it might be impossible to defeat both.

[169] Herbert to Lord Newton, 23 Aug. 1917 with minutes by Clerk and Cecil, FO 371/3060, no. 169535.

In August, the problem, on the face of it less perplexing, of a negotiated peace with Bulgaria arose. By the end of 1916 the Bulgarians had occupied most of the territory which they hoped to annex as an outcome to the World War and began to consider a separate peace based on the retention of these conquests. Bulgaria put out feelers which were at first directed almost entirely to Russia.[170] Owing presumably to the decline of Russian power some Bulgarian politicians turned to the other Entente powers. At the beginning of August, the Foreign Office received reports from a former British consul who had been lent to the Secret Service as its Bulgaria expert that peace overtures from that country were probably imminent.[171] Balfour drew the attention of the War Cabinet to these reports and that body authorized the Foreign Office 'to listen to any reasonable proposals' from Bulgarian sources.[172] A new problem had thus to be faced urgently. There was no question of depriving Bulgaria of any of the territory which she occupied when she entered the war in 1915 but beyond that was an entire range of questions. Which, if any, of Bulgaria's territorial aims should the British support as the price of a separate peace? If overtures came would their bearers be representatives of the Bulgarian government or of elements strong enough to seize power or would they prove to be powerless nonentities? Was Bulgaria trying to use Britain as a catspaw to obtain greater territorial concessions from Germany? Even if Bulgaria wanted peace, might not Germany be in a strong enough position to crush the government and set up an occupation regime?

A definite Bulgaria policy would also have to be correlated with Turkey policy. Though Bulgaria and Turkey were in theory allies, the enmity between them was bitter and deadly since each openly claimed territory from the other on their European border. There was, therefore, the possibility of coming to terms with one country and then combining its forces with those of the Entente to inflict speedy defeat on the other. Given a choice, Drummond would have preferred a negotiated peace with Bulgaria which would have put the Entente in a position to dictate whatever terms they chose to Turkey.[173] However, it was known that Bulgaria would not be

---

[170] A. Nekliudov, *Diplomatic Reminiscences* (1920), pp. 459–63; Logio, op. cit, pp. 162 ff.; Ulrich Trumpener, *Germany and the Ottoman Empire 1914–1918* (1968). pp. 153–6.　　　　　　　　　　　　　　　[171] See FO 371/2885, no. 158441.

[172] Roskill, op. cit. p. 420, quoting Hankey's diary, 3 Aug. 1917.

[173] Minute by Drummond addressed to Balfour, 2 Aug. 1917. FO 371/2885, no. 158441.

satisfied with annexations in European Turkey but would also demand at the very least Serbian Macedonia and the Greek towns of Drama, Serres and Kavalla. Serbia would only consent to the loss of Macedonia, if at all, in return for full allied support for her Yugoslav ambitions, thus practically making the dismemberment of Austria–Hungary an allied war aim. The complexity of the subject was recognized by Clerk:

The position then is this. It is probably easier to offer acceptable terms to Bulgaria than to Turkey. But peace with Bulgaria means a very serious break with Greece and Serbia and further it would oblige the allies to make the wresting of the Yugoslav provinces from Austria and their rendition to Serbia as definite an aim of the war as the evacuation of Belgium and the return of Alsace-Lorraine to France. It might also involve the despatch of a relatively large force to strengthen Bulgaria against simultaneous attack from Turkey and Germany.

On the other hand, peace with Bulgaria would mean the recovery of Rumania and would put Turkey in a position in which she would have to make peace on allied terms. Clerk concluded that in view of the complications in the Balkans and Austria of coming to terms with Bulgaria, a negotiated settlement with Turkey would, to his mind, be just as acceptable, and that if he favoured a concentration of efforts on Bulgaria, this was only because he doubted whether Talaat would make peace on the terms which the British would offer.[174]

In fact, during the next two or three months Bulgarian peace feelers were numerous whereas those from Turkey practically ceased and Austria confined herself to some leisurely overtures for a general peace through her legation in The Hague. The result was that during the early autumn of 1917 Bulgaria was the focus of British hopes for making a deal with one of Germany's allies.

About the middle of August, the Foreign Office learnt that the British and French military intelligence services in Switzerland were conducting negotiations with a 'Committee of National Defence' there which declared itself to be dedicated to the installation of a pro-Entente government in Sofia, while in Stockholm a British agent held talks with a Bulgarian 'socialist' politician. J. D. Gregory, who was considered to be one of the ablest young men in the office, was sent on a mission to France and Switzerland to report on the com-

[174] Minute by Clerk in ibid. 7 Aug. 1917.

mittee. His impression was favourable, and he extolled the plan which its leaders had outlined to him: the Entente would give a written promise of support for the union of all Bulgarians under the Bulgarian flag; the committee would then present this to Tsar Ferdinand as an opportunity to break with Germany and leave the war; if he refused other leaders would feel encouraged to carry out a coup.[175]

Hardinge was in favour of the adoption of this plan but Balfour commented shortly after its appearance in the Foreign Office that the credentials of all the persons who had so far approached the office conveying what they claimed were Turkish or Bulgarian peace feelers were insufficient for serious hopes to be built upon them.[176] He followed this by giving instructions for work on following up Gregory's mission to be suspended while Kühlmann's Madrid move was investigated.[177] Robertson, who thought that it was almost criminal to neglect the Bulgarian issue in this way and whose dearest single wish was, almost certainly, to end the Salonika expedition, wrote directly to Lloyd George, arguing that Serbia, Rumania and Greece should be 'compelled' to cede to Bulgaria whatever territory she demanded. 'We *must* detach some of the enemy countries if we possibly can', he repeated.[178]

Robertson did the Foreign Office something of an injustice. It had just drawn up a plan, already described and referred to above, which in effect sought to overcome the difficulties in the way of peace with Bulgaria outlined by Clerk less than two months before by setting aside many of Serbia's claims against Austria and making that country and a much-strengthened Bulgaria the lynchpins of a permanent anti-German bloc in the Balkans. Meanwhile Lloyd George was telling his colleagues that Bulgaria was war-weary and might yield 'for a price which deserves consideration'.[179]

As far as the British were concerned the time was now ripe for a

---

[175] See FO 371/2885 *passim*, especially no. 180915 which contains Gregory's report dated 15 Sept. 1917. There are some passages on this mission in Gregory's *On the Edge of Diplomacy: Rambles and Reflections 1902–1928* (1930), pp. 82–5, but these are so inaccurate as to be worthless.

[176] For Hardinge's views see his minute on Gregory's report as cited in previous note; for Balfour see his memorandum, 20 Sept. 1917, in D. Lloyd George, *War Memoirs*, ii. 1237–40.

[177] Balfour's instructions in Drummond to Hardinge, 21 Sept. 1917, FO 371/2885, no. 180915.

[178] Robertson to Lloyd George, 29 Sept. 1917, WO 106/1515.

[179] War Cabinet, 11 Oct. 1917, CAB 23/13.

climax but Gregory, on returning to Switzerland in October, found that the 'Committee of National Defence' had split into two hostile factions and that Tsar Ferdinand had reportedly lost all interest in coming to terms with the Entente. The possibility of a separate peace with Bulgaria thus faded but the Bulgarians could have re-activated it any time that they chose. Hardinge was irritated when the Rumanian, Serbian and Greek ministers made a joint protest against British consideration of Bulgarian overtures. 'It is clear', he wrote at the end of October, 'that we shall not fight for ever for Serbian, Greek or Roumanian extravagant claims.'[180]

[180] Minute by Hardinge, *c.* 29 Oct. 1917, FO 371/2885, no. 207195; for the above paragraph see also nos. 196738 and 200852.

IV

FROM THE LANSDOWNE LETTER TO THE GREAT GERMAN OFFENSIVE NOVEMBER 1917–MARCH 1918

I. WAR AIMS COME TO THE FORE

THE events discussed in this chapter cannot be treated apart from the British manpower and military situation in the winter of 1917–18. The Passchendaele offensive had a very sobering effect on Lloyd George's mind. It convinced him that, in addition to any humanitarian considerations, at least two more years of warfare would be needed to achieve military victory and that in this time British manhood might be so depleted as to impair permanently her power in the world. In October he confided these fears to Hankey.[1] The Prime Minister felt that even if military victory could finally be achieved with the build up of American troops in France and the adoption of his own strategic schemes for the East, the price might be so high as to make it pyrrhic.

As the offensive drew to a close, Haig 'unhesitatingly' recommended another massive offensive in France in 1918, expressing confidence that this would almost certainly ensure complete victory.[2] It was not only to Lloyd George that Haig's advice appeared transparently absurd. This is well shown by a minute which Milner made on a memorandum by Haig in which the Field Marshal argued that even if, as he admitted was probable, Germany moved thirty divisions from Russia to France early in 1918, thus making the allied (including American) and enemy forces there almost equal, he could still win a crushing victory:

How is this consistent with the fact that during the last two months although, as he himself says, the Germans have brought very few divisions from Russia, he has been able to make so little headway.

---

[1] Hankey, op. cit. ii. 697–707; cf. Lloyd George's remarks to the King on 18 Oct. 1917 in Harold Nicolson, *King George V: His Life and Reign* (1952), pp. 318–19.

[2] Haig to Robertson, 8 Oct. and 13 Nov. 1917, WO 106/1516, nos. 6 and 17.

The argument seems to be that since we can't overcome the un-reinforced Germans, ergo we may reasonably hope to overcome them strengthened by 30 divisions. It all rests on the 'quite inferior material' theory of which there is abundant assertion but no proof. This is all the more remarkable in view of his statements about the French [Haig had spoken pessimistically about French morale].[3]

At a War Cabinet meeting about the beginning of December, Derby, the Secretary of State for War and a staunch defender of the military High Command,[4] confessed: 'So far from there being any question of our breaking through the Germans, it was a question whether we could prevent the Germans breaking through us.'[5] Faced with what many of them regarded as proof of disastrous military incompetence, the politicians began to acquire the courage to resist the High Command. In November, owing to Lloyd George's initiative, the Inter-Allied Supreme War Council was set up as a new source of military advice and, for the British Prime Minister, a possible means of sidestepping the demands of the leaders of the British army. In December a Cabinet committee on manpower with Lloyd George as chairman began to sit and took little time to resolve that the British forces in France in 1918 should be on the defensive and that absolute priority should be given to avoiding wastage of manpower by means of fortifications and changes in tactics.[6] When Haig was summoned to the War Cabinet in early January he was reduced to arguing that he could only wage a successful defensive if his strength was not cut.[7]

While these deliberations were taking place, the Bolsheviks came to power in Petrograd and began negotiations for a separate peace, Italy seemed in imminent danger of collapse after her army had been routed at Caporetto and the prospect of large-scale American help remained a distant one. It was against this critical military and above

---

[3] Milner's minute on a copy of the letter from Haig to Robertson, 8 Oct. 1917, cited in note 2 above, Milner MSS. 125, Box AE 2.

[4] Cf. Milner's attitude as recorded above with that of Derby who on 25 Nov. 1917 wrote to Esher that 'Milner is intolerable' because he thought that soldiers 'were all damned fools'. Randolph Churchill, *Lord Derby: King of Lancashire* (1959), p. 293.

[5] Derby's remarks in a memorandum by Hankey, 8 Dec. 1917, CAB 27/14 M.P.C. 2.

[6] Final revised version of draft report of the Cabinet committee on manpower, 1 Mar. 1918, with covering note by Hankey, 2 Apr. 1918, G 185, CAB 24/4. On this policy see also Lloyd George's remarks at the first, third and fourth meetings of this committee, 10, 11 and 15 Dec. 1917, CAB 27/14.

[7] War Cabinet minutes, 7 Jan. 1918 in WO 106/425; Haig to Hankey, 9 Jan. 1918, WO 106/1517.

all manpower situation that the most important single British statement on war aims in the Great War, that by Lloyd George to a trade
union conference on 5 January 1918, was made.

Its indirect origins were both national and international but its
direct origins were purely international. On 4 August 1917, the third
anniversary of Britain's entry into the war, the National War Aims
Committee was founded with Lloyd George, Asquith, Bonar Law
and Barnes as presidents.[8] Utilizing the existing machinery of the
political parties in the constituencies, its objective, as set out in a
confidential memorandum, was: 'Generally to strengthen the
national morale and consolidate the national war aims as outlined by
the executive Government and endorsed by the great majority of the
people.' From this sprang such purposes as countering 'the insidious
and specious propaganda of pacifist publications', emphasizing the
economic advantages of victory, inspiring each individual worker
with a sense of personal responsibility for the war effort and stifling
all manifestations of class and party strife.[9]

Evidence of the importance of the new body, which distributed
literature to factories, churches and private individuals and arranged
meetings some of which were addressed by national leaders, is
revealed by the appointment of Carson as a member at the end of
August, giving the committee a representative in the War Cabinet.
However, the staff of professional bureaucrats attached to the committee were hindered from the first by the vagueness and repetitive-
ness of the leaders' public speeches on war aims. Lloyd George's
speech at the inaugural meeting was a plea for the entire nation to
concentrate single-mindedly on victory without pausing to consider
specific war aims.[10] The old reluctance to go beyond this survived
into the fourth year of the war. The committee soon began to report
that to organized labour this was no longer enough and that almost
everywhere trade unions were unwilling to co-operate in the setting
up of local committees for precisely this reason.[11]

More salutary than these pleas of which the public knew nothing,
was the Lansdowne letter published in the *Daily Telegraph* on 29
November 1917. The terms of this document, a call for the immediate enunciation of war aims of a very limited sort and for an

[8] For the founding of this body see *The Times*, 24 and 26 July 1917.
[9] Unsigned and undated memorandum, 'Aims of Home Publicity', T[reasury] 102/16.
[10] Speech by Lloyd George, 4 Aug. 1917.
[11] Memoranda by G. Wallace Carter, 25 Sept. and 10 Oct. 1917, T 102/16.

invitation to Germany to open negotiations, are much too well-known to require setting out here. Its significance was that those elements in British public life who openly called for a compromise peace now stretched across the entire political spectrum: to the Union of Democratic Control whose support lay in the non-socialist left and to the Independent Labour Party had been added the doyen of Conservative elder statesmen. It was a situation comparable to the one which in 1846 had elicited from Metternich the anguished cry that he had been ready for anything except a liberal pope. The Honourable Arthur Davidson, private secretary to Edward VII's widow, Queen Alexandra, confessed that the letter shook his faith in the value of 'high education and ancestral surroundings'.[12]

To Lloyd George, Lansdowne's action was a sovereign reason for *not* making a declaration on war aims. He told an allied conference in Paris at the beginning of December that he had arrived there prepared to agree to a public statement that the allies would be prepared to discuss the revision of war aims with a 'decent' Russian government but that he was now opposed to this as any such declaration would be looked upon as an endorsement of Lansdowne.[13] The British attitude was indeed one of a number of reasons which led House, who was in Europe for the conference, to despair of his hope that the United States and the Entente might draw up a joint programme of moderate war aims. Shortly afterwards, Lloyd George explained that Lansdowne's errors were two-fold. His action had been 'singularly ill-timed' (a reference to events in Russia and Italy) and he had failed to postulate victory. When taxed, Lloyd George was at a loss to define the circumstances which would constitute victory and this led his interlocutor to the conclusion that he 'had not really thought out our war aims and when he talked of victory was talking rhetorically unless he meant simply victory in the field which may not be attainable'.[14] Lloyd George was not at all convinced that victory was certain to come and an immediate reply to Lansdowne would have been impossible in view of the absence of a definite War Cabinet line on war aims. But neither of these points invalidates the conclusion that Lloyd George regarded the Lansdowne letter as a reason for not expending the necessary time and energy to formulate such a line.

[12] Davidson to Bertie, 3 Dec. 1917, FO 800/171.
[13] Inter-allied conference at Paris, minutes for 1 Dec. 1917, CAB 28/3 I.C. 35.
[14] Journals, 12 and 16 Dec. 1917, 50904.

What made the Prime Minister change his mind were the peace negotiations between the Bolsheviks and the Central Powers at Brest–Litovsk in which the latter expressed support for the principles of the allied governments' domestic opponents—self-determination, open diplomacy, no indemnities and so on—though always with qualifications such as saying that proof of the devotion of the inhabitants in the German colonies to their 'German friends' was so abundant as to make any testing of opinion before the restoration of German administration superfluous. Here was a threat to the loyalty of the working classes which could not be ignored. It was emphasized by continuing pressure for the definition of war aims from the War Aims Committee,[15] and by an energetic campaign which Henderson was waging to unite the Labour Party and the Trades Union Congress on a common programme of war aims as a first step toward an international socialist conference, a revival, in fact, of the Stockholm idea under the auspices of British socialism. There were also warnings, which Lloyd George took very seriously, that 'pacifist' propaganda was undermining the morale of British troops.[16] The Prime Minister declared that the Brest exchanges made a declaration on war aims necessary,[17] though he was also heavily influenced by the suggestion of the Austrian representative, Count Mensdorff, in his conversations with Smuts, discussed in another section, that the allies should restate their war aims with its implication that a moderate statement might have an important effect on Austrian and even German policy.

The War Cabinet began intensive discussion of war aims on the last day of 1917. Though it agreed to ask its chief military advisers whether there was in 1918 or 1919 any reasonable chance of a victory that 'would not leave the military domination of Prussia successful and intact'—an echo of the old dream of a crushing

[15] Cf. Wallace Carter's report, 8 Dec. 1917, and report on public reaction to the Lansdowne letter, no date, both in T 102/18.

[16] Such warnings were issued by Haig (Blake, pp. 274, 277, 290) and by Brigadier-General Cockerill, the Director of Special Intelligence (cf. Cockerill to Hardinge, 2 Jan. 1918, FO 371/3435, no. 1513). Cockerill refers to this memorandum, which called for a detailed statement on war aims written specifically to maintain the spirit of the troops, in his memoirs, *What Fools We Were* (1944), pp. 66–8. This was a reversal of previous propaganda policy toward the troops which had concentrated on denouncing Germany in general terms for 'bloodlust, cruelty, tyranny and every conceivable horror', ibid. p. 76. Lloyd George expressed anxiety on troop morale to the Manpower Committee, fourth meeting, 15 Dec. 1917, CAB 27/14.

[17] Journals, 28 Dec. 1917, 50904; War Cabinet, 11.30 a.m., 3 Jan. 1918, CAB 23/5.

military victory in which very few ministers or even General Staff
officers any longer believed—the emphasis was from the first on
drawing up a list of terms on which Germany could have peace
under her existing 'Prussian' regime though no one thought it likely
that she would yet be prepared to accept such terms. A joint reply
of all the allies was ruled out on the grounds that the result would
be a hopelessly unattainable catalogue of everybody's aims. Provisional agreement was reached that support should be expressed
for French aspirations in Alsace-Lorraine, for Italian claims only
where they were based on the national principle, and for the
restoration of Belgium, Serbia and Rumania, a formula which
omitted any endorsement of the desire of the Entente's Balkan allies
for expansion.[18]

As Robertson was to note in his memoirs, he had already supplied
an answer to the Cabinet's question in a memorandum of 27
December 1917. In this and in another paper six days later, he
opposed a compromise peace as merely a 'truce' in which Germany
would 'organize a fresh attempt for securing that world dominion
which she had failed to obtain in the present war'. If the Entente
armies could conduct a successful holding operation on the Western
Front until the Americans were present in strength, 'We may hope
to get eventually a favourable peace'. What is most significant is the
tone rather than the content of Robertson's advice. The bombast of
his reply to the Lansdowne memorandum just over a year before
was now totally absent. Ministerial questions as to whether the war
could be won which had then been denounced as unthinkable
aberrations were now described as natural expressions of anxiety.
No more than the politicians did Robertson think that there was any
great possibility of the war ending in military cataclysm for
Germany.[19]

Meanwhile, Lloyd George held consultations. On 28 December
the Labour Party produced a programme of 'anti-imperialist' war
aims and three days later the Prime Minister held conversations
with a party delegation from which he emerged with the impression
that its views were compatible with those expressed at the War
Cabinet on the same day.[20] He also consulted Asquith and Grey as
leaders of the Liberal party outside the government and obtained

[18] War Cabinet, 31 Dec. 1917, CAB 23/13.
[19] Robertson, op. cit. ii. 276–84 for these memoranda.
[20] Cf. War Cabinet, 31 Dec. 1917, CAB 23/4.

what Grey was to characterize as a 'general assent' to the terms of his speech.[21] The main discussions were, of course, in the War Cabinet. On 3 January Lloyd George outlined the sort of terms which, as he understood the matter, would be acceptable to his colleagues: to the aims which had been agreed upon three days previously, he would be inclined to add independence for Poland, autonomy for the subject races of Austria–Hungary and the proclamation for the German colonies and the occupied parts of Turkey of a doctrine of 'self-determination' under which chiefs and local notables would be called upon to announce their preference for British rule (see Appendix I, pp. 288–91).

A more difficult problem was that of Alsace-Lorraine which was 'disputable ground'. So far the British had succeeded in avoiding any official statement of support for French rule there and had confined themselves to statements of 'personal opinion'—that the restoration of the two provinces to France would be a very good thing indeed. During the previous autumn, pressure from the French for official support had mounted,[22] and some mention of the subject in a speech on war aims would clearly be unavoidable. Yet Lloyd George, while aware that merely equivocal British support might be disastrous for French morale, did not wish to pledge the country to fight on for the lost provinces. He therefore proposed that 'France should be promised support in so far as she was prepared to fight'.[23] To depart from chronology, it may here be mentioned that after delivering the speech Lloyd George proudly boasted that in his reference to Alsace-Lorraine he had achieved a double coup by replacing 'restore' with the more 'elastic' word 'reconsider' and yet had won more applause from the French than he would otherwise have received by deciding on the spur of the moment to turn to Albert Thomas, the distinguished French socialist, who was one of the platform guests, saying that Britain would stand by France 'to the death'. That the Prime Minister could not only behave in this way but preen himself on it afterwards sheds interesting light on his character as well as on British policy toward Alsace-Lorraine.[24]

---

[21] Grey to J. A. Spender, 26 Jan. 1932. Spender MSS., B.M. Add. 46389.

[22] *The Diary of Lord Bertie of Thame*, ii. 191–2; Cambon, op. cit. iii. 183–4; Cecil to Balfour, 19 July 1917, Lloyd George MSS. F/3/2/28 and to Lloyd George, 27 Dec. 1917, ibid. F/6/5/11; Bertie to Lloyd George, 24 Sept. 1917, ibid. F/51/4/40; E. L. Spiers to Lloyd George, 27 Dec. 1917, ibid. F/23/1/37.

[23] War Cabinet, 11.30 a.m., 3 Jan. 1918, CAB 23/5.

[24] Journals, 8 Jan. 1918, 50904.

The War Cabinet ended with Lloyd George remarking that though the forthcoming declaration was intended as a direct reply to what was being said at Brest–Litovsk, it could not take the form of a note since Britain did not recognize the Bolshevik government, and should be delivered as a speech. When the Cabinet resumed in the evening, it had before it two draft speeches on war aims by Smuts and Cecil as a basis for the Prime Minister's address.[25] In fact, the text of the speech was largely taken verbatim from these two papers. A careful comparison between them and the speech shows that of the pungent or fairly pungent expressions in the latter, the only one—apart from the 'to the death' interjection on Alsace-Lorraine—which was not plagiarized from Cecil or Smuts is a statement that Germany apparently proposed to set up 'one kind of independence for a great nation and an inferior kind of independence for a small nation.'[26] Lloyd George was apt to wax enthusiastic about small nations. He may well have been responsible for this phrase. Probably what happened was that the Prime Minister handed the two memoranda to one of his senior aides such as Philip Kerr and asked him to amalgamate them into a single address in which he then made alterations.[27]

Cecil and Smuts agreed on much. The gist of Smuts' argument was that the British Empire was fighting for the abandonment of aggression as a policy by all nations, and territorial rearrangements based on the national principle and self-determination; and that if Germany would agree to certain specified territorial changes Britain would look upon the militarist instinct in her as having been purged. These demands were the ones agreed to or mentioned by Lloyd George at the War Cabinet on 31 December and 3 January and were certainly moderate in Europe, threatening Germany with no losses except possibly that of Alsace-Lorraine and Austria–Hungary only with that of the comparatively small areas in which Italians were in a majority of the population. An independent Poland was indeed called for but opinion in British ruling circles was overwhelmingly that the inclusion of German territory in such

[25] Memoranda by Smuts and Cecil, both 3 Jan. 1918, G.T. 3180–1, CAB 24/37.
[26] D. Lloyd George, *War Memoirs*, ii. 1512. The text of this address is given on pp. 1510–17.
[27] On the authorship of this speech see in addition to the references above, W. K. Hancock and J. Van Der Poel, *Selections from the Smuts Papers*, iii (1966), 590; Ian Malcolm to Balfour, 5 Jan. 1918, Balfour MSS., B.M. Add. 49745; and Cecil to Balfour, 8 Jan. 1918, FO 800/207.

a state was outside the realm of possibility (see below). Smuts also gave an elaborate justification of 'self-determination' for the German colonies. He had already indicated his faith in this as a foolproof method of incorporating these colonies in the British Empire (see above, p. 74) and German leaders could not be so naive as to have any doubt about what was meant.

Cecil's paper was in a sense even more conciliatory. Implicit in his discussion of various territorial war aims was that these were all desirable changes but that none of them with the exception of the sacrosanct Belgian issue, was so important as in itself to justify continuance of the war. Smuts, Cecil and Lloyd George all made statements on the Middle East which accorded exactly with the terms which the British were prepared to grant Turkey in a separate peace (on which see Section 3 below).

Smuts and Cecil differed importantly in two respects. Smuts included a plea for Germany to become democratic in his draft while adding that the allies were not fighting to impose democracy on Germany and that the change could only be brought about by the German people of their own free will. Cecil was silent on this not because he dissented in the least from his colleague's views but because he felt that such a plea would be in modern political jargon 'counterproductive'. Lloyd George agreed with Smuts and coupled his expression of hope that the German people would reject autocracy with a hint that in that case the allies could afford to be less stringent in their peace terms.

In addition, Cecil proclaimed roundly: 'We could not willingly acquiesce in the establishment of a Lithuania or a Courland nominally independent, but in reality subservient to the German autocracy.' If his draft had been published as a statement of British war aims, German leaders would have been left with the impression that the prevention of any sort of German gains in Russia was as much a British aim as the retention of the German colonies on which Cecil declared, 'We do not desire to withdraw their future from discussion at the peace conference'. In private, Cecil was already saying that a peace settlement based on giving Germany a free hand in the Baltic area in return for losses or the *status quo* elsewhere 'cannot be regarded as a brilliant result of the war though it may turn out to be the best we can do'.[28] The key to his attitude lay in the military

---

[28] Commentary by Cecil on draft by Balfour of telegram for President Wilson, 28 Dec. 1917, Balfour MSS., B.M. Add. 49738.

situation. He had already characterized a proposal that the allies should publicly announce their readiness to revise the secret treaties as 'madness' (one of his favourite words) while adding that revision certainly was desirable.[29] Neither Cecil nor anyone else in the Foreign Office was ever resigned to recognizing German gains in Russia but they thought that if such a policy should become necessary it should not be announced until the allied military position had improved.

Smuts, in his donnish way, rather gently chided the Bolsheviks for negotiating with Germany from a position of military weakness and *implied* that the allies would not be prepared to rescue them from the consequences of their folly. To Lloyd George it seemed quixotic not to make all this explicit. He had been toying with the idea of abandoning Russia to Germany since at least September and the events of the previous three months were hardly calculated to induce him to abandon this idea. The only passage in his address which departs significantly from what either Smuts or Cecil said is the one on Russia. He declared that while Britain would be proud to fight alongside Russia, it was also the case that: 'If the present rulers of Russia take action which is independent of their Allies we have no means of intervening to arrest the catastrophe which is assuredly befalling their country. Russia can only be saved by her own people.'

Lloyd George had to fight very hard to gain the assent of his colleagues to the inclusion of this passage. He explained that not only was he anxious to leave the Bolsheviks in no doubt that they would receive no help from the allies if they persisted with the Brest negotiations but 'also that he wished to give a hint to the enemy in the same direction'. Few or no other ministers were prepared to wash their hands of Russia in this way but the Prime Minister gained his point, in return perhaps for agreeing to abandon a suggestion that the statements extracted from the memorandum by Robert Cecil, that the allies neither sought nor desired the break up of Austria–Hungary, should be rephrased in even more robust language.[30]

Such was the background to Lloyd George's address on war aims. Its most immediate and indeed most important purpose was to re-

[29] Minute by Cecil, *c.* 14 Dec. 1917, FO 371/3438, no. 12066.

[30] War Cabinet, 4 Jan. 1918, CAB 23/5. On 31 Dec. the War Cabinet had discussed the Russo–German peace negotiations and, by order of the Prime Minister, no minutes had been taken, note on War Cabinet, 31 Dec. 1917, CAB 23/13.

assure the British people that the government's war aims were ones which justified not merely the continuation but the intensification of the war effort. The fact that Lloyd George chose to deliver it at a trade union conference on manpower speaks for itself. As a programme for the eventual peace conference, he thought that it had real value.

In his opinion, however, the terms which we were bound to set out were not such as Germany could accept. He reminded the War Cabinet that at the moment Germany was in the hour of triumph and this was the atmosphere of the German people. In these conditions no German government could concede all that we were bound to insist on. Hence it was essential that this statement should be regarded rather as a war move than as a peace move.

Referring to the constant quest for a separate peace, he thought that its most important consequences might be in Austria or Turkey rather than Germany.[31]

The speech was a genuine statement of British aims. After delivering it Lloyd George wrote to Asquith: 'The nation can now go forward with a united front either to peace or to war as the Germans will'.[32] If Germany had offered to accept its terms and those of President Wilson's fourteen-point address three days later which set out conditions comparable with Lloyd George's except for Wilson's (vague) demand for 'freedom of the seas' and his (very clear) demand for the evacuation of all Russian territory,[33] the Prime Minister would certainly have favoured peace negotiations and probably allied concessions on Alsace-Lorraine and the colonies to say nothing of Russia. Probably he would have been able to carry most of his colleagues with him. Whether he could have won the assent of his allies, especially the France of Clemenceau, is much less certain. Clemenceau had rejected an urgent plea by Lloyd George that he should come to London for consultations on the war aims address.[34] Even the British Prime Minister was not prepared to make a further move toward peace unless Germany showed willingness to accept the sort of terms which he had set out and German policy on the fundamental issue of Belgium remained completely intransigent during the first nine months of 1918.[35]

[31] For the above paragraph see War Cabinet, 5 p.m., 3 Jan. 1918, CAB 23/5.
[32] Lloyd George to Asquith, 5 Jan. 1918, Lloyd George MSS. F/42/5/3.
[33] For a comparison between the two speeches see Mayer, op. cit. pp. 360–6.
[34] Cf. Lloyd George to Clemenceau, 2 Jan. 1918, FO 800/169.
[35] H. W. Gatzke, *Germany's Drive to the West* (1951), pp. 241 ff.

During the winter, there were important developments in two areas of British policy: the league of nations and the future of Poland. American participation in the war and the increasing unlikelihood, as it seemed, of being able to inflict total defeat on Germany made British leaders more friendly to proposals for a league of nations as a serious instrument for helping to preserve peace after the war. Hankey underwent an interesting metamorphosis. Wholly hostile to the league idea in 1916 (see above, p. 35), he was by January 1918 advocating a league in the first place as a war instrument (the economic war against the Central Powers would be centralized under league control and Germany would be threatened with permanent exclusion from world trade unless she accepted allied peace terms); but also as an instrument of peace which would include Germany and which would develop from international co-operation in the 'comparatively small matters' of finance, economics and education to dealing with international crises.[36] By this time, British ministers, aware of a great increase in public interest in the league since the entry of the United States into the war, were committing themselves in general terms in their speeches to the principle that there should be a league.[37] Yet the increased interest of the leadership was tempered with caution. Writing to Balfour at the end of December, Robert Cecil, whose position as the member of the government most interested in the league is well-known, remarked that he still thought that the only real guarantee of future security lay in the defeat of Germany or in a revolution there. 'The League of Nations may be a buttress to security but it is far too uncertain a project to be relied on as its foundation.'[38]

Discussion was in any case inhibited by President Wilson's known dislike for debate within the United States on the league and by his refusal to discuss plans for it with the British or anybody else.[39] British leaders were anxious not to offend the President and were convinced that the only possible chance for the success of the league lay in Anglo–American co-operation. The result was that in public

---

[36] Memorandum by Hankey, 16 Jan. 1918, G.T. 3344, CAB 24/39.

[37] H. R. Winkler, *The League of Nations Movement in Great Britain 1914–1919* (1952), pp. 53 ff., 240 ff.

[38] Cecil to Balfour, 28 Dec. 1917, FO 800/207. This letter helps to explain an earlier, curious remark by Cecil that he was omitting 'all question of measures to secure peace after the war' from a paper on war aims 'because whether effective or ineffective they are not likely to be contentious'. Memorandum by Cecil, 10 July 1917, FO 800/214.

[39] Cf. Drummond to Balfour, 15 Nov. 1917, reporting conversation with House, G.T. 2667, CAB 24/32; see also Seymour, op. cit., iv. 6–10.

they continued to repeat what they had themselves once genuinely believed: that it would be mistaken to discuss the details as opposed to the principle that there should be a league because of the danger that this would divert attention from the war effort.[40]

Shortly before repeating this argument, Cecil had written to Balfour suggesting the setting up of a committee to examine proposals for a league 'from a historic and juridical point of view'. The Foreign Secretary consented while observing that it would be 'sanguine' to expect that this would be very helpful at the peace conference.[41] Thus was born the Phillimore committee of Foreign Office experts and historians which was to do much work on the league question during the winter (see Chapter V below).

During the early months of the existence of the Provisional Government, the British relaxed their tendency to press for the internationalization of the Polish problem. The Foreign Office were pleasantly surprised by the liberal nature of the new government's statements on Poland and thought it unwise to tempt providence by asking for more. In addition, Balfour remained for some time a supporter of a Russo–Polish union which he saw as a means of maintaining Russian interest in European affairs should Germany remain a threat to peace after the war. In other respects, his views came nearer to what the Polish nationalists wanted. Reflecting the mood in which the allies had answered the German and American peace notes of the previous December, he declared it 'essential' at the Imperial War Cabinet that the future Polish state should include Posen.[42]

The steady decline of Russia during 1917 was a mixed blessing for the Poles, enabling them to be more importunate in pressing their demands on the western governments while making those governments less willing to contemplate a greater Poland with the frontiers, particularly on the west, that the nationalists wanted. In August 1917 a number of mostly right-wing Polish exiles set up a Polish National Council and immediately pressed the Entente and United States governments for recognition. France recognized it as an official Polish body entitled to represent Polish citizens in the

[40] Cf. Cecil's answer to parliamentary question by Mr. M'Curdy, *Commons Debates*, 5th series, XCIX, cols. 1369–70, 22 Nov. 1917.

[41] Cecil to Balfour, 20 Nov. 1917, with minute by Balfour, FO 371/3439, no. 53848.

[42] Imperial War Cabinet minutes, 22 Mar. 1917, CAB 23/43.

Entente countries in September. This fact, together with the declared intention of the council to set up a Polish army in France, left the British with little alternative but to take a similar step. They did so and, though it committed them to little, it led to a debate in the Foreign Office on what precisely constituted a war aim (see Introduction above). Although the result of this debate seemed to be that any British declarations to the Poles would be 'aspirations' rather than aims for which the war should, if necessary, be prolonged, the office were alarmed that the council, which had established a London office near Russell Square headed by Count Sobanski, one of its leading members, would exert continuous pressure for Britain to recognize the independence of Poland as an aim.

On one point there was virtual unanimity. Even J. D. Gregory, the staunchest champion of the Poles in the Foreign Office, thought that with Russia's collapse there was very little possibility of the allies being able to win the Polish-speaking areas of Germany for an independent Poland (see above, p. 2). One of the dearest wishes of the Poles was that their country when reconstituted should have a seaboard and this could only be achieved by annexations from Germany. Hence Cecil's violent opposition to a suggestion by Phillipe de Margerie, political director at the Quai d'Orsay, that the allies should issue a declaration of support for a united, independent Poland with access to the sea. 'At this stage in the war to adopt and proclaim as one of our war aims as essential as the restoration of Belgium, the creation of an independent Polish kingdom which would cut Prussia in two seems to me sheer lunacy.'[43]

At the inter-allied conference in Paris two months later which set up the Supreme War Council, the French Foreign Minister, Pichon, pressed for a declaration of support of the type suggested by de Margerie. Balfour supported him, explaining that 'access to the sea' need only mean an international regime on the Vistula and not Polish sovereignty in West Prussia or Danzig. Lloyd George disagreed, making it clear that his main fear was of an allied commitment to Poland standing in the way of a separate peace with Austria:

He hoped we would not increase our obligations at the very moment when our military strength was debatable. The suggestion was to set up a Polish state by military means. What would be the effect of this? Consider

[43] Minute by Cecil, *c.* 9 Oct. 1917, FO 371/3016, no. 193872.

the Italian position. If Austria would give all that Italy wanted, it would nevertheless be impossible to make peace unless Austria was willing to hand over Cracow and Lemberg districts which had always been perfectly well-governed and had been better treated by the Austrians than by the Russians during their short occupation. The present moment was most unpropitious when we had almost broken with Russia and had some hopes from Austria.

Soon the Foreign Office themselves were to look with favour on an 'Austrian solution' of the Polish problem (see Section 2 below). On this occasion the conference agreed to accept an alternative formula put forward by Balfour: 'The creation of a Poland, independent and indivisible, under such conditions as will ensure her free political and economic development, constitutes one of the conditions of a solid and just peace and of the regime of right in Europe.' He depicted this as a platitude: 'The propositions contained in it were undeniable and would not be embarrassing to us in the future.'[44] For precisely this reason the Polish National Council refused to endorse the declaration and it was never issued. Clerk explained that the council found it 'unpalatable', and feared that it would 'if published in Poland, do more harm than good'.[45]

During the early months of 1918 the British and the other allied powers made concessions to Polish nationalism which were not of so meagre a sort that the Poles declined to recognize them as such. This process began with the speeches on war aims by Lloyd George and Wilson at the beginning of the year, continued with public expressions of 'personal opinion' by Balfour that he favoured the reconstitution of an independent Poland including German territory and culminated in a note from the Entente and United States ministers at Jassy on 2 March to the Polish forces in Rumania, stating: 'That one of the principal aims of the Entente in the present war is the restoration of Poland, in her geographical and historical limits, having all necessary elements for a free national existence as well as for her economic development [and] that such restoration will be for the Entente in the event of victory an essential condition for the conclusion of peace.'[46]

All this was prompted by numerous reports that predominant opinion in Poland was despairing of any sort of allied support for

[44] Conference minutes, 1 and 3 Dec. 1917, CAB 28/3 I.C. 35.
[45] Minute by Clerk, 12 Dec. 1917, FO 371/3002, no. 234811.
[46] Komarnicki, op. cit. pp. 209–10.

the Polish cause and was turning to an accommodation with Germany.[47] Gregory remarked: 'If an allied nationality policy elsewhere constitutes a political *offensive*, an allied Polish policy is virtually a defensive policy, as events may so move that through lack of precaution we may find another and very inconvenient enemy in practice added to the rest.'[48]

As in the case of the Foreign Office's schemes for the future of the Balkans and the Turkish Empire, the background to these statements of support was thus one of military necessity and none of them was formally incompatible with the 'Austrian solution'. British policy toward Poland, as toward eastern Europe as a whole, was dictated by the need to find formulas which stood a reasonable chance of being durable and which would help to wear down Germany with the emphasis decidedly on the latter consideration.

2. AUSTRIA–HUNGARY: RETURN TO THE DIPLOMATIC APPROACH

The Italian defeat at Caporetto in late October 1917 put an end to the project for a diplomatic-military offensive against Austria. Only the purely diplomatic approach remained and the possibilities for its use were increased by the fact that American, French and British statesmen now looked upon Italian war aims with even less deference than before. Calls such as the one which Carson had made to Lloyd George just before Caporetto that British obligations to Italy should be emphasized in the public speeches of Cabinet ministers[49] were no longer heard. Indeed, in an address to an Anglo–American conference in London at the end of November, Lloyd George spoke of the 'collapse of Russia and Italy . . .'.[50] as though Italy were a spent force. The remarkable Italian recovery in the

---

[47] Particularly interesting is a letter from Cockerill as Director of Special Intelligence to Hardinge, 6 Nov. 1917, FO 371/3016, no. 215356. This gave the text of an intercepted letter from Clifford Sharp, *The Times* correspondent in Stockholm, to Wickham Steed in which he said that Esmé Howard, the British minister to Sweden, was worried and puzzled by the Foreign Office's failure to express any sort of support for Polish independence. The minister was convinced from his own numerous Polish contacts that this would drive the Poles into the German camp. He was therefore allowing Sharp to use the diplomatic bag to ask Steed to launch a campaign in Britain to publicize the error of the office's ways. Like so many, Howard was prepared to go behind the backs of colleagues and superiors on a political matter about which he felt strongly.

[48] Minute by Gregory, 18 Nov. 1917, FO 371/3002, no. 218943.

[49] Carson to Lloyd George, 17 Oct. 1917, Lloyd George MSS. F/6/2/47.

[50] Minutes of Anglo–American conference, 20 Nov. 1917, CAB 28/3 I.C. 33.

aftermath of Caporetto brought about a modification of this view but only a partial one. The French were positively eager that Italy should be forced to accept a scaling down of her war aims,[51] a symptom of that mistrust, amounting almost to hatred, which divided the two Latin nations during the war.

It also appeared that the United States favoured leniency to Austria. Cecil interpreted Wilson's speech declaring war on Austria early in December as being in reality an offer to the Monarchy for it to leave the war at almost any price,[52] an accurate interpretation.[53] Generally bleak prospects in the war as a whole led large sections of articulate British opinion to favour generosity to Austria and even to look upon its reputedly liberal-minded Foreign Minister, Count Czernin, almost as a hero.[54]

In the Foreign Office, Cecil held definite views on the future of eastern Europe as on most matters and these, as expressed in a private letter, are worth quoting in full as a corrective to any impression that the British sought peace with Austria as nothing more than an unwilling response to a desperate war situation:

As for terms of peace, some day or other I would like to discuss them with you. I must honestly admit to you that I am to some extent a heretic. I recognize, of course, that we must do all we can for the Poles and the Yugoslavs and the Czechs, but I must add that I cannot look forward with much enthusiasm to the success of our efforts. As far as I can see the Slavs have never shown the slightest capacity for self-government.

Steed and his friends would no doubt regard this as ignorant folly but they *will* treat this aspect of European politics from a crusading point of view. They believe in nationality as if it were a religion. I can only regard it as one of the great international forces which it would be folly to disregard. So far its achievements do not appear to me to have been very encouraging. It produced a united Germany, unfortunately for us, it has kept south-eastern Europe in a turmoil, it is responsible for very wild and unreasonable aspirations in Italy, and it is a perfect curse to us in Ireland.

All this, of course, is for your private eye alone and does not mean that I differ, except perhaps in degree, from the attitude you take about Austria, but it does emphatically mean I do not myself believe that a European peace founded only on nationality and without any other provisions, is likely to be durable or even in all respects beneficial.[55]

[51] Cf. Albert Thomas to Lloyd George, 13 Jan. 1918, Lloyd George MSS. F/50/2/7.
[52] Cecil to Lloyd George, 5 Dec. 1917, Lloyd George MSS. F/6/6/10.
[53] Mamatey, op. cit. p. 160.   [54] Hanak, op. cit. pp. 239, 254.
[55] Cecil to J. St. Loe Strachey, 13 Nov. 1917, FO 800/196. The Strachey MSS. do not appear to contain either the original of this letter or any communication which may have prompted it.

For Lloyd George, Balfour and other ministers the question of a separate peace was more a matter of expediency. In the original draft of a commentary on the proposals which Smuts took with him on his mission to Switzerland to meet Count Mensdorff, discussed below, Balfour included a rambling passage on the subject peoples. Here he admitted in effect that he did not know what could or should be done for them. He wisely crossed this out from the final version of the paper with the exception of a statement, 'It *may* be impossible to do anything for Bohemia or the Jugo-Slavs. But if so it is greatly to be deplored.'[56] The absence of fixed ideas in dealing with a problem which they had not considered before 1914 is not surprising; and it is certain that British ministers and their leading advisers had absolutely no conception that they were morally at fault or politically unwise in excluding the independence of the subject nationalities of the Monarchy from their war aims.

In November 1917, predominant opinion in the Foreign Office was that Austria was so bound to Germany politically and militarily that she could not conclude a separate peace and that a further decline in food and economic conditions would be needed to produce either a revolution or such discontent as would lead the ruling classes to break with Germany.[57] When, therefore, in late November Rumbold sent a message from the counsellor of the Austrian legation in Berne, Skrzynski—who represented himself as the personal emissary of Czernin and who was, however, acting without the knowledge of his chief, the envoy—that Czernin desired a meeting between British and Austrian emissaries of very high rank, the response in the Foreign Office was cool.

Balfour was at first opposed to any meeting and favoured asking the Austrian representative to set down his views in writing for the consideration of the British government, a method of procedure hardly calculated to lead to quick progress. However, at the Paris conference at the end of the month, Lloyd George spoke strongly in favour of a positive response to Austria (see above) and Balfour agreed that a representative should be sent.[58] The Prime Minister must, indeed, have looked back on this conference with some

---

[56] Balfour's original draft in Balfour MSS., B.M. Add. 49697; final version in FO 800/214; both papers are dated 15 Dec. 1917.

[57] Cf. Hardinge to Townley, 30 Nov. 1917, Hardinge MSS. XXXV; minute by Hardinge, 5 Dec. 1917, FO 371/2862, no. 230635.

[58] Undated minute by Balfour, FO 371/2864, no. 224082; and Bertie to FO, conveying message from Balfour, 29 Nov. 1917, ibid. no. 227704.

satisfaction. The Italian Finance Minister, Nitti, had told him that Sonnino's influence was on the wane and that Italy would now be prepared to continue fighting to gain only the Trentino and 'cultural autonomy' for the Italian population of Trieste—the kind of pleasing report that he was only too ready to regard as fact.[59] In addition, Sonnino, Clemenceau and House, the last-named without obtaining the permission of the President, gave their consent to a British probe of Austria's intentions.[60]

Lloyd George's first choice of emissary was Lord Reading who refused.[61] He then turned to General Smuts. An outstanding leader of a small nation who had personally become convinced that the best future for his people lay within the world-wide framework of the British Empire, Smuts could be expected even more safely than most men to see the Austrian problem in the 'overall' context of the war against Germany and not as presenting a separate set of ills in itself. Indeed, in the spring of 1917 he had written in some confidential notes with specific reference to Austria–Hungary: 'establishment of small nations not desirable.'[62] Balfour made a late plea for Smuts not to be sent on the grounds that a major move at the time would ruin what little chance there was of a separate peace with Austria while acknowledging that Lloyd George had set his heart on the project and that he had written his letter chiefly 'to liberate my soul'.[63]

Smuts journeyed to meet the Austrian representative, Mensdorff, with the conviction that military victory for the allies was 'improbable' even in 1919–20 and even with American help so that unless a 'counterpoise' could be found to Germany in central-eastern Europe, the war would end with a Mittel-Europa bloc in existence which would be a standing threat to the peace of the world. He believed that the counterpoise, to be effective, must be a single, strong power and that, given the eclipse of Russia, only Austria–Hungary could fulfil this role. In return for breaking with Germany, she should be offered 'the prospect both of ending her present sufferings and humiliations and also of future power and aggrandizement. In helping her in this way we are only helping ourselves both

---

[59] Cf. Hankey to Balfour, 5 Dec. 1917, giving message from Lloyd George, FO 371/3086, no. 231940.

[60] *Hankey Memorandum*, part III, p. 4; Seymour, op. cit. iii. 282–3.

[61] H. M. Hyde, op. cit. p. 232.

[62] W. K. Hancock and J. Van Der Poel, *Selections from the Smuts Papers* (1966), iii. 504.   [63] Balfour to Lloyd George, 4 Dec. 1917, FO 800/199.

now and in the future.' Specifically, Smuts recommended that Austria should cede Trentino to Italy and grant 'cultural autonomy' to Trieste and that Bukowina should pass to Rumania and possibly Herzegovina to Serbia. In return, Austrian and Russian Poland should be united into a 'third state' of the Monarchy and a united Serbia and Montenegro might become its fourth unit. Austria should also be offered allied (presumably United States) financial aid. Smuts' formula for overcoming Austria's insistence that she was only interested in a general peace was that the allies should make a perfectly genuine offer of such a peace to Germany so that if the Germans rejected it Austria could leave the alliance with a clear conscience. In return for evacuating the occupied territory in the west and accepting the loss of her colonies with the possible exceptions of the Cameroons and Togo which, together perhaps with the French Congo, might be returned, Germany would cede Strassburg and part of Lorraine to France, while the allies would recognize the independence of Finland, Courland and Lithuania. This would give Germany 'a fair field for her economic activities. . . . Such a peace practically recognizes the war map so far as the Russian front is concerned; but for that Russia has nobody but herself to blame.'[64]

Except for objecting strongly to the restoration of even the West African colonies to Germany on the grounds that this would threaten British trade routes, Balfour professed to be willing to conclude a peace with either Austria or Germany on these terms, but thought that both the Central Powers were so bloated with military victory that negotiations would very probably break down, producing discord and possible disintegration among the allies. At any rate, it was unrealistic to accept what was implicit in Smuts' recommendations: that Britain's allies should abandon almost all the aims for which they were fighting while the British Empire should make only the most minute nominal reductions in its aspirations in the German colonies and Turkey.[65]

The knowledge that within a year the war was to end with Austria–Hungary no longer in existence and Germany at the allies' mercy makes it difficult for the historian to convey the mood of the British leadership in the winter of 1917–18. They still sought the defeat of Germany's attempt to become a world power and this entailed the loss of the colonies and all but the purely Turkish parts

---

[64] Memorandum by Smuts on 'Peace Conversations', *c.* 12 Dec. 1917, FO 800/214.
[65] Memorandum by Balfour cited in note 56.

of the Ottoman Empire, Germany's Asian partner, but they had virtually lost hope for the reversal of the immensely strong position which German arms had won in Europe except for minor curtailments of Teutonic power on the western and south-western fringes of the Central bloc. The independence of France, Italy, a restored Belgium and a rump Russia on the edge of a Europe otherwise dominated by Germany could only be precarious. But the British now doubted whether there could be any other outcome to the war except perhaps by expending so many lives that Britain's population and economic and military capacity would be so reduced that she would sink to the status of a second-class power.

But if only Austria could be weaned away from Germany, it might still be possible to cripple German power in Europe. In these circumstances there could be no question of opposing a separate peace with Austria on principle. The question resolved itself into one of whether Austria would accept.

The attitude of the British toward Austria on the eve of the Smuts mission is nowhere better shown than in a paper which Drummond wrote reviving his federal scheme of the previous February and from which Smuts may have derived benefit in writing his memorandum on British policy. Asserting that 'a reconstituted and liberalized Austrian Empire' was 'even more desirable now than it had been in February', Drummond repeated the argument that it was the only means of blocking German expansion to the east and south-east: 'It seems unlikely that for many years to come Russia will be sufficiently strong or coherent to be capable of stemming the tide of German influence. The smaller Slav states cannot in the near future look to her as their protector against Teutonism.' He went on to adumbrate the scheme for a five-state federation (with Poland, Yugoslavia and Bohemia as the new units) which might so weaken Germany's position that even German Poland could be included in the Polish constituent. Drummond hoped that economic distress, discontent at German domination and the defeats inflicted on Italy and Rumania, which might make them willing to abandon most of their war aims, would lead Austria to accept such a scheme. Most eloquent of all is a passage on Austrian readiness to absorb West Prussia and Posen. Drummond thought this 'not unlikely to appeal to the Austrian Emperor whose dynasty have been distinguished in the past by the desire to extend their territory'.[66] That one of the

---

[66] Memorandum by Drummond, 10 Dec. 1917, G.T. 2976, CAB 24/35.

most senior (and also one of the most respected) men in London could write in such terms shows how very far removed the British were from any thought that Austria–Hungary might soon no longer exist.

Count Mensdorff had been ambassador in London in 1914 and was well-known for his ability to achieve good relations with members of the British ruling elite. Given Smuts' friendly attitude toward the Monarchy, the success of the talks on the purely personal level was guaranteed. Otherwise, they were almost barren. Mensdorff was adamant that Austria would never desert Germany while the war continued and responded to Smuts' suggestion that the British would favour a strong Monarchy including Russian Poland if Austria became truly independent of Germany by saying that this would provide an excellent basis for Anglo–Austrian relations *after* the war. The most positive result which Smuts could report was that his mission would probably induce Austria to put maximum pressure on Germany to limit her war aims.[67] Lord Hardinge thought that the mission had at least convinced Mensdorff that the allies did not seek the break up of Austria–Hungary,[68] a point which Smuts regarded as too obvious to state.

So far, the development of Anglo–Austrian contacts had been very much the personal affair of Lloyd George and Smuts. The Foreign Office had trailed behind reluctantly and most members of the War Cabinet had not even been consulted. These latter objected to their exclusion and about the end of December a War Cabinet was held at which the almost unique step was taken of ordering that there should be no minutes and that Hankey should be asked to leave the room. No doubt Lloyd George was called upon to defend both the manner in which he had dealt with Austrian approaches and his belief that they might lead to useful results. He seems to have been successful. On 2 January 1918 the War Cabinet gave its consent to a new renewal of the Smuts mission.[69]

Cecil proceeded to ask Smuts not to leave the Foreign Office in ignorance of his work—which must have been a humiliating action to have to take—and was told by the South African that he had no desire to do so—'I shall do my best to carry the P.M. with me,'

---

[67] Smuts' report in FO 371/2864, no. 246162; also in Lloyd George, *War Memoirs*, ii. 1478–89.   [68] Cambon, op. cit. iii. 206.
[69] *Hankey Memorandum*, part III, pp. 4–5; War Cabinet, 2 Jan. 1918, CAB 23/16.

promised Smuts.[70] Both Foreign Office and non-Foreign Office ministers, especially Cecil, were afraid that if Lloyd George was allowed to carry out another exercise in personal diplomacy, as in the Sixte affair, the results, which had then merely been negative, might be catastrophic, involving the departure from the war not of Austria but of Italy.

At Smuts' own suggestion the War Cabinet decided on 8 January to postpone the renewal of his mission until Germany and Austria had had time to digest Lloyd George's war aims speech.[71] Shortly after this, Rumbold sent the spectacular news that Czernin had been so impressed by Lloyd George's address that he wished to have a personal interview with the British leader. This led Cecil, speaking undoubtedly for predominant opinion within the Foreign Office, to explain at length why he favoured extreme caution in dealings with Austria despite his complete willingness in principle to come to terms with her: the Austrian overtures might be a diplomatic smoke-screen for German–Austrian plans to renew the offensive against Italy while the Italians themselves were suspicious by nature and might regard *any* Anglo–Austrian contacts as tantamount to a betrayal. If the overtures were genuine, Italy should be informed but should not be allowed to veto Britain from responding to them. However, only if internal conditions in the Monarchy were dreadful could they be true, and, 'If it be true we shall increase and not diminish the pressure by holding off.'[72] The difference between the Foreign Office and most non-Foreign Office ministers in dealing with Austria was essentially one of timing. Throughout January 1918, the Foreign Office urged caution in treating with Austria. Yet Hardinge and two other senior members of the staff, Clerk and Gregory, who were much concerned with Poland in their daily work, were writing that 'eventually' the 'Austrian solution' to the fate of Russian Poland 'may prove the best'—a line of argument which only made sense in the context of Smuts' 'counterpoise' to Germany.[73] This point is not invalidated by the impression which the student sometimes has that for the Foreign Office mind the right moment would *never* come.

---

[70] Smuts to Cecil, 2 Jan. 1918, FO 800/198.
[71] War Cabinet, 8 Jan. 1918, CAB 23/16.
[72] Minute by Cecil, c. 11 Jan. 1918, FO 371/3133, no. 7760.
[73] Minute by Hardinge, 6 Jan. 1918, and minutes by Clerk and Gregory, 28 Jan. 1918, FO 371/3277, nos. 3361 and 16767.

On 18 January the War Cabinet agreed that whether the proposal was genuine or not it would have to be taken up and that Czernin should be offered a meeting with Smuts.[74] At this point the story of overt Foreign Office attempts to block this peace move begins. On the 28th, Balfour told the War Cabinet that he had decided not to send the telegram agreed to ten days before because he wished to consult Orlando, the Italian Prime Minister, who was currently visiting London; and because a new problem had arisen in that the Austrians were making overtures to the United States both in speeches by Czernin and in secret conversations on the possibility of a separate peace between George D. Herron and Professor Lammasch, unofficial agents of the American legation in Berne and the Emperor Karl.[75]

The War Cabinet now decided that Wilson should be asked whether he wished Britain to pursue peace talks with Austria and should be informed that the British government, for their part, favoured such talks. At the next discussion of the Austrian problem a week later it transpired that Balfour had again quite simply not sent a message which the Cabinet had specifically asked him to send. Scope for procrastination had, however, lessened since on the 2nd Rumbold had wired a statement from Skrzynski that Austrian policy had undergone a fundamental change and that the Monarchy now sought a separate peace. Even Lloyd George responded to this report with scepticism and said that he favoured a positive reply chiefly to keep Austria militarily inactive for as long as possible. Nevertheless, the War Cabinet drew some cautious encouragement from this latest Austrian move and again asked Balfour to send to Washington the telegram which had been agreed to a week before.[76] Balfour at last acted, informing President Wilson that there were signs that Austria wanted a separate peace and suggesting that if this were so it would probably be best for the United States to undertake the

---

[74] War Cabinet, 18 Jan. 1918, CAB 23/16.

[75] M. P. Briggs, *George D. Herron and the European Settlement* (1932), pp. 79–85. Herron passed all his information on to the Foreign Office and War Office: ibid. pp. 31–3. For Austro–American peace contacts see also May, op. cit. ii. 586–7; Mamatey, op. cit. pp. 226–7; and Seymour, op. cit. iii. 383 ff.

[76] War Cabinet, 28 Jan. and 4 Feb. 1918, CAB 23/16; *Hankey Memorandum*, part III, p. 7. The one-upmanship of regarding these reports as fraudulent and as designed to divert the British from military preparations yet appearing to treat them seriously as a means of diverting the Austrians from military exertions on *their* part was suggested to Lloyd George by Count Horodyski at the beginning of 1918: record of their conversation in FO 371/3440, no. 21235.

necessary negotiations. He added the familiar refrain that he advised holding back from any action for some time so that conditions in Austria might deteriorate still further.[77]

At this point knowledge of Smuts' mission in December became public property as Balfour had feared would happen. Its existence was mentioned in an article published in the newspaper of the British Social Democratic Party on 7 February and it was then denounced by a member of Parliament who declared that even before this article appeared, Smuts' activities had been 'well known to many in this House and to many outside'. Balfour replied that he 'entirely refused' to subscribe to the doctrine that 'no effort should ever be made to detach a single enemy from the coalition with whom you were at war'.[78]

It was no doubt this blaze of publicity which led the Monarchy's most powerful single opponent in Britain, Wickham Steed, to try to commit Britain to a policy of breaking it up by announcing to the subject peoples that the British government supported their liberation. This was doomed to failure even though Steed enlisted the formidable support of Northcliffe as head of the government department responsible for propaganda to the enemy countries in Europe. Balfour, advised by Drummond, blandly replied that it was a matter of unconcern whether the war ended with 'the complete break up of the Austrian Empire or its de-Germanization under Hapsburg rule' and that a decision in favour of propaganda promising liberation would not be given unless all hope of coming to terms with Vienna was seen to have vanished. In the meantime, Northcliffe's department should confine itself to propaganda in general terms designed to sow disaffection among the subject peoples without promising them anything.[79]

It is clear from these exchanges that Balfour had no sympathy with Steed's fervently anti-Hapsburg attitude but he was again the most cautious person present at the next War Cabinet debate on Austria on 1 March. There was a great deal to consider: the Herron–Lammasch talks were continuing and Austria had made a formal approach to the United States for talks on a general peace through

[77] Drummond to Wiseman conveying message from Balfour to Wilson, 6 Feb. 1918, Balfour MSS., B.M. Add. 49687.

[78] *Parliamentary Debates*, 5th series, CIII, cols. 163–9, 13 Feb. 1918.

[79] Printed memorandum of correspondence between Balfour and Northcliffe in FO 800/209; see also memorandum by Drummond addressed to Balfour, 25 Feb. 1918, FO 800/213.

the Spanish Foreign Ministry; Skrzynski had offered to furnish documentary proof that Austria sought a separate peace; and the French seemed to be reviving their interest in negotiations with Vienna. They sent to Berne a new ambassador, Emil Dutasta, whose reputation was that of a pronounced Austrophil.[80] Balfour remarked that he was certain that Britain would be unable to negotiate peace with Austria but hinted that he thought that the United States might be able to do so. Other ministers were torn between fear of a 'trap' and a longing for a separate peace with the Monarchy. Bonar Law 'asked if we were not jeopardizing the position we had so long desired to reach, namely that Austria should be willing to make a separate peace'.[81] All of them, even Cecil, were quite unwilling to follow Balfour's advice and entrust such a matter to Wilson.[82] It was agreed to ask Skrzynski for more details about Austria's readiness for peace.

Almost as soon as the legation in Berne contacted him, the Austrian agent replied that Czernin wished to know whether Britain would enter into negotiations if Austria gave an assurance that she only wished to discuss terms concerning herself. This was the latest of a number of pleas of this sort extending over nearly a month which indicated seriousness in at least some influential quarters in the Austrian capital. In addition, Milner[83] and Hankey[84] sent strongly-worded protests against Foreign Office footdragging on this issue to the Prime Minister. Lloyd George was thus encouraged to overrule Balfour and Cecil when they argued that a high-level meeting of the sort sought by Czernin was intended to attract publicity and damage relations between Italy and her allies. It was decided that Philip Kerr should go to Switzerland to undertake a preliminary probe of Austrian intentions. The following day when Drummond, deputizing for Balfour who was unwell, suggested that the peace exchanges between Washington and Vienna showed promise and that the Kerr mission should therefore be abandoned, the War Cabinet refused to agree.[85]

An insight into Balfour's reasons for preferring the United States

[80] Memorandum by Bertie addressed to Lloyd George on the new French ambassador to Switzerland, 14 Feb. 1918, FO 800/201. France was at this time the only country which maintained diplomatic relations with Switzerland at embassy level.
[81] War Cabinet, 1 Mar. 1918, CAB 23/16.   [82] Ibid.
[83] Milner to Lloyd George, 27 Feb. 1918, Lloyd George MSS. F/38/3/16.
[84] Hankey to Lloyd George, 2 Mar. 1918, CAB 23/16.
[85] War Cabinet, 5 and 6 Mar. 1918, CAB 23/16.

rather than Britain to handle Austrian feelers is provided by a memorandum which Harold Nicolson wrote as Kerr was actually travelling to Switzerland and which was designed to furnish the new chief of the General Staff, Henry Wilson, with a guide to Foreign Office thinking on the international situation. He argued that American–Austrian negotiations stood most chance of success, partly because America could offer Vienna financial help and partly because of President Wilson's immense prestige which 'rests on a basis at once more solid and more spiritual than that of the older belligerents'. Also, the United States were unhampered by commitments to Italy which meant that, while Italy would almost certainly leave the war if Austria made peace, she would not have the same sense of betrayal as if Britain were responsible, and would probably be a reasonably contented power in the post-war world. All this assumed that Austria was really interested in a separate peace. If she were anxious to induce the allies to promise to abandon their treaty commitments to Italy so that Rome could then be presented with evidence of betrayal which would cause her to leave the war, the manoeuvre might work in the case of Britain but hardly in that of the United States because, again, of the absence of commitments to Italy. If this approach to the Austrian problem were adopted, Nicolson, writing what was intended as a composite Foreign Office view, had no objections to the most extensive concessions to Austria. He spoke favourably of the 'Austrian solution' in Poland and of 'dazzling Austrian ambitions with prospects of the return of non-Polish Silesia and the succession to the moral heritage of Slav hegemony.'[86]

Despite his misgivings, Balfour had to dictate a set of instructions for Kerr. These were that he should try to discover for whom Skrzynski spoke (Czernin, Karl, both or neither), whether his activities were known to Germany, whether Austria really wanted a separate peace and, if so, what were her terms. Kerr was absolutely forbidden to promise any Austrian that the Entente would enter into negotiations in return for a promise that a separate peace was acceptable.[87]

On arrival in Berne, Kerr found that Skrzynski was awaiting instructions and would not therefore see him. This did not stop him from sending a telegram to Lloyd George in which he said that he

[86] Memorandum by Nicolson, 10 Mar. 1918, FO 371/3440, no. 40497.
[87] Balfour to Kerr, 6 Mar. 1918, FO 371/3133, no. 41211.

was convinced that Skrzynski truly spoke for Czernin and that the latter wanted a separate peace. Kerr received a personal message from Lloyd George who declared himself 'much encouraged' and authorized Kerr 'definitely' to arrange talks between Czernin and Smuts if, 'of course, it is understood that there is no question of discussing terms with Germany'.[88] Even the Foreign Office were now prepared to co-operate sincerely in trying to ensure the success of the proposed negotiation instead of arguing the sovereign virtue of further delay. Hardinge minuted Lloyd George's message to Kerr that the office would have to work hard without delay to draw up terms that Smuts could take with him; while at the same time Balfour informed House that if the consent of Orlando, who was due in London the following day, could be obtained, Smuts would immediately set out to negotiate peace with Austria.[89]

Two days after Kerr's message had been received all these hopes were dashed when he actually met Skrzynski. The Austrian diplomat, whose new instructions obviously ordered him to take a very different line from his previous one, told him that Austria would always be allied with Germany. It was this *volte-face* and not, as is usually thought, the insults which Clemenceau and Czernin were to exchange a few weeks later, that marked the end of negotiations between the allies and Austria in the Great War. A proposal by Rumbold to refuse to have any more dealings with Skrzynski was accepted to the accompaniment of many sad little minutes that all hope of peace with Austria was ended.[90] At the same time Czernin was busily ending his peace contacts with the United States.[91] The Austrians had clearly decided to place all their hopes on the success of the German offensive in France.

On the same day that Kerr had his interview with Skrzynski, Smuts submitted to Lloyd George that in the forthcoming negotiation a 'liberalized' Austria should be offered not merely Russian Poland and Serbia but also the Ukraine![92] Kerr in his report on his mission, did not accept that there was no longer any hope of peace

[88] Cf. Rumbold to FO, 11 Mar. 1918 and FO to Rumbold, 12 Mar. 1918, FO 371/3133, no. 45538.

[89] Cf. Drummond to Wiseman, 12 March 1918, Balfour MSS., B.M. Add. 49687.

[90] Rumbold to FO and FO to Rumbold, 25 and 28 Mar. 1918 respectively, with minutes, FO 371/3133, no. 55733.   [91] Mamatey, pp. 231–2.

[92] Smuts to Lloyd George, 14 Mar. 1918, Lloyd George MSS. F/45/9/10. This letter was written from the Savoy Hotel. Lloyd George's memory was simply at fault when he wrote in his *War Memoirs*, ii. 1500, that Smuts actually travelled to Switzerland with Kerr in March 1918.

with Austria. He recommended that the government should draw up a complete set of peace terms with Austria so that a treaty could be signed within a few days of the opening of negotiations. He also argued that it was very much an open question whether any measure of federalization at all should be included in such terms.[93] Lloyd George, Smuts and Kerr had hoped for much from Austria and it was natural that they should be slow in realizing that there was a new situation. But such was the case and the way was open for very significant changes in British policy in eastern Europe.

3. TURKEY AND BULGARIA

The Bulgarian peace overtures which had given rise to considerable hopes in some British circles in the early autumn practically ceased during the winter so that little attention was paid to that country. However, Smuts did not neglect to include proposals for ceding Serbian Macedonia and South Dobrudja to Bulgaria as an addendum to the peace terms which he favoured for Austria in December 1917,[94] while in the new year the General Staff tried to obtain government acceptance of a scheme by which Bulgaria would, in return for a promise that she should have Macedonia after the war, secretly agree to be militarily inactive on the Salonika front while still nominally remaining in alliance with the Central Powers.[95] It was generally felt that as long as the United States were not only at peace with Bulgaria but actually continued to maintain diplomatic relations with her, this was the most that could be hoped for.[96]

With Turkey there were very serious efforts to negotiate peace terms. There were two quite distinct sets of approaches, one of them involving the orthodox channels of the British legations in Switzerland and Greece and the other one of the most bizarre episodes in the history of secret diplomacy. Both took place against a background of conflicts between the civilian and military leaders which was a direct continuation of the split over Austria policy in the summer. All Lloyd George's hopes of peace had then been concentrated on Austria. He remarked to an inter-allied conference in Paris at the end

[93] Kerr's report, 19 Mar. 1918, copy in Milner MSS. 108, Box A1.
[94] See above, pp. 161–2.
[95] Robertson to Lloyd George, 1 Jan. 1918, WO 106/1517; 'Note by Director of Military Intelligence', 14 Feb. 1918, G.T. 3646, CAB 24/42.
[96] Cf. War Office intelligence report from Berne, 7 Nov. 1917, FO 371/2185, no. 222370.

of July, 'To get Turkey out of the war was important but to get Austria was infinitely more so'.[97] When his Austrian hopes suffered eclipse two months later his mind immediately turned to Turkey.

While on holiday at his home in Wales in mid-September, he decided to press for a concentration of all important allied military efforts against Turkey.[98] He was heartened and aided in coming to this conclusion by Milner who joined him and agreed that it was 'absolutely essential to knock out one or more of the allies [i.e. of Germany] and the most promising one by far was Turkey' because she was exhausted and too distant from Germany to be easily helped.[99] He added a cautionary note that no plan, no matter how well-conceived, could succeed if the press and public, who had 'an almost superstitious belief in Robertson', opposed it or if large numbers of the public came to regard it as an imperialist adventure to expand the Empire.[100]

There were indeed still other problems such as Woodrow Wilson's failure to respond to a suggestion by Lloyd George in September that it might not be wise to concentrate the whole of America's military effort on the Western Front.[101] But the main difficulty was the high command, above all Robertson. In January 1917 Robertson had spoken favourably of military operations in Turkey the following winter if the war had not by then been won in the west:

If the war goes on into next winter it will mean that we have not had any very striking success during the summer. The public will become impatient and we shall have to do something to keep the war alive. Moreover it will begin to look more like stalemate than it does at present, in which case it will be necessary that we should pick up any territory we can. The autumn and winter are good seasons for you and if we are still fighting then my desire is to give you a really big show and to let you do as much as you can and go as far as you can into Turkish territory.[102]

---

[97] *Hankey Memorandum*, part II, p. 9.

[98] Hankey, op. cit. ii. 697.

[99] Memorandum by Milner, 9 Oct. 1917, with note by his secretary, 31 Oct. 1917, that it was the result of Milner's conversations with Lloyd George in Wales in September, CAB 21/59.

[100] Memorandum written at Criccieth, 17 Sept. 1917, unsigned but almost certainly dictated by Milner, Milner MSS. 148.

[101] David F. Trask, *The United States in the Supreme War Council: American War Aims and Inter-Allied Strategy 1917–18* (1961), pp. 13–15.

[102] Robertson to Murray, 31 Jan. 1917, Robertson–Murray correspondence, p. 189, B.M. Add. 52463.

This sounded like Lloyd George speaking and what a happy man the Prime Minister would have been if this had actually been Robertson's line in the autumn of 1917! In fact, Robertson was uncertain and vacillating in his attitude toward policy in Turkey. In late September he wrote to Haig in sympathetic terms about the desire of 'the whole Cabinet' to give the Turks 'as hard a knock as possible this winter' so that they could then be induced with moderate terms to make peace.[103] Shortly afterwards, he wrote a memorandum declaring that the possibility of inducing Turkey to make peace was so problematical that it would not justify any concentration of military efforts in Palestine.[104] Yet a month later he and Macdonagh urged the Foreign Office to press for the immediate abrogation of the Asia Minor agreement with Italy precisely to facilitate peace with Turkey. Hardinge replied soothingly that Britain would renounce the St. Jean agreement, in so far as she was committed to it, as soon as Turkey showed a serious disposition toward peace.[105]

At times, then, Robertson seemed to support Lloyd George's policy: extensive military operations in Turkey with the maximum objective of forcing the enemy power to leave the war and the minimum aim of occupying substantial amounts of territory. But when matters came to a head, he became cold. In a paper written in the middle of November and clearly prompted by the early successes of Allenby's first great offensive in Palestine, he argued that there was very little possibility of Turkey's leaders coming to terms so that Allenby's ultimate objective should be the establishment of a position in front of Jaffa and Jerusalem, that is the latter should not be occupied. Robertson's advice may have owed something to War Office intelligence reports but it owed a great deal more to his desire that there should be no great British victory in Palestine since he would then be faced with pressure to transfer troops from the West Front to exploit it. Jerusalem fell on 3 December and Robertson's task became accordingly more difficult with some ministers, including Lloyd George,[106] talking deliriously of advancing to Aleppo. By a strange paradox Robertson, who looked upon the war with Turkey almost as a triviality, found himself in alliance with those

[103] Robertson to Haig, 24 Sept. 1917, Robertson, ii. 253–4.
[104] Robertson, op. cit. ii. 179–81.
[105] Macdonagh to Hardinge, 6 Nov. 1917, Hardinge MSS. XXXV; Hardinge to Robertson, 8 Nov. 1917, WO 106/1516, no. 5.
[106] Cf. Lloyd George to Robertson, 14 Dec. 1917, Robertson MSS. I/19/13.

like Curzon and Mark Sykes to whom the Middle Eastern war was the most important part of the whole conflict, to be carried to a successful conclusion at all costs.[107]

Throughout the winter a debate over how far, if at all, Allenby should be ordered to advance and what reinforcements, if any, in terms of men and material, the latter chiefly for railway-building, should be sent him, continued. It took the form virtually of a personal duel between Lloyd George and Robertson whose action in criticizing the Prime Minister at the end of January before foreign leaders on this issue was probably decisive in making Lloyd George summon the courage to dismiss him the following month. The council agreed that the British should carry out offensives in the Middle East in the coming year providing their strength on the West Front was not reduced for this purpose. Allenby, reinforced from Mesopotamia and by Indian cavalry from France, resumed his advance in February.[108]

The struggle continued in a more muted form under the new chief of the General Staff, Henry Wilson. He criticized a suggestion by Smuts, who had been sent by the War Cabinet to Egypt and Palestine in February to make policy recommendations, that Allenby should be reinforced, chiefly from Mesopotamia, so that he could press on to Aleppo or drive the Turks into making peace, whichever happened first. Wilson proposed much smaller reinforcements which would probably not do more than enable Allenby to complete the conquest of northern Palestine and suggested that it would be even better to adopt a passive policy so that troops could be withdrawn from Palestine to France or Salonika if necessary or used in the Holy Land in the winter of 1918–19 if such withdrawal had proved unnecessary.[109]

The German offensive in France in late March ensured that this policy must be adopted. Before that the predominant impression in official London had been that the military situation would develop in such a way as to reinforce any inclination on the part of the Turks to accept British terms. Their own war was not going well for them. They simply could not raise the necessary forces to launch their

---

[107] Cf. memorandum by Robertson on 'Situation in Turkey', 15 Nov. 1917, G.T. 2630, CAB 24/32; for Curzon's opposition to a separate peace see his memorandum of 16 Nov. 1917, G.T. 2648, CAB 24/32; for Sykes's opposition see his letter to Hankey, 14 Nov. 1917, copy in FO 371/3057, no. 225559.

[108] Cf. Guinn, op. cit. pp. 283–90, 297–8 for a summary of these developments.

[109] Report by Smuts, 1 Mar. 1918, with covering note by Wilson, WO 106/1545.

much-heralded autumn campaign to recapture Baghdad while the British under Allenby carried out a successful advance into Palestine which promised even greater results. It was therefore possible to hope that they would be more impressed by their own defeats than by Germany's victories in Italy and Russia (a view which ignored the fact that during the first two years of the war Russia had been a more formidable and successful military opponent of Turkey than the British). Both Lloyd George and the Foreign Office shared this hope.

After becoming Prime Minister, Lloyd George had acquired a secret channel to the Turkish War Minister, Enver. In June 1917 Abdul Kerim, an agent of Enver's, submitted a plan to Basil Zaharoff by which Abdul Kerim, Enver and certain other Turkish leaders were to be bribed to lead Turkey out of the war in four stages, involving the departure of the Turkish forces from the different fronts and finally Turkey's exit from the war. A total of ten million dollars would be demanded beginning with a 'down payment' of two million dollars.[110] Zaharoff approached Sir Vincent Caillard, a director of Vickers, a firm in which Zaharoff had very large interests, and he in turn approached Lloyd George.

Caillard had been president of the Ottoman Public Debt Council for sixteen years and afterwards divided his time between business and writing short stories and songs including a musical setting to Blake's *Songs of Innocence*.[111] This was an interesting *curriculum vitae* but it pales into colourlessness by comparison with that of Zaharoff, an international armaments manufacturer of Greek extraction who had become a figure of European legend (or demonology) long before his death in 1936. Stories that Zaharoff secretly controlled the governments of both the Entente and Central Powers during the First World War and prolonged the struggle at a cost of millions of lives to increase the profits of his armaments factories clearly belong to the same category as the *Protocols of the Elders of*

---

[110] See memorandum by Abdul Kerim, 27 June 1917, annexed to letter from Caillard to Lloyd George, 12 Jan. 1918, Lloyd George MSS. F/6/1/8. I have not been able to trace the origins of this episode before June 1917. Zaharoff had almost certainly been working for some time to interest Enver in a separate peace. In 1915 Asquith had entrusted Zaharoff with a mission to bribe Greek politicians into taking their country into the war. In June 1916 he had submitted to a sceptical Asquith a scheme to buy up the entire Young Turk party for £4 million in return for which they would hand over Constantinople and the Straits and flee to the United States. Roskill, p. 239.

[111] *Who's Who.*

Zion of which Zaharoff himself is said to have been an avid reader. While much concerned that the war should end without damage to his factories or, as he put it, 'without permitting industrial chaos in Europe',[112] he threw in his lot with the Entente and worked sincerely for its victory. He was a personal friend of Bonar Law and Walter Long to say nothing of having 'many of the leading French politicians in his pocket' according to Lord Bertie.[113] Also, he became a friend of Lloyd George while he was at the Ministry of Munitions to the limited extent that the Prime Minister was capable of friendship, and in 1918 undertook on his behalf a fact-finding mission to Germany, disguised as a Bulgarian army doctor whom he apparently took the precaution of murdering.[114]

In 1917 this last episode still lay in the future. The information which Lloyd George received from Zaharoff, who was normally resident in France, through Caillard, no doubt prompted a remark to the War Cabinet in June 1917 that he was confident that Turkey would leave the war in return for financial compensation but that first he wanted the British to occupy Palestine to make sure of obtaining that prize.[115] On 1 August Caillard wrote to the Prime Minister that Abdul Kerim was demanding the down payment of which half a million dollars was to be his and one and a half millions Enver's, the money to be deposited in Swiss accounts. On 17 August he wrote for a decision on whether the money might be used—which indicates that in the meantime Lloyd George had authorized the transfer of two million dollars from Secret Service funds for this purpose.[116]

There was no further action until 23 November when Caillard told the Prime Minister that Turkey wanted a separate peace and that her main condition would be nothing more than a guarantee of the Ottoman Public Debt.[117] Partly because of this and partly because of a meeting with Zaharoff in Paris a week later,[118] Lloyd George became very active on the Turkish issue. He was in the French capital to attend an inter-allied conference at which he emphasized that owing to the Bolshevik revolution all question of

---

[112] Donald McKormick, *Pedlar of Death: the Life of Sir Basil Zaharoff* (1965), pp. 118, 126, 144.
[113] Memorandum by Bertie on Zaharoff, 24 June 1917, FO 800/175.
[114] McKormick, op. cit. pp. 132, 153–9.
[115] War Cabinet, 8 June 1917, CAB 23/16.
[116] Caillard to Lloyd George, 1 and 17 Aug. 1917, Lloyd George MSS. F/6/1/1–2.
[117] Caillard to Lloyd George, 23 Nov. 1917, ibid. F/6/1/3.   [118] Roskill, p. 466.

depriving Turkey of Constantinople had ceased and that this opened the way to a separate peace.[119] He obtained what he called a 'free hand' from Clemenceau, who said that it was a matter of complete indifference to him whether the French flag ever flew in Syria, to negotiate any terms of peace with Turkey.[120]

In a speech in Parliament on 20 December he again said, this time publicly, that no one now wished to deprive Turkey of Constantinople.[121]

By this time the Zaharoff peace move was well under way and Lloyd George played a fantastic double game in his handling of it. On the one hand, he presented it to the Foreign Office and to at least some of his other colleagues including Zaharoff's friend, Bonar, as a means of submitting peace terms to Enver of much the same sort that the office was giving to a man who was believed to be the agent of Talaat, the other Turkish leader. Arabia was to become independent; Mesopotamia and Palestine were to become nominally independent protectorates of Britain like Egypt before 1914; Syria and Armenia were to be autonomous; the capitulations were to remain abolished; and Turkey was to receive generous financial assistance.[122]

On the other hand, there is no evidence that Lloyd George allowed the Foreign Office to know that he was actually trying to bribe Enver to lead Turkey out of the war though they may well have had their suspicions as is suggested by a letter which Cecil wrote to the Prime Minister early in January stating that he had heard a rumour that Lord D'Abernon was to be sent on a peace probe to the Turks in Switzerland and that he hoped that this was not true since actions of this sort, undertaken without the Foreign Office's knowledge, would make its work impossible.[123]

Zaharoff had written to Caillard on 15 December asking for

---

[119] Inter-allied conference at Paris, minutes for 1 Dec. 1917, CAB 28/3 I.C. 35.

[120] Hankey to Balfour, 5 Dec. 1917, enclosing memorandum by Lloyd George, 28 Nov. 1917, FO 371/3086, no. 231940.

[121] Text in J. B. Scott, op. cit. pp. 216–20. But cf. a War Cabinet decision the previous day that Turkey must be deprived of effective control over the Straits in any peace settlement. War Cabinet, 19 Dec. 1917, CAB 23/4.

[122] Cf. Bonar Law to Lloyd George, 7 Dec. 1917, Lloyd George MSS. F/30/2/27. It was presumably the scheme as thus set out which Crewe urged Balfour to support in a letter of 5 Dec. 1917, FO 800/210. In January the terms which Zaharoff was authorized to put forward were amended so that Turkey was definitely assured that she might retain nominal suzerainty in Mesopotamia and apparently also Palestine but with no voice in administration. Caillard to J. T. Davies, 16 Jan. 1918 and copy of Caillard to Zaharoff, 16 Jan. 1918, Lloyd George MSS. F/6/1/9–10.

[123] Cecil to Lloyd George, 8 Jan. 1918, ibid. F/6/5/13.

permission to proceed with the scheme.[124] There is no copy of Lloyd George's reply but it was clearly affirmative. On 1 January he was informed by Caillard that the money sent to Zaharoff in August had now been deposited in the two Turks' Swiss accounts,[125] and J. T. Davies, the Prime Minister's secretary, informed Caillard that further payments would be made as the Turks carried out the plan for withdrawal in stages, culminating in the abandonment of the naval defences of Constantinople.[126] In this way, for a mere *pourboire* of ten million dollars, Lloyd George hoped to succeed where the Gallipoli expedition had failed. Zaharoff made contact with Enver in Switzerland on 2 February though the Turkish leader refused a face-to-face meeting and insisted on using Abdul Kerim as a messenger between their respective hotel rooms. Enver said that he wished to have nothing more to do with the scheme on the grounds that there was no possibility of inducing the essential co-operation of Talaat who had been heartened by the collapse of Russia and Rumania. Enver returned his one and a half million dollars though Abdul Kerim insisted that he was going to keep his half million.

The fact that this curious episode has, apparently, never previously been brought to light owes much to Zaharoff's undoubted skill in secret intrigue, to the fact that both Enver and Zaharoff returned the money to its source and to Enver's evident belief that Zaharoff was not a British agent and was working for the French.[127] The impression of Lloyd George's attitude toward the conduct of foreign policy that emerges from the Sixte affair is reinforced. No doubt a scheme of this sort requires absolute secrecy but the British Foreign Office has always been adept at guarding its secrets from outsiders and, as Cecil said, private initiatives of which it was ignorant threatened to make its work—in this case its own attempts to come to terms with Turkey—impossible.

By the time that Allenby marched into Jerusalem the Foreign Office had for some time been dealing with a new set of Turkish peace overtures. Since the late summer a number of reports had reached the office that the Turks were prepared to accept the

[124] Cf. 'Zed-Zed' to 'Brother Mine', 15 Dec. 1917, ibid. F/6/1/5.
[125] Caillard to Lloyd George, 1 Jan. 1918, ibid. F/6/1/6.
[126] Note marked 'Given to Sir Vincent Caillard' by J. T. Davies, 9 Jan. 1918 and Davies to Caillard, 21 Jan. 1918, ibid. F/6/1/7 and 11.
[127] Cf. Caillard to Lloyd George, 10 Oct. 1918, and Zaharoff to Caillard, 3 Oct. 1918, ibid. F/6/1/21.

'autonomy' formula as a graceful means of acknowledging that the British had won for themselves a position in Arabia and southern Mesopotamia which they intended to keep.[128] In London almost everyone concerned with eastern policy considered changes in the direction of 'autonomy' to be inevitable in order to meet the anti-annexationist clamour at home and in the United States and to provide a basis for dealings with Arab nationalists. To allow the Turks to retain nominal sovereignty or suzerainty over parts of their empire proclaimed autonomous hardly involved a sacrifice except in terms of prestige.

The Foreign Office pinned its (slender) hopes of making peace with Turkey on Talaat and on Rahmi Bey, the semi-independent 'vali' or governor of Smyrna. Rahmi was a powerful man and he never attempted to conceal his pro-Entente sympathies but nobody in the office thought that he would be strong enough to lead Turkey out of the war except in alliance with Talaat. Enver was considered to be completely pro-German,[129] a false interpretation to judge from his dealings with Zaharoff.

The first of the renewed Turkish overtures came from Rahmi who at the end of October sent an interned Frenchman, Giraud, on parole on a mission to the British legation in Athens. Alec Waugh, a diplomat there who knew Rahmi, reported that he favoured peace on the basis of autonomy for Armenia, Mesopotamia and perhaps Syria with a small extension of Turkey-in-Europe at the expense of Bulgaria. Hardinge thought that these proposals were 'sensible' and recorded that they 'corresponded generally except in a few details to those held here'. Both he and Balfour added that the time to discuss such terms with the Turks was not yet; Rahmi's 'sensible' proposals would have to come from a higher source before the Foreign Office would listen.[130]

---

[128] Rumbold to FO, 29 Aug. 1917, FO 371/3060, no. 169829; 25 Oct. 1917, FO 371/3061, no. 203875; 16 Nov. 1917, FO 371/3058, no. 223845. Yet in September-October 1917 the Porte successfully pressed Germany to sign a formal treaty promising not to make a peace in which Turkey did not recover full sovereignty over all territory which she ruled in 1914. Trumpener, op. cit. pp. 163-5. Neither Professor Trumpener nor, apparently, any other writer in a western language provides a full account of the attitude of the Turkish leadership on the question of a separate peace.

[129] Memorandum on Turkish peace overtures by Lord Drogheda, 20 Nov. 1917, CAB 21/59.

[130] Macdonagh to Hardinge, 27 Oct. 1917, FO 371/3057, no. 20748; Granville (minister to Greece) to FO, 30 Oct. 1917 enclosing a memorandum by Waugh to which are attached a minute by Hardinge and a memorandum by Balfour, no. 208753 in ibid.

The office soon moved to a slightly less passive attitude owing at least in part to prodding from Milner. Balfour's apparent intention to ignore Rahmi's move prompted him to argue that it would be a grave error not to couple the stick of Allenby's advance into Palestine with the carrot of a diplomatic offensive to Turkey designed to assure her that the allies did not seek her complete dismemberment and that if they would come to terms they could 'save most of what is left to them'. Milner had an answer to Curzon's argument that Germany had promised Turkey so much that she would not be interested in allied terms: 'Yes but she has promised a lot which she has not been able to perform. My contention is that the Turks might prefer a bird in the hand to a sackful of promises.' To Robertson's assertion that there was little chance of coming to terms with Turkey he replied that this might well be so but that the only way to be sure was to launch probes. This was a platitude but it was as sophisticated a reply as Robertson's argument deserved.[131]

Whatever the precise impact of Milner's pressure, Balfour authorized Waugh, who was due to go to Smyrna on a prisoner of war mission, to say to Rahmi, if the latter raised the subject, that it was his personal opinion that Britain would make peace on the basis of independence for Armenia and Arabia including Mesopotamia and of 'real autonomy' for Syria and Palestine meaning 'only purely formal recognition of Turkish suzerainty'.[132]

A Turkish leader was thus for the first time given an opportunity to learn British peace terms. The purely nominal nature of the proferred concessions is emphasized by the proclamation on 2 November of the Balfour Declaration, adding a major commitment to British aims in the Middle East, and by a speech by Balfour a few days later in which he pleaded: 'Do not let us put altogether out of sight one of the objects which we ought to aim at . . . the duty of taking away from under Turkish rule people who are not Turks, who have been tyrannized over by the Turks, whose development has been stopped by the Turks and who would . . . flourish under their own rule . . . if they were given the chance.'[133]

How little the British were really prepared to concede is shown by

---

[131] War Cabinet memorandum by Milner, 12 Nov. 1917; and minutes by Milner on copies of the papers by Curzon and Robertson cited in note 107 above. Milner MSS. 108, Box A2.

[132] Minute by Balfour with telegram from FO to Granville based on the minute, 20 Nov. 1917, FO 371/3057, no. 220306.

[133] *Parliamentary Debates*, 5th series, XCVIII, col. 2042, 6 Nov. 1917.

the fact that the offer of 'autonomy' for Palestine rather than 'independence' was made not as a concession to Turkish feeling but because it was believed that: 'The Turkish flag would help to eliminate French and Italian participation in the administration and leave us in virtual possession.'[134] The only territorial concession of substance that the British were prepared to make was the abandonment of Italian claims in Asia Minor and possibly French in Cilicia. It was believed that Britain's overwhelming role in the war against Turkey justified this cavalier treatment of her allies. Hardinge,[135] Milner, Cecil and probably Balfour thought that there was a real chance of inducing a Turkey demoralized by British victories and economic exhaustion to make peace on these terms.

When Smuts went to Switzerland in December his instructions were to sound out the Turks as well as the Austrians and he deputed the Turkish part of his work to Philip Kerr. On the basis of an interview on 18 December with Parodi, the Egyptian middleman whom Rumbold invariably used in his dealings with both Turks and Austrians, Kerr reported that there was a pro-Entente minority within the Committee of Union and Progress which might be able to seize power if conceded certain terms: an independent Arabia, real autonomy for Syria, Palestine and Mesopotamia with these territories paying tribute to the Turkish treasury; the fate of Armenia to be decided by the Entente; and Turkey to be allowed to write off her £300,000,000 debt to Germany. He advised that Parodi should be informed of British peace terms and authorized to convey them to the Turks whom he knew.[136] These reported Turkish terms bore an encouraging resemblance to those which Waugh had taken with him to Rahmi. This, together with the fact that an Anglo–Turkish prisoner of war conference in which the Turkish delegation was led by Mouktar Bey, a close associate of Talaat, was currently taking place at Geneva, produced some excitement in the Foreign Office.

On 21 December Rumbold was informed of the terms drawn up for Rahmi and that he could convey them to any important Turks

---

[134] Minute by Ronald Graham, *c.* 22 Dec. 1917, FO 371/3057, no. 242085. Graham added that in his opinion this belief was 'altogether fallacious' and that the best prospect for obtaining complete British control lay in demanding 'independence' for Palestine. It is worth pointing out that Graham conducted the Foreign Office's day-to-day Palestine policy during Allenby's conquest.

[135] Cf. Hardinge to Granville, 19 Nov. 1917, Hardinge MSS. XXXV.

[136] Report by Kerr, 18 Dec. 1917, FO 371/2864, no. 246162; also in D. Lloyd George, *War Memoirs*, ii. 1504–9.

who made enquiries.[137] In response to a suggestion by Smuts that
Mouktar should actually be approached, Cecil gave his consent for
Parodi to do this, perhaps the first time ever that the Foreign Office
had violated the rule that any peace moves must originate with the
enemy.[138] When Mouktar showed a distressing reluctance to discuss
peace, Cecil ordered that the Turks should be offered a free hand to
take what territory they could from Bulgaria as an additional bait,
and when Mouktar at last agreed to meet Parodi, Cecil, taking as it
were a leaf from Lloyd George's book, laid down that bribery almost
without limit might be offered. There was even a hint of genuine
concessions to Turkey in the Arab East: 'We are very anxious to
secure peace with Turkey if possible and you should try to obtain
a counter-proposal from the Turks if ours is unacceptable.'[139] Indeed, at this time the King was recommending that 'every inducement' should be made to Turkey to break with Germany.[140]

During January 1918 Mouktar remained in Switzerland but still
showed little inclination to discuss peace terms seriously. There was
a growing fear that Turkey was resigning herself to the loss of her
Arab territories only to prepare for the creation of a new empire in
Persia and Moslem Russia. Partly because of this, the junior staff at
the Foreign Office felt little enthusiasm for negotiations.[141] Then at
the end of the month came a report that Mouktar had said that
Turkey was prepared to be conciliatory on Arabia and Iraq and
favoured a 'referendum' in the old Armenian vilayets—an indication
that his qualities included a sense of humour. Drummond suggested
to Balfour that Mouktar's terms provided a basis for a 'reasonable
settlement' with Turkey.[142] The matter was shortly afterwards submitted to the War Cabinet when Mouktar announced his readiness
to travel to Talaat to obtain his permission to conduct peace talks
with a high-ranking British delegation. Ministers authorized negotiations with Mouktar in which Turkey would be offered the terms
sent to Rumbold on 21 December.[143]

[137] FO to Rumbold, 21 Dec. 1917, FO 371/3057, no. 241322.

[138] Cf. Rumbold to FO, 22 Dec. 1917, and FO to Rumbold, 25 Dec. 1917, with
minute by Cecil, ibid. no. 242085. For the 'rule' that the enemy must make the first
approach see Hardinge to Sir M. Findlay, 16 Mar. 1917, Hardinge MSS. XXX.

[139] Telegrams drafted by Cecil to Rumbold, 26 Dec. 1917 and 1 Jan. 1918, FO
371/3057, nos. 243608 and 245518.

[140] King George V to Lloyd George, 25 Dec. 1917, Lloyd George MSS. F/29/1/52.

[141] On this theme see below, ch. v, section 3.

[142] Rumbold to FO, 31 Jan. 1918, with minute by Drummond addressed to Balfour,
2 Feb. 1918, FO 371/3388, no. 20082.   [143] War Cabinet, 4 Feb. 1918, CAB 23/16.

Mouktar, after presumably seeing Talaat, informed the British a month later that he would expect a substantial financial reward for his services and, more to the point, that he must know whether they would be prepared to listen to Turkish counter-proposals to any British terms.[144] Balfour told the War Cabinet that the newly-signed treaty of Brest–Litovsk under which Russia ceded substantial frontier districts in the Caucasus to Turkey imposed a great obstacle to peace since it was clear that Turkey was intent on absorbing Russian Armenia, a development to which Britain could never consent as it would amount to counter-signing the death warrant of the remnant of the Armenian people. However, he had no objections to a preliminary probe and it was agreed that Kerr should sound out both the Austrians and the Turks in Switzerland. As in the case of Skrzynski, not the least important of his tasks would be to determine whether Mouktar really did represent anybody other than himself.[145]

Kerr set out on his mission with the conviction that the Austrian part of his business was much the more important and that if Austria made a separate peace the Turkish problem would virtually solve itself,[146] an attitude almost certainly shared by the War Cabinet. The revelation of Austria's change of attitude in the middle of the mission led to a brief increase of interest in Turkey. A suggestion by Rumbold that the autonomy formula should be extended to cover Mesopotamia as well as Syria was accepted after some delay though with the proviso that 'independence' should now be claimed for Palestine.[147] Nothing came of this. On the same day that he wrote his optimistic report on continuing peace prospects with Austria, Kerr commented nonchalantly on the Turkish side of his mission that the Turkish agents in Switzerland were in no hurry to respond to British peace terms of which they were well aware and that it had to be remembered that they had acquired ambitions on

[144] Rumbold to FO, 6 Mar. 1918, FO 371/3388, no. 42760.

[145] War Cabinet, 8 Mar. 1918, CAB 23/16.

[146] Rumbold to FO, conveying message from Kerr, 11 Mar. 1918, FO 371/3388, no. 45537.

[147] Rumbold to Balfour, 11 Mar. 1918, and FO telegram, drafted by Ronald Graham, to Rumbold, 19 Mar. 1918, ibid. no. 48753. This change clearly reflects Graham's conviction that it was more important to ensure British rule in Palestine than in Mesopotamia. In a letter written in August 1918, Balfour, while recording that the autonomy formula had been extended to Mesopotamia in March, a change which he now considered to have been mistaken and suitable for reversal, said that there had been no change in autonomy as the condition which Britain would demand from Turkey in Palestine in a separate peace. Balfour to Beaverbrook, 9 Aug. 1918, FO 800/206.

their north-east frontier which would preclude their consent to an independent Armenian state.[148]

In reality, the Austrians and Turks were now adopting exactly the same attitude, that of severing their channels of communication to Britain and their other enemies in anticipation of a German victory in France. Kerr's thinking on international problems was based in part on race. He wanted the victorious white powers (i.e. excluding Japan) to form a club to maintain 'order' in the post-war world.[149] No doubt this helps to account for his zest for negotiations with Austria rather than Turkey but, on the whole, racial antipathy on the part of the British cannot be held to explain the failure of attempts to come to terms with Turkey. Even Lloyd George had been driven to try to negotiate with a Turkish leader and was prepared to forego the crushing military defeat whose prospect had given him so much pleasure during the first two or three years of the war. There was no essential difference between British determination to deprive Germany of her colonies and Turkey of her 'colonial' domain beyond the Asia Minor homeland of the Turkish people, while readiness to forego the total military defeat of Turkey as an object lesson to all aggressors involved a decision as serious as the virtual abandonment of the aim of crushing Germany militarily.

Assuming that Mouktar really spoke for Talaat, two questions would have arisen in detailed Anglo–Turkish negotiations. The British would hardly have maintained their demand for the autonomy of Turkish Armenia in view of the fact that the Armenian population had been virtually wiped out in a series of massacres and deportations culminating in 1915 but the prospect of an otherwise satisfactory peace which left Russian Armenia at Turkey's mercy would have presented a very painful moral dilemma. It is perhaps fortunate that the British were never put to this test. Another intriguing but unanswerable question is whether they would have been prepared to make other than nominal concessions to Turkey in the Arab areas. In all probability they would not have done so.

---

[148] Report by Kerr, 19 Mar. 1918, FO 800/206.
[149] J. R. M. Butler, *Lord Lothian* (1960), pp. 68–70.

V

THE CRISIS OF THE WAR, MARCH–SEPTEMBER 1918

---

1. GERMANY, RUSSIA AND THE BRITISH EMPIRE IN THE EAST

IN the early part of December 1917 the Bolshevik government of Russia and the Central Powers began peace negotiations at Brest–Litovsk. These pointed unmistakably to the imposition by Germany upon Russia of a conqueror's peace and such a peace was signed three months later. The Soviet government abandoned its claim to all the western, non-Russian borderlands of the Tsarist Empire including the Ukraine, together also with some territory in the Caucasus. Long before this, fear had become widespread in British ruling circles that the Germans and the Turks would be able to march across a prostrate Russia and threaten the British Empire in India, thus undoing the painful work that British arms had accomplished against Turkey in blocking Germany's supposed ambitions for eastward expansion. On 3 December 1917, the War Cabinet resolved to finance 'loyal' Russian forces in the Caucasus and Persia,[1] and three weeks later it decided that in order to block the expansionist designs of the Turks and Germans British policy should aim at independent Georgian and Armenian states, preferably in federation with one another.[2]

In January a first step to establish a 'line' to the Caspian to keep the Turks out of Persia was taken with the despatch of 'Dunsterforce' under General Dunsterville to Enzeli on the Persian shore of the Caspian.[3] Fears naturally mounted with the signature of the treaty of Brest–Litovsk and the corresponding treaty of Bucharest between the Central Powers and Rumania. The latter treaty prompted Balfour to call for an investigation as to whether Germany

---

[1] War Cabinet, 3 Dec. 1917, CAB 23/4.
[2] War Cabinet, 26 Dec. 1917 in ibid.
[3] C. H. Ellis, *The Transcaspian Episode* (1963) for a recent account of Dunsterforce.

could use her new-found rail access to Odessa to send forces across the Black Sea to the Caucasus and on to Central Asia and Afghanistan.[4] Curzon feared that Germany would actually do this.[5]

The massive German offensive in France on 21 March complicated the problem by forcing the British to concentrate all efforts on defending the Western Front and leaving them with little room for manoeuvre to meet a military emergency in any other theatre. One result was that the British came to attach increased importance to inducing the Japanese to intervene in Siberia. Henry Wilson argued that if the Germans gained western Siberia they would also have access to Turkestan and would thus be able to threaten India: 'The problem was in fact part of the same problem as that raised by the danger to Persia. It was a question of pulling Siberia out of the wreck in order to save India.' He was opposed by those ministers who believed that the Bolsheviks might still be able to put up some resistance and that intervention in Siberia would be virtually an admission of writing off European Russia.[6] The British desire for Japanese intervention in Siberia was less irrational than has often been supposed.[7] It was possible that if, as was expected, the war continued for a considerable time and if Japan did not occupy western Siberia, the Germans would enter and would send agents to instigate tribal wars against the British in Afghanistan and on the north-west frontier of India. The British were unrealistic only in supposing that Japan could be induced to conduct operations in west Siberia instead of merely occupying the east in the hope of bringing it under her permanent control.[8]

On the same day that the Germans launched their great offensive in the west, Balfour remarked that although Dunsterforce had had to withdraw because of threats to its communications, a mobile force of 1,300 men with armoured cars would have to be sent into north-west Persia to keep out the Turks. Curzon agreed and said that whereas the government had previously considered withdrawing the South Persian Rifles, a British-officered gendarmerie in the south, it would now be necessary to strengthen it so that these two

---

[4] Memorandum by Balfour, 7 Mar. 1918, G.T. 3840 in CAB 24/44.
[5] War Cabinet, 6 Mar. 1918, CAB 23/5.
[6] War Cabinet, 21 Mar. 1918 in ibid.
[7] Cf. R. H. Ullman, *Intervention and War* (1961), pp. 95–6, 128–30, 202, 229, 331–2.
[8] But see a memorandum by Balfour, 14 Feb. 1918, in which he pointed out that it was possible that the Japanese would refuse to advance beyond the Far Eastern provinces of Russia, Balfour MSS., B.M. Add. 49699.

British forces could exert sufficient pressure on the Teheran regime to dissuade it from lending itself to German–Turkish schemes.[9] Montagu joined in this chorus of fear the next day.[10]

The military policies which the British actually pursued in the East after Brest–Litovsk and the German attack in France were sensible and contrasted with the frenetic reaction of the Government of India.[11] Henry Wilson thought that the German attack would have to be defeated where it had been launched, on the Western Front, that Germany would have to make very lengthy preparations, which could not be concealed, before sending any troops to Asia and that she was likely to confine herself to penetration by agents.[12] His plans, as outlined to British commanders in Egypt, Mesopotamia and India, were for encouragement of Japanese intervention in Siberia, maintenance of the existing position in Mesopotamia and an advance in Palestine, and the building up of 'local organizations on a foundation of military strength' from Baghdad to the Caspian and into the Caucasus, together with a military mission to Turkestan.[13] This policy was adopted by the Eastern Committee of the War Cabinet on 6 May where it was supported by General H. Cox, military secretary at the India Office.[14]

In the thinking of ministers, the efforts to induce Japan to intervene in Siberia, with the maximum objective of rallying 'loyal' Russians and the minimum ones of keeping the Germans out of Central Asia and the Japanese firmly in the alliance against the Central Powers, rapidly became more important than operations against Turkey (except for the 'line' to the Caspian which was all of a piece with Japanese intervention). Thus policy in the Middle East, Trans-Caucasia and Central Asia was deputed to a cabinet committee under Curzon, the Eastern Committee to which reference has already been made, while the War Cabinet continued to control policy in Siberia directly 'as a matter of imperial policy of the first moment'.[15] Indeed, in the light of the events of 21 March in France,

---

[9] War Cabinet, 21 Mar. 1918, CAB 23/5.
[10] War Cabinet, 22 Mar. 1918, CAB 23/40.
[11] Cf. Chattar Singh Samra, *India and Anglo-Soviet Relations* (1959), pp. 23–5.
[12] Memorandum by the chief of the General Staff on the defence of India, 30 Apr. 1918, G.T. 4401, CAB 24/50. Intelligence reports confirmed that this was the German–Turkish intention: cf. Political Intelligence Department memorandum, 8 May 1918, G.T. 4576, CAB 24/51.
[13] War Office telegram, 14 Mar. 1918, Appendix A to memorandum by Wilson cited in note 12 above. [14] Eastern Committee, 6 May 1918, CAB 27/24.
[15] Memorandum by Curzon, 13 Mar. 1918, G.T. 3905, CAB 24/45.

offensive operations in the Middle East by the British became impossible. Allenby's orders, which had been broadened on 6 March to provide for a maximum advance, were revoked three weeks later when he was instructed to be ready to send two of his three British divisions to France and on 21 June it was decided that the remaining British divisions in Palestine should be transferred to the West Front leaving only one white division of Australian cavalry. It was recognized that any reverses in Palestine would endanger the entire eastern position including India, but it was also felt that if the West Front collapsed, the East would be lost in any case. However, with the defeat of the Austrian offensive in Italy, this decision was revoked five days later, though only provisionally in Henry Wilson's absence, and it was agreed to treat the three British divisions in Italy as a reserve for the front in France. Lloyd George declared that there must at all costs be no retreat in Palestine,[16] and according to Hankey he had set his heart on a campaign in Palestine and Syria in the autumn.[17]

Without military operations in Syria and northern Mesopotamia, the possibility of carrying out allied war aims in those areas appeared slight. Equally slight, however, were the chances of conducting such operations while predominant military opinion continued to be that offensive operations in the East should be confined to building up the 'line' through Persia to the Caucasus,[18] and while Britain's military resources were stretched to the limit. This latter factor was graphically illustrated in a remark by the Director of Military Operations, General Radcliffe, to the Imperial War Cabinet, that no troops could be spared from India for Siberia and that while it might eventually be possible to send a division from Mesopotamia this could not be done yet as the Caspian had not been cleared of the enemy.[19] As Hardinge put it, Britain was playing 'a big game of bluff in northern Russia and Central Asia' with limited forces. 'The fact that we are able to carry on this bluff is a good indication of the straits in which the Germans find themselves at present.'[20] It is fortunate that British plans for the defence of their position in the East in the spring and summer of 1918 were never put to a serious test.

[16] Imperial War Cabinet, 21 and 26 June 1918, CAB 23/44.
[17] Hankey, op. cit. ii. 821.
[18] Cf. memorandum produced in British section of the Supreme War Council, 28 July 1918, G.T. 5295, CAB 24/59.
[19] Imperial War Cabinet, 12 Aug. 1918, CAB 23/44.
[20] Hardinge to Wingate, 28 Aug. 1918, Hardinge MSS. XXXVIII.

Fear that in 1919 Germany might launch a great offensive against India persisted into the autumn. On 11 September the General Staff informed the British section of the Supreme War Council of its opinion that a major Turkish attack on the Baghdad–Resht line was likely to be carried out soon at the instigation of the Germans who were surely anxious to make as many gains in the East to offset their defeats in the West as possible 'quite apart from her post-war aspirations for domination or control in the East'. It was, therefore, imperative to strengthen defences along the route to the Caspian.[21] When Smuts expressed similar conjectures a few days later,[22] he provoked a division of opinion in the Eastern Committee between Curzon and General Cox, who agreed with him, and Henry Wilson and Balfour who thought that the threat was receding.[23] Not until 18 October did Curzon announce to his colleagues that he was satisfied that the German–Turkish threat to advance into Central Asia had been defeated,[24] and it is remarkable that at this time General Thomson of the Supreme War Council was still writing about the need to reconstitute an eastern front in Russia in 1919 to prevent the Germans from exploiting the resources of Siberia and from crossing the Caspian.[25]

The concern of the British with what they considered to be a serious threat to their eastern empire was less important for military operations and war aims against Turkey than for British thinking on the question of a compromise peace with Germany at the expense of Russia. In the case of north Mesopotamia a sudden awareness in ministerial circles of the area's importance on account of its oil deposits led the government to favour a resumption of operations in the late summer[26] while in Palestine Allenby made plans for an offensive with his existing forces whose strength was maintained with Indian drafts. Originally he envisaged a limited campaign which would complete the conquest of northern Palestine while allowing most of the Turkish troops there to escape. In August he changed his plans. Aware of Turkish weakness and confident of his own ability and that of the forces under his command, he made plans for

[21] General Staff memorandum, 11 Sept. 1918, CAB 23/5.
[22] Memorandum by Smuts, 16 Sept. 1918, G.T. 5700, CAB 23/63.
[23] Eastern Committee, 18 Sept. 1918, CAB 27/24.
[24] War Cabinet, 18 Oct. 1918, CAB 23/8.
[25] See the papers with a covering note by Thomson, 14 Oct. 1918 in CAB 25/123.
[26] See V. H. Rothwell, 'Mesopotamia in British War Aims 1914–1918', *Historical Journal* xiii (1970), 273–94.

a campaign of annihilation which, if successful, would make the problem of occupying Syria one of supply only. This plan was executed almost without fault in late September and Damascus was occupied on 2 October.[27]

No aspect of British war aims in the First World War is more important or more fascinating than the problem of whether the British were at any time prepared to make a compromise peace with Germany which allowed her to retain her conquests in Russia in return for the *status quo* of 1914 in the west and the loss of at least some of her colonies, and none has been the subject of greater misunderstanding. The entire idea was a non-starter in the sense that even if the British government had adopted it as their policy it is unlikely that they would have been able to win the support of their two main allies. The Clemenceau government was opposed to any compromise with Germany though it is true that there were less intransigent elements in French public life and that the position of the government was not unassailable. More important, President Wilson was very strongly opposed to German ambitions in Russia. He made this clear in the Fourteen Point address and at the same time Spring-Rice reported that there was much talk in Washington that the President was specially concerned not to drive the Russians into the arms of Germany.[28] He periodically repeated his views though he chose to speak to the French rather than the British, apparently fearing that they would be tempted to agree to anything in return for an offer on Alsace-Lorraine. In August, he told the French ambassador, Jusserand, that 'for his part he was confident it would be madness to let the Germans do as they liked in Russia. They might obtain many Alsace-Lorraines there for the one they gave up to France.'[29]

Within the British government itself the most serious, if not the only serious, proponent of such a policy was Lloyd George.[30] He was restrained only by the reluctance of his colleagues and by the absence of indications from Germany that she was prepared to abandon her aims in the west though there were a few encouraging signs from that quarter such as an intelligence report in November

---

[27] Cf. Cruttwell, op. cit. pp. 619–22; and Archibald Wavell, *Allenby* (1940), pp. 265–6.

[28] Spring-Rice to FO, 8 Jan. 1918, FO 371/3435, no. 6061.

[29] Cecil to Balfour, 5 Aug. 1918, reporting an interview with M. De Fleuriau of the French Embassy, FO 371/3436, no. 136946.

[30] See above, pp. 148–51, 212–14.

1917 that Kühlmann regarded the idea of making concessions to France in Alsace-Lorraine in return for the Baltic provinces of Russia as 'a business proposition which no responsible statesman could refuse to entertain'.[31]

Lloyd George was so vehement that everyone in the highest official circles had to come to some opinion on the question of a peace on these lines. Opinion in the Foreign Office was that if such a peace was necessary it should not be announced until the military position of the allies had much improved,[32] a view with which Robertson agreed.[33] Haig, however, felt that the time had already come to turn Germany 'in the direction of Russia for her future'. He evidently thought that the Germans would encounter so many military obstacles in establishing their rule in all or part of Russia that they 'would be taken off the path of the British Empire. . . . He was strongly in favour of an early peace on those lines.'[34] Admiral Hall, the head of naval intelligence, favoured in a muddled sort of way a peace at the expense of Russia.[35]

Greatest interest attaches to the attitude of Lord Milner who has often and wrongly been looked upon as the leading exponent of this idea.[36] It is regrettable that Milner's latest biographer allows himself to conclude: 'When the Germans were beaten in the West and no longer threatened the Empire in an immediate sense, Milner had no objection to the conditions established at Brest–Litovsk to the "free hand" in the East for Germany.'[37] This assertion is hardly supported by the pieces of evidence which Mr. Gollin himself has laboriously assembled and which fall into two categories. Firstly, there are those in which Milner, from shortly after the time of his entry into the War Cabinet, expressed fear that the war was not going at all well, that the allies ought to be prepared to make sacrifices to induce the lesser enemy states to make peace and that it was unlikely that, at the conclusion of hostilities, it would be possible to deprive Germany of much with the exception of the colonies. Milner was early in

[31] Department of Information memorandum on the views of Kühlmann and Czernin, 9 Nov. 1917, G.T. 2588 in CAB 24/31.   [32] See above, pp. 151–2.

[33] Robertson, *Soldiers and Statesmen*, ii. 277 ff.

[34] Smuts to Lloyd George, 22 Jan. 1918, reporting conversation with Haig. Hankey added a minute confirming the accuracy of Smuts' report, Lloyd George MSS. F/45/9/9.

[35] *The Diary of Lord Bertie of Thame*, ii. 293.

[36] The latest discussion is in A. M. Gollin, *Proconsul in Politics* (1964), Chapter XX where detailed references are given to previous writings on the subject, notably in *The History of The Times* and in works by E. H. Carr and A. J. Mayer.

[37] Gollin, op. cit. p. 577.

coming to these views but by the late autumn of 1917 they were shared by almost all his colleagues. Secondly, there are assertions that Milner favoured a compromise peace between the British and German empires at the expense of Russia and all of these can be traced to certain passages in the published diaries of Beatrice Webb.[38] Early in March 1918 the Webbs had certain conversations with Lloyd George and Haldane in which the two politicians hinted clearly at a peace at the expense of Russia and said that they hoped that the Webbs would help to enlist Labour support for such a policy. They suggested that the Webbs should have further conversations on the subject with Milner. The Webbs never in fact met Milner but nevertheless they, or at least Beatrice, came to the conclusion that he was the *eminence grise* behind the proposal. This would appear to be the only solid piece of evidence anywhere that Milner favoured a compromise peace at the expense of Russia. Against it must be set Milner's opposition to such an idea when Lloyd George originally put it forward in September 1917.[39] The following March, shortly after Lloyd George had made his invitation to the Webbs to meet Milner of which so much has been made, Milner wrote to the Prime Minister about the 'very serious' position in the East. Some Austrian prisoners, he remarked, were reported as having been seen at Meshed in north-east Persia. 'That shows what comes of the collapse of the Power which used to cover our whole Asian flank.'[40] This is hardly the language of a man who was thinking of allowing Germany a 'free hand' in Russia. Beatrice Webb was an intelligent and witty woman but she was hopelessly at a loss to understand the mind of a man like Milner whose ideas were both complex and different from her own. She thought that he was a lover of autocracy and Prussian-style efficiency and that therefore in the nature of things he must be attracted to the idea of an alliance with the present enemy against revolutionary Russia. Contemporaries like the journalist Clifford Sharp to whom she expressed her views and later historians have made the same assumption.

Milner's whole attitude to Russia after the overthrow of the Tsardom was indeed one of hostility. As early as April 1917 he detected 'ominous cracks' in the social structure of every European country and feared that the recent revolution in Russia was par-

[38] Margaret Cole, ed., *Beatrice Webb's Diaries 1912–1924* (1952), pp. 111–16.
[39] See above, p. 108.
[40] Milner to Lloyd George, 20 Mar. 1918, Milner MSS. 145 (VII).

ticularly likely to precipitate 'the dissolution of all human society'.[41] This hostility naturally deepened when the Bolsheviks with their aim of world social revolution came to power and led Russia out of the war. Milner could not understand how anyone in the remaining allied states could feel tenderness toward Russia who 'has let us all down in the most abominable way and has been rewarded with a tremendous pat on the back from [President] Wilson'.[42] Yet Milner, unlike Lloyd George, always realized that a negotiated peace at the expense of Russia would involve risks that were too great and that Germany might treat a position of dominance in Russia as merely a staging-post for further schemes of world power.

There is some evidence on Milner's thinking in the mid-winter of 1917–18. A few days before Christmas he went with Cecil to Paris to discuss with the French a joint policy in Russia. Both sides agreed that it was vastly more important to keep the Central Powers out of southern Russia than out of the north, partly because it was only in the south that they could obtain substantial supplies of foodstuffs and raw materials and partly because if the Germans and Turks gained control in the south there would be no 'barrier against the development of a Turanian movement that will extend from Constantinople to China and will provide Germany with a weapon of even greater danger to the peace of the world than the control of the Baghdad railway'.[43]

Milner himself remarked: 'If it came to the point we would keep in with the Ukraine and let the Bolsheviki join up with Germany.'[44] Two months later he said in the War Cabinet that 'in the near future Russia would have a German-controlled government at Petrograd either under the Bolsheviks or under a pro-German czar' and that what mattered in Russia policy was to intervene energetically in the south and Siberia without paying heed to the protests of a central government which would soon join Britain's enemies.[45] Milner clearly thought that if a Bolshevik government in north Russia chose to become a German vassal, British interests would not be vitally affected. However, it was manifestly clear that Germany had ambitions in south Russia and the Caucasus and also the capacity to

---

[41] Milner to Arthur Glazebrook, 21 Apr. 1917, Milner MSS. 144 (VI).
[42] Milner to Balfour, 15 Mar. 1918, FO 800/204.
[43] Memorandum read by the British side in minutes of Anglo–French conference at the Quai d'Orsay, 23 Dec. 1917, FO 371/3086, no. 243036.
[44] Conference minutes as cited in note 43 above.
[45] War Cabinet, 25 Feb. 1918, CAB 23/5.

pursue them. A peace based on concessions in the north was therefore not a practical proposition. Probably what Milner had in mind
was that eventually Germany might be so far defeated as to be ready
genuinely to abandon all her more grandiose aspirations and to claim
only the non-Russian Baltic provinces of the former Empire as a
field for her ambitions. Milner certainly would have been prepared
to make peace on those terms. There was, indeed, a widespread
assumption that the war might end on that basis. In March General
Studd of the British section of the Supreme War Council spoke
about 'the Power which will dominate north-west Russia and which
according to present prospects must necessarily be Germany'.[46] At
the same time, Milner's disciple, Amery, was writing hopefully that
Germany could be expected to acquiesce in the loss of her colonies
in return for concessions in the Baltic: 'From the German point of
view the Baltic provinces are a much better colony than any African
colony could be for the expansion of the German race.'[47] As late as
August 1918, the Political Intelligence Department of the Foreign
Office which was, to say the least, hardly staffed by appeasers was
declaring that Lithuania and Courland could safely be left as a
German sphere and that it would only be necessary to block
German designs in Esthonia and Finland.[48]

The treaty of Brest–Litovsk and subsequent actions by Germany
such as the penetration of the Caucasus by her agents showed that a
deal with Berlin would be impossible for at least some time to come
and virtually put a stop to discussion of a peace at Russia's expense
in responsible British quarters.

The change in attitude can be seen most clearly in the case of
Smuts. In November 1917 he told C. P. Scott that if Russia made a
separate peace and if Germany offered to restore Belgium, to give
up the colonies and to reach a compromise on Alsace-Lorraine on
the condition that the allies would accept the Russo–German treaty:
'It would be difficult to resist such a proposal.' By the following
August, Smuts was speaking to Scott of his fear that Germany
would adopt defensive tactics in the west so that she could concentrate upon the domination of Persia and Afghanistan and upon

[46] Undated minute but written in Mar. 1918, CAB 25/48.
[47] L. S. Amery, 'Political Aspects of the Campaign of 1919', 21 Mar. 1918, CAB
25/73. See also Appendix II, pp. 292–3.
[48] Political Intelligence Department memorandum, 15 Aug. 1918, G.T. 5493,
CAB 24/61.

threatening India. He continued: 'The real difficulty in reaching a settlement was in the East. We could not accept the Brest–Litovsk and Rumanian treaties. They must be placed on the table of the peace conference for revision.'[49]

Long before this, it had become a commonplace that Germany intended to exploit her triumph in Russia by attacking the British in Asia and what made the matter frightening was the possibility that with the resources of Russia under her control she would actually be able to make a serious effort in this direction. In May 1918, Cecil, at what would today be called a press conference, declared that he thought that Germany would soon make insincere peace moves to give herself time to complete her economic domination of Russia: 'They believe that if they really establish themselves with a Germanophil government in Russia once on its legs, with the resources of Russia and the possibilities of a wealthy country there is no reason why they should not fight the world for ever and be unconquerable.'[50]

Just over a month later, Milner, then Secretary of State for War, who had been asked by Balfour to furnish him with military as opposed to political arguments to present to President Wilson in order to gain his support for Japanese intervention in Siberia—without which Japan refused to act—wrote: 'If Germany is allowed to help herself to anything she wants in all Russia—not only supplies but ultimately men—then Germany cannot possibly be beaten.' Japanese intervention might rally enough Russians to resist the small forces with which Germany would otherwise be able to occupy and exploit the whole of Russia. 'I don't know whether the above are "military" arguments. What I do know is that the recognition or non-recognition of the importance of these considerations is going to determine the result of the war.'[51]

In an interview at the end of June with Arthur Ponsonby—a radical ally of his youth in, among other things, Russophobia—Lloyd George could still say, 'Russia . . . must be left to take care of

---

[49] Journals, 12 Nov. 1917, 50904, and 6–8 Aug. 1918, 50905.

[50] Record of Cecil's remarks to journalists, 3 May 1918 in FO 371/3436, no. 120309.

[51] Milner to Balfour with covering note by Milner stating that the letter was written in mid-June 1918 and never sent, Milner MSS. 146 (VIII). Milner almost certainly decided not to send this letter because of his pronounced views on Balfour's incompetence as Foreign Secretary rather than because he had second thoughts on the validity of its arguments. Balfour's request for 'military arguments' is in Balfour to Milner, 18 June 1918, FO 800/205.

herself'.[52] In reality, he had undergone the same change of attitude as Smuts. In his opening address to the second Imperial War Cabinet a few weeks before his interview with Ponsonby, the Prime Minister said that Germany definitely did have ambitions to dominate Asia and that consequently Brest–Litovsk could not be accepted,[53] whereas in his opening address to the previous imperial gathering in March 1917, he had merely said that the then Secretary of State for India, Austen Chamberlain, *might* be right in thinking that Germany was intent on using the Turkish Empire as a gateway to the East.[54] A fortnight later Curzon made a powerful speech on the folly of acquiescing in the Brest–Litovsk treaty[55] and this had a considerable impact,[56] chiefly no doubt because it expressed in clear language what many in ruling circles were thinking.

The following month Lloyd George asked Lord Reading to inform President Wilson that Britain wanted a liberal and democratic Russia for the benefit of the Russian people and also from 'the point of view of the peace of the world and of the peace and security of the Indian frontier. Reactionary Russia is certain to be aggressive and in close alliance with Germany.'[57] During the main Imperial War Cabinet debates on war aims, Balfour announced his wish for the complete reconstitution of Russia, excluding Poland, as a democratic, multi-national federation[58] and, observing that Germany continued to build up a system of puppet states in Russia, declared: 'The breaking down of the Brest–Litovsk treaty must be an essential part of our policy. That would be the most effective way of disposing of the dangers in the Middle East with regard to which Lord Curzon had warned the Imperial War Cabinet.'[59] Lloyd George stated that he agreed with his Foreign Secretary.[60]

---

[52] Memorandum by Arthur Ponsonby on interview with Lloyd George, 27 June 1918, Ponsonby MSS. I wish to thank Lord Ponsonby of Shulbrede Priory for allowing me to make use of this document and Dr. M. Ekstein Frankl for drawing my attention to its existence. [53] Imperial War Cabinet, 11 June 1918, CAB 23/43.

[54] Text of address in D. Lloyd George, *War Memoirs*, i. 1047–57, especially p. 1051.

[55] War Cabinet, 25 June 1918, CAB 23/43.

[56] Cf. E. S. Montagu to Lord Chelmsford, 3 July 1918, India Office Library: EUR. MSS. D 523.2; General Macdonagh's remarks to Eastern Committee, 4 July 1918, CAB 27/24.

[57] Telegram Lloyd George to Reading, 18 July 1918, based in part on a letter from Balfour to Lloyd George, 16 July 1918, Balfour MSS., B.M. Add. 49692. Cf. *War Memoirs*, ii. 1907, and Ullman, op. cit. pp. 221–3.

[58] Imperial War Cabinet, 13 Aug. 1918, CAB 23/43.

[59] Ibid. 14 Aug, 1918, CAB 23/42.

[60] Ibid. 14 Aug. 1918, minutes in CAB 23/43.

By this time the British leaders were dwelling much on the role of Turkey in Germany's supposed plans for expansion to the east. It was thought that Turkey, both working as Germany's conscious tool and pursuing her own ambitions, sought the unity under her leadership of the Turkish-speaking peoples of Russian Central Asia, parts of Persia and Afghanistan. Such a state or confederation, Arnold Toynbee had warned, 'would threaten India in the gravest way. It would create a vast anti-British hinterland behind the anti-British tribes on the north-west frontier.'[61] Turkey's Pan-Turanian ambitions were worrying the War Office, conscious of its responsibilities for the defence of the Indian Empire, by 1916 at the latest.[62] But fear of Pan-Turanism did not become sharp until toward the end of 1917 when British victories in Palestine and Mesopotamia began to seem irreversible and when the collapse of Russia was seen to open up vistas of a *Drang nach Turanien* into middle-Asia.[63] The Turkish leadership were in fact turning more and more in that direction.[64]

The attitude of the British to German ambitions in Russia might have been very different if Germany had lacked a powerful Asian ally. As it was, the middle months of 1918 saw the death of the idea of a negotiated peace with Germany at Russia's expense, an idea which had probably never been entertained seriously by any British statesman except Lloyd George and which was finally killed by a conviction that acceptance of Brest–Litovsk would lead, if nothing worse, to 'a vast accretion to the resources of the Central Powers and an insidious but certain weakening of Great Britain's position in India'.[65]

2. MANPOWER PROBLEMS AND GERMAN PEACE MOVES

If a negotiated peace at the expense of Russia was unacceptable the immense casualties which the British Empire had suffered in the war and the near-certainty, as it was thought, of the struggle continuing into 1919 or 1920 produced a mood approaching anguish

[61] A. J. Toynbee, 'Report on the Pan-Turanian Movement', Oct. 1917 in *Eastern Report*, XLIV, 29 Nov. 1917, CAB 24/144.
[62] Cf. minute by W. H. Gribbon, 25 Sept. 1917, on memorandum by General Moberly, Indian Army, WO 106/1418.
[63] Minute by H. Nicolson, 26 Jan. 1918, FO 371/3388, no. 16415; cf. memorandum by Toynbee cited in note 61 above.
[64] Emin, *Turkey in the World War* (1930), pp. 181 ff.
[65] Supreme War Council memorandum by General C. B. Thomson, 10 Aug. 1918, CAB 25/122.

among the imperial statesmen as they assembled in June 1918. The keynote for military-political discussion was set by Henry Wilson who argued that few satisfactory results had been achieved on the West Front so far and that, while the 'final push' would have to be made there in 1919, 'We ought to exploit the outside theatres as much as we can, so that at the peace conference we, the British anyhow, will not be so badly off.'[66]

The main discussions on this theme began on 31 July when Lloyd George, Milner and Smuts made clear their disillusion with the West Front in no uncertain terms. The Prime Minister repeated a fear which he had expressed to Hankey the previous October, this time arguing that if the attrition tactics were persisted in, the British army would by the end of 1919 be reduced to twenty-three divisions compared with 120 American divisions and even forty for the French so that the American President would be able to dictate the peace settlement with effortless ease. He declared that the only hope of winning the war lay in the reconstitution of Russia though he was again toying with the idea of a knock-out blow from Italy against Austria as another short-cut to victory.

Lloyd George's attitude toward the High Command is sufficiently indicated by his point-blank refusal to accept the General Staff estimate that at the end of 1919 the strength of the army would be forty-three divisions. He insisted on a figure of twenty. Perhaps because of the Prime Minister's strictures, the War Office shortly afterwards sent Hankey a revised estimate on manpower according to which the strength of the army by mid-1919 would be 311,000 compared with a previous estimate of 400,000, while by the end of the year, assuming that Ireland were not conscripted, it would fall to 275,000. In August 1918 its strength was 575,000.[67] These appalling figures speak for themselves and what gave them especial poignancy was the almost universal belief that the war would last well into 1919 though in retrospect the tide had begun to turn decisively with Foch's successful attack between Soissons and Château-Thierry on 18 July.[68]

The need to achieve British imperial war aims thus combined with humanitarian considerations to dictate a major change in strategic policy and this was reflected in the report which Hankey

[66] Imperial War Cabinet, 18 June 1918, CAB 23/43.
[67] Cf. Radcliffe to Hankey, 13 Aug. 1918, CAB 25/85.
[68] Cruttwell, op. cit. pp. 543-7.

drew up for the Imperial War Cabinet. It recommended that there should be no major offensive on the West Front in 1919, that the possibility of operations in Italy should be examined, that offensive operations in the Middle East should be in Mesopotamia and not Palestine and should aim at capturing the oil-bearing areas, that control of the Caspian should be strengthened and that, while Russia was 'the most promising' alternative to the West Front there was at present no bright spot there except for the Czech legions.[69]

A deep contradiction was implicit in this policy. It would, if successful, ensure the defence of the eastern empire and the achievement of many British territorial war aims. This was pointed out by Lloyd George who added that if the western strategy continued to be applied, 'Of course, we could continue to fight resolutely, but there would be no chance of achieving our war aims and retaining the islands of the south Pacific and South-West Africa if we had no army at the end.' This sally was intended for the Dominion leaders, especially Hughes of Australia who was not convinced that the war should not still be fought in France with the old vigour. Lloyd George was speaking more from the heart when he entered a reservation against the recommendation in the conference report that there should be no offensive in Palestine: 'There would be considerable advantage in acquiring the whole of Palestine prior to any peace negotiations in which the Turks might take a part. It would be easier for the Turks to give up something they had lost than to withdraw troops from territory they had occupied.'[70]

However, all this was, by the Prime Minister's own definition, only nibbling at the real problem of the war which was that of carrying out the extremely desirable objective of inflicting signal military defeat on Germany. This, he reaffirmed, was more important than any specific terms of peace.[71] Perhaps he was uneasily aware of this contradiction when, after assenting to the conference report with its argument that victory in France would be too costly and that the allies should look to the defection of Austria and the revival of Russia to wear Germany down, he made the robust statement that he looked forward to a really resounding military victory in 1920.[72]

Lloyd George and other statesmen hoped to square this circle by

[69] The Imperial War Cabinet military debates from 31 July 1918, and Hankey's report on the conference, 15 Aug. 1918, are in CAB 23/44.
[70] Imperial War Cabinet, 16 Aug. 1918.   [71] Ibid. 31 July 1918.
[72] Ibid. 15 Aug. 1918, minutes in CAB 23/42.

14

leaving it to the Americans and the French to win the final victory on the West Front while the British rested on their laurels except for undertaking campaigns in the East which would bring permanent political advantage to themselves. This policy was advocated openly by Milner[73] and it found a clear echo in the recommendation in the conference report that the British army in France should be reduced to thirty-six divisions so that the remainder might be withdrawn to the East with losses in those which stayed being made up by bringing in American troops.[74]

Whether it would have been possible to implement these strategic schemes if the war had lasted into 1919 is obviously impossible to say. The first step, the replacement of Haig, the most implacable champion of the western doctrine, was much discussed behind the scenes at the Imperial Cabinet but became impossible on 6 August when he won a notable victory, freeing the railway line between Montdidier and Amiens.[75] It was also clear that the British would have a hard time convincing their allies that they should be allowed to carry out their plans. Making use of a report on British manpower by a French officer, one Major Roure, Clemenceau protested that the British military effort was inadequate and that another million men could be mobilized without greater efforts being involved than those which France was already making.[76] Foch as generalissimo of the allied armies in France insisted that by April 1919 Britain must have as many troops on the West Front as in the previous summer. When told that this could not be done without striking serious blows at British shipbuilding and coal production, he replied predictably that he wanted men and not coal. While Lloyd George felt that Britain's bargaining position at the peace conference would depend above all on the then size of her armed forces, Foch reminded him that the exertions made while the war was still being fought would count for much. He was informed by one of his military advisers: 'I understand the French view is that if when the time for discussion of peace arrives we have reduced the number of our divisions while they have not, we shall not have the same weight in council.'[77]

[73] Imperial War Cabinet, 31 July 1918, minutes in CAB 23/44.
[74] Conference report, 15 Aug. 1918.
[75] Hankey, ii. 816, 828–9.
[76] Derby to FO, 17 Aug. 1918, FO 371/3443, no. 142880.
[77] Sackville-West (British representative on the Supreme War Council) to Hankey, 27 Aug. 1918, Lloyd George MSS. F/23/3/10.

The Prime Minister was unconvinced. He asked Lord Reading, whom he had sent to Paris to try to reach agreement with the French on the British manpower question, to inform Clemenceau that the British could not possibly maintain their existing number of divisions even by reducing strengths. The French government had finally to accept that the British must make their own dispositions on manpower while bearing French views carefully in mind.[78] Shortly after this, Lloyd George assured the Canadian Prime Minister, Borden, 'Nothing has happened to force us to change fundamental views in regard to manpower.'[79] At an Entente conference in Paris on 7 October the British and French Prime Ministers exchanged sharp words over British manpower allocations for the West Front in 1919. Then, abruptly, the armistice with Germany consigned the new strategic-political plans of the Imperial War Cabinet to oblivion.

During the summer of 1918 the British political leadership, to say nothing of that of the thinly-populated overseas Dominions, were almost desperately anxious to conserve manpower. Yet their plans for meeting the situation did not include an investigation of the question of a negotiated peace with Germany. When a possibility of this arose at an Anglo–German prisoner-of-war conference at The Hague in June, they ran away from it in some panic.

On 16 May 1918 Balfour made a speech in the House of Commons in which he promised that the British government would listen carefully to any serious peace offers from any of the enemy powers. It has been suggested that this was a peace feeler to Germany.[80] In view of Balfour's absolute refusal to entertain the feelers which the Germans themselves made at The Hague a few weeks later, this interpretation is clearly false. It is likely that he was trying to convince those elements in the nation with latent 'pacifist' tendencies that the government's attitude toward Germany was more flexible than was really the case.

Lloyd George's attitude was more complicated. On 6 June he decided to send instructions to the Home Secretary, Sir George Cave, who was leading the British delegation at The Hague, that

[78] Reading to Lloyd George, 4 Sept. 1918, ibid. F/43/1/16; Lloyd George to Reading in FO to Derby, 5 Sept. 1918, FO 371/3443, no. 153289; message from Reading in Derby to FO, 6 Sept. 1918, ibid. no. 153756.
[79] Lloyd George to Borden, 11 Sept. 1918, Lloyd George MSS. F/5/2/21.
[80] Guinn, op. cit. p. 308.

he should listen to any German peace offer without committing himself or the government in any way. The Prime Minister said that during his recent visit to France he had learned that the working classes were depressed by Clemenceau's determination on a fight to the finish and his opposition to even an honourable peace offer.[81] This was manifestly a hint by Lloyd George to his more intransigent colleagues not to make the same mistake. He was speaking at a discussion prompted by a telegram from the British minister to the Netherlands, Sir Walter Townley, that the appointment of a member of the government to head the British delegation to the forthcoming conference had convinced the Germans that the British wished to discuss peace. There was, he added, reliable information that their peace terms would be more reasonable than was generally expected.[82] There had been other portents such as a report from Rumbold at Berne that the disappointing results of the current offensive and economic distress were inducing a feeling in Germany that peace must be sought.[83]

The response in the Foreign Office could hardly have been cooler. Howard Smith commented on Townley's telegram: 'The belief of the Germans may help us to get better terms for the prisoners.' Balfour put a special gloss on Lloyd George's instructions for Cave by remarking upon the 'absurd' German supposition that he had been appointed to head the British delegation so that peace could be discussed.[84] In a speech in Parliament a fortnight later, the Foreign Secretary scoffed at the idea that the British might be prepared to make peace with Germany on the basis of nothing more than the restoration of Belgium.[85]

Shortly afterwards, Kühlmann made a sensational speech in the Reichstag in which he stated that complete military victory for the Central Powers had become unattainable while at the same time, the leader of the German delegation at The Hague, Prince Hatzfeldt, approached Cave with a request for confidential talks on peace. The Home Secretary advised acceptance if only to facilitate the prisoner negotiations which were 'dragging terribly'.[86] Cave was immediately

[81] War Cabinet, 6 June 1918, CAB 23/6.

[82] Townley to FO, 5 June 1918, FO 371/3442, no. 100113.

[83] Rumbold to FO, 21 April 1918, FO 371/3436, no. 70977.

[84] Minute by H. Smith and FO (drafted by Balfour) to Townley, 6 June 1918, reference as in note 82 above.

[85] Speech by Balfour, 21 June 1918, in J. B. Scott, pp. 338–42.

[86] Cave to Balfour, 28 June 1918, FO 800/201.

recalled and Lord Newton, deputy leader of the delegation who took his place, was given no instructions whatever on how to deal with peace approaches. Left to his own devices, he listened to a German delegate who described what he claimed to be German peace terms, and reported this to Lloyd George on 25 July, the earliest date on which he could secure an interview after returning to London.[87]

After a leisurely interval, Newton was asked to report to the Foreign Office where he told J. W. Headlam-Morley that he was convinced that the Germans truly wanted a compromise peace on the terms which had been mentioned to him: satisfaction of allied demands in the west and in the German colonies, concessions to the Entente in Turkey and a free hand for Germany in eastern Europe. Lord Newton, who had been approached after Kühlmann had been deposed, thought that it was significant that Germany was continuing to pursue this line despite the fall of the Foreign Minister on whose dismissal the High Command had insisted in view of his Reichstag speech.[88]

The Foreign Office were totally unwilling to act upon this information. Light is cast on their attitude toward Germany at this time by the reception given to the reports of George D. Herron, an American intellectual living in Switzerland who acted as intermediary between the United States legation there and the American embassy in Paris and numerous Germans and Austrians who wished to discuss peace.[89] The bleak message which he invariably conveyed —that it was necessary that military defeat should be inflicted on Germany and that it would be idle to expect the United States to be interested in a separate peace with either of the Central Powers— much commended itself to the office. Tyrrell was prompted by one of Herron's reports to suggest to Hardinge that British agents should be advised to reply to German peace feelers in the same uncompromising terms as Herron used, while Hardinge minuted that Herron's opinions 'appear absolutely sound'. Cecil joined with Hardinge in praising Herron but thought that the government could not adopt his tactics as the result might be a pacifist

---

[87] Lord Newton, *Retrospection* (1941), pp. 261–2.

[88] Memorandum by Headlam-Morley, 8 Aug. 1918, FO 800/201.

[89] The fact that Herron sent all his reports to both the Foreign Office and the War Office seems to have been unknown to his interlocutors: cf. Briggs, op. cit. p. 36 n.

reaction at home.[90] Balfour was another admirer of Herron.[91]

At the same time the office moved to veto a suggestion by the Dutch Prime Minister, Loudon, who sought to act as intermediary between Britain and Germany, that he should arrange a continuation of the peace contacts begun at The Hague.[92] Drummond minuted a letter from Loudon, 'Such a meeting could only be dangerous in the present circumstances' and suggested that it should be rejected. Balfour minuted his assent and wrote accordingly to Cave.[93] Shortly afterwards a member of Parliament submitted a question asking whether any enemy peace overtures had recently been received by the government. Howard Smith drafted a reply for Balfour that only unofficial approaches had been made and that official approaches would, if made, be considered carefully. Balfour altered this to a simple statement that no enemy government had made approaches.[94] Even more revealing, he refused to say anything when, after giving this answer in the House if Commons, he was asked to say whether the government welcomed such peace feelers as it had received unofficially.[95]

Foreign Office attitudes showed signs of reverting to the extreme ones of 1916. Cecil described as 'admirable' a statement drawn up in the Political Intelligence Department for publication by a Swedish journalist as an actual interview with Cecil, which made the Assistant Foreign Secretary say that Germany was divided into two nations: the unrepentant militarists and the liberals who were anxious to 'acknowledge guilt' and who, it was to be hoped, would bring themselves to the fore in their country's life.[96] There were thus hopes of a basic change of system in Germany, a development which was recognized as only being possible as the result of very severe military defeat.

One reason why the Foreign Office were unwilling to consider German peace overtures was, as always, the suspicion that they were a trap, designed to weaken the war-will of the allied peoples. It was widely thought in the office that Kühlmann's Reichstag speech was a direct attempt to aid the Lansdownite movement which was very

[90] Note by Tyrrell to Hardinge, 2 July 1918, on a report by Herron, 14 June 1918, with minutes by Hardinge and Cecil, Lloyd George MSS. F/3/3/26.

[91] Ibid. minute by Balfour; also Briggs, p. 33.

[92] Loudon to Cave, 15 July 1918, FO 800/201.

[93] Ibid. Balfour to Cave, 22 July 1918.

[94] Minutes by Balfour and Smith and text of parliamentary question, FO 371/3436, no. 137700.   [95] *House of Commons*, 5th series, CIX, col. 907, 5 Aug. 1918.

[96] See text of this statement and various minutes in FO 371/4367, no. 339.

strong in Britain during the first half of 1918.[97] Reports that Germany was trying to induce prominent Englishmen to enter into peace talks in neutral centres so that these could then be publicized to the embarrassment of the British government[98] lent support to this suspicion.

Beyond this point the historian must indulge in the dangerous pastime of conjecture. It would probably not be unduly cynical to suggest that the British were more ready for a protracted struggle after the Imperial War Cabinet debates when it was, in effect, decided to try to ensure that future casualties would be predominantly American and French, not British. In the case of Lloyd George there was also the constant fear that if he moved toward peace, the Asquithians in Parliament and the generals would form an alliance against him which might well bring down the government. The Prime Minister was prevented from trying to strengthen his political position by means of a general election as he lacked a party machine. Asquith controlled most of the Liberal machine while Bonar Law, in charge of the Conservative apparatus, remained unwilling to consent to a general election until September 1918. Lloyd George, in any case, did not feel confident of the outcome of such an election and with good reason: war weariness, the problem of Irish conscription, labour unrest and the uncertainty of the women's vote made the result of an election, held when victory was apparently not in sight, doubtful.[99]

Behind the parties and generals loomed the press. On 24 May Northcliffe wrote to a member of the editorial staff of *The Times*, of which he was proprietor, 'Lloyd George has been with Haldane lately and also with Sidney Webb. If there is any sign of wobbling or peace talk, please deal with the PM drastically.'[100] A few weeks later, the foreign editor of *The Times*, Wickham Steed, learning of the reports which the War Cabinet had received that Germany might make overtures at The Hague, obtained Northcliffe's consent to a sensational leading article in the *Daily Mail*, another Northcliffe newspaper, on 18 June which specifically condemned the only

[97] Cf. minute by Headlam-Morley, c. 26 June 1918, FO 371/3436, no. 114172. For the Lansdowne movement in 1918 see Lord Newton, *Lord Lansdowne: A Biography* (1929), pp. 473–5.

[98] Cf. copy of War Office intelligence report headed 'Plan for Anglo–German Meeting', Geneva, 1 July 1918, FO 371/3223, no. 120339.

[99] Cf. the analysis in Barry McGill, 'Asquith's Predicament 1914–1918', *Journal of Modern History*, xxxix (1967), 283–303, especially pp. 300–3.

[100] R. Pound and G. Harmsworth, *Northcliffe* (1959), p. 641.

sort of compromise peace which was conceivable—one based upon the satisfaction of allied aims in the west and of German aims in the east.[101]

Even more important was a conviction that the war and all the sacrifices so far made would be futile unless it was continued to a point where Germany realized that for her it had been a failure. This was emphasized by the Prime Minister in his interview with Arthur Ponsonby at the end of June. Since neither Lloyd George nor probably anyone else in the highest ranks of leadership had a clear definition of what would constitute the point at which Germany recognized her failure, the government's conduct on the fundamental question of war or peace was one of drift. Giving his impression of government policy after several hours' conversation with Lloyd George, Ponsonby wrote:

The real obstacle is that they believe that at present Germany has won, knows she has won against overwhelming odds and that our generals think she has won. This they were apparently determined not to submit to. They will not take any advantage of more favourable statements on the part of Germany but they will go on, not expecting anything in the nature of a decisive military victory, but hoping that prolongation may by improving our position and showing a readiness to go on indefinitely at least make the German militarists adopt a more resigned attitude.[102]

A subsidiary though not wholly negligible reason for the British government's rejection of the peace feelers which Germany made in the middle of 1918 was the influence exercised by a new department of the Foreign Office, the Political Intelligence Department. This was set up in January 1918 by the transfer of the Intelligence Bureau in the Department of Information to the Foreign Office. Unlike the other branches of the Information Department, which were concerned with propaganda, the work of the Intelligence Bureau consisted in compiling periodical summaries of events and trends in important foreign countries, based largely on Foreign Office telegrams and despatches. Its transfer to the office could therefore be justified as logical,[103] but it also reflected a recognition of the need

[101] Wickham Steed, op. cit. ii. 217–19.

[102] Memorandum by Arthur Ponsonby on interview with Lloyd George, 27 June 1918, Ponsonby MSS. Cf. a letter which Smuts wrote to a friend, 1 June 1918: 'I want no overwhelming victory but a certain measure of military victory is so necessary to ensure the victory of what we all hold dear.' Hancock and Van Der Poel, op. cit. iii, no. 832.

[103] Cf. note by Balfour circulated to the King and War Cabinet, 5 Jan. 1918, G.T. 3547, CAB 24/41.

for expertise in dealing with the foreign political problems of the war and thus, indirectly, with war aims. With the exception of its head, William Tyrrell, all the members of the new department held their positions as specialists on given problems. The assistant head, J. W. Headlam-Morley, had been transferred to the Foreign Office from the Board of Education because of his great knowledge of Germany.[104] Other members included R. W. Seton-Watson (Austria–Hungary), L. B. Namier (Poland and Austria–Hungary), A. J. Toynbee (the Middle East) and Alfred Zimmern (Germany and economic policy). All these men were or were destined to become outstanding figures in British public and intellectual life. In addition, there was a substantial number of other members, such as Professor J. Y. Simpson, a writer on Russia, who worked conscientiously in their particular fields.

The powers of the new department were a source of no little confusion and of anger to those outside it who thought that their own functions were being usurped. In April Eustace Percy, another distinguished member, observed to Tyrrell that British missions abroad were showing signs of restiveness because the Political Intelligence Department was preventing any attention being paid to their views. He wrote a circular letter, which Hardinge agreed to sign, describing the department as 'a permanent, integral part of our organization. ... The primary duty of the new Department is to collect information and to take, to some extent, off the shoulders of the administrative departments the task of keeping up to date, in a readily available form, the knowledge of foreign countries which should exist here.' Information from the overseas missions was more important than ever and suggestions for the improvement of the Department's work would be welcomed.[105]

Problems continued to arise because of the difficulty of writing papers which only gave information and did not make policy recommendations, a difficult and irksome distinction for men with minds as lively as those of the members of the new department. On one occasion Percy was at pains to emphasize that a recent memorandum of his could not be construed as touching upon policy.[106] On another occasion Toynbee 'pleaded guilty' to 'having incidentally

[104] A. J. Toynbee, *Acquaintances* (1967), pp. 161–3.
[105] Percy to Tyrrell, 20 April 1918, and circular letter written by Percy and signed by Hardinge, 5 May 1918, FO 371/4363, no. 74.
[106] Minute, 22 June 1918, FO 371/4360, no. 209.

suggested policy' and promised not to repeat the offence.[107] In practice, this distinction proved impossible to maintain and a procedure was evolved by which members could make policy recommendations. They would submit these to Hardinge or Clerk via Tyrrell who would make such comment as he saw fit.[108] Members thus had a recognized means of influencing policy even though they were only expected to do so 'in very exceptional cases'.[109]

The more outstanding members of the Political Intelligence Department all had pronounced views on the subjects about which they wrote as well as the capacity to present their views persuasively. The most brilliant and the most effective though not the most popular member was undoubtedly Namier. He was responsible for a real change in policy toward Poland—discussed below—whereas it is doubtful whether even so distinguished a man as Professor Seton-Watson brought about any changes in foreign policy which would not have occurred in any case. Namier's writings in the Foreign Office show a none-too-subtle blend of factual information with special pleading and he occasionally made statements which were simply absurd such as that the German aristocracy in Courland and Esthonia had 'poisoned' all aspects of Russian life[110] whereas it would be nearer the truth to say that they were one of the best elements in it. In this he was not different from his fellow intellectuals in government. The only difference was one of effectiveness.

The staff of the new department had one common concern—that Germany should be crushed. The German peace feelers in the early summer produced a frantic reaction. It was claimed that an analysis of the German press showed that even the less extreme newspapers 'look forward to a compromise which will assign to England as regards Germany the position of Austria after 1866 and 1871'.[111] Kühlmann's speech was interpreted as having been made at the orders of Hindenburg and Ludendorff in order to prepare the German people not for peace but for a long continuation of the war. Finally, a bill to broaden the notoriously restrictive Prussian franchise was declared to necessitate greater vigilance in dealing with

---

[107] Toynbee to Tyrrell, 19 Aug. 1918, FO 371/4363, no. 231.

[108] Cf. Clerk to Tyrrell, 26 June 1918, FO 371/4366, no. 299.

[109] Headlam to Tyrrell, 17 July 1918, reference as in note 107.

[110] Memorandum by Namier, 'Remarks on "The Problems of Central and Eastern Europe"', 14 Sept. 1917, FO 371/3016, no. 194676.

[111] Political Intelligence Department memorandum on a 'peace offensive' in the German press, 15 June 1918, FO 371/3436, no. 110382.

German overtures: if it was passed the Kaiser would face less pressure from Pan-German conservatives and so would be freer to put forward peace terms which were dressed as a compromise but really gave Germany all that she desired.[112] In this way some of Britain's leading intellectuals made their small contribution to ensuring that there would be no compromise peace.

By 1918 many of the junior staff of the Foreign Office hoped that the peace conference, when it finally came, would solve all international problems and not those raised by the war only.[113] Such idealism, amounting almost to a desire for a new heaven and a new earth, was reinforced by the establishment of the Political Intelligence Department. At the end of the war Eustace Percy concluded a memorandum on suggested policy toward Africa that it was regrettable that some 'sore spots' such as the Portuguese colonies were too delicate an issue to be dealt with at the peace conference.[114] It might well be thought that with so many other problems before them, the bright young men of the Foreign Office would be pleased that they did not have to concern themselves with the Portuguese colonies!

Such attitudes were not universal within government circles. They were less strong among senior Foreign Office staff and were absent without trace in many departments of state. Charles Strachie, nominated as Colonial Office representative at the peace conference, was infuriated by Percy's proposals for colonial powers in Africa and elsewhere to bind themselves to rule their possessions according to an international code whose implementation would be supervised by an international commission. This was 'unnecessary' and 'fantastic':

If only the authors of these schemes would ask themselves at intervals 'what is the object of the peace conference?' and give themselves the answer 'to make peace' it might help them to discard a mass of projects which may conceivably be desirable but seem to be introduced on the principle that the making of peace is not a sufficient task and that the opportunity should be taken for doing a great many other things as well.[115]

---

[112] Memorandum by ibid. on Kühlmann's resignation, 22 July 1918, and on the Prussian Franchise Bill, 14 July 1918, FO 371/4357, nos. 250 and 247.

[113] Cf. H. Nicolson, *Peacemaking 1919*, pp. 16–17, 31–3, 36–8, 41–2.

[114] Memorandum on colonial policy, undated and unsigned but with covering letter by Percy, 18 Nov. 1918, stating his authorship, C[olonial] O[ffice] 532/18, no. 3437 18/19.   [115] Memorandum by Strachie, 12 Dec. 1918 in ibid.

However, there was much discussion at the highest level of one project which smacked of idealism, the league of nations. The deliberations of the Phillimore committee during the winter were marked by a split between the historians (J. Holland Rose and J. S. Corbett) and the Foreign Office men (Crowe and Tyrrell supported by Phillimore himself) with the latter arguing that conferences of the Powers to settle disputes should act only as mediators and conciliators and above all that there should be no majority voting on recommendations as to terms of settlement. They were prepared to modify this only to the extent of agreeing that recommendations might be made provided that they were supported by all parties except those directly involved in the dispute. Even this much compromise was unfortunate according to Crowe: 'We may be sure that in the hands of the German government, for instance, the manipulation of a conference for the purpose of producing majority reports directed against their enemies, notably against this country, would become a grateful (*sic*) and fairly easy task.'[116]

The Phillimore committee produced interim and final reports in the spring along these lines with, also, the provision that any party to a dispute could apply for the league procedures for its settlement to be waived on the ground that immediate, unilateral action was essential to achieve the reparation or restitution sought.[117] This approach was dictated partly by pure caution, a determination not to compromise Britain's sovereignty as the basis for upholding her international position. Crowe who, rather than Phillimore, dominated the committee, was contemptuous and hostile toward the advice of the many societies and individuals who were campaigning for a league of nations. He dismissed them as wild amateurs and argued that in so far as 'responsible ministers and (their) competent advisers' needed help, '*the* great amateur conference is the British Parliament which has its proper place and functions.'[118] Also important was a belief, held most strongly by Cecil, that international disputes could almost invariably be prevented from leading to war by nothing more than delay during which leaders would have time to cool their heads and international opinion to assert itself to demand peace. Hence, in Cecil's words, 'the real trouble is how are we

[116] Minute by Crowe, 28 Mar. 1918, FO 371/3439, no. 53848.
[117] H. R. Winkler, *The League of Nations Movement in Great Britain 1914–1918* (1952), pp. 236–9 for the terms of this report.
[118] Minute by Crowe, 12 Oct. 1918, FO 371/4365, no. 425.

to secure that disputants *shall* bring their disputes before the council of the nations? For that purpose, according to the Phillimore scheme, coercion is to be employed.'[119]

The committee did in fact recommend much stronger procedures for bringing parties to an arbitration conference than for ensuring acceptance of its proposals. Military and economic sanctions were to be used against any state which refused to attend the conference and instead went to war.

The Phillimore reports were regarded as documents of major importance by both Cecil and Balfour. The former confessed that he would be 'pretty near despair' if nothing could be done along the lines recommended by them while Balfour favoured an immediate conference of the chief allied powers to draw up joint proposals on the league.[120] After the reports had appeared, Eustace Percy assumed responsibility for further work on the league in the Foreign Office under Crowe's supervision.[121] Very little further progress was made before the end of the war. This resulted in large measure from President Wilson's continuing refusal, despite a great deal of pressure from the British, to comment in detail on the Phillimore reports or otherwise to reveal his thoughts on the league question. At the same time he urged the British government not to publish the reports or to encourage public discussion of the league question.

In April 1918, in a letter—whose contents were perhaps meant to reach the highest political quarters in London—to a British editor, Wilson argued that the time had not come to draw up a constitution for the league. This would provoke jealousies among the allies and would otherwise not be desirable since it would obscure the 'essential objects' of a 'mutual guarantee of political independence and territorial integrity and also, as you suggest, of the binding and sacred force of treaty agreements.' The President continued that it was unlikely that the war would make nations unwilling to assume commitments which might lead to renewed war and that he thought that it would convince them of the need for collective security arrangements.[122] This belief may have contributed to Wilson's

---

[119] Cecil to Colonel House, 22 July 1918, FO 371/43,65 no. 259; also in Seymour, iv. 39–42.

[120] Cecil to Wiseman, 17 May 1918, FO 371/3439, no. 92255; and minute by Balfour, early July 1918, ibid. no. 122551.

[121] Cf. minute by Hardinge, 24 July 1918, FO 371/4365, no. 253.

[122] Woodrow Wilson to J. St. Loe Strachey, 5 Apr. 1918, Strachey MSS. Strachey passed this letter to Cecil with permission to show it to Balfour if he was interested but not to anyone else: ibid. Strachey to Cecil, 29 Apr. 1918.

evident conviction that there was no great urgency in discussing the league issue.

In August the President gave William Wiseman a comprehensive explanation of his negative attitude. If he said anything in public on the league it would displease both those who felt that it went too far and those who felt that it did not go far enough. His own ideas were as yet in flux. Publication of the Phillimore report would leave him with no alternative but to issue a statement rejecting it as 'having no teeth', in this way probably reviving the old Anglophobia in the United States. Finally, if a league were set up during the war: 'It would inevitably be regarded as a sort of Holy Alliance aimed at Germany. This would not be the purpose of the American people. Germany should be invited to join the family of nations providing that she will behave according to the rules of the Society.'[123]

The President was intelligently aware of a crucial problem, that of the position of Germany in relation to the league. At the same time that he was outlining his attitude to Wiseman, Percy was writing:

To try to define publicly the position of Germany in connection with the League of Nations is to expose oneself to the choice between a weak overture and a sordid threat. The first weakens the alliance; the second forfeits our leadership of liberal opinion in our country and all over the world. All we can safely or wisely say is that Germany's position will be that to which her character entitles her. . . . At present those who try to think out these things in a practical way live in constant fear of some statement by one or other of His Majesty's Ministers portraying in threatening language the exclusion of Germany from a League—which HMG has as a matter of fact no desire to form or even to think about![124]

The flourish with which Percy concluded his observations was quite unjustified. The leaders did want a league and early in October they agreed that it was a matter of the first importance and urgency to obtain President Wilson's views.[125] Even so it was true that as a result of the American attitude and the problem of policy toward Germany, the British government, as Cecil put it less than a month before the end of the war, still had 'no policy' on the league of nations.[126] What they did have was a collective attitude which the

[123] Wiseman to Reading, 18 Aug. 1918. Balfour MSS., B.M. Add. 49741; incomplete account in Seymour, iv. 51–3.

[124] Minute by Percy, 15 Aug. 1918, FO 371/4365, no. 309.

[125] Record of War Cabinet discussion, 2 Oct. 1918, no. 410 in ibid.

[126] Minute by Cecil, 18 Oct. 1918, no. 446 in ibid.

Phillimore reports had crystallized. This, as Cecil outlined it in a notable speech at Birmingham University on 12 November 1918 was a faith after four years of war against autocratic powers, that if only an international body could 'delay and discuss' conflicts, the force of public opinion would ensure a peaceful settlement.[127]

3. THE WANING OF THE QUEST FOR A SEPARATE PEACE

The spring and summer of 1918 were uneventful in British policy toward the Turkish state though not toward the Arab areas under British occupation for which a new department of state in London, the Middle East Department, was planned, involving 'really founding an administrative department for dealing with a new empire' according to Cecil.[128]

Owing to the collapse of Russia it was difficult not to believe that, whatever else Turkey might yield in return for a separate peace, she would retain the foothold which she had won in the Caucasus and north-west Persia, many of whose peoples were of the same racial stock as the Ottoman Turks, and would embark on a full-scale Pan-Turanian programme designed to establish for herself a new empire in south-east European Russia, Central Asia and Persia.[129] A report in July that Turkey was negotiating with Germany and Austria for the Caucasian railways to be connected with those of Anatolia was seen as strong evidence of Pan-Turanian ambitions in Russia, Persia and ultimately India[130] even though none of Britain's Moslem subjects in India belonged to the Turkish group of peoples. In August 1918, Harold Nicolson, who was then concentrating on work connected with the Middle East, pronounced Pan-Turanism the chief argument against a separate peace with Turkey.[131]

The contribution of the new Political Intelligence Department was likewise dampening to the idea of peace with Turkey. Its Middle East expert, Toynbee, argued that Turkey would not easily abandon her war aims in the Caucasus, Persia and Egypt since they were 'expressions of the corporate interests of Turkish officialdom': the

---

[127] Cf. the remarks which Cecil was making privately on the league of nations about this time. In a letter to St. Loe Strachey on 2 November he referred to 'the central idea of providing for a delay'. To the same correspondent he wrote on 22 November 1918, 'I rely on delay and not on decisions'. Strachey MSS.

[128] Cecil to Balfour, 23 Aug. 1918, Balfour MSS., B.M. Add. 49738. The industrious Cecil was to be head of the new department.   [129] See above, p. 197.

[130] War Trade Intelligence Department to FO, 17 July 1918, FO 371/3381, no. 126065 and minutes in ibid. and in no. 136548.

[131] Memorandum by H. Nicolson, 11 Aug. 1918, Cecil MSS., B.M. Add. 51094.

more territory Turkey ruled the more jobs there would be for members of the official class and their sons. Toynbee added that the information at his disposal indicated that since Brest–Litovsk the Committee of Union and Progress regime had recovered confidence in Germany's ability and willingness to recover Palestine and Mesopotamia for the Turks after achieving a crushing victory in France and that the opposition elements in Turkey were most unreliable. The most important at present was one Shukri who had withdrawn his support from the regime in 1917 when it had dismissed him for embezzling money intended for the education of the orphans of Turkish soldiers killed in battle.[132]

Yet the British were still entirely willing to come to terms with Turkey. Lloyd George suggested buying the Turks out of the war with concessions in the Caucasus[133] while Balfour hinted at acquiescence in Turkey's gains in north-west Persia.[134] At the end of June Rumbold wrote that he had heard rumours that the Entente were prepared to cede Constantinople to Bulgaria and that he would like to know whether this was true since if so it would make it idle for him to have dealings with Turkish peace emissaries. Cecil minuted this letter: 'There is, of course, no truth in the report.' Hardinge assured Rumbold that the peace terms which the British had been prepared to offer Turkey six months previously remained 'precisely the same'.[135]

The Foreign Office, indeed, continued to be prepared to hold out these terms until the armistice with Bulgaria made Turkey's position hopeless though Balfour modified them in August by laying down that Britain should demand the 'independence' of Mesopotamia rather than its full autonomy within the Turkish Empire—a result undoubtedly of the energetic campaign which Hankey waged at the Imperial War Cabinet for British control of the Mesopotamian oil deposits.[136] From the beginning of June Rumbold sent reports of

---

[132] Memorandum on 'The Present Mind in Turkey', 25 May 1918, FO 371/3381, no. 96681.

[133] War Cabinet, 24 June 1918, CAB 23/6. These minutes record a furious outburst by Curzon and it is possible that Lloyd George was being flippant and was indulging his well-known taste for 'baiting' Curzon.

[134] Eastern Committee, 24 June 1918, CAB 27/24.

[135] Rumbold to Hardinge, 28 June 1918, and Hardinge to Rumbold, 6 July 1918, Hardinge MSS. XXXVIII.

[136] Roskill, op. cit. pp. 583, 585–7; Balfour to Beaverbrook, 9 Aug. 1918, FO 800/206; V. H. Rothwell, 'Mesopotamia in British War Aims 1914–1918', *Historical Journal*, xiii (1970), 287–90.

renewed Turkish peace overtures by agents claiming to speak for Talaat and the new Sultan who, in contrast to his feeble-minded predecessor, was said to have ambitions of overthrowing Enver and ruling the country himself. These attracted little interest and less excitement in the office.[137] Apart from fears of Pan-Turanism, there had been too many of these unofficial approaches for them to be taken very seriously and the British had real hopes of making peace with Bulgaria.

The Foreign Office received few peace feelers from opposition elements in Bulgaria during the late autumn and winter of 1917–18 and it avoided involvement in conversations which were known to be taking place between the American chargé in Berne and Shipkoff, a close friend of Tsar Ferdinand.[138] After the shock of Bulgaria's entry into the war in 1915 and the failure of the peace moves of the autumn of 1917, the Foreign Office finally seem to have decided to have nothing more to do with 'Foxy Ferdinand'.

The revival of interest in Bulgaria in the spring of 1918 sprang from two sets of factors. Firstly, two other governments, the War Office as well as the Crewe House Committee which, under Northcliffe's chairmanship, was responsible for propaganda to the enemy countries in Europe, had agents at work in France and Switzerland actively probing for openings for a separate peace with Bulgaria. If anything came of this activity it was clear that the Foreign Office would have to play a part in trying to bring about a successful result. Secondly, the office themselves thought that one of these openings might be important. The men with whom the Crewe House agents dealt were the same as those with whom Gregory had had contact during his two missions the previous year; that is exiled members of the Bulgarian political 'establishment' who retained links with powerful figures still in the country and who claimed to be in a position to carry out a revolution if only the Entente would promise support for Bulgarian war aims. As an added inducement they were now saying that they would welcome a British prince on the Bulgarian throne.[139] After the lesson of the previous year, the Foreign Office did not take these approaches seriously and induced

[137] Cf. Rumbold to FO, 5 June 1918, FO 371/3388, nos. 101107 ff.

[138] Memorandum by Nicolson, 4 Apr. 1918, FO 371/3442, no. 64251.

[139] For the activity of Crewe House agents see FO 371/3148, nos. 124195, 129416 and 132078.

Northcliffe to instruct his chief agent that Bulgaria would have to break off relations with Germany *before* any promise of the type desired could be given. They should also be informed that 'the idea of a British prince for the Bulgarian throne would have no attraction here'.[140]

Balfour had already rejected a suggestion by Northcliffe for a firm line on propaganda in the Balkans promising a greater Bulgaria and compensation to Serbia from Austrian territory by replying that it would be better to concentrate on threatening Bulgaria with the dire punishment that would ensue if she continued in the war.[141] There were many good reasons for this reply: disbelief that the propaganda department's peace probes would yield results; fear that its activities would obstruct the Foreign Office's own strategy for bringing Bulgaria to terms; the danger of alienating Serbia and Greece by such a propaganda line; and, perhaps not least, a suspicion that Northcliffe and Steed in Crewe House and Beaverbrook in the parallel Ministry of Information which conducted propaganda to Turkey, were trying to take a controlling hand in aspects of foreign policy—which was inadmissible as Balfour informed Northcliffe in no uncertain terms.[142]

The War Office agents included Dame Leila Paget who spent most of 1918 in France and Switzerland having a most exhilarating time which caused her husband to complain of the boredom and un-importance of his work at the Copenhagen legation. Ostensibly and in part genuinely, she carried out Red Cross work but she also transmitted to the Director of Military Intelligence reports on Bulgarian matters from other agents who were in actual contact with Bulgarians in Switzerland. Like the men with whom Crewe House had contact these were members of the Bulgarian ruling class.[143] Early in September 1918, a representative of the Bulgarian government, one Gueschoff, asked Lady Paget to act as mediator for a separate peace. She reported this to the War Office but Bulgaria's speedy collapse overtook events.[144] Like so many aspirant peace-

[140] Cf. FO to Rumbold, 9 Aug. 1918, FO 371/3436, no. 13552.

[141] D. Collins, op. cit. pp. 245–7, for an account of this episode.

[142] Balfour to Northcliffe, 9 July 1918, FO 800/212.

[143] Cf. copies of Lady Paget's telegrams to the War Office in the notebook which she kept from April to September 1918, Dame Leila Paget MSS., B.M. Add. 51262.

[144] Cf. memorandum by Lady Paget, 10 Sept. 1918, B.M. Add. 51261. It is not clear whether the man referred to was I. M. Gueschoff, a former prime minister and one of Bulgaria's leading politicians.

makers in the First World War, Lady Paget's moment of glory never came.

The War Office attached more importance to the ideas of a Bulgarian Social Democratic politician, Doctor Bomboloff, who in the spring of 1918 approached the United States legation in Denmark with very detailed and apparently serious plans for a revolution in his country, to be followed by a separate peace. His proposals had novelty for, while he wanted South Dobrudja and European Turkey west and north of the Enos–Midia line to be annexed by Bulgaria, he professed to favour the internationalization of Macedonia rather than its outright annexation as demanded by almost all other Bulgarians who had put forward peace plans. The military attaché at the legation took him to London and the American embassy there put him in touch with the War Office and the Foreign Office, both of whom were very interested by his plans.[145]

Indeed, Bomboloff brought about a change of policy toward Bulgaria. Shortly before the Foreign Office had become aware of him, it had sent instructions to Wiseman to press the United States to declare war on Bulgaria while at the same time issuing a propaganda statement that they had no quarrel with the Bulgarian people.[146] This would most probably have served as a long-term means of wearing down Bulgarian morale. There had been much emigration from Bulgaria to the United States before 1915 with many of the emigrants returning home to buy land with their savings and the United States were held in high esteem. However, it was known in London that there was very little possibility of American forces joining the allied contingents at Salonika.

In mid-June Wiseman's instructions were amended: the United States should be urged at first only to threaten war and then to declare it after an interval of several weeks during which the shock of the American threat might enable Bomboloff and his associates to carry out their revolutionary plans. The office was certainly still reluctant to negotiate with Tsar Ferdinand. At the end of July Balfour told the British minister in Athens that there could be no talks with Bulgaria until Ferdinand had been deposed.[147] They had clearly been unimpressed by his recent action in dismissing his Germanophil Prime Minister, Radoslavoff, and appointing in his

---

[145] Cf. Macdonagh to Hardinge, 8 June 1918, FO 371/3148, no. 102860.
[146] Cecil to Wiseman, 29 May 1918, no. 106735 in ibid.
[147] Balfour to Lord Granville, 30 July 1918, copy in Milner MSS. 108, Box A2.

place Malinoff who had the reputation of being mildly pro-Entente.

House, whom Wiseman asked to convey to the President the British suggestions, was evidently unenthusiastic and did not raise the matter with Wilson until 17 August. The President professed to be willing in principle to declare war on Bulgaria but unable to think of a pretext. He was unwilling to declare war on Turkey because he feared massacres of the Christian population.[148] It may well be, as Lansing had some weeks previously told Reading, that American reluctance to accede to the British suggestions on Bulgaria stemmed from a desire to protect her missionary interests in Turkey, ruling out war with that country. Lansing said that the United States 'could not declare war against Bulgaria, a Christian country, without also including Turkey, a Moslem Power'.[149] The problem of the Christian missions did in fact rule out an American declaration of war on Turkey though Wiseman reported that the President, if not his Secretary of State, was open to persuasion on the merits of declaring war on Bulgaria.[150]

During the last summer of the war, the British pinned almost all of such hopes as remained of a separate peace upon Bulgaria. Balfour wanted the United States to declare war on Turkey immediately as a means of making the threat of war on Bulgaria more vivid rather than as an act of policy toward Turkey itself.[151] The Foreign Secretary even thought of offering Constantinople to Bulgaria 'as compensation for the surrender of territory elsewhere to Serbia and Greece'. Hardinge, in an argument which Balfour evidently found convincing, opposed this not because of the Turks but because the Greeks had aspirations of their own to possess the city and would never willingly consent to its absorption by their traditional enemies, the Bulgarians. He suggested that instead Bulgaria should be offered the Rodosto–Midia line in European Turkey.[152] The significance of this was that previously the Foreign Office had usually thought of giving Bulgaria the Enos–Midia line at Turkey's expense. The new line would give Bulgaria most of the remainder of European Turkey except Constantinople itself. When information was received of a

---

[148] V. S. Mamatey, 'The United States and Bulgaria in World War I' in *The American Slavic and East European Review*, xii (1953), 236–57, especially p. 251.

[149] Reading to FO, 6 May 1918, FO 371/4363, no. 104.

[150] Evans, op. cit. pp. 36–42; Wiseman to Drummond, 28 Aug. 1918, FO 800/225. Wiseman described Wilson's solicitude for the Christian missions in Turkey as 'curious'.

[151] Balfour to Wiseman, 27 July 1918, FO 371/3148, no. 131129.

[152] Hardinge to Balfour, 31 July 1918, no. 132078 in ibid.

serious quarrel between Bulgaria and Turkey in which the latter demanded the return of the districts ceded to Bulgaria in 1915 as compensation for Bulgarian acquisitions from Rumania in the treaty of Bucharest, the Political Intelligence Department suggested an attempt to woo the Bulgarians by offering them allied support to keep the gains of both 1915 and March 1918 and also to advance their frontier with Turkey to the Enos–Midia line.[153] This was recommended in preference to utilizing Turkish discontent on this and other issues.[154] However, it must be repeated that peace with Turkey was still acceptable in principle and that the chief reason for the concentration of hopes on Bulgaria was simply that moves from that quarter seemed more promising.

Balfour took a personal interest in Bulgaria policy at this time. He was prepared to agree to extensive territorial concessions to her and favoured a United States declaration of war as the only means of convincing her that the allies would win the war[155] though he was, as always, more concerned than most of his colleagues and staff with the need not to alienate the allies whose interests would be affected by a separate peace with an enemy power—in this case Serbia and Greece.[156] An added complication for British policy was that no help could be expected from the French in putting pressure on the Americans. When allied leaders met at the Supreme War Council early in July, the French opposed Cecil's call for an attempt at a negotiated peace with Bulgaria and Foreign Minister Pichon described her as an inveterate aggressor who could only be taught the ways of peace by a crushing military defeat.[157] The expeditionary force at Salonika had been inactive for years and the French were determined to use it in major operations as quickly as possible.

Until the sudden Bulgarian collapse in late September, Balfour continued to put pressure on the United States to accept the policy which the British favoured though without trying to hurry them or to depict the matter as one of very great importance.[158] While this

[153] Political Intelligence Department memorandum, 28 Aug. 1918, G.T. 5606, CAB 24/63.
[154] For these see *Eastern Report*, LXVIII, 16 May 1918, CAB 24/145; and Political Intelligence Department memorandum, 4 Oct. 1918, G.T. 5908, CAB 24/66.
[155] War Cabinet, 11 June 1918, CAB 23/14; and Supreme War Council, 4 July 1918, CAB 24/4 I.C. 70.
[156] War Cabinet, 9 July 1918, CAB 23/41; and Imperial War Cabinet minutes for 13 Aug. 1918 in both CAB 23/42 and 43.
[157] Supreme War Council, 11 July 1918, CAB 25/122, no. 274.
[158] Mamatey, 'United States and Bulgaria', pp. 251–2; Seymour, iv. 57–8.

episode in Anglo–American diplomacy was taking place, there was much discussion within the Foreign Office of peace arrangements in the Balkans. It was still thought that the national characteristics of the Bulgarians were somehow such that they would always be the strongest power there, and that Bomboloff's proposals for the internationalization of Macedonia were therefore to be favoured as the only alternative to a Bulgarian conquest of the disputed territory at some future date. Harold Nicolson expressed this conviction and continued:

> Bulgaria being the only strong power in the Balkans any solution which will leave her unsatisfied but still dominant will entail the indefinite maintenance of our 'protectorate' of Greece and Serbia, will thereby perpetuate Bulgarian and Turkish dependence on the Central Powers and thus render the Near East infinitely more inflammable than before the war.

Cecil agreed:

> It is as hopeless to try to settle the Balkan question according to Balkan ideas as it is to settle Ireland according to Irish ideas. The only chance is for some intelligent outsider—preferably England—to decide what is a just and reasonable settlement and enforce it. I am myself disposed to agree with Mr. Nicolson.[159]

Cecil's faith in British sagacity was such that he really would, no doubt, have preferred British solutions for all international problems. However, there was wide recognition by the middle of 1918 that peace arrangements would be far more durable if the United States played a part in both framing and upholding them—a recognition which was by no means wholly reluctant. It was Cecil himself who told the United States ambassador that America's role in the peace conference would be of

> decisive importance and that in no field of international controversy will this role be of more value than in the Near and Middle East. So long as America abstains from declaring war against the common enemy in these regions, inference will certainly be drawn by friends and foes alike that she means the various phases of the Eastern Question which must come up at the peace conference to be settled without her intervention. H.M.G. would regard this as a great misfortune.[160]

[159] Minutes by Nicolson, 5 July 1918, and Cecil, no date, FO 371/3148, no. 117931.
[160] Cf. FO to Reading, 18 May 1918, FO 371/4363, no. 104. This telegram, which gives the substance of a note from the Foreign Office to the United States embassy, is unsigned but Cecil identified it as his work in Cecil to Wiseman, 29 May 1918, FO 800/222. There is a paraphrase of this telegram in Evans, *United States Policy and the Partition of Turkey*, p. 41 n., where authorship is incorrectly ascribed to Balfour.

This early attempt to involve the United States in the Balkans failed, and what remains most striking in British Balkan policy is her support for at least some Bulgarian aspirations until the very moment that her collapse took the matter at least temporarily out of British hands. As late as 27 September 1918, Drummond suggested that Bulgaria should be given the Uncontested Zone in Macedonia: 'To insist on Bulgaria abandoning what may be termed her legitimate national aspirations would mean that Balkan unity could never be obtained.'[161]

Foreign Office hopes in the case of Bulgaria contrasted with its attitude toward Austria–Hungary. The break-down of Kerr's mission in March, the early German successes in their offensive in France shortly afterwards which naturally heartened the Austrians, and an exchange of insults between Clemenceau and Czernin in April as to the authenticity of Karl's letter to Sixte of 24 March 1917 which the Austrian Foreign Minister foolishly tried to deny all did their work. The publication of Karl's letter led Balfour to conclude: 'The French have now destroyed any chance of allied mediation with the Austrian Emperor.'[162] Czernin now resigned while Karl moved closer to Berlin to try to restore the damage done by his Alsace-Lorraine comment in the letter to Sixte.

Yet old attitudes died hard. A report that the Vatican was very anxious that Austria should be preserved led Hardinge to observe: 'We also would like a strong and independent Austria as a barrier to Germany but this is only feasible as a federated empire in which the Slav states enjoy complete autonomy.'[163] An Austro–German military pact for closer collaboration the following month finally convinced the Permanent Under-Secretary: 'All our attempts to detach Austria have come to nought. The meeting of the two Emperors seems to have resulted in a further tightening of the German bonds and we must now face the prospect of fighting it out, while doing all we can to encourage the subject races to revolt against the German–Magyar domination.'[164]

Lloyd George was even more reluctant to face reality. In the draft of a speech which he was to make at Edinburgh on 24 May 1918 he

[161] Minute in FO 800/200.
[162] Minute by Balfour, *c.* 13 Apr. 1918, FO 371/3134, no. 65250.
[163] Minute by Hardinge, 18 Apr. 1918, no. 68566 in ibid.
[164] Lord Hardinge to Rumbold and to Arthur Hardinge, 23 May 1918, Hardinge MSS. XXXVII.

wrote that Austria had become a complete German satellite and was therefore beyond redemption. Yet in the speech itself this passage was excluded, indicating that he wanted to keep the door open for any moves from Vienna.[165] About a month later Hankey, who had been closely associated with the Prime Minister's active Austria policy of 1917, urged him to make a pro-Austria statement in one of his speeches, offering terms if she would end her 'humiliating' dependence on Germany.[166] Lloyd George himself denounced Clemenceau's 'extreme folly' in publishing Karl's letter.[167] In the Imperial War Cabinet's discussions on military policy Lloyd George spoke in favour of a concentration of efforts in Italy.[168] Presumably he still hoped to detach Austria by combined diplomatic and military pressure but he was aware that he was swimming against the tide and he assumed a passive attitude toward policy in eastern Europe during the crucial middle months of 1918.

About the middle of May Balfour informed the British envoy in Washington, Lord Reading, of a change in Austria policy:

Policy of trying to detach Austria from Germany *at present time* seems to us both inopportune and impracticable. Recent meeting of Emperors obviously led to bonds between the two empires being tightened. We think the best plan is to give all possible support to oppressed nationalities in Austria in their struggle against German–Magyar domination . . . *Austria may thus be reduced to a reasonable frame of mind.*[169]

The change in British east European policy was thus based on expediency and not on ideological conviction. Yet there was now a situation in which the Monarchy's opponents, who were by this time in official positions in Crewe House and in the Political Intelligence Department, found most of their political superiors ready to listen to them. They were aided by two extraneous factors. The first was a partial reconciliation between the Yugoslavs and the Italians. With Steed acting as midwife, the Croat leader, Trumbic, and Doctor Andrea Torre, the representative of a powerful group of liberals in Italian public life, signed a pact in London on 9 March 1918 promising reciprocal support for Italian and Yugoslav unity.

[165] Lloyd George's notes for his speech at Edinburgh, Lloyd George MSS. F/235; cf. report of his speech in *The Times*, 25 May 1918.
[166] Hankey to Lloyd George, 22 June 1918, Lloyd George MSS. F/23/2/42.
[167] Journals, 26–7 June 1918, 50905.
[168] Imperial War Cabinet, 31 July and 1 Aug. 1918, CAB 23/44.
[169] Balfour to Reading, 21 May 1918, FO 800/222. My italics.

The Italian government was in no way bound by this but it consented to the holding in Rome the next month of a 'Congress of Oppressed Peoples' of Austria–Hungary and it was widely believed that Orlando was only prevented from endorsing its call for the complete break up of the Monarchy on national lines by the opposition of Sonnino. After this conference there was a continuing split in the Italian government between those, led by Sonnino, whose opposition to the Yugoslavs was inveterate and those, believed to include Orlando, who favoured accommodation which necessarily implied the limitation of Italian territorial aims. The Austria specialists in the Political Intelligence Department and indeed those in the Rome embassy who shared their views naturally called for the British government to support the Italian liberals, arguing that this would strengthen their hands decisively.[170]

Still more important was the prospect that the subject races or rather the Czechs alone might afford really significant military assistance to the allies. The most important elements in this respect were the celebrated Czech legions of former Austrian prisoners in Russia whom the Entente hoped to use, together with the Japanese, to keep the Central Powers out of Siberia and to provide a focal point for those in Russia who are variously described in the official British documents of the time as 'patriotic', 'decent' and 'loyal'. The fate of the Czechs in Siberia was out of the hands of the British but there were many Czechs and other Slav prisoners in Italian camps as well as large numbers of Czechs in the Anglo–Saxon countries and in France. British officers had a high opinion of these men. One staff officer wrote: 'Although the Czechs in the British Armies are comparatively few in number, they afford material of uncommonly high standard. So that all questions referring to them are well worthy of solution.'[171] Steed and the great Czech leader, Benes, played upon this point for all that it was worth, arguing to every politician and officer who would listen that if only the British and French governments would agree upon a definite policy of supporting the subject races, the Austro–Hungarian army would virtually dissolve.[172] It

---

[170] Political Intelligence Department memorandum on Baron Sonnino, 3 July 1918, FO 371/4363, no. 214; Erskine (chargé at Rome) to FO, 20 July 1918, copy in Milner MSS. 108, Box A3.

[171] Memorandum by N. I. Thisch, General Staff, on 'Czechs in the British Army: Why They Are Dissatisfied', 25 June 1918, WO 106/678.

[172] Cf. memorandum by Lt.-Col. Stanhope on conversations with Mr. Stead (*sic*) and Dr. Benish (*sic*), 22 Apr. 1918, G.T. 4414, CAB 24/50; Wickham Steed to Lloyd George, 30 May 1918, Lloyd George MSS. F/41/8/15.

was fortunate for them that Delmé Radcliffe, chief of the British military mission with the Italian army and an acquaintance of Steed, supported this line strongly.[173]

Some time in April 1918 a policy decision was taken in the Foreign Office to give official encouragement to the Czech National Council and the various Czech armed forces. Action was only delayed while an attempt was made to gain American support for a declaration and when this proved not to be forthcoming, it was decided to act alone.[174] The British action took the form of a letter to Benes which, in essence, gave the Czechs the same very limited measure of recognition that had been accorded the Polish National Council the previous October—a measure of recognition already accorded the Czechs by France and Italy. The British government now recognized the Czecho–Slovak *movement* in allied countries and the Czech armed forces as a single unit operating on the allied side.[175] Cecil circulated this to the War Cabinet with a covering note stating that the letter had been drawn up in such a way that it 'will not commit us to any increased war obligation'.[176] Thus assured, the War Cabinet approved the letter on 27 May. At that time predominant opinion in the office was that Britain should go no further in recognizing Czech nationalism.[177] At an Anglo–French conference in London on 28 May Lloyd George and Cecil joined to oppose a suggestion by Pichon that the independence of Poland and Bohemia should be proclaimed allied war aims. 'All thought of a separate peace with Austria was over', declared the French Foreign Minister, adding that the allies 'should use every means to make difficulties for the Austrian government. They should support the Slavs and non-Austrian or non-Magyar elements in the Empire.' This moved the Prime Minister to a quite eloquent outburst:

The allies must not give pledges that they could not realize. To raise hopes that could not be fulfilled was to turn these small nations into our deadly enemies, he instanced the rancour of the Boers against the Germans after the Boer War as an example. We must be very careful not to make

[173] Delmé Radcliffe to Macdonagh, 22 and 24 June 1918 in WO 106/824 and 825 respectively. On propaganda to the Austro–Hungarian army on the Italian front from March 1918 see A. J. May, op. cit. ii. 607–9.

[174] Cf. minutes on a report by Col. B. Granville-Baker, 30 Apr. 1918, FO 371/3135, no. 8216 and minutes by Clerk and Cecil, 20 May 1918, no. 89425 in ibid.

[175] Draft of letter in ibid.

[176] Note by Cecil, 23 May 1918, G.T. 4647, CAB 24/52.

[177] Cf. minutes by Hardinge, Cecil and Nicolson, FO 371/3135 no. 90542.

use of these peoples and expose them to all the horrors of retribution and yet fail to carry out what they wanted. . . . We would try to free them but we could not say that the independence of Poland and Bohemia was one of our war aims.[178]

A few days later at the Supreme War Council, the French resumed their advocacy of 'liberation' in eastern Europe; Clemenceau sent a message that if there were Czech troops fighting on the West Front, knowledge of this would produce a revolution in Prague.[179] The British had no need to be vocal on this occasion since Sonnino absolutely vetoed any declaration of support for the Yugoslavs' independence and it was felt that this ruled out a declaration on behalf of the Czechs. Hence the declaration on policy in eastern Europe which the conference issued on 3 June called for the independence only of the Poles and in the case of the Czechs and Yugoslavs merely associated the Entente Powers with a recent statement by Lansing that the United States felt 'earnest sympathy' with their national aspirations.

According to Steed, Balfour was distressed by the Italian attitude on this occasion.[180] His views on policy in eastern Europe were certainly undergoing a change in the direction of support for a policy of 'liberation'. One reason for this was clearly the eclipse of hopes of peace with Austria and the new opportunities for making military use of the subject races. He was attracted by a plan put before the British government by Drummond's friend, Count Horodyski, for simultaneous risings by the subject races of eastern Europe. He thought that if the Polish and Czech National Councils would co-operate a great deal might be achieved.[181]

Another consideration was a change in American policy. At the end of May President Wilson told Wiseman that Clemenceau's action in the affair of Karl's letter was:

A thousand pities. . . . Now we had no chance of making a separate peace with Austria and must look to the other way—the way which he disliked most intensely—of the Austrian people against their own government by plot and intrigue. We were not good at the work and generally

[178] Conference minutes in CAB 28/3 I.C. 62–3.

[179] Supreme War Council, 3 June 1918, CAB 28/4 I.C. 66. At this time the French were pressing for the transportation of the Czech legions in Siberia to the Western Front. The British argued very strongly that they would be much more usefully employed in Siberia. [180] Wickham Steed, op. cit. ii. 214.

[181] Balfour to Derby, 13 June 1918, Balfour MSS., B.M. Add. 49743; memorandum by Drummond, 8 June 1918, Drummond MSS. FO 800/329.

made a failure of it but he saw no other way. He intended to support the Czechs, Poles and Jugo-Slavs.[182]

This was a complete reversal of American policy and it apparently left the President almost lachrymose. However, it was not long before he became a genuine convert to the cause of dismembering the Monarchy.[183]

These two developments are alone probably enough to account for the change in Balfour's attitude. It is also possible that he underwent a real change in intellectual conviction comparable with his conversion to Zionism. In a speech to the Dominion Prime Ministers in August he expressed full support for the break up of the Monarchy because of the rise of nationalism among the subject peoples and in view of the mathematical equation that it was better that Germany should be augmented by the addition of the eleven million Germans of Austria (non-Prussian and therefore peace-loving to boot!) than that it should have an appendage empire of 51 millions.[184] Writing to Amery, the Foreign Secretary gave another reason, that peace arrangements in eastern Europe would be vital for the peace of the world during the next fifty years. This seemed to imply that it would even be worthwhile to continue the war for the specific purpose of securing peace arrangements there which were, from a long-term point of view, desirable, rather than accepting a compromise of any sort.[185]

At all events the British were to find that once they had embarked on a policy of declaring support for the subject races it was difficult to turn back. During June 1918 the word 'depressed' often occurs in Foreign Office minutes on the reaction of the Czechs and Yugo-slavs to the tepid allied declaration of 3 June. The feeling grew that they must be more strongly encouraged unless the allies were to lose their support *and* all chance of coming to terms with Vienna. It was hoped that a speech which Pichon was to make at the end of June when presenting colours to the Czech forces in France would redress the balance and when he did not act upon a suggestion by Balfour, who had been sent an advance copy of the speech, that he should

[182] Wiseman to Drummond, 31 May 1918, FO 371/3443, no. 101715.
[183] Mamatey, *The United States and East-Central Europe*, pp. 333-4.
[184] Imperial War Cabinet, 13 Aug. 1918, reference as in note 156 above; three months later Balfour strongly reaffirmed this argument in a letter for the King, Balfour to Lord Stamfordham, 11 Nov. 1918, FO 800/200.
[185] Balfour to Amery, no date but Aug. 1918, FO 800/207.

mention the Yugoslavs as well as the Czechs he sent the French Foreign Minister a telegram of congratulations, 'rejoicing' that alongside the allies there were 'not merely Czecho-Slovaks but Jugo-Slavs and Poles bravely fighting in the cause of freedom'.[186] Shortly before this, on 28 June, Lansing had issued a new declaration in which the United States announced unreserved support for the complete independence of all the Slav peoples. This fact must undoubtedly have weighed heavily in Balfour's mind.

In mid-July, Benes requested British recognition of the Czech National Council as the government of an independent state, arguing that the contribution which the Czech legions in Siberia were making to the allied cause warranted granting them favourable treatment in this way and that the prospect of such a reward might spur the Poles and Yugoslavs to make similar military exertions. Much doubt was felt about the wisdom of putting the Czechs in a favoured position and even Namier opposed it on the grounds that when Bohemia truly became independent a regime might come to power which repudiated the National Council. Cecil supported Benes' request for the humanitarian reason that it might deter the Austrians from executing Czech prisoners who had deserted from the Austrian army.[187]

Whatever the precise weight given to political and humane considerations, a document of recognition was drawn up based on a Czech text which was only slightly watered down. The Czecho-Slovaks were recognized as an allied nation and their three armies in France, Italy and Siberia as one force waging regular warfare against the Central Powers and under the supreme authority of the National Council. Cecil favoured official endorsement of this formula.[188] The National Council was thus not explicitly recognized as a government but this was chiefly the result not of British reluctance but of a wish to avoid complications with the Poles and Yugoslavs and with Italy.[189] A declaration was issued on 9 August. Steed claimed to have smoothed over final difficulties between the Foreign Office and the Czechs who wanted their council to be recognized as 'the basis of' the future government of Czechoslovakia

[186] For this paragraph see FO 371/3135, nos. 111985 and 115851.
[187] Letter from Benes to Steed, 16 July 1918, and the numerous minutes in ibid. no. 127473.
[188] Text of Czech and British draft declarations and minute by Cecil, late July 1918, in ibid. no. 132422.
[189] Cf. minutes by Drummond, 30 July 1918, and by Balfour, no. 135132 in ibid.

by substituting the words 'as trustee for' which the office found more palatable.[190]

As the war moved toward the phase of enemy collapse, the British had gone far to meet the national wishes of one of the two major groups of underprivileged peoples in Austria–Hungary. However, this process had only been partial and most British leaders would probably have agreed with Cecil that it was reversible. Early in September he minuted: 'Our recognition of the Czechs was very carefully worded and though it would undoubtedly be consistent with the dismemberment of Austria it does not in fact bind us to that solution.' At the same time he was opposing the grant to the Yugoslavs of the same measure of recognition as that extended to the Czechs not only because of the attitude of Italy but also because, according to him, they were at a 'lower stage' of social development than the Czechs.[191]

Cecil had lost none of his disdain for small Slav nations. He still wanted Austria–Hungary to become a federation and to suffer no losses except that of Trentino with Italy having economic rights (which were in fact of no interest to her) in Trieste. He hoped that she would come to the conference table before final collapse so that the allies would then have a chance of preserving her along these lines.[192] These views had become unfashionable by the summer of 1918 but they were, in their own way, as doctrinaire as those of Wickham Steed and they emphasize what a fund of good-will the Dual Monarchy would have been able to draw upon if it had seriously sought a separate peace.

Whereas the Czechs and in lesser degree the Yugoslavs made gains in their relations with the allied governments in the spring and summer of 1918, the Poles virtually stood still after their advances of the previous winter.[193] The declaration at Versailles on 3 June in favour of an independent Poland with access to the sea hardly added to what had already been said especially in the light of the fact that Balfour assured the Italians, who were unwilling to accept the formula on access to the sea, that this did not necessarily mean

---

[190] Wickham Steed, op. cit. ii. 231–3. There is no reason to doubt this assertion though I have seen no reference to it in contemporary documents.

[191] Minute by Cecil, no date, FO 371/3136, no. 152102; and memorandum on interview with the French ambassador, 9 Sept. 1918, FO 371/3137, no. 15848.

[192] Memorandum, 7 Aug. 1918, Cecil MSS., B.M. Add. 51105.

[193] See above, pp. 157–8.

possession of a seaboard and might only mean rights such as Germany possessed on the Rhine in the Netherlands.[194] Yet the Versailles declaration convinced Hardinge, 'We have really gone as far as we reasonably can in helping the Poles.'[195] The one real gain for the cause of an independent Poland was that the virtual loss of hope for a separate peace with Austria had the effect of discrediting the 'Austrian solution' of the Polish problem. But this, as Clerk astutely pointed out, was of benefit to the Czechs and Yugoslavs rather than the Poles who had received such favourable treatment from Vienna as hardly to qualify as a subject people. 'The Austrian solution', he wrote, 'in realit7 means the Poles making a bargain with the Austrian government at the expense of the Czechs and Jugo-Slavs. It is that tendency which, as it is, prevents the full effect of the actual moral collapse of the Austrian administration.' Hardinge, who had favoured the 'Austrian solution' in January, added quietly, 'The Austrian solution is not ours'.[196]

On the British side, this lack of progress was owing in no small measure to a crisis of confidence as to whether they were supporting the right elements among the Poles. The political situation in Poland in 1918 was complicated. Following their promise to restore Russian Poland as an independent kingdom in 1916, the Central Powers set up native legislative and executive bodies, known respectively as the Council of State and the Regency Council, with limited but real powers and in April 1918 held elections for the Council of State which, rather astonishingly, seem to have been free. The party of pro-German Poles won only eight seats out of fifty-two while thirty-seven went to an Inter-Party Union of right-wing parties whose policy was, in effect, that they would not co-operate with the occupiers so long as there was hope that Germany might lose the war. The socialists boycotted the elections and, by adding almost as many nominated members to the legislature as there were elected ones, the Germans were able to obtain a Regency Council largely favourable to themselves.[197] However, the Regency Council thus formed was not a puppet and when, in May, it suggested,

[194] Memorandum by Balfour on interview with the Italian ambassador, 13 Mar. 1918, FO 371/3277, no. 46350.
[195] Undated minute, FO 371/3278, no. 10851.
[196] Minutes by Clerk, 23 July 1918, and Hardinge, no date, FO 371/3281, no. 135129.
[197] This account of developments in Poland is based largely on a memorandum by Namier, 23 Apr. 1918, FO 371/3278, no. 84, and a minute by the same author, 16 Sept. 1918, no. 154236 in ibid.

presumably through its agents in Switzerland, that it should appoint an official emissary in London the idea was only rejected by the Foreign Office after much thought and was not considered at all ridiculous.[198]

The office's dealings had always been with the right-wing Poles whose most outstanding figure was Roman Dmowski, who had set up the Polish National Council in exile in 1917 and who had links with some members of the Council of State within Poland. Once the Political Intelligence Department had been set up, Namier was in a much better position than before to expound his very decided views on these men: that they were liars and rogues whose sole policies were anti-semitism, an imperialist desire for expansion to the east into territory where the only Poles were a small minority of land-owners, and personal enrichment. Namier was concerned above all with the immorality, indeed criminality as he saw it, of these men. His argument to British policy-makers was that if they ruled Poland they would pursue a policy of expansion in the Ukraine and Byelorussia which would sooner or later lead them into alliance with Germany. He tried to give those around him some conception of the economic and social basis underlying foreign policy in a part of the world about which they knew little. To prove the point that the race of their landlords was a matter of indifference to east European peasants he quoted a rhyme sung in some districts of Posnania by German colonists:

> Michel sagt zu seinem Sohne:
> Hol' der Teufel die Barone,
> Ob die Deutsche oder Polen,
> Soll sie all' der Teufel holen.[199]

Namier's method was to combine an almost awe-inspiring knowledge of the human geography and politics of the three parts of Poland with occasional incisive recommendations such as that financial aid to the Polish National Council should be stopped. A clumsy attempt by the council to forge a Russian–German treaty in the spring of 1918 in which Poland was depicted as the victim of these two great powers with the Polish socialists acting as their agents provided Namier with a field-day and gives a good illustration of his technique. Having shown by textual analysis that the 'treaty'

---

[198] Cf. ibid. nos. 9813 and 10851.
[199] See ibid. no. 148264.

was a forgery, he was moved to mirth when the Poles produced an 'improved' version: 'To defend the authenticity of both would be like the ready-witted apologist who, at the time of the Reformation, defended the genuineness of two skulls attributed to the same saint by saying that the smaller was his skull as a child and the other his skull when he was grown up.'[200]

The Dmowski Poles were well aware of who Namier was and of what he was doing and their campaign against him was conducted on a bitter personal level. He accused them of inciting the extreme right-wing *Morning Post* against him and of publishing his real name (Bernstein) and the address of his family in Galicia in one of their newspapers for the information of the Austrian police.[201]

Namier's views were so extreme as to be automatically suspect but they were argued so well that they could not be dismissed. Many in the Foreign Office began to wonder whether they should, as he suggested, support the temporarily submerged radical and socialist elements in Poland and even whether the Poles were the kind of people who were worth supporting at all. By July 1918, Hardinge, Cecil and Tyrrell had come to the conclusion that all Poles were, not to put too fine a point upon the matter, inveterate liars.[202] One particularly distasteful feature of the Polish National Council was its anti-semitism. In 1918 there were reports that it was trying systematically to oust Jewish officers from the Polish forces in France including those who had accepted baptism as Christians.[203] The Board of Deputies of British Jews made incessant demands to the Foreign Office for it to extract assurances from the Polish National Council that in the Poland of the future Jews would not be treated as second-class citizens and Cecil for one felt that, owing to the world-wide importance of the Jews, it was more important to be on good terms with them than with the Polish National Council.[204] By August he had lost all faith in what he called 'the reactionary Polish elements'.[205]

The appointment of a British officer, Captain Leveson-Gower, to the Paris embassy in June 1918 to maintain liaison with the Polish

---

[200] Minute by Namier, 1 July 1918, FO 371/3281, no. 92306; cf. minutes by Balfour and Hardinge, *c.* 4 May 1918, no. 74548 in ibid., praising Namier's work.

[201] Namier to Tyrrell, 15 May 1918, FO 371/4363, no. 137.

[202] Minutes in FO 371/3281, nos. 135129 and 140466.

[203] Cf. FO 371/3277, no. 146278.

[204] Minute by Cecil, late Mar. 1918, FO 371/3280, no. 47304. See this jacket and no. 166791 for the pressure of Jewish organizations on the British government.

[205] Minute, 15 Aug. 1918 in ibid. no. 148973.

16

National Council and, in effect, to make sure that they spent the subsidies which they received on political work and not on providing themselves with a high standard of living[206] was a victory for Namier. A much more crucial point arose in October at a time when it was certain that there would soon be an independent Polish state. The British government had decided to recognize the Polish army on the Western Front as a co-belligerent army following a similar action by France and it was felt that this must be combined with a more general statement of policy toward Poland. Recognition of the National Council as the government of that country was advocated by J. D. Gregory who maintained daily contact with its London office and who was perhaps the one man in the Foreign Office who had been left completely unmoved by Namier's influence. Gregory conceded that a feeling had arisen that the British had 'backed the wrong horse' in supporting the council. This, however, was mistaken. The council represented the great mass of Polish opinion and opposition to it came only from 'Jews, Bolshevists and from partisans of a more or less pro-Central Powers solution of the Polish Question.'[207]

Eric Drummond who, despite all his other duties, never lost interest in policy toward Poland, had likewise not changed his views but he had come to respect Namier, whose dismissal from government service or transfer to non-political work he had recommended a number of times in the past, and laid down that Gregory's draft statement should be sent to Namier before Balfour saw it so that 'the Secretary of State may come to a decision after hearing both parties'.[208] Namier, in his advice to Balfour, recognized that the National Council would have to be acknowledged as the supreme authority over the Polish army in France since there was no other body which could fulfil this role but argued that recognition should only be provisional and should not involve a commitment that the council was the legitimate government of Poland.[209] Balfour used Gregory's text as the basis for the letter which he sent to Count Sobanski on 11 October but drafted a crucial last paragraph which accorded with Namier's advice. The British government 'looks forward to a time when the present provisional arrangements will come

---

[206] Cf. minutes in FO 371/3277, nos. 102644 ff.
[207] Minute by Gregory, 6 Oct. 1918, FO 371/3280, no. 167666.
[208] Drummond to Ronald Graham, 7 Oct. 1918 in ibid.
[209] Namier to Tyrrell, 9 Oct. 1918 in ibid.

to an end; and a Poland free and united will shape its own constitution according to the wishes of its people.'[210]

It is obviously true that the extent to which political developments in Poland could be influenced by letters dictated in the British Foreign Office was limited. Even so, Namier's achievement was considerable. British policy on which elements to support in Poland had been reversed despite the advice of the Foreign Office's two chief, professional Poland experts, Gregory and the powerful Drummond. At the time of the armistices Esmé Howard, the British minister in Stockholm, visited London and noted with surprise a change in attitude toward the Polish National Council in official circles so that it was now generally regarded as undemocratic and preoccupied with imposing Polish rule on non-Poles.[211] This change was undoubtedly largely Namier's work. Considering that he had been in the Foreign Office less than a year the results which he had achieved were remarkable.

[210] This letter can be seen at various stages of drafting in ibid.
[211] E. Howard, *The Theatre of Life* (1936), ii. 649–52.

VI

THE ARMISTICES, SEPTEMBER–
NOVEMBER 1918

1. THE LESSER ENEMY POWERS

IN September 1918 the Salonika expeditionary force, with the grudging assent of the British government, at last began major offensive operations. After only a few days of fighting Bulgaria decided to seek an armistice. It is said that she only delayed doing so in order to have time to force Germany, Austria and Turkey to cede to her their rights in the northern Dobrudja, an important piece of Rumanian territory including the mouths of the Danube, which had been made a condominium of the four victorious powers in the treaty of Bucharest. All of them had aspirations there and they had been unable to agree on its fate. Having gained the assent of their allies on this point, the Bulgarian government then immediately informed them that it was suing for an armistice on the grounds that the military aid which they were supplying was insufficient. At first the Bulgarian emissaries approached the commander of the British forces, General Milne, who, in accordance with normal etiquette, referred them to General Franchet d'Esperey as supreme commander in the Macedonian theatre. After very brief negotiations, Franchet, on 29 September, signed an armistice on highly satisfactory terms which allowed the allies to make whatever use they wished of Bulgarian territory for operations against the Central Powers or Turkey.

Bulgaria's sudden surrender—for such it virtually was—took all other belligerents by surprise. The initial reaction of the War Cabinet when Milne reported that he had been approached was not to take the Bulgarian overtures seriously and to hope that the current offensive in the Balkans would not be halted because of them. Lord Milner, who was bedridden at the time, wrote to his colleagues, begging them to make a serious attempt to conclude peace with Bulgaria. Always ready to be generous to the lesser enemies where British interests were not affected, Milner favoured offering Bulgaria

Adrianople and the Enos–Midia line at Turkey's expense if she would actually change sides in the war but felt that she could no longer be allowed to claim Greek or Serbian territory.[1]

As usual, it is difficult to trace Milner's exact influence on foreign policy. It may have been responsible for the sending of instructions the next day to the British ambassador in Paris that the French government should be urged to prolong the armistice talks even if the Bulgarians proved uncooperative and to agree to a full-scale peace conference with Bulgaria if she demanded one. A prior Entente conference would settle the terms which could be offered and which must not 'violate the legitimate claims of our Balkan allies'.[2]

Franchet's swift conclusion of an armistice irritated the British because he had failed to consult Milne while the French found a source of grievance in the attempts of the Bulgarian government and the United States minister in Sofia to induce President Wilson to mediate between Bulgaria and the Entente.[3] Balfour tried to soothe the feelings of both parties, arguing to his colleagues that France's exclusive role in the armistice was unimportant as it need have no bearing on the final peace terms with Bulgaria and that the French should be informed that the British government did not wish to pick a quarrel with the United States on Bulgaria policy or any other issue. The War Cabinet agreed to send a message to the French government along these lines.[4] Balfour felt that if the Americans wished to play a role in Balkan peace-making, they must be allowed to do so. It is probable that he himself would have welcomed such a development but with Lloyd George expressing sympathy with Clemenceau's vexed attitude toward them, he may have thought it unwise to say so.[5]

At all events, the war with Bulgaria was at an end. No British interests had ever been directly involved and Bulgaria policy receded to being of interest chiefly to the Balkan specialists in the Foreign Office such as Harold Nicolson who lamented that emotional feeling might prevent territory being ceded *to* Bulgaria in the peace settlement, as indeed was to be the case, and so prolong instability in the Balkans.[6]

---

[1] War Cabinet, 27 Sept. 1918, CAB 23/14 with copy of letter from Milner to Balfour, 27 Sept. 1918; original in FO 800/200.

[2] FO to Lord Derby, 28 Sept. 1918, copy in Milner MSS. 108, Box A3.

[3] Cf. Derby to FO, 30 Sept. 1918, copy in Lloyd George MSS. F/52/2/34.

[4] War Cabinet, 1 Oct. 1918, minutes in CAB 23/8 and 42.

[5] War Cabinet, 3 Oct. 1918, CAB 23/14.

[6] Minutes by Nicolson and Graham on memorandum presented to the Foreign Office by Noel Buxton and others, 25 Oct. 1918, FO 371/3448, no. 179302.

By September 1918 the allied leaders had become far too wary to believe that the Bulgarian collapse might lead or contribute to the defeat of the entire enemy alliance within six weeks as actually happened. They therefore immediately began considering what long-term operations they should undertake to exploit their victory over the least of their opponents. A week before the Bulgarian armistice Lloyd George had sent the uncharacteristic instructions to the chief of the General Staff that the official announcement of the Palestine victories 'must not be given by an unbalanced orientalist who does not know that there is more than one point in the compass'.[7]

The Prime Minister knew that Sir Edmund Allenby's magnificent victories in Palestine were too far from the centres of Turkish power for them alone to bring about her collapse. He may also have been influenced by a number of papers prepared by General Thomson of the Supreme War Council since July 1918. These called for landings on the coast of Thrace and for an attack on Constantinople so that Turkey would quickly be forced to yield, and warned that if a satisfactory peace became possible in the west owing to allied victories Britain might be accused of continuing the war for imperialist motives if the campaigns in the east were allowed to drag on.[8] The feasibility of the Thrace project clearly increased with the Bulgarian armistice and Lloyd George advocated it at the Entente conference in Paris in early October while attributing it to the Greek Prime Minister, Venizelos.[9]

Nothing came of this project. The French had different plans for following up the Bulgarian armistice. The instructions which their War Ministry sent to Franchet envisaged the liberation of Serbia, the isolation of Turkey and the establishment of a front from the Adriatic to the Black Sea to be followed by an advance into Rumania as an essential step toward bringing her back into the war. Most British and French troops in the Balkans would probably have to be brought to the West Front and be replaced by troops of the Entente's Balkan allies.[10] Presumably, the front thus established would be used for operations against Austria–Hungary. It was certainly clear that

[7] Note to H. Wilson, 24 Sept. 1918, Lloyd George MSS. F/47/7/44.

[8] Memoranda by C. B. Thomson, 20 July and 5 Sept. 1918, CAB 25/122, nos. 280 and 321.

[9] Minutes of Entente conference, 5 Oct. 1918, CAB 28/5 I.C. 76.

[10] See the *Dossier pour M. Lloyd George* of French documents on military policy given to him in Paris in early October and Clemenceau to Lloyd George, 1 Oct. 1918, Lloyd George MSS. F/50/3/28–29.

France did not favour a major offensive against European Turkey in the near future.

Anglo–French disagreement on this as on a number of issues connected with manpower and strategy was cut short by the rapidity of the enemy collapse. Immediately after the Bulgarian armistice came into force the War Cabinet took steps to prepare for Turkish overtures. The First Sea Lord, Sir Wester Wemyss, announced that he was sending two Dreadnoughts to the Aegean in case it became necessary to exert force against a tottering Turkey and the cabinet instructed Wemyss and Henry Wilson to draw up naval and military terms of armistice with Turkey.[11]

Turkish feelers were soon received. Rumbold informed London that they were coming to him from three quarters: from self-proclaimed representatives of Talaat and the Sultan and from the military attaché at the Turkish legation who, however, probably did not represent anyone other than himself. He stated his intention of having nothing to do with these men unless they provided proof that they represented elements who were in power in Turkey.[12] This was indeed the perennial problem but the War Cabinet were sufficiently interested in an earlier Berne report of Turkish feelers to take a decision that it would be best if negotiations were carried out in Palestine.[13] The British were already showing signs of what was to be their main concern in the Turkish armistice negotiations—that they alone should negotiate with Turkey.

On another important point, they had already made up their minds: a separate peace with Turkey was no longer acceptable. Balfour minuted a report that the Committee of Union and Progress had taken a secret decision to seek peace on the British terms of the previous winter, 'An armistice is the right course'.[14] Ronald Graham commented upon renewed peace overtures from Rahmi Bey, the pro-Entente governor of Smyrna, which envisaged the retention of Turkish suzerainty over the Arab provinces: 'These terms might possibly have been considered if we were in an unfavourable position and wished to bring Turkey out. As it is they are preposterous and deserve no consideration.'[15] Rahmi was told, rather curtly in view of his Ententophil record, that if he wished to discuss

[11] War Cabinet, 1 Oct. 1918, CAB 23/8.
[12] Rumbold to Cecil, 7 Oct. 1918, FO 371/3444, no. 172071.
[13] War Cabinet, 2 Oct. 1918, CAB 23/14.
[14] Minute on Rumbold to FO, 1 Oct. 1918, FO 371/3448, no. 165602.
[15] Minute, c. 7 Oct. 1918, no. 167738 in ibid.

peace he must seize power in Constantinople and that even then the allies would only be prepared to grant an armistice.[16]

There was no longer any military need to be prepared to make concessions to Turkey and this caused the British to show themselves in what might be described as their true colours. Lloyd George toyed with the idea of an immediate peace treaty with Turkey—only to find the French unwilling to co-operate—for reasons which are revealing. He told Robert Cecil that he wanted to frighten the French into thinking that unless the United States were excluded from the Middle East settlement they would claim Syria and Palestine. He hoped that France, in order to save her position in Syria, would at once sign a peace and, in her haste, allow Palestine to pass to Britain. Cecil talked him out of this harebrained scheme.[17]

On this same occasion, the conference in Paris, Lloyd George did obtain some less spectacular victories. After an argument with Clemenceau in which the two men 'spat at one another like angry cats',[18] the French Prime Minister agreed that Milne should command any land operations against Constantinople. The conference also endorsed the terms for an armistice with Turkey which had been drawn up by Admiral Wemyss and Henry Wilson, making only minor amendments.[19] Finally, it agreed that President Wilson should not be informed of these terms.[20] Balfour regretted this decision and quickly obtained French and Italian consent for it to be reversed.[21] Even before this, the Foreign Secretary had sent a message to Washington 'that there is no question of arranging any secret or separate terms of peace'.[22]

Less easily resolved was the issue of naval command in any operations against Constantinople which, it was thought, might be vital in finally bringing Turkey to terms. The British were on rather weak ground in claiming such command for themselves. Both the allied naval commander in the Mediterranean, Gauchet, and the senior naval officer in the Aegean, Amet, were French while French naval strength in the latter sea was greater than British.[23] Against

[16] Cf. Derby to FO, 8 Oct. 1918, no. 169081 in ibid.
[17] Cecil to Balfour, 7 Oct. 1918, FO 800/201.   [18] Letter cited in note 17 above.
[19] Cf. Lloyd George's report to War Cabinet, 11 Oct. 1918, CAB 23/42.
[20] Cf. Derby to Drummond, 7 Oct. 1918, Balfour MSS., B.M. Add. 49738.
[21] Drummond to Derby, 8 Oct. 1918 in ibid.; and FO to Derby and Rodd, 11 Oct. 1918, FO 371/3444, no. 171512.
[22] Balfour to Barclay, 10 Oct. 1918, FO 371/3442, no. 169743.
[23] Henry Newbolt, *History of the Great War based on official Documents: Naval Operations*, v (1931), 352–3.

this the British could only argue that they had borne the overwhelming brunt of the war against Turkey and that it ought, therefore, to be their privilege to deliver the *coup de grâce*. As well as rushing naval reinforcements to the Aegean, Wemyss spent an entire evening with Lloyd George impressing this point upon him. He also sent out a British officer, Calthorpe, who was senior to Admiral Amet.[24] Meanwhile, Anglo–French naval conversations in Paris reached total deadlock on this issue.[25]

Wemyss again urged the need not to give ground.[26] However, Lloyd George needed no convincing[27] and wrote a minatory letter to Clemenceau.[28] 'A very good letter' minuted the normally cold Balfour on his copy of this document.[29] Unsurprisingly, Clemenceau's reaction was 'decidedly unfavourable'[30] though a showdown with the French was delayed until the next allied conference, again in Paris, which did not begin until 29 October.

This gave British leaders several days in which to devise a strategy on two points: how to induce French acceptance of British naval command in the Aegean; and what concessions, if any, could be granted to Turkey from the terms which Wemyss and Wilson had drawn up. Every day it became clearer that Turkey's collapse could not long be delayed. A new government had come to power with the obvious aim of seeking peace while the Committee of Union and Progress proclaimed its own dissolution as a party.[31] A major concern of the British now was that Enver Bey, the one Turkish leader whom they feared and in a sense respected as a genuine anti-British zealot rather than an opportunist, would retreat to the Caucasus and launch guerrilla warfare against a Turkish regime which had 'treacherously' signed an armistice with the allies.[32]

What complicated matters was that the Prime Minister was anxious for the earliest possible conclusion of an armistice because of belated realization that there was a good possibility of forcing the Central Powers themselves to yield on allied terms before the end of the year. He felt that the chances of this happening would be much

---

[24] Wemyss to Eric Geddes, 3 Oct. 1918, ADM 116/1809.
[25] Supreme War Council discussion of naval command in the Aegean, 10 Oct. 1918, G.T. 5972, CAB 24/66.   [26] Memorandum, 12 Oct. 1918, ADM 116/1810.
[27] Riddell, op. cit. p. 379.
[28] Lloyd George to Clemenceau, 15 Oct. 1918, G.T. 6016, CAB 24/67.
[29] Undated minute, FO 800/206.   [30] Derby to FO, 18 Oct. 1918 in ibid.
[31] Ahmed Emin, *Turkey in the World War* (1930), pp. 267–8.
[32] Cf. FO 371/3448, nos. 173983 and 179182.

increased if the allies could gain a free military hand in the Balkans including European Turkey and the Black Sea, enabling them speedily to inflict defeat on Austria–Hungary and to follow this up by an attack on Germany from the south. Henry Wilson gave his powerful backing to such a policy. 'In short', he wrote, 'if we can get Turkey out of the war in the near future I can see no reason why we should not inflict a final crushing defeat on German soil.'[33] This heady prospect produced renewed thoughts of making concessions to the Turks to bring about their early departure from the war. Once again there was a question of endangering British political aims in Turkey because of the overall needs of war strategy.

On 20 October Townshend, the British general who had surrendered to the Turks at Kut in 1916, arrived at Mudros on Mitylene, the chief allied naval base in the Aegean, together with some Turkish emissaries, and grandiloquently announced that the Turks had asked him to go to London to negotiate a treaty of peace between the two countries based on autonomy for the areas already under allied occupation. At the same time the new Turkish government of Izzet Pasha presented a formal request for peace talks to the French ambassador and the British minister in Berne. This produced alarm among the eastern specialists in the Foreign Office, based on their understanding of oriental psychology and of how the British as a ruling nation should respond to it. Ronald Graham wrote:

The Turks are making this final effort to save their face in the East before the Mohammedan world—they wish it to appear that they have not been beaten, but have secured a negotiated peace and for this they will offer considerable sacrifices and might even attack the Germans in Constantinople—after which they would declare to the eastern Moslem world that they had come in on the winning side and that the final allied victory was due to their help. There is absolutely nothing the Eastern world will not believe. I have no wish to crush the Turks or humiliate them unduly but, apart from any of our obligations to the subject races whom they have so disgracefully mishandled, it is absolutely essential for us, if we wish for future peace and order in India, Egypt and the Moslem world, to show with unmistakable clearness that the Turk is beaten and is forced to accept such terms as we choose to offer. This is vital.[34]

Graham need not have worried. Ministers had no difficulty in agreeing that a separate peace could not even be discussed and they

[33] Some notes by H. Wilson, 21 Oct. 1918, WO 106/1433.
[34] Minute by Graham, *c.* 22 Oct. 1918, FO 371/3448, no. 177193.

wished to exclude the rather discredited Townshend from any negotiations.[35] However, the War Cabinet debate on this occasion produced a three-way split among those present. Bonar Law and Milner were prepared to make very large concessions in the interests of an early armistice. Curzon and Chamberlain upheld the armistice terms already agreed to as an essential minimum. Finally, the majority of members including Lloyd George, together with Henry Wilson and Wemyss, argued that if only the British could gain control of the Straits, Turkey would be at their mercy and so it would be unnecessary to insist on anything else until the Central Powers had been defeated.

Meanwhile the Turks who had accompanied Townshend were pressing the British at Mudros to enter into armistice talks and, gratifyingly, were making it clear that they did not wish to have any dealings with the French. On 22 October the War Cabinet decided to instruct Admiral Calthorpe to commence such negotiations. He should try to gain acceptance of all the twenty-four clauses in the Wemyss–Wilson armistice terms but need only insist on the first four. All of these, with the exception of one based on humanitarian considerations which demanded the earliest possible release of allied prisoners, were concerned with military and naval control over the Bosphorus forts, the Straits and the Black Sea.[36] When Wemyss asked what Calthorpe should be instructed to tell his French colleague, Austen Chamberlain 'suggested that the French Admiral could be told that he would be doubtless informed by his own government in due course as to the character of the negotiations'.[37]

Negotiations proper thus began with the French unceremoniously excluded. The next day Balfour reported the inevitable French protest to a meeting attended by Lloyd George, Wilson, Milner and Reading. It was agreed to send Milner on a mission to Paris to try to win over Clemenceau to British views on giving Turkey more generous terms than originally intended if necessary, and on French exclusion from their negotiation.[38] A good choice had been made. Milner always got on well with Clemenceau. In addition, whereas most British leaders wanted to exclude the French from these

[35] Cf. ibid. nos. 175315, 175330 and 175349; and War Cabinet, 21 Oct. 1918, CAB 23/14.
[36] Newbolt, Appendix III(D), pp. 418–23 for the texts of the original armistice terms drawn up on 7 Oct., the four essential conditions wired to Calthorpe on 22 Oct. and the terms signed by Turkey on 30 Oct.   [37] War Cabinet, 22 Oct. 1918, CAB 23/14.
[38] Record of this conversation, 23 Oct. 1918, CAB 23/17.

negotiations to enhance British prestige among the eastern peoples and to put her in a dominating position in the Middle East at the peace conference, Milner favoured such exclusion for reasons which could more easily be mentioned to a foreign leader. He was afraid that if France and other powers joined the armistice negotiations the Turks might become frightened and break them off. At any rate, talks would be prolonged and the military benefits of an early armistice would not materialize.[39] Milner found the French Prime Minister ready to assent to a scaling-down of armistice terms but insistent that France must have a hand in their negotiation.[40] He did not finally yield until the end of the month when Lloyd George, again in Paris, made it clear that this was an issue on which he was prepared to split the Entente.[41]

This, however, is to depart from chronology. At the time of the Milner mission Balfour decided on another concession to Turkey: that her negotiators might be assured that she would never be deprived of Constantinople.[42] The 'hawks' on eastern policy then made their counter-attack. Curzon, supported a little hesitantly by Austen Chamberlain, protested against the decision to insist only upon the opening of the Straits if this appeared essential for an early armistice. Outside the War Cabinet, the Secretary of State for India, Montagu, was protesting against his exclusion from any part in drawing up armistice terms for Turkey and against any scaling-down of the original terms. Lloyd George was unmoved. He insisted again that control of the Straits would put Britain in effective control of Turkey and that it would be well worthwhile to pay such a price in order to create a new front against Austria. He added a gentlemanly consideration: Milner would be made to look foolish if the British stiffened their minimum terms after he had visited Clemenceau to press for the acceptance of those terms.[43]

Whether Lloyd George really believed that Britain would be able to impose whatever peace terms it chose upon Turkey with the proposed minimum armistice conditions is open to doubt. On 24 October the War Cabinet decided that Allenby and Marshall, who

[39] Milner to Balfour, 21 Oct. 1918, FO 800/206.
[40] Cf. War Cabinet, 25 Oct. 1918, CAB 23/14.
[41] Inter-allied conference, 30 Oct. 1918, CAB 28/5; cf. D. Lloyd George, *War Memoirs*, ii. 1974-7.
[42] War Cabinet, 24 Oct. 1918, CAB 23/14.
[43] War Cabinet, 25-6 Oct. 1918, in ibid.; memorandum by Montague, 24 Oct. 1918, G.T. 6127, CAB 24/68.

knew nothing about the Mudros talks except that they were taking place, should if possible occupy Aleppo and Mosul before the armistice was signed. This would hardly have been necessary if the ministers truly felt confident that the minimum terms would put the allies in complete effective control of Turkey. It is likely that once again the majority of them were prepared to subordinate eastern policy to the needs of the war against the Central Powers.

Admiral Calthorpe, a distinguished servant of the state, conducted the Mudros negotiations with great skill. He was courteous to the Turkish delegates, led by Raouf Bey, the Minister of Marine, but at the same time he impressed upon them that they were the vanquished party and that they could only hope for minor concessions.[44] As a result of Calthorpe's conduct and the fact that the Turkish delegates were unable to establish wireless contact with Constantinople and so could not appeal to their government against British demands to which they particularly objected, the Turks finally accepted practically the full original terms drawn up by Wemyss and Henry Wilson three weeks before, a development which the War Cabinet greeted with surprise and delight.[45] It was mean, though characteristic of human nature, that once the war had ended on all fronts ministers began to complain of the very limited concessions which Calthorpe had made such as the omission of a clause that Constantinople should be available to the allies as a naval base.[46] This point was one of form only and there was an ample corrective in another clause which laid down that the allies could claim ship-repair facilities in all Turkish ports.

The British government's handling of the Turkish armistice negotiations was marked by an element of perversity which was typical of Lloyd George's war-time administration. During the ten or twelve days before the armistice was signed on 30 October, the British were prepared to make real concessions to Turkey which might have made it impossible to impose a comprehensive peace settlement of their choosing on the Ottoman Empire. At the same time, they were, with deadly seriousness, threatening to end the Entente unless France abandoned any claim to a role in armistice-making with Turkey. During October 1918 they only made one

[44] This impression emerges from the (incomplete) minutes of the Mudros negotiations and from Calthorpe's report on them, 10 Dec. 1918, both in ADM 116/1823.

[45] War Cabinet, 31 Oct. 1918, CAB 23/14; cf. Newbolt, op. cit. pp. 354–7.

[46] Cf. Cecil to Derby, 31 Oct. 1918, and the various minutes in FO 371/3449, no. 186944.

concession to France's desire to play such a role. In the middle of
the month, the War Cabinet abandoned their earlier preference for
negotiations to be conducted by Allenby in Palestine on the grounds
that the specific reference of Turkish emissaries to Allenby would
alienate the French.[47] More characteristic of Anglo–French relations
was the British response to Turkey's formal request for peace talks
to the British and French envoys in Switzerland. This was not discussed by the War Cabinet and was dealt with as a matter of Foreign
Office routine. Lord Acton, the chargé in Berne, was told in 'rare
and curt' messages that there must be no negotiations there, and
when he suggested that Britain and France should work to draw up
a joint position, Hardinge reminded him of France's exclusive role
in the Bulgarian armistice and of Britain's predominant part in the
war against Turkey. He suggested, 'This may throw some light for
you on what has passed in Switzerland'.[48]

The French were humiliated and it may be that the refusal of
France and Britain's other war-time allies to co-operate in implementing the treaty of Sèvres of 1920, which represented the ideal
of what they wished to do with Turkey, can be traced to British
treatment of them during the armistice negotiations and before. The
Lloyd George government was always ready to be generous to its
lesser enemies at the expense of its own allies and this attitude was
hardly calculated to prepare the ground for the all-embracing settlement of international problems for which most British politicians
and diplomats hoped by November 1918.

These last acts of war-time policy toward Turkey had a counterpart in the occupied Arab areas. Immediately after the armistice, the
young Arnold Toynbee in the Political Intelligence Department
wrote a number of memoranda which proved to his own satisfaction
that, whatever might have been the case in 1915–16 when the Sykes–
Picot agreement was drawn up, it was now just and desirable if not
absolutely essential, for the sole outside influence in the territory of
the old Ottoman Empire to be British. His superiors agreed and only
regretted that it might prove impossible for this to be achieved.[49]
The rise of such attitudes is a different story from the one traced

[47] War Cabinet, 17 Oct. 1918, CAB 23/8.
[48] Acton to Hardinge, 31 Oct. 1918, and Hardinge to Acton, 5 Nov. 1918, Hardinge
MSS. XXXIX.
[49] Memoranda and minutes by Toynbee and minutes by Cecil, Hardinge and Eyre
Crowe, all written in November and December 1918, FO 371/4368.

here but the history of the Turkish armistice negotiations is an important and unduly neglected backcloth to it.

The first sign that the Central Powers were ready to acknowledge defeat came in a note which the Austrian government addressed to the United States on 15 September 1918, suggesting that all parties in the World War should feel free to enter into peace discussions with anyone and without any preconditions—an ingenious compromise between suggestions of a separate and a general peace. Balfour and President Wilson made speeches rejecting the Austrian offer out of hand.[50]

Those who had hoped so fervently in the past for peace with the Dual Monarchy were irritated. When Balfour made his anti-Austrian speech he may have had in his possession a letter from Cecil of the same date appealing for the Austrian offer to be treated seriously and for Vienna to be told that they could only have peace on the basis of the allied note to President Wilson of 10 January 1917. The language of that note was compatible with the preservation of the Monarchy as a federation and there is no doubt that this is what Cecil wanted.[51] Lloyd George was irritated by Balfour's speech which was made without consulting him. He did not think that Austria's offer should have been accepted but he regretted that it had not been given more consideration. 'Here was a formal approach from a Great Power on a vital matter.'[52] Austria–Hungary was thus still a great power to the Prime Minister. This opinion was evidently shared by the rulers in Vienna who, according to an intelligence report in early October, were offering Italy Trentino and some territory west of Trieste though not the city itself together with their good offices to mediate the cession of Alsace-Lorraine to France![53]

During the following weeks the Dual Monarchy moved rapidly and visibly toward total collapse. There was very little that the allies could do to influence events and the British government adopted no comprehensive policy toward it at this time. No doubt Cecil had his tongue in his cheek when he wrote to Lloyd George in mid-October that he did not know what allied war aims in eastern Europe were

[50] J. B. Scott, op. cit. pp. 386–96, for text of Austrian note and of these speeches.
[51] Cecil to Balfour, 16 Sept. 1918, FO 800/200.
[52] Journals, 18 Sept. 1918, 50905.
[53] Rodd to FO, 1 Oct. 1918, FO 371/3448, no. 166032.

but: 'I dare say the Cabinet have a complete answer to these and similar queries. But as far as I know the answer is not recorded.'[54]

In the absence of a War Cabinet directive policy was formulated within the Foreign Office. Balfour endorsed a suggestion from the Political Intelligence Department that the American State Department should be informed that the British government would not be prepared to treat with the Austro–Hungarian government except as regarded German-speaking Austria and the Magyars.[55]

War Cabinet ministers were concerned with the purely military aspects of the Austrian collapse. Lloyd George was powerfully attracted by the idea, which he outlined to his colleagues on 21 October, of an attack on Germany from the south from neutral Austrian territory. This, he was convinced, would enable the allies to inflict utter defeat on Germany in 1919.[56] The chief of the General Staff, who had at first doubted the feasibility of such a project,[57] now supported it strongly.[58] On 5 November, after returning from Paris, the Prime Minister told the War Cabinet with relish of the plans which Marshal Foch had drawn up for a southern campaign against Germany.[59] In the case of Austria as in that of Turkey, Lloyd George was chiefly preoccupied with the problem of defeating Germany and, no doubt, with the vindication of strategic policies which he had advocated since the earliest months of the war.

The armistice terms which the allied leaders required Austria to sign were drawn up in Paris on 29 and 30 October and were signed by the tottering Imperial government of Austria on 3 November. They provided for the free movement of allied troops through Austrian territory and for the occupation of strong points within the Empire to protect what were described as the 'oppressed nationalities'. However, by that time the 'oppressed nationalities' were well able to look after themselves. During the weeks before and after this armistice the only aspects of developments within the Monarchy's area which the British could significantly influence were those concerning the Yugoslavs.

Early in September the Italian government had informed its allies

[54] Cecil to Lloyd George, 15 Oct. 1918, Lloyd George MSS. F/6/5/42.
[55] Headlam to Drummond, 15 Oct. 1918 and FO to Barclay (chargé in Washington), 16 Oct. 1918, FO 371/3444, no. 173441.
[56] War Cabinet, 21 Oct. 1918, CAB 23/14.
[57] War Cabinet, 1 Oct. 1918, CAB 23/42.
[58] Memorandum by H. Wilson, 21 Oct. 1918, G.T. 6069, CAB 24/67.
[59] War Cabinet, 5 Nov. 1918, CAB 23/8.

that it supported 'the movement of the Jugo-Slav peoples for the acquisition of their independence and for their constitution in a free state'. Later in the month *The Times* 'leaked' this message by publishing it. From the point of view of relations with Italy, there was no longer an obstacle, therefore, to British recognition of the Jugo-Slav Committee on the lines of that granted to the Czechs. However, action was delayed by a quarrel between the Croat leader, Trumbic, and the Serbian leader, Pashitch, who made no effort to conceal that he looked forward to Serbian domination of the Croats and Slovenes whom the Jugo-Slav Committee represented.[60]

At the Paris conference early in October Baron Sonnino was in true form. Setting aside the policy which his government had adopted the previous month, he repeatedly interrupted the discussion of armistice terms with Germany by irrelevant comments on Austria and even complained that if there was an armistice with Germany alone the other allies would leave Austria and Italy to fight on in isolation. Likewise, he opposed any recognition of the Yugoslavs until after an armistice had been signed and demanded that the Austro–Hungarian fleet in its base at Pola, which had just been seized by Yugoslavs who wished to put it at the disposal of the allies, should be treated as an enemy force and required to surrender under a white flag.[61]

The American, British and French governments finally obtained a compromise under which Italy agreed not to attack the fleet which would be instructed to surrender to the senior allied naval commander in the Adriatic who, fortunately for the self-respect of the Yugoslavs, was not an Italian.[62] The Serbs used the renewed Italian hostility to bludgeon the Croats and Slovenes into accepting Yugoslav unity on Serbian terms.[63] At the same time, the Yugoslavs were quick to protest against Italian landings in Dalmatia to occupy territory promised in the treaty of London.[64] It was clear that a long period of Italian–Yugoslav enmity lay ahead in which Britain would be heavily involved but the way was at least open for the speedy establishment of the kingdom of Yugoslavia.

During the last few weeks of the war a debate took place in the Foreign Office about policy in the disintegrating Monarchy which,

[60] Minutes by A. W. A. Leeper and Drummond, 21 Oct. 1918, FO 371/3137, nos. 169690 and 176378.
[61] Inter-allied conference, 29 Oct. and 1 Nov. 1918, CAB 28/5.
[62] Mamatey, *United States and East-Central Europe*, pp. 364–6.
[63] Ibid. pp. 371–5.   [64] Cf. Rodd to FO, 7 Nov. 1918, FO 371/3137, no. 185131.

though irrelevant to events there, has interest. Everything seemed to bear out the contention of the Austria specialists in the Political Intelligence Department, Seton-Watson and Namier, that 'no constitutional reform within the boundaries of Austria is possible': the German Austrians might offer this but would be insincere; the Magyars would probably not even be prepared to make a pretence of acceptance; the subject races were determined to become independent.[65]

Leo Amery for one was unconvinced. Making much of the inconsistency in the Czech argument that they claimed Slovakia on ethnographic grounds and German-speaking Bohemia on those of strategy, he turned to one of his favourite themes, the division of the world into a few huge, closely-knit blocks. National states in eastern Europe, he thought, could never be viable and at the peace conference the allies should work to undo the current disintegration and to facilitate 'the inevitable coming of the larger non-national superstate'—a federated Austria–Hungary in federation with Germany.

Namier, aided by Harold Nicolson, put forward arguments which opponents of the Monarchy had used many times. The possession of some German territory in Bohemia was essential for a Czech state. There was absolutely nothing that could be done to reverse Yugoslav or Rumanian unity in sovereign states. Germany and the German Austrians would be totally uninterested in such a union unless they could dominate it in which event 'so far from restoring a balance against Germany, an Austrian federation under German leadership would merely increase the difficulties caused by the collapse of Russia'. Finally, the only steps which the allies could take to reverse the break up of Austria–Hungary on national lines would be anti-Czecho–Slovak: they could force the Czechs to allow Germany to absorb the whole of German Bohemia and they could help the Magyars to preserve their oppressive domination of the Slovaks—which would be quixotic.

On the question of the security of the new states Namier voiced the hopes of the younger men in the office when he asked:

Have the new states which we propose to create to be created on bases strategically and economically such as were required previous to this war, or is the League of Nations going to become something real which

[65] Political Intelligence Department memorandum, 18 Sept. 1918, G.T. 5794, CAB 24/64.

will change the face of European politics just as the introduction of a municipal or government police has made it possible for people to do away with iron shutters in their houses?

Robert Cecil who at first felt 'considerable sympathy' with Amery was later impressed by the line of argument of Namier and Nicolson which 'seems very sound'.[66] It was a process familiar to the historian of policy formulation. The leaders' advisers argued their respective points of view while the leaders themselves, not endowed with a great deal of knowledge and anxious only for arrangements which would be stable, were swayed now one way, now another.

2. GERMANY

The allied leaders were slow to realize that Germany was nearing the point where she would accept an armistice on their terms. Those of their advisers professionally concerned with analysing German policy were likewise slow to discern signs of impending collapse. In early September 1918 Political Intelligence Department reports were still in the vein that any German peace moves would be mere snares[67] and that annexationism and militarism were still completely in the ascendant.[68] When Haig told Milner as Secretary of State for War that he was sure that the war could be brought to a satisfactory conclusion very soon, Henry Wilson recorded in his diary on 23 September that this merely had the effect of leaving Milner fearful that Haig intended to embark upon 'another Passchendaele'.[69]

One of the first indications that it was realized that matters might be changing was a statement in an intelligence report on 25 September that the German people were becoming so war-weary that the military chiefs were losing their grip.[70] Four days later Ludendorff and Hindenburg advised the Kaiser and his government that it was essential to seek an armistice, advice which was unquestioningly accepted.[71]

On 3 October a new government in Germany, headed by Prince

[66] Memorandum by Amery, 20 Oct. 1918, and minutes by Namier, 22 Oct., and Namier and Nicolson, 7 Nov. 1918, and Cecil, no date, FO 371/3136.

[67] *Foreign and General Report*, LXXXV, 11 Sept. 1918, CAB 24/149.

[68] Memorandum on German war aims with covering note by Political Intelligence Department, 5 Sept. 1918, G.T. 5615, CAB 24/63.

[69] C. E. Callwell, *Field Marshal Sir Henry Wilson: His Life and Diaries* (1927), ii. 125–6.   [70] *Foreign and General Report*, LXXXVII, 25 Sept. 1918, CAB 24/149.

[71] H. R. Rudin, *Armistice 1918* (1944), pp. 49–55. This is by far the best of a number of books on the armistice with Germany.

Max of Baden, sent a note to President Wilson suing for peace on the basis of his fourteen-point address. Throughout the armistice negotiations the Germans clung to the hope that they could obtain more favourable treatment from the United States than from the Entente, a supposition which betrayed their natural ignorance of the extremely war-like mood of the American nation by the end of the First World War. Wilson had to take account of this mood even though it distressed him.[72]

On this same date, 3 October, although unaware of the German move, the Political Intelligence Department addressed themselves for the first time to the serious possibility that Germany might soon make a genuine offer of peace on terms unfavourable to herself. The department was chiefly concerned that the government should not put themselves in the 'very awkward and delicate position' of putting forward the democratization of Germany as a super war-aim above territorial and economic objectives, partly because what mattered were changes in spirit rather than constitutional form and these could not be assessed with any great accuracy, but chiefly because 'the weapon is one which might be used also by others and we may easily find that we are playing into the hands of international socialism or international labour'.[73] This paper bears the hall mark of Headlam-Morley who was afraid of a social revolution taking place in Germany which would spread to France and Italy and perhaps Britain: 'Even in this country it might have a serious echo.' He conceded that peace terms to Germany must be harsh but he advocated winning the support of the German middle classes by promising that no crippling economic burdens would be placed on the country and informing the German government that allied troops would be available to it 'to preserve order'. He was convinced that revolutionary upheavals were certain to end in the establishment of military dictatorships.[74]

Headlam was unusual in coming to the conclusion, almost at the very moment when Germany began to acknowledge defeat, that a new struggle must at once be begun to preserve the existing social structure of Europe which was the very last thing that the rulers of Germany during the First World War had wished to disturb. Not

[72] H. R. Rudin, *Armistice 1918* (1944), pp. 101–4, 167–8, 173–5.
[73] Political Intelligence Department memorandum, 3 Oct. 1918, G.T. 5883, CAB 24/65.
[74] Headlam to Tyrrell, 12 Oct. 1918, FO 371/3444, no. 172800; cf. Headlam to Tyrrell, 28 Oct. 1918, FO 371/4368, no. 477.

everyone in the Foreign Office, to say nothing of ruling circles as a whole, accepted this analysis. Eyre Crowe welcomed the prospect of a social democratic government in Germany and did not agree with Headlam that it would be a puppet or dupe of international Bolshevism. It would, on the contrary, be a welcome blow to the 'Junker regime in Prussia'. Cecil wrote: 'I cannot imagine any conditions in which our intervention in the internal affairs of Germany would be wise.'[75] Balfour, with the admixture of complacency and purely academic interest with which he was apt to regard problems before he had really thought about them, wrote: 'The revolutionary prospect in the Central Powers is disquieting. But they have brought it on themselves and I rather fear upon us also.'[76]

The increasing readiness, even eagerness, of British ministers to conclude an armistice during the last month of the war stemmed partly from human excitement that Germany really was desperately anxious for peace and partly also from a wish to minimize social upheavals summed up in the word 'Bolshevism'. In late October, Smuts called for the immediate conclusion of a full peace treaty, partly—and not wholly—because 'to-day the grim spectre of Bolshevist anarchy is stalking to the front' so that, 'It would be wrong merely for the sake of still further and more adequately punishing Germany for her misdeeds to continue the war'.[77] When the armistice was finally signed Henry Wilson wrote crisply, 'Our real danger now is not the Boches but Bolshevism'.[78] This factor is difficult to trace and can easily be exaggerated in an age like the present one which is fascinated by social interpretations of history. Even so, it was definitely there.

The French intelligence service intercepted the first German peace note before the United States government officially conveyed it to the Entente on 7 October. The Entente political and military leaders were by then already discussing their response at a conference in Paris which lasted from 5 to 7 October. Although Lloyd George for one was sceptical as to whether the German note was sincere, these leaders drew up detailed armistice terms based on the evacuation by Germany of all occupied territory in the west and of

---

[75] Minutes by Crowe and Cecil, 16 Oct. 1918, FO 371/3444, no. 172800.
[76] Minute by Balfour, *c.* 15 Oct. 1918, no. 173441 in ibid.
[77] Memorandum by Smuts, 24 Oct. 1918, G.T. 6091, CAB 24/67; cf. W. K. Hancock, *Smuts: the Sanguine Years* (1962), pp. 491–5.   [78] Callwell, op. cit. ii. 148.

her own territory west of the Rhine. In addition, on the grounds that Germany was unique among European states in that, 'Its word cannot be believed and it denies any obligation of honour', a number of towns in the evacuated territory and the island of Heligoland should be occupied by the allies and the blockade should be maintained to provide safeguards that Germany would do as she promised.[79]

These terms were not harsh after over four years of total war and both Lloyd George and Clemenceau thought that it would be wrong to continue the war if an armistice could be signed on satisfactory conditions, in other words those under which Germany would find it militarily impossible to resume hostilities. Lloyd George's old fears that the endurance of the troops on the West Front might reach breaking point revived now that it was public knowledge that Germany was suing for peace. He and Bonar Law spoke against a proposal by Clemenceau that there should be a three-day armistice in which Germany would be required to assent to all essential allied peace conditions on the grounds that the fighting men could not be relied upon to take up arms again if the Germans refused to assent.[80]

At a conference at the Quai d'Orsay on 9 October Lloyd George skilfully dissuaded Clemenceau from his wish to ignore President Wilson's reply to the German peace note with the argument that its language implied that Germany should be granted an armistice in return for the evacuation of occupied territory and acceptance of the Fourteen Points as the basis of the peace settlement and that the Entente should not allow these terms to be accepted by default. A note was duly despatched to Washington.[81]

This dual concern on the part of the Prime Minister with vigorously pursuing the opportunity of concluding an armistice and with relations with the United States was reflected in his report to the War Cabinet on 11 October on the Paris conference. He thought that maintenance of the blockade would alone be enough to make it impossible for Germany to resume hostilities. The Cabinet agreed with him that the closest co-operation with the United States should be sought.[82] Balfour had already responded to a warning that the American Administration suspected the Entente of seeking to draw up armistice or peace agreements with all the enemy powers without

[79] Rudin, op. cit. pp. 93–6.
[80] Entente conference, 7–9 Oct. 1918, I.C. 78, CAB 28/5.
[81] Minutes in ibid.; cf. Rudin, op. cit. pp. 106–8.
[82] War Cabinet, 11 Oct. 1918, minutes in CAB 23/8 and 42.

consulting the United States by a categorical assurance that this was not the case.[83] Wiseman reported that the President was satisfied with this assurance.[84]

The wish of ministers for close co-operation with the United States was not reciprocated by President Wilson. When the French and Italian ambassadors and the British chargé in Washington agreed that ambassador Jusserand should suggest to the President that his fears about the Entente's intentions in Paris would be allayed if he sent a representative—meaning in effect Colonel House—to Europe to be present at future discussions, he at first refused. Confessing almost openly to an instinctive distrust of Europe, he said: 'Your ministers are in close touch with their own countries. Any American I could send over would soon lose contact with American atmosphere. He would fall under local influences and lose the point of view of the United States.' Cecil drew up a reply to this report which showed considerable exasperation in the face of American coldness. The only way of meeting the President's fears 'would appear to be to have relays of American representatives who should succeed one another at short intervals, but that might very likely be difficult to arrange.' (In the message actually sent to Washington this was altered to the more diplomatic: 'I do not know whether the President can suggest any satisfactory method of meeting the difficulty.')[85]

The President's attitude was distressing. British politicians could never grasp that, from the time when America entered the war, the preservation of her diplomatic independence had, to President Wilson, been an objective second only to the defeat of Germany. They regarded his silence on political matters as leaving the door open to a post-war Anglo–American alliance, to be cemented, hopefully, by American acceptance of colonial-type responsibilities in parts of the Turkish Empire and the German colonies, notably German East Africa. The intense diplomatic activity of the armistice period revealed clearly this hope and also the more cautious attitude of the professional diplomats. Thus Crowe, a few weeks after the armistice, commented upon an argument by Smuts that the British Empire should regard the United States rather than France as her

[83] Barclay to FO, 10 Oct. 1918, and FO (drafted by Balfour) to Barclay, 10 Oct. 1918, FO 371/3442, no. 169742.

[84] Wiseman to Reading and Drummond, 13 Oct. 1918, copy in Balfour MSS., B.M. Add. 49741.

[85] Barclay to FO, 10 Oct. 1918, FO 371/3444, no. 170667; FO to Barclay, 13 Oct. 1918 and draft telegram by Cecil, no. 171764, in ibid.

main ally: 'We must remember that our friend America lives a long way off; France sits at our door.'[86] In the middle of October, Crowe had supported a French suggestion that the two countries should formulate a complete joint approach to the often obscure meaning of each of the Fourteen Points. Cecil was doubtful. He wrote: 'It is part of the policy of the French government to detach us from the USA and bring us into the "European" fold.' Balfour favoured a reverse procedure. The War Cabinet should adopt a policy in consultation with Colonel House and should then discuss it with France and Italy though it was doubtful whether much could be achieved in view of Italian–French enmity and Italy's insistence on her claims under the secret treaties, many of which the United States would certainly reject as contrary to 'natural justice'.[87]

The difficulties in the way of an Anglo–American entente did not lie wholly on the American side. British rejection of President Wilson's insistence on Freedom of the Seas was also to prove a formidable obstacle. However, before battle was joined on this the British leadership discussed the fundamental question whether they wanted an armistice with Germany at all in preference to fighting her until she surrendered unconditionally, thus heaping the maximum degree of discredit and humiliation on militarism. On 13 October, at the country home of his friend the newspaper proprietor, Lord Riddell, Lloyd George remarked to his colleagues that there was much to be said in favour of demanding a peace of unconditional surrender on the analogy of the struggle between the Roman Republic and Carthage which the Romans had finally won by annihilating their enemy. No doubt it occurred to the Prime Minister that the German people could not be exterminated or sold into slavery as those of Carthage had been. At all events, it is clear from his behaviour at the recent conference in Paris that he himself favoured an armistice. His remark was clearly intended to sound out the views of his colleagues. Bonar Law, Balfour, Milner and Henry Wilson all spoke against unconditional surrender[88] and Lloyd George said afterwards that he thought his ministers and leading advisers definitely wanted an armistice.[89]

[86] Minute, 7 Dec. 1918, FO 371/3451, no. 200881; Smuts' views are expressed in his memorandum of 3 Dec. 1918, copy in Cecil MSS., B.M. Add. 51076.
[87] Minute by Crowe, 16 Oct. 1918, and minutes by Cecil and Balfour, FO 371/3444, no 173395.   [88] Minutes of conference, 13 Oct. 1918, G.T. 5967, CAB 24/66.
[89] Riddell, op. cit. p. 372.

Ministers then turned to the more specific task of convincing the American President of the validity of British views on the Freedom of the Seas and the future of the German colonies.[90] The British were receiving re-assuring reports as to President Wilson's views on the armistice conditions which Germany must be forced to accept. Eric Geddes, the first lord of the Admiralty, who was on an American mission, told them that Wilson had said to him that the armistice terms must be such as to make Germany militarily impotent—precisely the British doctrine—that anything harsher would be 'inexcusable' and that he had no definite views on the Freedom of the Seas. All this was good. But Wilson's policy seemed to be swinging like a pendulum from the reply to the first German note, with its suggestion of granting Germany an armistice on inadmissibly light terms, to his satisfactory remarks to Geddes and then on to his reply to the second German note which the War Cabinet discussed at the same time as they discussed Geddes' report on 15 October. This note warned that the United States and the Entente powers must alone decide the military conditions of the armistice and added the condition that the overthrow of 'arbitrary power' in Germany would be 'fundamental' in deciding the terms of peace. This demand caused general consternation in the War Cabinet where it was feared that the President was seeking something which the Germans would not give and which was not at all essential to end the fighting. Ministers fell back on the hope that, as Balfour said, the note was badly drafted and that the demand on arbitrary power was not to be taken seriously.[91]

By the middle of October, ministers were becoming cautiously confident of the end of the war. On the 17th they had asked Reading to find someone to compose the British brief for negotiations at the inter-allied conference which, it was thought, would precede a full peace conference at which Germany would be represented. The departments of state were also to draw up memoranda on their peace desiderata.[92]

At the same time, while no one shared President Wilson's suspected wish to demand internal changes in Germany as an armistice

[90] War Cabinet, 14 Oct. 1918, CAB 23/8.
[91] War Cabinet, 15 Oct. 1918 in ibid.; cf. the much fuller minutes in Thomas Jones, *Whitehall Diary*, ed. K. Middlemas, i. 68–70; there is a full report by Geddes on his interview on 13 Oct. in ADM 116/1809; on Wilson's second note to Germany see Rudin, pp. 131–2.
[92] War Cabinet, 17 Oct. 1918, CAB 23/8.

condition, there was a division within the leadership between those who wanted the earliest possible armistice and those who favoured insistence on certain demands at the cost if necessary of a prolongation of the fighting. On the 19th Haig advised a gathering at which Lloyd George, Milner, Balfour and Bonar Law were present in favour of granting an armistice on very limited terms: the evacuation of occupied Belgium and northern France and also of Alsace-Lorraine though without most of the latter being occupied by the allies. The gist of his argument was that if it was decided to fight on for harsher conditions such as bridgeheads on the Rhine, Britain would not benefit and yet the British army would have to bear the brunt of casualties.[93] Milner supported Haig as did Lloyd George who said that the Field Marshal's terms, combined with continuation of the blockade and possession of the colonies, would surely put the allies in a position to obtain all that they wanted at the peace conference. Referring to a factor which had haunted him for the past year, he expressed doubt whether the British army would fight for anything more than the terms which Haig had mentioned. When Balfour tentatively suggested fighting on until Germany would accept an independent Poland, his colleagues replied plainly that British lives could not be sacrificed for the sake of the Poles. If changes in eastern Europe had become a war aim for Balfour, they were not, even at this late date, such for the other leaders. Less easy for the 'doves' to dismiss was Sir Wester Wemyss' repetition of Admiralty demands for stern naval terms.[94]

The views of the 'doves' were stated most strongly by Milner who had given a newspaper interview, published two days previously, in which he was reported as saying that the Germans should not be driven by allied harshness to make a desperate stand which would cost the allies dear, that such a policy would foster Bolshevism in Germany and that there were many signs that the German people were now adopting democracy and repudiating militarism. At the conference at Lord Riddell's home he had 'expressed the view that German militarism was already overthrown'. His colleagues dissociated themselves publicly from his remarks.[95]

Milner's own explanation of this affair in a private letter to a friend was that it sprang from a double conviction. Firstly:

[93] Blake, op. cit. pp. 332–4.
[94] Ministerial conference, 19 Oct. 1918, CAB 23/17.
[95] Gollin, op. cit. pp. 566–74; G.T. 5967 referred to in note 88 above.

The defeat and destruction of a military autocracy which recognized no law but that of might, was the great object of the war and that if this were accomplished everything else was of minor consideration. . . .

Secondly, Germany had already suffered so much that:

One thing certain is that if the German people are so wedded to Junker government that this debacle does not sicken them of it, nothing we can do or say will eradicate it from their hearts. Certainly they will not be converted by the fulminations of those who in the same breath that they denounce the Hohenzollerns also denounce the whole German nation, represent them as monsters of iniquity.

If this analysis was correct—if the Germans were either purged of militarism or incapable of being purged of it—then it would be 'blood guiltiness' indeed to force them to continue the war with the loss of thousands more American, French and British lives to serve no purpose except that of satisfying the passions of armchair fanatics at home.[96]

Three days before writing this letter, Milner had told the American representative on the Supreme War Council, General Bliss, that he opposed the demobilization of the German army on the grounds that 'Germany may have to be the bulwark against Russian Bolshevism' which he envisaged as a military as well as a psychological threat.[97] Immediately after the armistice had finally been signed, he was to plead with Lloyd George for the demobilization of the British army on a limited scale only, in order, presumably, that there would be substantial forces available to deal with 'the revolutionary tendency, greater or less, in all countries'.[98] Yet it must be recorded that Milner's main concern while the fighting still continued was to prevent the useless loss of life. He deplored the prospect of social revolution and feared aggression by the Russian Bolsheviks into east-central Europe. But this was secondary. There was a general feeling in the War Cabinet—most clearly revealed by ministers' reactions to President Wilson's second note to Germany— that it would be morally wrong to let the war drag on because of inessential points. Even Balfour was anxious for Germany to surrender very extensive territory in an armistice because he did not believe that it would be possible to maintain the economic blockade

[96] Milner to Sir Hugh Thornton, 31 Oct. 1918, Milner, MSS., Additions I.
[97] Seymour, op. cit. iv. 118–19.
[98] Milner to Lloyd George, 13 Nov. 1918, Milner MSS. 145 (VII).

for long afterwards and that territory would be needed as a hostage to force Germany to accept the final terms of peace.[99]

The difficulty on the British side to granting Germany an armistice increasingly became one of the British Navy's insistence on severe naval terms. There were two issues involved in this. The first and one on which the naval leaders and the politicians saw eye-to-eye was the need to exclude the Freedom of the Seas from the armistice conditions. What President Wilson meant by this phrase, the second of his Fourteen Points, was never at any time to become clear.[100] Many British leaders suspected that it was a formula for curtailing and even virtually abolishing naval warfare and therefore one which would leave the British Empire without security. As the Admiralty was to put it in December 1918, naval power was '. . . not the measure of our offensive power, it is not even only a measure of our relative strength as compared with other nations for the purpose of safeguarding our national interests and honour. It is the very source of our national life, the maintenance of which is an act of self-preservation.'[101] In October, the First Sea Lord, Sir Wester Wemyss, put the most unfavourable possible interpretation upon the mysterious phrase: that there must in wartime be no acts of war at sea except between actual warships. He thus had no difficulty in demonstrating its utter unacceptability.[102]

Secondly and much more controversial, the Royal Navy were insistent that the armistice terms concerning the German fleet must be very severe. Admiral Wemyss wanted the whole of the German submarine fleet and part of the surface fleet to be surrendered.[103] Sir David Beatty, the commander of the Grand Fleet, came to London to join him in pressing for these terms.[104] However, it was left to the old Sea Lord, Admiral Fisher, to utter the last word in naval intransigence. He called for the surrender of the entire High Seas fleet, 'every' submarine, the islands of Heligoland, Borkum and Sylt and, for good measure, '. . . no spot of German Jesuitry in the world to be permitted—it would infallibly be a submarine base'.[105]

[99] Memorandum by Balfour, 20 Oct. 1918, G.T. 6045, CAB 24/67.

[100] Gelfand, op. cit. p. 304.

[101] 'Limitation of Armaments: Admiralty Memorandum for War Cabinet', Dec. 1918, ADM 116/1863.

[102] Memorandum by Wemyss, 17 Oct. 1918, G.T. 6018, CAB 24/67.

[103] Memorandum by Wemyss on 'Naval Conditions of Armistice', 19 Oct. 1918 G.T. 6042, CAB 24/67.   [104] War Cabinet, 21 Oct. 1918, CAB 23/14.

[105] Memorandum by Fisher, 22 Oct. 1918, G.T. 6065, CAB 24/67; also in A. J. Marder, ed., *Fear God and Dread Nought*, iii (1959), 554.

It was not appreciated that Germany's condition was becoming so desperate that such terms were unlikely to present a major obstacle to an armistice. This is shown by a conversation between Lloyd George, Balfour, Milner, Wilson and Reading on the 23rd, when they discussed Milner's forthcoming mission to Paris. It was agreed that while his main task was to convince Clemenceau of the wisdom of British views on armistice conditions to Turkey, he should also 'talk straight' to Colonel House on the refusal of the American army in France to co-operate with other forces: 'Unless a change was made the same thing would happen next year. The result would be that brave men would die like flies without achieving any considerable results.'[106]

Meanwhile, events outside British control were leading toward an armistice. On 23 October President Wilson sent another note to the German government informing them that he felt bound to refer their request for an armistice to the Entente governments so that they could take action on it. Two days later at a conference at Senlis, Foch and Pétain agreed that Germany should be granted an armistice if she would evacuate all territory west of the Rhine including the principal crossings of that river, surrender very large quantities of munitions and rolling stock, withdraw her surface fleet to the Baltic and surrender fifty submarines. Haig and the American commander, Pershing, dissented from this advice, the former because he thought it unnecessarily severe and Pershing because he wanted Germany to be forced to surrender unconditionally.[107] The allies and the United States then agreed to hold a major conference in Paris to settle the final armistice terms that Germany must accept or reject.

On the 26th the War Cabinet discussed the line which Lloyd George and Balfour should take in Paris. They were afraid that, despite the very harsh language which President Wilson had recently used towards Germany, the correspondence between the German and United States governments had followed such a course that either could claim at the peace conference that all belligerents were committed to a peace based on the Fourteen Points. There were also reports from the Paris embassy that France and the United States were secretly preparing a joint anti-British front on the terms of

[106] Ministerial conference, 23 Oct. 1918, CAB 23/17.
[107] Rudin, op. cit. pp. 171–3, 177–8, 183–6.

peace.[108] Ministers agreed that, while any reservations on most of these points could be set aside until after the armistice, Freedom of the Seas must be repudiated beforehand. This was unanimous. Lloyd George clarified another point by renewing talk of a Carthaginian peace. No one wanted this and so he could go to Versailles confident that there would be no opposition to an armistice on 'good' terms.

It was naval terms which produced real acrimony. The Prime Minister opposed the surrender of even the whole submarine fleet as an essential condition. Geddes suggested the surrender of one third of it which, he said, would probably be the proportion of the whole that was seaworthy. Policy toward the surface fleet was more difficult. Lloyd George could not see that it was essential to mention it at all while Bonar Law, Chamberlain and Balfour supported Admiralty views. The War Cabinet had to leave the matter open by adopting a formula proposed by Curzon: 'The naval conditions of the armistice should represent the admission of German defeat by sea in the same degree as the military conditions recognized the corresponding admission of German defeat by land.'[109]

Lloyd George went to Versailles muttering curses against 'our stupid admirals'.[110] Convinced that the fate of the surface fleet was irrelevant to the objective of making Germany helpless before the allies, he was for a short time as afraid of the admirals as he had been throughout his premiership that the army High Command might denounce his leadership to the country and seek the establishment of a semi-military regime. In an open clash, the Royal Navy would have been able to make a powerful appeal against him to the British nation and they would probably have had the support of some leading politicians. Balfour, a former first lord of the Admiralty, remarked during the early stages of the Paris conference on 29 October, that he did not think that Germany would accept the naval armistice terms which Lloyd George had brought with him until she had suffered considerable further defeats.[111] He nevertheless accepted a suggestion by Wemyss that he should throw the full weight of his authority behind the demand of the Allied Naval Council—the counterpart of the Supreme War Council—for

[108] Derby to Balfour, 23 Oct. 1918, Lloyd George MSS. F/52/2/44.
[109] War Cabinet, 26 Oct. 1918, CAB 23/14.
[110] J. L. Hammond, *C. P. Scott of the Manchester Guardian* (1934), p. 228.
[111] Seymour, op. cit. iv. 120.

stringent naval terms.[112] Despite this problem, the Prime Minister left London convinced that the odds were two-to-one in favour of the forthcoming conference leading to an armistice.[113]

The story of the Versailles conference, beginning on 29 October, can be briefly told since its minutes have long been available in published form.[114] Lloyd George presented Colonel House with a draft accepting the Fourteen Points in principle, providing that the Freedom of the Seas was set aside. Foch's military terms were likewise endorsed on 1 November despite misgivings by Lloyd George that they were unnecessarily harsh. This left the Freedom of the Seas as the dominant problem which, House confessed, occupied 'almost every minute'[115] of his time outside the conference though, in addition, the French were insistent that Point III on economic matters was unacceptable as possibly restricting their right to claim indemnities from Germany. House finally accepted a suggestion by Lloyd George on 3 November by which the British government accepted the Freedom of the Seas as a fit subject for the 'freest discussion' at the peace conference.

The task of drafting naval terms proved more long drawn out. Foch announced that he would be satisfied with the surrender only of the German submarine fleet. Lloyd George, opposed by Geddes and the British naval representatives and supported ironically by the Anglophobe American admiral, Benson, was ready to compromise on the terms with which the Admiralty had equipped him by which Germany would have to surrender 150 submarines, ten battleships and six battle cruisers. With the agonizing thought in his mind that countless lives might be lost owing to the Royal Navy's determination on an immediate settling of naval accounts with Germany, he put forward one formula after another: that only the six battle cruisers should be surrendered, the ten battleships being interned in a neutral port, on the grounds that Germany was stronger in the battle cruiser arm than in battleships; then that the entire surface fleet should be interned in place of the surrender of part of it. On 4 November the Allied Naval Council endorsed this latter proposal

---

[112] Admiral Wemyss's diary, 1 Nov. 1918, quoted in Lady Wester Wemyss, *The Life and Letters of Lord Wester Wemyss* (1935), p. 388; Balfour to Lloyd George and to Bonar Law, 1 Nov. 1918, FO 800/199 and 201.

[113] Journals, 26 Oct. 1918, 50905.

[114] Cf. Rudin, op. cit. pp. 268–319. The official British minutes are in CAB 28/5; cf. Newbolt, op. cit. v. 370–5 for an account of the naval side of negotiations based on official documents.   [115] Seymour, op. cit. iv. 181.

on the understanding, which Lloyd George accepted,[116] that the surface fleet could never be restored to Germany.

In contrast to the tension which had marked the drawing up of the naval terms at Versailles, the War Cabinet on 6 November accepted quietly a French suggestion that since it was doubtful whether any neutral country would accept so onerous a duty as that of interning the German High Seas fleet, the armistice should provide for their internment in allied ports if no neutral would accept this duty.[117] The armistice terms were duly altered and three days after Germany had signed them the Foreign Office asked the ambassador in Madrid to approach the Spanish government on the internment of the German vessels while at the same time stipulating conditions which the Admiralty had recommended as virtually certain to bring about a Spanish refusal.[118] Spain having, as hoped, refused this undertaking, the allies ordered the German fleet to proceed to Scapa Flow without consulting any other neutral. In this way, the Royal Navy gained the final victory for which it had worked so ardently.

The armistice negotiations had brought to the fore a problem which the British had strangely neglected, that of naval war aims. Throughout the war there had been in British official circles an assumption that, as the Official Naval Historian put it, it was 'surely axiomatic that the German fleet should be practically abolished by the peace treaty'.[119] With certain exceptions such as Sir Henry Jackson's memorandum of October 1916, which had been drawn up on the instructions of the Prime Minister, this assumption had taken the place of detailed discussion.[120]

The possibility that the War Cabinet would sanction insufficiently harsh naval terms had prompted Sir David Beatty in October to remark that the surrender of the German surface fleet was 'more important' than the fate of the submarines and was essential for the reduction of the position of 'the continental nation of Germany to that of a second-rate naval power, corresponding to her geographical

---

[116] War Cabinet, 7 Nov. 1918, Cab 23/8.

[117] War Cabinet, 6 Nov. 1918, CAB 23/44.

[118] FO to A. Hardinge, 14 Nov. 1918, FO 371/3446, no. 188838.

[119] Newbolt, op. cit. v. 373.

[120] But cf. a questionnaire which Balfour circulated to 'high naval authorities' in September 1916 seeking their views on the future of Heligoland, G. 142, CAB 24/3.

position and requirements'.[121] However, Beatty had not thought out what should be done after this and on the very day of the armistice wrote to Geddes: 'The question of the peace terms from the naval point of view I am going into and will let you have them as soon as I can get them formulated.'[122]

It was not until 7 November that Eric Geddes invited the planning staff at the Admiralty to submit and discuss their views on naval peace terms. An important Board of Admiralty meeting on this subject was held two days later.[123] In general the naval staff were inclined to follow the advice of one of their number who submitted that only such terms should be demanded as would ensure future security and that Germany should not be gratuitously humiliated.[124] They did not recommend the destruction of the Kiel Canal and, though favouring the reduction of Heligoland to high-water level by explosives, rejected a suggestion that the remnant of the island should be reannexed by Britain as a symbol of victory. Otherwise their recommendations were stringent and included the handing over of the entire German mercantile marine as partial compensation for lost allied tonnage, the balance to be paid in cash, the destruction of all German submarines and the outlawing of submarine warfare. 'The submarine is essentially the weapon of the weaker naval power and this would undoubtedly be in the interests of Great Britain.' The officers hoped that if an 'all-powerful League of Nations' were set up it would enforce the outlawry of submarine warfare—a curious and extreme example of a desire to put a world organization to purely national, partisan uses.

It was not until January 1919 that the Admiralty submitted to the Cabinet its recommendations on the future of the German surface fleet. These were that almost all of it should be sunk and that Germany should be left with only enough vessels, most of them obsolescent, as were needed 'for self-protection and police duties while not giving her naval predominance in the Baltic'.[125]

Before coming to an end, the Paris conference decided upon a procedure for presenting the armistice terms to Germany by which

[121] Record of Beatty's remarks to ministers, 26 Oct. 1918, ADM 116/1651.
[122] Beatty to Geddes, 11 Nov. 1918, ADM 116/1809.
[123] Note by Geddes, 7 Nov. 1918, and record of meeting on 9 Nov. 1918, ADM 116/1852.
[124] Memorandum by Director of Plans, 9 Nov. 1918, ADM 116/1861.
[125] Admiralty memorandum for Cabinet, 6 Jan. 1919, ADM 116/1810.

President Wilson would suggest to the German government that it should send emissaries to Marshal Foch. The conference also made plans for continuing the war if necessary including Lloyd George's cherished scheme for an attack on Germany from the south. It discussed a proposal, also put forward by the British Prime Minister, that air bases should be set up in Bohemia to bomb Berlin.

While the conference took place there was only one important War Cabinet meeting. This was on 1 November when Hankey returned from Paris to report on the negotiations. The ministers present agreed that Lloyd George should be advised to seek assurances from House on Point III of the Fourteen Points and on the German colonies.[126] He carried out the advice on Point III by fully supporting Clemenceau's successful demand that France could only accept it as a basis for discussion. On the German colonies he did not add anything to what he had told House on 29 October: that if the southern Dominions did not retain the colonies which they occupied there would be a revolution against the British Empire.[127]

When the Prime Minister reported to the War Cabinet on the recent conference on 5, 6 and 7 November, his actions on this and other points were criticized by the Australian Prime Minister, Hughes, who had been resident in Britain since the Imperial War Cabinet of the previous summer. Hughes accused him of betraying the interests of the Dominions not only on the German colonies but also by committing them to a league of nations and to Point III with its implication of compulsory low tariffs and, finally, of insulting them by inadequate consultation.[128]

These complaints had little substance. There is no reason to doubt the sincerity of Lloyd George's reply that the wide wording of the Fourteen Points, combined with the actual possession of the colonies by the allies, would make it impossible for the United States to dictate their fate. Furthermore, according to Balfour, it had been agreed at the conference at Riddell's home on 13 October that the colonial claims of the Dominions must be met.[129] However, Hughes

---

[126] War Cabinet, 1 Nov. 1918, CAB 23/14.   [127] Rudin, op. cit. p. 270.
[128] War Cabinet, 5 Nov. 1918, CAB 23/8, and 6 Nov. 1918, CAB 23/44; cf. the correspondence between Lloyd George and Hughes in Lloyd George MSS. F/28/2/7-10 and 20; Hughes made his complaints public in a speech and in a communication to *The Times*, cf. *The Times*, 8–9 Nov. 1918.
[129] War Cabinet, 14 Oct. 1918, CAB 23/8. No Dominion representative was present on either of these occasions and so there is no reason to read a propagandist intention into Balfour's remarks.

was right in the sense that Lloyd George never felt enthusiasm for their absorption into the British Empire, a point on which there is ample testimony from himself and others.[130]

The defeat of Germany remained to the end the major British war aim and, once the Germans showed themselves ready to acknowledge defeat, British leaders were anxious to end the slaughter as quickly as possible. It was only the fear that under the formula of the Freedom of the Seas the United States would impose a crippling blow to British security—setting out conditions which had not existed before the war—that troubled their pleasure at this prospect. Concern at the possibility that there might conceivably be some loophole under which the Empire would not be able to annex German East Africa or German New Guinea was not a major factor.

Ministers continued until the very last moment to wonder whether Germany would sign the allied armistice terms. At a War Cabinet meeting on the evening of 10 November, Balfour told George Barnes that he was inclined to think 'that no men who could stand upright could so humiliate themselves as to sign the document which had been presented to them'.[131] After Germany had signed and her helplessness had become fully apparent the mood of British leaders, who had always drawn a distinction between the German people and their rulers and who had for a time been forced to consider a peace settlement which would have left Germany dominant on the continent of Europe, became vindictive. The psychology of victory is well expressed in a letter on the post-armistice situation in Germany written by Lord Hardinge, the Permanent Under-Secretary of State at the Foreign Office. After stating a belief that militarists were still secretly in control of the new German Republic, he continued: 'Our terms under these circumstances cannot be too hard and when the allies have made up their minds as to what those terms should be they must be forced upon the Germans without discussion. The big stick is what bullies like them understand better than anything else.'[132]

[130] Journals, 26 Oct. 1918, 50905; D. Lloyd George, *War Memoirs*, ii. 1930-1, and *Memoirs of the Peace Conference*, i. 30, 32–3; H. Nicolson, *Peacemaking 1919*, pp. 83, 89.   [131] G. N. Barnes, *From Workshop to War Cabinet* (1924), p. 216.
[132] Hardinge to Wingate, 28 Nov. 1918, Hardinge MSS. XXXIX.

VII

ECONOMIC WAR AIMS

SIDE by side with the military struggle, the allied powers in the First World War waged an economic war designed to contribute to victory by cutting off economic and financial relations between the enemy powers and neutrals as well as the allied states. The present discussion is concerned not with the economic war as such but with certain narrower questions: British official thinking on the possibility of using the threat of the maintenance and intensification of the economic war after military hostilities had ceased to force Germany into an early peace on allied terms; and whether the British had long-term economic war aims designed to block Germany's bid to become a world Great Power commercially as well as politically. The entire question is closely bound up with the conflict between Free Traders and Protectionists in pre-war domestic politics, with relations with the self-governing Dominions and with the policies of Britain's allies, above all the United States. None of these factors can be fully treated in these pages.

During the first two years and more of the war the doctrine that victory could only come through military struggle was virtually unchallenged in ruling circles. In October 1916, Hankey, the one leading figure who believed that 'in the last resort' victory could be won by economic rather than military pressure, confessed that he was almost alone in this view.[1] More typical were the attitudes of the Foreign Office's leading expert on the economic war, W. G. Max Müller, who believed that victory through this instrument, the reduction of the German people to defeat by privation and actual starvation, could almost certainly never be achieved.[2]

[1] Hankey, 'General Review of the War', 31 Oct. 1916, CAB 42/22/14. For Hankey's faith in the efficacy of the economic weapon see Hankey to Drummond, 25 Feb. 1915, FO 800/90.

[2] Memorandum on 'Economic Position of the Central Powers', 26 Oct. 1916, CAB 42/22/9. Müller was holding strongly to this view two years later. Cf. his memorandum of 11 June 1918, FO 371/4364, no. 160.

This view of the limited results which could be achieved by economic warfare went hand-in-hand with the notion that it would be immoral to starve the Germans into surrender or at least that victory achieved by this means would somehow not discredit aggression and militarism in the same way as would defeat in the field.[3]

Even so, by the second year of the war the Board of Trade were discussing in strictest secrecy post-war economic measures against Germany.[4] In 1916 a Board committee reported that it was essential that British industries which had been dependent on imports from Germany before the war and which had striven to find alternatives to this dependence since its outbreak must be protected.[5] Austen Chamberlain announced government endorsement of this recommendation.[6] At the same time a committee under Eyre Crowe was expressing remorse for the Foreign Office's pre-war neglect of British trade interests overseas and urged the adoption of national economic policies to be pursued with as much vigour as the political aspects of foreign policy.[7]

What prompted this activity was a belief, held almost as an article of faith in official circles though unsupported by the slightest concrete evidence, that Germany was making elaborate plans to launch an 'economic offensive' as soon as the war ceased to achieve complete ascendancy in markets where she had long been challenging British trade. It was this belief which led Asquith to abandon his Free Trade scruples and consent to the establishment of a system of economic controls,[8] and which was to lead Bonar Law in the debates on the resolutions of the Paris economic conference to say that he was convinced that the Germans were employing vast numbers of their womenfolk to produce goods for this end.[9] Subsidiary considerations

---

[3] Cf. Balfour to Hankey, 17 Feb. 1915, Balfour MSS., B.M. Add. 49703.

[4] W. J. Ashley to Bonar Law, 21 Dec. 1915, Bonar Law MSS. 52/1/50; Runciman to Balfour, 14 Oct. 1915, Balfour MSS., B.M. Add. 49716.

[5] This report was published as Cd. 8181, Jan. 1916, *State Papers 1916*, XV.

[6] Cf. *Commons Debates*, 5th series, LXXXII, col. 1680, 13 May 1916.

[7] Report in Cd. 8715, 1917, *State Papers 1917–1918*, XXIX.

[8] Spender and Asquith, op. cit. ii. 224–5.

[9] *Commons Debates*, 5th series, LXXXV, cols. 395–6, 2 Aug. 1916; see also paragraph 51 in Cd. 8181 for a typical expression of this assumption. The historian, H. W. C. Davis, who was working in the War Trade Intelligence Department and who was, therefore, well-placed to give an opinion, was one of the very few to point out this lack of evidence and to proceed to argue that it was most improbable that at the end of the war Germany would be in any condition to launch an 'economic offensive'. Davis expressed these views in a pamphlet which, though it was published on behalf of the government Stationery Office, can have made little impact on opinion, official or popular.

included pressure from the French for the Entente to found a post-war economic alliance against Germany on the same grounds of preventing her from flooding world markets with cheap goods,[10] and from some Dominion leaders. The most notable of the latter was the Australian Prime Minister, Hughes, who, always at something of a loss to understand the territorial issues involved in the war, was convinced that, 'Putting it fairly, the struggle between the two races [i.e. British and Germans] is for economic domination or supremacy.'[11] In England during the first six months of 1916 Hughes made countless speeches calling for the utter elimination of German trade and finance from the British Empire.

Finally, a further factor behind the government's decision in March 1916 to participate in an inter-allied economic conference in Paris lay in the support which the Conservatives gave to French pressure for such a gathering. Bonar Law urged Grey to discuss post-war economic measures as a means of fostering imperial unity in trade[12] while doubting whether it was feasible to formulate a permanent economic policy toward Germany while the war was still taking place.[13] Bonar Law exerted very considerable pressure upon Asquith for his inclusion in the British delegation to this conference, arguing that his position as Colonial Secretary and Conservative leader made it necessary, and he was successful in the end.[14]

After some delay, the conference finally met in Paris in June 1916 under the chairmanship of the French Minister of Commerce, Albert Clémentel. The British delegation was led by Walter Runciman, the President of the Board of Trade, and included Bonar Law and Hughes. The conference resolved that the governments of the Entente powers should encourage trade among themselves, pool their resources and strive to make themselves economically independent of the Central Powers. Except for the denial to the enemy states of Most Favoured Nation treatment for a number of years, to be decided upon later, after the war, the conference was vague in

Summary of Information Furnished by the War Trade Intelligence Department Relating to German Trade After the War, compiled and with an introduction by H. W. C. Davis (1916).

[10] Memorandum by Bertie on remarks by the French prime minister, Briand, at inter-allied conference in Paris, 27 Mar. 1916, FO 800/175.

[11] Imperial War Conference minutes, 26 June 1918, CAB 32/1/2.

[12] Bonar Law to Grey, 14 Feb. 1916, FO 800/91.

[13] Bonar Law to J. P. Croal, 25 Mar. 1916, Bonar Law MSS. 53/6/66.

[14] Bonar Law to Asquith, 25 Mar. 1916, ibid. 53/6/65; Asquith to Bonar Law, 25 Mar. 1916, ibid. 52/4/27; Walter Long to Bonar Law, 24 Mar. 1916, ibid. 52/4/28.

laying down the economic terms to be imposed in the peace treaties. It merely stated that there should be further discussions on reparations and that 'special rules' of a discriminatory nature should be applied against enemy commerce for, again, a term to be specified later. The essentially defensive nature of these recommendations is reflected in a secret annex to them which suggested that the allied governments should seek to ascertain the resources in raw materials and manufactured goods of the Central Powers which they had built to launch an 'export drive' after hostilities had ceased.[15]

The Paris economic conference of 1916 was the only major attempt by the allied powers in the First World War to draw up a common post-war economic policy. Signs soon appeared that it had failed. The Russian government, anxious for the resumption of its pre-war trade with Germany, refused to ratify the conference resolutions without the addition of a protocol in effect allowing signatories to ignore those provisions which they considered detrimental to their interests.[16] A few months later, the entry of the United States into the war virtually ended hope of drawing up a common programme of economic war aims (see below). The conference was also of little use in achieving Bonar Law's aim of preparing the ground for imperial economic unity and ultimately a protective tariff. Canadian susceptibilities over their non-representation at prime minister-level made it necessary to give an assurance that 'This conference will be only preliminary and of no practical value'.[17] However, the doctrine that during the 'Reconstruction' period after the war there must be extraordinary economic measures against probable German commercial aggression continued to be conventional in official discussions.

This policy was endorsed in a memorandum which the Board of Trade produced in October 1916 in response to Asquith's call two months previously for the departments to express their views on war aims. Apart from supporting what seemed the self-evident wisdom of making the allied states completely independent of Germany as far as possible, its recommendations were moderate. Those on indemnities, which were the work of Philip Ashley and J. M. Keynes, called for reparations to be in kind and not money

---

[15] The resolutions of the conference were published at the time, Cd. 8271, 1916, *State Papers 1916*, XXXIV; there is a copy of the resolutions with the secret annexes in CAB 16/36.   [16] Foreign Office memorandum, 1 Jan. 1917, FO 800/214.

[17] Bonar Law to the Governor-General of Canada, 8 Apr. 1916, Bonar Law MSS. 50/2/3. Canada was represented by her Minister of Commerce, Sir G. Foster.

and to be claimed only for certain specific objects—merchant shipping losses, the materials needed to repair the invaded territories and also the supply of certain materials of industry for which the allies would otherwise be dependent on the Central Powers, notably potash—rather than for the whole or part of the entire cost of the war. A lump sum to cover the whole of the indebtedness of enemy nationals in allied states, estimated at £150 million, was also recommended.[18] At the same time, Balfour was writing that with certain exceptions, similar to those in the Board paper, indemnities should not be imposed as they were 'needlessly humiliating even when they are not onerous; and when they are onerous they are sure—sooner or later—to be broken'.[19]

This set the keynote for those aspects of economic policy toward Germany which were not international in scope and in which the British could decide their policy without negotiating with their allies. A committee under Milner on economic war aims set up by the Imperial War Cabinet in April 1917 agreed that British reparation claims should be modest and declared it more desirable that Germany should repair Belgium as a symbol of atonement for her war-guilt than that British claims should be met.[20] In June 1917 the War Cabinet decided, subject to discussion with its allies, that at the peace conference Britain should demand 'ton for ton' compensation for merchant shipping losses[21] and did not decide to claim compensation under any other heads while the war continued. In January 1918 it adopted a Board of Trade report which suggested complete state regulation of the dye industry to make it self-sufficient.[22]

This industry was considered to be a unique case owing to the very great degree of its dependence on imports from Germany before 1914.[23] The larger question of complete economic self-sufficiency *vis-à-vis* Germany involved wide questions of relations with the self-governing Dominions. The ideal of such self-sufficiency could only be realized if adequate markets were available in the Dominions for British goods and if they excluded Germany from any share in their agricultural or mineral wealth.

[18] Memorandum by Board of Trade, 27 Oct. 1916, CAB 29/1.
[19] Memorandum, 4 Oct. 1916, printed in D. Lloyd George, *War Memoirs*, i. 523–9.
[20] Report of Milner committee, 24 Apr. 1917, CAB 29/1.
[21] War Cabinet, 7 June 1917, CAB 23/3.
[22] War Cabinet , 23 Jan. 1918, CAB 23/5.
[23] Economic Offensive Committee minutes, 2 Nov. 1917, CAB 27/15; and Board of Trade memoranda E.O.C. 24 in ibid. and E.O.C. 53 in CAB 27/16.

At the Imperial War Cabinet in March and April 1917, the Dominions showed themselves unwilling to yield an inch of their political autonomy for the cause of imperial federation. Likewise, in the economic field, they were lukewarm to the British government's proposals for national ore and metal trading companies to be set up in each Dominion with an international company for overall super-vision in order to exclude foreign, particularly United States and German, interests from controlling imperial mineral resources on the grounds that this would detract from their 'local autonomy'. They were equally unwilling to undertake not to restore trade relations with Germany after the war. Only the New Zealanders spoke in favour of refusing such resumption. (Hughes of Australia who was absent would undoubtedly have taken the same line as New Zealand.) It is interesting that at the same time as the imperial gathering was taking place, the British War Cabinet agreed that the resolutions of the Paris economic conference were undesirable as adversely affecting certain industries such as coal and Yorkshire woollens which had been dependent on German markets before the war.[24]

Before dissolving, the Imperial War Cabinet and Conference passed resolutions calling for imperial self-sufficiency in foodstuffs, for the principle of imperial economic preference and encouragement of emigration from Britain to the Dominions, for the control of the Empire's wool and mineral resources in order to exclude Germans and for protective measures to prevent the 'dumping' of enemy goods as part of the anticipated economic offensive after the war.[25]

These resolutions gave a more grandiose impression of the achievements of the meeting than was warranted by the facts. How-ever, economic planning within Whitehall had been given a spur; for instance, the Board of Trade had recommended that the length of the 'interim' period during which German trade was to be sub-jected to special disabilities should be five years.[26] Planning con-tinued afterwards though at first on something of a shoe-string. In July 1917 Long complained to Balfour that Professor Hewins, an influential Conservative backbencher who had been entrusted with planning the implementation of the preference resolutions of the

[24] War Cabinet, 3 Apr. 1917, CAB 23/2.
[25] The minutes of the Imperial War Conference discussions on economic policy, 2, 4, 23, 25 and 26 Apr. 1917 are in CAB 32/1/1; the resolutions were published in Cd. 8566, May 1917, pp. 109–15.
[26] Board of Trade memorandum, no date but Mar. 1917, G.T. 310, CAB 24/9.

Imperial War Cabinet, was carrying out his work with no resources so that Long personally had had to lend him £200.[27] Momentum was to gather with the setting up of an Economic Offensive Committee of the War Cabinet under Carson in September and later a special department under A. Steel-Maitland to secure British exports after the war.

The increasing pre-occupation of the British with the economic implications of the war had two aspects. It reflected a desire to do permanent damage to Germany's commercial position in the extra-European world as a desirable war aim. As early as August 1914, when it became clear that Japan intended to enter the war, the Board of Trade informed E. F. Crowe, the commercial attaché at the embassy in Tokyo, that the government were considering helping British firms to capture permanently German trade with Japan. The attaché found it heartening to know that 'the government are so full of confidence that they are prepared to consider schemes of this sort'; while the ambassador, Sir C. Greene, referred to 'the attempt which is to be made to oust German firms from the position they occupy in Japanese commerce'.[28] A similar policy in China was favoured in the Far Eastern Department of the Foreign Office though not by the British minister in Peking.[29] In September 1915, a junior Foreign Office official commented that Japan could not be condemned for trying to use the war to expand her trade: 'We ourselves desire to seize the opportunity to capture German trade.'[30] In Japan the industrious Crowe was asserting by 1916 that he had reduced German trade to 'very small dimensions' by 'private steps', among which he listed persuading the Ministry of Communications to instruct Japanese steamers not to carry enemy cargo and the Yokohama Specie Bank 'to eschew anything with an enemy taint'.[31]

In February 1916 a secret War Office memorandum recommended that British traders should be encouraged to take advantage of the Trading with the Enemy Acts and the reduction of German trade

[27] Long to Balfour, 20 July 1917, FO 800/207.
[28] E. F. Crowe to T. Worthington Evans, Director, Commercial Intelligence Branch, Board of Trade, 18 Aug. 1914; despatch by Sir C. Greene, 21 Aug. 1914, both in FO 371/2020, no. 54444.
[29] Cf. J. N. Jordan, minister in Peking, to Sir W. Langley, head of Far Eastern Department, 4 and 19 Aug. 1915, FO 800/31.
[30] Minute by Charles Wingfield, 29 Sept. 1915, FO 371/2390, no. 140227.
[31] Despatch by H. Norman of the British embassy, Tokyo, 25 Aug. 1916, enclosing a memorandum by Crowe, 22 Aug. 1916, copy in BT 55/8.

on account of the war to establish themselves in markets formerly held by Germany:

By checking German shipping and German imports of raw materials during the period immediately subsequent to the declaration of peace, by the establishment on British territory of manufactures of such commodities as aniline and potash of which Germany up to the present has held the monopoly and by the formation of syndicates, cartels and trusts to compete with similar German organizations, much may be done to assist British trade to retain the advantages which it has gained. The British Empire can supply everything which is needed for trade or manufacture, and if properly organized should have nothing to fear from the competition of Germany, Austria–Hungary, Bulgaria and Turkey which Germany is seeking to unite in a central European economic alliance.[32]

In November 1917 the Foreign Office sent a circular to British representatives in Spain, Latin America, China, Siam and Morocco, instructing them to do everything that they could to prevent German economic recovery there after the war: 'It is pointed out that allied firms and subjects abroad should take the fullest advantage of war conditions and the effect of the statutory list to destroy or capture German trade in those countries and prevent the accumulation of supplies for post-war shipment to Germany.'[33] Shortly before this Cecil had noted with satisfaction that German trade in the Far East had been shattered, that good work toward the same end was being accomplished in South America and that it would probably be possible to force the remaining neutral countries to end their financial relations with the Central Powers.[34]

Yet it would be mistaken to look upon this notion of driving German trade out of world markets—in a sense an attempt to turn the clock back to the early and middle decades of the nineteenth century—as a settled policy. The uncertainty of political and economic relations with the Dominions and with the United States (on which see below) ensured that only spasmodic progress would be made in this direction. The survival of an attitude of *laissez faire*, of an unwillingness to try to put British traders in overseas markets in a privileged position, which has recently been traced through the

[32] 'Secret: Note on Restrictions of German Trade', unsigned but probably written by the Director of Military Intelligence, Macdonagh, 25 Feb. 1916, WO 106/1510, no. 18.
[33] L. S. Amery's remarks in *Western and General Report*, XLIII, 21 Nov. 1917, CAB 24/147.
[34] Memorandum by Cecil, 28 Sept. 1917, G. 159, copy in FO 800/214.

World War to the time of the Great Depression,[35] was important. So also was a realization that the allies would make nonsense of their hopes for the emergence of a democratic and peaceful Germany if they subjected her to crippling economic disadvantages. The Milner committee in April 1917 felt that five years might be too long a time for the transition period of extraordinary economic measures against Germany after the war because of 'possible changes in a democratic direction in the form of government in Germany'.[36]

What really mattered to the British was the elimination of the practice of using economic means to obtain sinister political influence in which Germany was considered to have indulged. In a paper on policy toward Turkey written in October 1917, William Tyrrell said: 'Almost every country has discovered as a result of the war that there was a political and sinister side to the apparently innocent commercial and industrial enterprise of Germany in its territories and that the introduction of German capital and applied science was intended to be made the basis of economic vassalage and ultimately of political servitude to Germany.' Germany had thus obtained 'a predominating influence over national economy' in Italy, Russia, Switzerland, Belgium, Bulgaria, Rumania and above all Turkey by 1914. He recommended various measures to counter this such as the establishment of a British bank and compulsory open bidding for public utility contracts, while specifically accepting that German trade could not be excluded from Turkey after the war under any circumstances. The 'paramount object' should be rather 'to remove the political sting from any German economic enterprise in Turkey'.[37] Tyrrell, a major figure in the formulation of British foreign policy, thus did not envisage that Britain's immense sacrifices in the war against Turkey should lead to any advantages in trade other than those which would accompany the abolition of commercial practices unfairly favouring other nations.

A second economic consideration and one which weighed more heavily in the minds of ministers was to use the allies' practical monopoly, once the United States was a belligerent, of many vital raw materials to force Germany to make peace on allied terms by

[35] D. C. M. Platt, *Finance, Trade and Politics: British Foreign Policy 1815–1914* (1968), pp. xxx–xxxix, 142–8.

[36] Milner committee, minutes of second session, 17 Apr. 1917, CAB 29/71; cf. also T. Jones, *Whitehall Diary*, pp. 30, 32.

[37] Memorandum on 'Turkey in Europe and Asia', 22 Oct. 1917, FO 800/214. For the attribution of authorship to Tyrrell see n. 168 to Chapter III above.

threatening to continue to deny her those materials after the war. This reflected a growing lack of faith that the war could be won by military means and must be sharply distinguished from the policy of trying to starve and weaken Germany into submission by the economic blockade of her shores and frontiers while the war went on. Those who knew Lloyd George well noted that even when he felt most pessimistic about military prospects he did not believe that the economic blockade of Germany could bring her to her knees.[38] He was constantly seeking short-cuts to win the war and the blockade was clearly not one of those. The long if bloodless haul involved in primary reliance on the economic weapon no more appealed to the Prime Minister's mind than did the strategy of attrition in France and Flanders. Even Milner, with a less mercurial mind than Lloyd George, feared that if the war were allowed to drag on until Germany was starved it would last longer than the public would be prepared to accept.[39]

What more and more attracted the leadership during the last eighteen months of the war was the possibility that the threat of denying Germany vital raw materials after the war would strike such a blow as to compel her to make peace on allied terms. One of the first public figures to advocate such a policy had been Henry Wickham Steed in April 1916.[40] A year later disillusionment with military prospects and a stream of reports that German opinion was desperately afraid of such an outcome to the war[41] won the idea important adherents. While Balfour was in Washington, Cecil passed on to him one of these reports and urged him to suggest to the United States administration that they should make use of this 'powerful and humane weapon'.[42] A month later the American ambassador, Walter Page, summarized a new consensus of official opinion in London: 'If Germany can be made to see that practically the whole world will discriminate against her trade after the war she will be the more likely to give in at some early time.'[43] About the same time Lloyd George was speaking favourably of using economic threats 'as a means of forcing the enemy to come to terms, giving say

[38] Harold Spender, *The Prime Minister* (1920), pp. 181–2; Hankey, op. cit. ii. 703–7.
[39] Milner to E. B. Poulton, 8 June 1917, Milner MSS. 144 (VI).
[40] Wickham Steed, op. cit. ii. 95.
[41] E.g. Townley, minister at The Hague, to FO, 1 Oct. 1917, FO 371/2941, no. 191285.
[42] Cecil to Balfour, 17 May 1917, FO 800/208.
[43] B. J. Hendrick, *The Life and Letters of Walter H. Page*, iii (1924), 378.

six months notice that if they did not surrender the economic boycott would be used against them'.[44]

At the time of the War Cabinet debates on the papal peace note, Cecil outlined to his colleagues a scheme suggested to him by Clémentel for threatening to deny Germany those essential raw materials in which the allies had a virtual monopoly unless she made peace on their terms. Ministerial opinion was far from unanimously favourable. On the analogy that the British people would respond to such a threat by doubling their war efforts, it was suggested that the Germans might do the same. It was also argued that if Germany rejected the scheme it would become an encumbrance: in the event of complete victory it would fetter their freedom to impose whatever terms they chose while in the event of a compromise peace Germany would be able to demand its abandonment. Even so it was agreed that the scheme should be kept under review.[45]

Though the initial reception of this scheme was thus mixed, it had powerful friends in Cecil and Hardinge,[46] and in Bonar Law.[47] Balfour, commenting upon the Lansdowne letter, also felt that it would be justified to threaten Germany with post-war economic sanctions if that country 'shows herself to be utterly unreasonable'.[48] The idea continued to find favour in Foreign Office and propaganda circles during 1918. Hankey and Cecil coupled it with the league of nations, hoping that machinery would be built up for it which could be bequeathed to a world body for use against future aggressors.[49] H. G. Wells, during his brief spell in Lord Northcliffe's propaganda organization in Crewe House drew up elaborate plans in the middle of the year by which Germany would be offered a secure economic future in return for acknowledging defeat and acquiescing in territorial losses.[50] Eustace Percy and Alfred Zimmern, the economic specialists in the Political Intelligence Department, recommended economic threats as uniquely likely to have a disintegrating effect on the mass of Germans who, it was explained, hoped that the war would give them a more secure and comfortable economic life rather than for military grandeur.[51]

[44] Journals, 50904, 9–11 Aug. 1917.   [45] War Cabinet, 20 Aug. 1917, CAB 23/3.
[46] See the minutes by them, *c.* 27 Aug. 1917, FO 371/2864, no. 166940.
[47] Seymour, op. cit. iii. 232–3.
[48] Memorandum by Balfour on Lansdowne, Dec. 1917, copy in FO 800/213.
[49] Memorandum by Hankey, 16 Jan. 1918, G.T. 3344, CAB 24/39; Cecil to House, 22 July 1918, FO 371/4365, no. 259, also in Seymour, op. cit. iv. 39–42.
[50] Wickham Steed, op. cit. ii. 222–4.
[51] See their memoranda, 14 June 1918, FO 371/4357, no. 174 and 1 Aug. 1918, FO 371/4367, no. 434.

However, such threats were never actually uttered in official form. When in April 1918 Cecil suggested that the time had come to resort to them, Hankey had to inform the Foreign Office that the War Cabinet had reached no decision on which such a declaration could be based.[52] In addition to the doubts about their feasibility expressed in the War Cabinet in August 1917, very slow progress was made in planning machinery for the control of raw materials after the war. A committee on United Kingdom trade relations within the Empire, set up in October 1917 under the chairmanship of Long, drew up two largely identical lists of raw materials, comprising those in which the Empire would need to acquire adequate stocks for the Reconstruction period and those which could be used as bargaining counters with enemy states. Further action had to await the endorsement of this report by the second Imperial War Conference in the summer.[53] This was given and the conference also approved an Imperial Mineral Resources Bureau which had been provisionally set up in June. However, the Dominions again showed themselves hyper-sensitive toward any British control of their economic resources. Indeed, they insisted that the word 'control' in the report of the Long committee should be replaced with 'command' which was considered less offensive. Walter Long, though an ardent imperialist, was left thinking that the prospects for a solid economic block within the Empire were bleak.[54]

More difficult still was the danger that economic threats would be misunderstood in the United States and by working-class opinion at home as selfish long-term schemes for the benefit of British capitalism. In August 1917, the Labour Party and the Trades Union Congress announced their opposition to anything which smacked of a continuation of the war by economic means after fighting ceased.[55] The leaders fell back on the policy that economic threats should be presented in the genuine guise of measures that the allies would have to take after the war in the interests of their own economic well-being and security. The sole element of threat would be that if the war were prolonged the shortage of raw materials would become more

[52] Minute by Cecil, *c.* 2 Apr. 1918, FO 371/3381, no. 52478. This seems to have formed the basis for a letter which Hardinge sent to Hankey three weeks later, 25 Apr. 1918, CAB 21/108; Hankey's reply, 27 Apr. 1918, is in CAB 24/49 G.T. 4368.

[53] Report of this committee and conference resolution upon it in CAB 32/1/2, xii, 209–57.

[54] Long to Cecil, 15 Nov. 1918, Cecil MSS., B.M. Add. 51094.

[55] Winkler, op. cit. p. 179.

acute so that there would be correspondingly less that the allies could spare from their own needs for Germany. In January 1918, Carson, the War Cabinet minister most concerned with economic warfare and planning, triumphantly boasted that the public were pre-occupied with 'a controversy which, so far as the government is concerned, does not exist': whether there should be punitive measures against Germany after the war. All the proposals of his Economic Offensive Committee were in the first place genuinely concerned with the needs of British and allied reconstruction and with resisting the economic offensive which Germany would surely launch after the war.[56] It was on this understanding that the Dominion statesmen in the summer assented to the British government's proposals for central direction of raw materials.[57] It must be emphasized that the British were acting in good faith. As early as December 1916 a strong committee under Lord Balfour of Burleigh had recommended that it was essential on purely economic grounds for the British Empire and its allies to control commodities which they produced and of which there would be a post-war shortage.[58]

The capital difficulty in the way of economic threats against Germany lay in relations with the United States. President Wilson's views on this aspect of economic policy were really similar to those of the British leaders. In January 1918, echoing an analysis which was often put forward in Whitehall, he told Wiseman that while Germany had all the military advantages, Britain and the United States held all the economic advantages and that he intended to use the undoubted post-war scarcity of raw materials to force the German military party to give way at the peace conference—an interesting sign that, again like the British, he was becoming reconciled to dealing with the existing rulers of Germany.[59] In certain of his addresses, notably those of 4 December 1917 and 27 September 1918, he hinted that if it did actually prove necessary to negotiate with a regime in Germany which was deemed militarist, then the

[56] Memorandum, 21 Jan. 1918, G. 190, p. 11 in CAB 24/4.

[57] Cf. statements by Borden, 19 June 1918, and Hughes and Ward, 26 June 1918, CAB 32/1/2. Hughes said: 'I think if we get, as General Smuts says, enough for ourselves really the thing [i.e. economic sanctions against Germany] settles itself because there is not enough for ourselves and for them.'

[58] 'Committee on Commercial and Industrial Policy: Interim Report on . . . Exports . . .', 14 Dec. 1916, Cd. 9034, 1918, *State Papers 1918*, XII. This argument was maintained in the final report, 3 Dec. 1917, G.T. 2891, CAB 24/34.

[59] Memorandum by William Wiseman on interview with President Wilson, 23 Jan. 1918, Balfour MSS., B.M. Add. 49741.

democratic nations would be obliged to deny her a full place in the community of nations including a denial of economic rights. Again, this corresponded with the circumstances, ones in which there was manifestly a possibility of Germany resuming military aggression, in which the British thought that it would be necessary to wage a permanent economic struggle against Germany as part of a policy of denying her every possible advantage.[60]

However, Wilson suspected the British of harbouring the most sinister economic war aims. Like many Americans, he misunderstood the resolutions of the Paris economic conference of 1916 which he regarded as a blueprint for Entente, chiefly British, world economic domination,[61] though his self-righteous hostility to what he took to be British economic aims had not prevented him, during the early months of the war, from initiating a policy by which his administration would aid American businessmen in replacing German and British trade in the western hemisphere.[62] Balfour and Cecil were from the moment of America's entry into the war anxious to dispel the sort of impression of the 1916 resolutions held by the President,[63] but were dealing with a field in which Americans were peculiarly prone to believe the worst about their new allies. The British for their part, were unable (on account of relations with the French) or unwilling to denounce the Paris resolutions which alone might have made possible Anglo–American economic co-operation both on reconstruction needs and on threats to level against Germany. In May 1918 Bonar Law publicly reaffirmed that the government still adhered to the Paris resolutions.[64] A few weeks later Victor Wellesley, the head of the commercial department at the Foreign Office, wrote to the Board of Trade that unity on post-war economic policy among the allies would be certain 'to produce a

[60] Text of the President's speeches in Scott, op. cit. pp. 193–202 and 399–405. Cf. a memorandum by Percy, 26 Apr. 1918, FO 371/4360, no. 81, in which he spoke of a British intention to disrupt German financial and commercial operations after the war 'in the event but only in the event of an unsatisfactory and inconclusive peace'.

[61] For the virulent American distrust of British economic aims which Wilson shared in full see L. W. Martin, op. cit. pp. 112, 128–9, 176–7.

[62] William Diamond, 'The Economic Thought of Woodrow Wilson', pp. 135–6, 151–2, 154 in *The Johns Hopkins University Studies in Historical and Political Sciences*, vol. lxi (1943).

[63] Memorandum circulated by Balfour to members of his American mission on 'What it is and what it is not expedient to say on several questions which are known to be of interest to Americans', no date, FO 800/208; memorandum by Cecil, 31 Aug. 1917, FO 800/198.

[64] *Commons Debates*, 5th series, CVI, cols. 30–1, 13 May 1918.

profound and depressing effect in the mind of the enemy'. 'Mr. Balfour', he added, 'is of opinion that this is a point to which too much importance can hardly be attached.'[65] However, this could only be a pious aspiration.

Under these circumstances no purpose could be served by clumsy manoeuvres such as Cecil's remarks to an American press agency in mid-July in which he attempted to depict a policy of threatening Germany with post-war economic sanctions unless she abandoned her 'restless and aggressive policy' as one which had been enunciated by President Wilson and which the British were merely anxious to follow.[66] During the summer of 1918, Percy and Cecil corresponded with certain members of the British embassy staff in Washington on the probable food and raw material needs of the United States in the reconstruction period.[67] This had to serve as an indirect substitute for Anglo–American negotiations even on the straightforward economic needs of the allies.

A crisis in relations with the United States arose just as the British, tired of waiting for an American response to their pleas, were moving toward a unilateral policy of drawing up a scheme for the control of raw materials which was to be given sufficient publicity for it to become widely known in Germany.[68] Wilson, greatly annoyed by a speech by Lloyd George which he took to mean that Britain sought a post-war trade boycott of Germany, warned that he would openly denounce such a proposal if the British adopted it officially.[69] He coupled this warning with a statement of his readiness to use economic threats to force Germany to make concessions in peace negotiations—which was little different from what the British wanted. However, their rather frantic attempts to reassure the

[65] Wellesley to Board of Trade, 2 July 1918, BT 11/15, no. 6194.

[66] These remarks, which concluded with an appeal for Britain and the United States to co-operate on the practical details of such a policy, are in *The Times*, 19 July 1918. They were actually drawn up by Percy in two versions, the first a simple exposition of the advantages of this type of scheme, the second altered to make it seem that the British were taking their cue from Wilson. Cf. Economic Defence and Development Committee minutes, 2 July 1918 and memoranda 5 and 9 by Percy, CAB 27/44. Wilson disliked Percy, who had served in the Washington embassy, because he considered him over-clever, a not unjustified judgement.   [67] Cf. FO 371/4367, especially no. 364.

[68] Economic Defence and Development Committee minutes, 13 Aug. 1918, CAB 27/44. This committee was the successor to the Economic Offensive Committee.

[69] Wiseman to Reading, 16 Aug. 1918 in Seymour, iv. 62–4. The full text of Lloyd George's speech is in *The Times*, 2 Aug. 1918. According to Wiseman the sort of fears which Wilson was to express were not general in administration circles. Cf. Wiseman to Reading, 5 and 7 Aug. 1918, FO 800/225.

President of their intentions, asserting that what they sought in their post-war economic plans was simply to provide for their own needs while making it clear to Germany that if she prolonged the war those needs would leave little surplus for the Central Powers, drew attention to the impossibility of trying to frighten Germany into peace with economic threats without American co-operation.[70]

The essence of this crisis if such it can be called was whether economic means should be used to try to extract political concessions from Germany while the war continued or at the peace conference. This hardly involved a matter of supreme principle and indeed some British leaders including Carson favoured Wilson's line. Throughout the war they would have looked upon the abandonment of almost all economic war aims against Germany as a small price to pay for her transformation to the ways of democracy and peace. The German collapse in October 1918 which left her with absolutely no bargaining position at the peace conference exposed the leadership to demands from their own public, from the French and also from the primitive-minded Hughes[71] for sweeping economic as well as political claims against Germany, especially payments of reparations, but that is another phase in history.

[70] For the British reply to the United States on economic policy see FO to Washington, 21 Sept. 1918, copy in C[olonial] O[ffice] 532/121, no. 46641; text in part in a note from the British embassy, 15 Oct. 1918, *Foreign Relations 1918, Supplement I, The World War*, i (1938), 612–14.

[71] In November and December 1918 Hughes was chairman of an Imperial War Cabinet committee which recommended that Germany should be made to pay the entire cost of the war to the allies estimated at £24,000 million. Report and minutes in CAB 27/43. Cf. a contemporaneous Board of Trade memorandum, November 1918, which advised allied acceptance of a lump sum compensation to the allies of not more than £2000 million to repair devastated territory and make up merchant shipping losses resulting from 'illegal' enemy action, CAB 29/1, no. 33.

CONCLUSION

THERE are still serious writers who treat the First World War as an incomprehensible catastrophe which, once it had begun, continued of its own momentum with cynical and myopic leaders, obsessed by lust for territorial and economic booty, hoodwinking the peoples that the war was being fought for purposes large enough to justify the immense cost which it entailed.[1] The fallacy of such an interpretation in the case of the Central Powers has been amply demonstrated. German ruling circles formulated extensive annexationist ambitions to offset demands for social and political reforms at home and so preserve the existing order there, as well as to make Germany economically and strategically stronger.[2] This interpretation also falls down in the case of the opponents of the Central Powers including Britain. British leaders and their advisers did indeed discuss the territorial issues raised by the war almost *ad nauseam* and there was a general assumption that everyone ought to gain something out of it. In 1917 the Mallet committee recommended that France should be asked to cede the small islands of St. Pierre and Miquelon to Newfoundland, partly because otherwise the British Dominions in North America 'would receive no reward for their sacrifices'.[3] Only a minority of politicians like Balfour and of civil servants like Sir Hamilton Grant realized that the jealousy of other nations toward the British Empire was itself a factor for international instability so that it was a desirable war aim to expand the British Empire as little as possible on account of the war.[4]

[1] Cf. Leon Wolff, *In Flanders Fields* (Corgi Books ed., 1966), pp. 29, 43–4, 87, 289.
[2] Cf. Gatzke, pp. 27–8, 65–6, 128–31, 165–6, 187–8, 214, 250–1.
[3] Mallet committee, third interim report, 28 Mar. 1917, CAB 16/36.
[4] For Balfour's views see minutes of Anglo–French conference, 26 Dec. 1916, CAB 28/2 I.C. 13; Eastern Committee minutes, 24 Apr. and 16 Dec. 1918, CAB 27/24 E.C. 5 and 43; memorandum, 2 May 1918, CAB 24/53 G.T. 4774; Imperial War Cabinet minutes, 13 Aug. 1918, CAB 23/42. For Grant's views see his undated memorandum, apparently written in the middle months of 1918, in Grant MSS., India Office Library, EUR MSS. D. 660. Grant, who was Foreign Secretary to the Government of India, wrote: 'We have bitten off as much of the world as we can chew and we shall be running on the rocks if we continue our policy of attempting to exclude everyone else from places in the sun on strategical, political and commercial grounds.'

Yet the leaders were always clear in their minds that territorial issues—the frontiers of Germany, the future of the German colonies, the fate of the Austro–Hungarian and Ottoman Empires—were subordinate to the need to defeat the renegade nation of Germany which they regarded as the chief and possibly even the only obstacle to a peaceful world order. To use A. J. P. Taylor's illuminating distinction, pressures from their allies and from the Dominions obliged the British to spend much time 'defining solutions for the problems which would follow the defeat of Germany' but they were always more interested in 'the objects for which Germany should be defeated.'[5]

The British were convinced that Germany in the First World War had ambitions so large that they could probably only be satisfied in full if Britain resigned herself to becoming a German client state. The need to resist appeared self-evident under these circumstances. Behind it lay a great fear and a great hope. The fear was the knowledge that Germany's great power status could not be abrogated. In August 1918 Balfour told the Imperial War Cabinet: 'Even if the whole of the war aims he had indicated in Europe were fulfilled, Germany would still remain the biggest military power in Europe and that those war aims were therefore such as Germany could in the last resort accept if beaten.'[6] Balfour almost seemed to be apologizing in advance to Germany for depriving her of Alsace-Lorraine and German Poland which he once defined as 'almost our maximum demand from Germany'.[7] Plans such as those which France entertained in 1916 and 1917 for depriving Germany of the Rhineland were deprecated both in public and private by the British leaders who thought that it was a fantasy to believe that Germany could be permanently deprived of territory whose population was wholly German.[8]

The hope was that if German power was shattered, albeit temporarily, a new Germany would arise, democratic, peaceful and above all not hostile to the *status quo*. This hope fed on the belief that the war was directed against what Lloyd George called 'the worst elements in Germany',[9] and that for many years before 1914

[5] A. J. P. Taylor, 'The War Aims of the Allies in the First World War' in *Essays to Namier*, ed. R. Pares and A. J. P. Taylor (1956), pp. 475–505.
[6] Imperial War Cabinet minutes, 15 Aug. 1918, CAB 23/42.
[7] Minute by Balfour on letter from Drummond, 29 Mar. 1917, FO 800/206.
[8] Cf. Balfour in *Commons Debates*, 5th series, C, col. 2017, 19 Dec. 1917.
[9] Speech by Lloyd George at Bangor, 28 Feb. 1915 in *Through Terror to Triumph*, ed. F. L. Stevenson (1915), p. 86.

German leaders had been divided between militarists and pacifists. The defeat of Germany would surely give the latter permanent ascendancy. In truth, all the leaders including even a man of profoundly liberal views like Grey, sometimes wondered whether this dichotomy really existed and whether all Germans with only negligible exceptions were really devotees of militarism.[10] However, the hope that it might be possible to induce Germany as a nation to a 'reasonable' frame of mind was one reason why the British kept their war aims against her within the bounds of what an historian striving for impartiality might well describe as just.

At least as important in explaining this limitation of aims was Germany's strength which showed few signs of waning until the very last months of the war. Uncertainty as to when and under what circumstances the war would end accounts largely for the relative absence of attempts to draw up programmes of war aims in the first two years of the war and for the failure of the attempts that were made in 1916–17 to draw up a detailed programme of what the nation was fighting for. There were various pressure groups at work —the Foreign Office, the admirals, the General Staff, the radical-imperialist circle around Milner and Amery—who, not at all sure that the war would end in a complete victory which would enable all of them to achieve their aims, were unwilling to give priority to the cherished objectives of anybody else.

It is curious that the British did not seriously consider a negotiated peace until after the United States had entered the war. For all the importance which they attached to relations with America, they had not yet learnt to respect her power to the extent of believing that once she was with them, final victory was only a matter of time. They were more impressed by German victories in Russia and Italy and by the impending exhaustion of their own manpower reserves. They formulated war aims which could serve either to spur on the British and allied peoples—many of them doubtful whether the war was being fought for aims of which they could approve—to make further efforts or to provide a basis for a negotiated peace. To Lloyd George the great merit of his war aims speech of 5 January 1918 was this flexibility and the fact that the whole speech could if necessary be repudiated. Four weeks after making it, he urged allied statesmen not to draw up a joint declaration of war aims and to confine them-

---

[10] Preface by Grey, 22 Sept. 1917, to Gilbert Murray, *The Way Forward* (1917), pp. 7–14, especially pp. 8–10.

selves, if they must say anything at all, to speeches: 'Nobody was bound by a speech.'[11]

Even in the dark winter of 1917–18 the prospect of a negotiated peace was a chimera. British ministers were divided on the terms and timing of such a move. They did not even begin to face the problems of drawing their allies into it. Above all, there was no sign from Germany of readiness to abandon any of the five streams—sea power based on annexations in the west, a Mitteleuropa bloc under German leadership, dominance in the Middle East, an African colonial empire and agricultural colonization in western Russia—into which one official British writer divided her war aims.[12] By the middle of 1918 the leaders were returning to the earlier line of seeking victory, though the military situation remained apparently bleak.

The issues at stake in the war were such as to preclude independent treatment of Germany's European allies, Austria–Hungary and Bulgaria. The problems of nationality which so exercised a vocal minority in British public life during the war interested ruling circles as a whole only in so far as support for the 'liberation' of the subject peoples of eastern Europe was likely to contribute to the defeat of Germany. A break between Germany and Austria always seemed a surer means to this end and so the British preferred to encourage it whenever there seemed even a faint chance that it might be possible to bring it about.

And yet, as Professor Carr once said, British policy in Europe has always been one to 'amuse cynics and infuriate rivals'.[13] With no ambitions on the continent of Europe save the overall one of preventing any one power from becoming dominant there, Britain has traditionally been able to pose as honest broker, striving for such equitable political arrangements as would reduce the risk of disputes, involvement in which might tempt one of the Great Powers to aim at European supremacy. Ministers and leading members of the Foreign Office were indeed unable to adopt a policy of seeking to come to terms with the Dual Monarchy without convincing themselves that it was doubtful whether its subject nationalities wanted full independence or at least that they ought to be denied it for their own good. It is important that in the case of the Poles, the one

[11] Supreme War Council minutes, 2 Feb. 1918, CAB 25/120, no. 80.
[12] Memorandum by E. R. Bevan, 12 July 1917, FO 371/3077, no. 138664.
[13] E. H. Carr, *Ambassadors at Large: Britain* (1939), p. 125.

submerged nation whose wish for statehood was undeniable, informed British official opinion always hoped strongly that the war would end with this wish fulfilled though before March 1917 this could only be seen within the framework of a Russo–Polish confederation.

Evidence available at the time and since indicates that the suspicion that most of the 'subject peoples' did not really want full independence was partly justified but that the reasoning that went with it, the belief that Austria was or might become capable of breaking with Germany, was wholly unwarranted.

For the British the only part of the war against Germany's allies which had a separate reality was that with Turkey. The decision on military grounds to foster an Arab revolt and the consequent need to arrive at an understanding as between the conflicting political claims of the Arabs, the French, the Italians and the British themselves led in 1915–16 to plans for the break-up of the Turkish Empire which would have given Britain effective control over much of it. Yet it is difficult to believe that even if decisions had been entirely in the hands of the British government they would not have retreated from the early reluctance to extend British responsibilities which was manifest in the War Council debates on the Russian claim to Constantinople and in the deliberations of the De Bunsen committee. Even at that early stage the British were determined to insulate the Arabian peninsula from the influence of all powers other than themselves. Later the possibilities for economic development in the rest of the Arab world—seen before 1918 more in terms of agricultural production than of oil—together with the glamour of building an empire in famous lands conquered by British blood gave birth to distinctly *British* ambitions in Mesopotamia, Palestine and finally Syria.

But there as elsewhere, the policy-makers in London, if not the officials on the spot, saw matters in a world context oriented toward Germany. In August 1917 the Director of Military Intelligence, Macdonagh, warned that unless the war ended with Germany's position in the Middle East and the Balkans smashed, she 'will then prepare for the next struggle against the British Empire and for the mastery of the world'.[14] The reaction of ministers to the treaty of Brest–Litovsk showed that well-nigh all of them shared this fear of

---

[14] 'Notes on Allied Strategy' by Macdonagh, no date but Aug. 1917, WO 106/1514, no. 15.

what Germany might do if she was not completely defeated in the Middle East and the vast southern stretches of the old Russian Empire if nowhere else. British offers to Turkey on a separate peace did not and could not include anything of substance in terms of restoring her rule over areas lost in the war. What would have happened if Britain had offered Turkey a peace based on the *status quo* of 1914 is obviously impossible to say though it is interesting that Turkey unlike Austria–Hungary was largely successful in maintaining her political, economic and military independence of Germany throughout the war.[15]

The reasons which British leaders in the Great War gave as its justification were spurious in that they were often presented as primarily beneficial to other countries or to mankind in general rather than to Britain herself. As the Political Intelligence Department put it in November 1918 in a fascinating discussion of British policy toward Belgium—the symbol of allied, especially British, moral superiority—that country might seek a reconciliation with Germany after the war. If so she would have to be coerced into an anti-German policy if the allies failed in their 'main aim in this war [which] has come to be the "civilization" of international relations by the creation of an inter-state authority.' Only if Germany became a willing partner in such an authority could the allies 'safely remain loyal to the principle of "self-determination" and leave the Belgian people to denounce its Guaranteed Neutrality and adhere as it certainly would to the League of Nations'.[16] An effective system of collective security would have benefited Britain and Belgium alike but few in official London would have dissented from the conclusion that in an imperfect world in which alliances and guarantees were the best instruments available for preserving peace, Belgium should if necessary be forced to play her part in them. Always one comes back to the point that British foreign policy in the era of the First World War was truly concerned only with the interests of the British Empire.

[15] Ulrich Trumpener, *Germany and the Ottoman Empire 1914–1918* (1968), pp. 366 ff.
[16] Political Intelligence Department memorandum on the International Status of Belgium after the War, 4 Nov. 1918, CAB 24/69 G.T. 6214.

THE BRITISH AND SELF-DETERMINATION

THE leading British statesmen were only attracted to the principle of self-determination outside Europe as a matter of expediency and because they were convinced that it would work in their favour.[1] The original impetus which drove them to endorse the principle came from a bleak war situation. The prospect of a negotiated end to the war, rather than one brought about by complete allied victory, made the argument that the inhabitants of territories occupied by the allies wished to remain under their new rulers seem a good one for bargaining purposes. Its value was enhanced by the belief that Woodrow Wilson was dedicated to a peace settlement based on self-determination which thus became the most important if not the sole means of enlisting American support for Entente territorial war aims. After leading the United States into the war, the President broke his silence on war aims occasionally to inform the British and French in confidence that his old views on the need for a peace settlement free from forcible annexations or punitive indemnities remained unchanged.[2] The government was also aware that self-determination had a strong attraction for the political left in Britain. In some draft notes for a speech to trade unions on 18 January 1918, designed to show that Germany had responded negatively to his war aims speech, Lloyd George wrote: 'What has happened? Put forward terms substance of which corresponded to yours

= Belgium

= Right of self-determination.'[3] The implication appears to be that Lloyd George thought that these two issues were the only ones for which organized workers were prepared to fight.

British ruling circles had already shown their alarm at the series of statements which the Bolsheviks issued in November and December 1917 calling for the grant of immediate independence to *all* colonial peoples. The government acted against the publication of these proclamations—

[1] Louis, op. cit. pp. 97–101.

[2] See for example Wiseman to Drummond and Balfour, 4 Feb. 1918, Balfour MSS., B.M. Add. 49741.

[3] These notes are in Lloyd George MSS. F/235. There is no comparable statement in the actual speech as recorded in *The Times*, 19 Jan. 1918.

one of which was described by Sir Thomas Holderness, Permanent Under-Secretary in the India Office, as 'potentially mischievous in the highest degree'—in the British press or their dissemination in India, China, Japan, the United States and the Netherlands East Indies.[4] However, such statements could not be kept secret for long and, together with the factors mentioned above, they created an atmosphere. By January 1918, even the ultra-conservative Chichele Professor of Modern History at Oxford, Charles Oman, then working in Whitehall, was writing that anything which smacked of annexationism or imperialism must be eliminated from allied policy because of its deplorable effect on world public opinion.[5]

The War Cabinet decided that the risks involved in meeting this problem fully, by declaring that the British Empire was based on self-determination, were too great. Afraid that if the principle were proclaimed in general terms it might cause the British trouble in one or two possessions, such as Cyprus, where the level of political consciousness was already high—if nowhere else—they agreed that the references to self-determination in Lloyd George's speech on war aims should be drawn up so as to apply only to the peace settlement in Europe, the German colonies and Turkey.[6]

This decision set the keynote for the execution of the 'self-determination' exercise in the German colonies. The Colonial Office sought from the governments of South Africa, Australia and New Zealand, and the administrators of German East Africa and the British-occupied parts of Cameroon and Togo 'evidence of anxiety of natives to live under British rule' which was carefully sifted to present British policy in a purely altruistic light and, as Sir Louis Mallet had previously suggested, to conceal any arguments for the retention of occupied territory 'which suggest that we are capable of being influenced by motives other than the highest'.[7] Accordingly, a letter from the Administrator of South West Africa and a memorandum from the South African Cabinet which made it clear that South Africa was determined to retain South West Africa for her own security, were omitted from a British Blue Book on the wishes of the natives in the German colonies on the grounds that—as Sir G. V. Fiddes, Permanent Under-Secretary at the Colonial Office, put it—they could serve no purpose except to show the real reasons why the Empire must retain South West Africa.[8]

[4] Holderness to Sir Frank Swettenham (of the Press Bureau), 7 Dec. 1917, India Office Library: Political and Secret subject files 1918: 1: file 4. See this file generally for the evidence to support the above statement.

[5] Memorandum by Oman, 8 Jan. 1918, CAB 25/42.

[6] War Cabinet, 5 p.m. on 3 Jan. and 4 Jan. 1918, CAB 23/5; cf. Hankey, ii. 737.

[7] Mallet to L. S. Amery, no date but February 1917, FO 371/2859, no. 42658.

[8] Administrator's letter, 21 Jan. 1918, C[olonial] O[ffice] 532/109, no. 13045; memorandum from South African Cabinet, 26 Mar. 1918, CO 532/110, no. 21452; Fiddes's

In the case of Australia, whose record in colonial administration was considered execrable by the Colonial Office, it proved impossible to obtain any statements of the type desired in German New Guinea. An official British memorandum for the Paris peace conference could only suggest: 'The natives are of a backward type and hardly capable of appreciating the position.'[9] More privately, a Colonial Office member was writing that the Germans could make a 'crushing case' against allowing Australia to retain New Guinea solely on the criterion of native wishes.[10] In German East Africa feeling in the Colonial Office was that German standards of administration had, at least during the six or seven years before 1914, reached tolerable standards so that a really convincing case for denying her the colony on grounds of native interests could not be made.[11]

The tiny German Pacific island of Nauru was a special case. With the partial exception of Mesopotamia, it was the only territory which the British coveted during the First World War for chiefly economic reasons. It had huge phosphate deposits and in September 1918, moved by this consideration, Sir Charles Fielding of the Board of Agriculture and Fisheries wrote to Austen Chamberlain, chairman of the Economic Defence and Development Committee,[12] arguing for the retention of the island. Chamberlain agreed to exert himself in this matter.[13] In response to a request from his committee, the Colonial Office, which had already obtained a petition from the chiefs of Nauru proclaiming their wish to remain under the protection of King George V 'as his children who are newly born in the year 1914', sought to make assurance doubly sure by asking the administrator of the island to obtain a formal request from its entire population for British rule. A fortnight later he proudly replied that such a request had been signed by everyone of the island's inhabitants.[14]

The very fact that the expurgated statements on native wishes published in November 1918 were not spontaneous but had been obtained on

---

minute, no date, CO 532/118, no. 54874; cf. 'Correspondence relating to the Wishes of the Natives of the German Colonies as to their Future Government', Cd. 9210, Nov. 1918, *Accounts and Papers*, 1918, xvii.

[9] Memorandum on the German colonies, undated but apparently Jan. 1919, CAB 29/1, no. 34.

[10] Minute by G. E. A. Grindle, late Nov. or early Dec. 1918, CO 532/112, no. 56594.

[11] Cf. Sir H. Read to Fiddes, 1 July 1918, CO 532/111, no. 29889.

[12] On this see Chapter VII above.

[13] Fielding to Chamberlain, 25 Sept. 1918, and (for Chamberlain's attitude) Clement Jones to Colonial Office, Foreign Office and Board of Trade, 28 Sept. 1918, CO 532/127, no. 46950.

[14] For these events see CO 532/128, no. 51563. The request for British rule was published in the State Paper cited in note 8 above (enclosure 16) without, of course, any indication that the British had themselves solicited it.

instructions issued by the Colonial Secretary, Walter Long, the previous January was carefully concealed.[15] Besides the artificial self-determination argument, British leaders attempted to justify the loss to Germany of her colonies with several arguments in which they sincerely believed: that Germany would use them to set up black armies and submarine bases for aggression; that the inhabitants were and knew themselves to be better off under British than under German rule; and that the southern Dominions had set their hearts on retaining the colonies which they themselves had occupied. During the last eighteen months of the war, Bolshevik propaganda and the strict letter of Wilsonian idealism though not perhaps its true spirit, seemed to call for another justification: 'a plebiscite of negroes which is absurd',[16] as Balfour put it. The British leaders set about manufacturing evidence that they had provided such a justification.[17] Their consciences were clear in view of the larger purposes which their dissimulation was meant to serve: the cohesion and security of the Empire, retention of the loyalty of the left in Britain and a demonstration to the United States that Britain did not base her policy on imperialist greed and was therefore a fitting partner in world affairs.

[15] Minutes by Read and Long, no date but late October or early November 1918, on Long's telegram to the Dominions of 4 Jan. 1918, CO 532/118, no. 54874. It should be added that the main propaganda document included reports from German East Africa and the British-administered Cameroon which dwelt on the difficulty of ascertaining the political wishes of peoples at a primitive stage of development: Enclosures 11 and 13 in Cd. 9210.

[16] Minute by Balfour, late Oct. 1917, FO 317/3077, no. 203035.

[17] The British were rather more serious in discussing the applicability of self-determination to the Arab Middle East with its more advanced population. That subject is not treated here.

L. S. AMERY'S VIEWS ON LONG-TERM POLICY IN RUSSIA, 1918

IN January 1918 Amery wrote that it was 'of vital importance for the future that Germany should not after the war dominate Russia or Turkey in a political, economic or military sense. The domination of Russia will make her all-powerful economically.'[1] By March he had decided: 'In the political or racial sense, we must arrive if possible at clearly marked boundaries between the spheres of British and enemy control', the British minimum being a line from the Mediterranean to the Caspian which would leave most of the Arab and Persian world in the British sphere.[2] Shortly after this he came forward with the argument that the final area of the German sphere would be decided by the war map which, he felt, would at the conclusion of hostilities leave Germany in possession of almost all European Russia and Britain in possession of almost all non-Turkish parts of the Ottoman Empire. He talked vaguely about giving Turkey a new sphere in the Caucasus and Turkestan while at the same time saying that Britain should try to include Trans-Caucasia in her own sphere though this was not an essential interest. He made no mention of the fate of Siberia.[3]

Three months later Amery put forward some more geopolitical musings, this time addressed directly to Lloyd George.[4] The military defeat of Germany, the reconstitution of Russia and even the liberation of the subject nationalities of eastern Europe were desirable and might prove possible of achievement but it was also possible that the war would end in a stalemate in which Germany would hold European Russia except perhaps the Caucasus, together with Siberia as far as a line from the Caspian to the Yenisei or even Lake Baikal. Western Siberia would thus fall to Germany while Japan would assume control in eastern Siberia. Essential British interests would not suffer in this arrangement since the

---

[1] Amery, 'The Turkish and South Russian Problem', 4 Jan. 1918, CAB 21/4.
[2] Memorandum by Amery, 20 Mar. 1918, CAB 25/72.
[3] Memorandum by Amery, 21 Mar. 1918, CAB 25/73.
[4] Amery to Lloyd George, 19 June 1918, Lloyd George MSS. F/2/1/25; the argument is repeated in a memorandum by Amery of 1 Aug. 1918, copy in Milner MSS. 126, Box AF2.

new British position in the Arab world, Persia and Central Asia would safeguard her position in Egypt and India. He concluded that the results of the campaigns of 1919 would decide whether the British must accept such an outcome to the war. At the Imperial War Cabinet in August he reaffirmed that his ideal preference was for Germany to receive a sphere of economic influence in central Europe and the western borderlands of Russia only.[5]

Amery had a mind which was in many ways very doctrinaire and he believed that it was inevitable that the world would be divided into a small number of very large power blocks. He felt fairly certain in his mind of the form which this division would take but Russia was an enigma even to him. Late in August he concluded a letter to Balfour on his favourite topic of geopolitics: 'I have left Russia a blank for the moment. It may become a sphere of its own or it may become largely an annex of one or other of the new greater groupings.'[6] His views on the future of Russia have been relegated to an appendix because from March 1918 onwards they diverged sharply from those of the British leadership whom it was his work to advise. It is certain that, despite the long-standing personal and political ties between the two men, they were unacceptable to Milner.

[5] Amery, *My Political Life*, ii. 162–3. Amery distinguished sharply between annexations by Germany and the acquisition by her of a sphere of economic dominance in central Europe. Cf. his comment in the 'Enemy Affairs' section of *Western and General Report*, XXXII, 5 Sept. 1917, CAB 24/147: 'In Germany the annexationist as against the Middle Europe tendency has no doubt been greatly strengthened by the capture of Riga.'

[6] Amery to Balfour, 22 Aug. 1918, Balfour MSS., B.M. Add. 49775.

BIBLIOGRAPHY

I. UNPUBLISHED SOURCES

1. *Records of the Departments of State*

PUBLIC RECORD OFFICE:
Admiralty
Board of Trade
Cabinet Office
Colonial Office
Foreign Office
Treasury (contains records of the National War Aims Committee)
War Office

INDIA OFFICE LIBRARY:
India Office: Political and Secret Department

2. *Papers of Public Figures*

PUBLIC RECORD OFFICE (COLLECTIONS IN THE FOREIGN AND WAR OFFICE FILES):
Balfour MSS.
Bertie MSS.
Robert Cecil MSS.
Drummond MSS.
Grey MSS.
Macdonagh MSS.
Arthur Nicolson MSS.
Reading MSS.
Spring-Rice MSS.

BRITISH MUSEUM:
Balfour MSS.
Robert Cecil MSS.
Egypt 1916–1917: Private Letters between General Sir William Robertson and General Sir Archibald Murray (privately printed, London, 1932), B.M. Add. 52463.
Operations on the Western Front 1916–1918 (The 'Haig Memorandum'), B.M. Add. 52460.
Leila Paget MSS.
Ralph Paget MSS.

C. P. Scott MSS. (Journals and letters)
J. A. Spender MSS.

BEAVERBROOK LIBRARY:
Bonar Law MSS.
Lloyd George MSS.
St. Loe Strachey MSS.

CENTRE FOR MILITARY ARCHIVES, KING'S COLLEGE, UNIVERSITY OF LONDON:
Kiggell MSS.
Robertson MSS.

INDIA OFFICE LIBRARY:
Hamilton Grant MSS.
Montagu-Chelmsford correspondence 1917–1918

HOUSE OF LORDS RECORD OFFICE:
Herbert Samuel MSS.

UNIVERSITY LIBRARY, CAMBRIDGE:
Hardinge MSS.

BODLEIAN LIBRARY, OXFORD:
Milner MSS.

PRIVATE SOURCE:
Arthur Ponsonby MSS.

II. PUBLISHED SOURCES

The published literature on the First World War is enormous and a very great part of it contains material from which the student of war aims and war-time diplomacy can derive benefit, albeit in many cases indirect. This bibliography is, therefore, largely confined to works actually cited in this study. However, a small number of works which, though not so cited, are highly relevant have been included. There is a good recent bibliography of published literature on the military and political history of the war in the book by Paul Guinn cited below. The place of publication is London, Oxford or Cambridge unless otherwise indicated.

1. *Parliamentary Debates: Commons*
Selective use has been made of this source for the period of the war.

2. *The Times*
Likewise, selective use only has been made of *The Times* newspaper.

20

3. *Primary Works* (collections of documents and speeches, official histories, records of personal experience including authorized biographies).

AMERY, L. S., *My Political Life*, vol. ii, 1953.

AMIGUET, P. *Vie du Prince Sixte de Bourbon*, Paris, 1934.

ASQUITH, EARL OF OXFORD and, *'Justice of Our Cause' and 'The Duty of Everyman': Four Speeches*, 1914.

—— *Memories and Reflexions*, 1928.

BALFOUR, A. J., *Chapters in Autobiography*, 1930.

BARNES, G. N., *From Workshop to War Cabinet*, 1924.

The Diary of Lord Bertie of Thame 1914–1918, Lady Algernon Gordon Lennox, ed., 1924.

BLAKE, R., ed., *The Private Papers of Douglas Haig 1914–1919*, 1952.

BRÉMOND, ÉD., *Le Hedjaz dans la Guerre Mondiale*, Paris, 1931.

BUTLER, J. R. M., *Lord Lothian*, 1960.

CALLWELL, C. E., *Field Marshal Sir Henry Wilson: His Life and Diaries*, 1927.

CAMBON, PAUL, *Correspondance*, Henri Cambon, ed., vol. iii, Paris, 1946.

CHURCHILL, RANDOLPH, *Lord Derby: 'King of Lancashire'*, 1959.

COCKERILL, GEORGE, *What Fools We Were*, 1944.

CURZON, G. N., *The War: A Speech Delivered in Harrow Speech Room, 14 October 1914*, no date.

Documents on British Foreign Policy, first series, vol. iv, 1952.

DUGDALE, B. E. C., *Arthur James Balfour*, 1936.

—— *Sir Maurice De Bunsen: Diplomat and Friend*, 1934.

Journals and Letters of Reginald, Viscount Esher, M. V. Brett, ed., vol. iv, 1938.

FIDEL, C., *La Paix Coloniale Française*, Paris, 1918.

GREAT BRITAIN, *Command Papers*: Cd. 8181, Jan. 1916, *State Papers 1916*, XV; Cd. 8271, 1916, *State Papers 1916*, XXXIV; Cd. 8715, 1917, *State Papers 1917–18*, XXIX; Cd. 9034, 1918, *State Papers 1918*, XII.

—— 'Correspondence relative to the Peace Proposals made by His Holiness the Pope to the Belligerent Powers on 1 August 1917. August–October 1917', *British and Foreign State Papers 1917–1918*, CVI, 1921, pp. 575–89.

GREGORY, J. D., *On the Edge of Diplomacy: Rambles and Reflexions 1902–1928*, 1930.

GREY OF FALLODON, VISCOUNT, preface to Gilbert Murray, *The Way Forward*, 1917.

—— *Twenty-Five Years 1892–1916*, People's Library edition, no date.

GWYNNE, S., ed., *The Letters and Friendships of Sir Cecil Spring-Rice*, 1929.

HAMMOND, J. L., *C. P. Scott of the Manchester Guardian*, 1934.
HANCOCK, W. K., *Smuts: the Sanguine Years 1870–1919*, 1962.
—— and VAN DER POEL, J., eds., *Selections from the Smuts Papers* vol. iii, 1966.
HANKEY, LORD, *The Supreme Command*, 1961.
Old Diplomacy: the Reminiscences of Lord Hardinge of Penshurst, 1947.
HENDRICK, B. J., *The Life and Letters of Walter H. Page*, 1922–5.
HERBERT, AUBREY, *Mons, Anzac and Kut*, 1930.
HOWARD, ESMÉ, *Theatre of Life*, 1936.
JONES, THOMAS, *Whitehall Diary: Volume I 1916–1925*, K. Middlemas, ed., 1969.
KELLY, DAVID, *The Ruling Few*, 1952.
KENWORTHY, J. M., *Soldiers, Sailors and Others*, 1933.
LLOYD GEORGE, COUNTESS, *The Years That Are Past*, 1967.
LLOYD GEORGE, DAVID, *Through Terror to Triumph: Speeches and Pronouncements of the Right Honourable David Lloyd George*, 1915.
—— interview in *Pearson's Magazine*, XXXIX, March 1915, pp. 258–67.
—— *War Memoirs*, Odhams Press edition, no date but 1938.
—— *My Memoirs of the Peace Conference*, New Haven, 1939.
LONG, WALTER, *Memories*, 1923.
MALCOLM, IAN, *Lord Balfour: A Memory*, 1930.
—— *Vacant Thrones*, 1931.
MANTEYER, G. DE. See Sixte De Bourbon, Prince.
MARDER, A. J., ed., *Fear God and Dread Nought*, vol. iii, 1959.
NEKLIUDOV, A., *Diplomatic Reminiscences*, 1920.
NEWBOLT, HENRY, *Naval Operations*, vol. v, 1931.
NEWTON, LORD, *Lord Lansdowne: A Biography*, 1929.
—— *Retrospection*, 1941.
NICOLSON, HAROLD, *Sir Arthur Nicolson, Bart.*, 1929.
—— *King George V: His Life and Reign*, 1952.
—— *Peacemaking 1919*, University Paperbacks edition, 1964.
OLIPHANT, LANCELOT, *An Ambassador in Bonds*, 1947.
PERCY, LORD EUSTACE, *Some Memories*, 1958.
POLONSKY, J., *Documents Diplomatiques Secrets Russes 1914–1917*, Paris, 1928.
POUND, R., and HARMSWORTH, G., *Northcliffe*, 1959.
READING, SECOND MARQUESS OF, *Rufus Isaacs: First Marquess of Reading 1914–1935*, 1945.
Journal d'Alexandre Ribot et Correspondances Inédites 1914–1922, Al. Ribot, ed., Paris, 1936.
Lord Riddell's War Diary, 1933.
ROBERTSON, W. R., *From Private to Field Marshal*, 1921.
—— *Soldiers and Statesmen*, 1926.
ROSKILL, STEPHEN, *Hankey: Man of Secrets Vol. I 1877–1918*, 1970.

SAMUEL, VISCOUNT, *Memoirs*, 1945.

SCOTT, J. B., ed., *Official Statements of War Aims and Peace Proposals, December 1916–November 1918*, Washington, 1921.

SEYMOUR, CHARLES, ed., *The Intimate Papers of Colonel House*, 1926–8.

SIXTE DE BOURBON, PRINCE, *L'Offre de Paix Separée de l'Autriche (5 Décembre 1916–12 Octobre 1917)*, Paris, 1920. (This work was published in English as G. De Manteyer, *Austria's Peace Offer*, 1921).

SPENDER, J. A., and ASQUITH, C., *Life of Herbert Henry Asquith, Lord Oxford and Asquith*, 1932.

SPENDER, HAROLD, *The Prime Minister*, 1920.

TABOUIS, GENEVIEVE, *Jules Cambon: Par l'Un des Siens*, Paris, 1938.

TOYNBEE, A. J., *Acquaintances*, 1967.

TREVELYAN, G. M., *Grey of Fallodon*, 1937.

Beatrice Webb's Diaries 1912–1924, Margaret Cole, ed., 1952.

WEMYSS, LADY WESTER, *The Life and Letters of Lord Wester Wemyss*, 1935.

WICKHAM STEED, HENRY, *Through Thirty Years*, 1924.

4. *Secondary Studies*

BONHAM CARTER, VICTOR, *Soldier True: the Life and Times of Field Marshal Sir William Robertson*, 1963.

BRIGGS, M. P., *George D. Herron and the European Settlement*, Stanford, 1932.

CARR, E. H., *Ambassadors at Large: Britain*, 1939.

COLLINS, DOREEN, *Aspects of British Politics 1904–1919*, 1965.

CRUTTWELL, C. R. M. F., *A History of the Great War*, edition of 1936.

DIAMOND, WILLIAM, 'The Economic Thought of Woodrow Wilson' in *The Johns Hopkins University Studies in Historical and Political Sciences*, LXI, Baltimore, 1943.

EKSTEIN FRANKL, MICHAEL G., 'The Development of British War Aims August 1914–March 1915' (University of London, Ph.D. thesis, 1969).

ELLIS, C. H., *The Transcaspian Episode*, 1963.

EMIN, AHMED, *Turkey in the World War*, New Haven, 1930.

EVANS, LAURENCE, *United States Policy and the Partition of Turkey*, Baltimore, 1965.

FISCHER, FRITZ, *Germany's Aims in the First World War*, 1967.

FORSTER, KENT, *The Failures of Peace*, Washington, 1941.

GATZKE, H. W., *Germany's Drive to the West: A Study of Germany's Western War Aims during the First World War*, Baltimore, 1950.

GELFAND, L. E., *The Inquiry: American Preparations for Peace 1917–1919*, New Haven, 1963.

GILBERT, MARTIN, ed., *A Century of Conflict 1850–1950: Essays for A. J. P. Taylor*, 1966.

GOLLIN, A. M., *Proconsul in Politics: A Study of Lord Milner in Opposition and in Power*, 1964.

GORDON, B. K., *New Zealand Becomes a Pacific Power*, Chicago, 1960.

GOTTLIEB, W. W., *Studies in Secret Diplomacy during the First World War*, 1957.

GUINN, PAUL, *British Strategy and Politics 1914 to 1918*, 1965.

HANAK, HARRY, *Great Britain and Austria–Hungary during the First World War: A Study in the Formation of Public Opinion*, 1962.

—— 'The Government, the Foreign Office and Austria–Hungary 1914–1918', *Slavonic and East European Review*, xvii (1969), 161–97.

The History of The Times, vol. iv, Part i, 1952.

HOWARD, H. N., *The Partition of Turkey: A Diplomatic History 1913–1923*, Norman, Oklahoma, 1931.

HYDE, H. MONTGOMERY, *Lord Reading: the Life of Rufus Isaacs, First Marquess of Reading*, 1967.

IKLÉ, F. W., 'Japanese–German Peace Negotiations during World War I', *American Historical Review*, lxxi (1965), 62–76.

JOHNSON, HUMPHREY, *Vatican Diplomacy in the World War*, 1933.

JOHNSON, PAUL BARTON, *Land Fit for Heroes: The Planning of British Reconstruction 1916–1919*, Chicago, 1968.

KEDOURIE, ELIE, *England and the Middle East: the Destruction of the Ottoman Empire 1914–1921*, 1956.

—— 'Cairo and Khartoum on the Arab Question 1915–1918', *Historical Journal*, vii (1964), 280–97.

KOMARNICKI, TITUS, *The Rebirth of the Polish Republic*, 1957.

KURTZ, HAROLD, 'The Lansdowne Letter', *History Today*, xviii (1968), 84–92.

LAUNAY, J. DE, *Secrets Diplomatiques 1914–1918*, Brussels, 1963.

LINK, A. S., *Wilson: Confusions and Crises 1915–16*, Princeton, 1964.

—— *Wilson: Campaigns for Progressivism and Peace 1916–1917*, Princeton, 1965.

The Listener, 9 June–14 July 1966. A series of six articles on attempts to end the First World War by negotiation, Robert Blake, ed.

LOGIO, G. C., *Bulgaria: Problems and Politics*, 1919.

LOUIS, W. R., *Great Britain and Germany's Lost Colonies 1914–1919*, 1967.

MAGNUS, PHILIP, *Kitchener: Portrait of an Imperialist*, Grey Arrow edition, 1961.

MAMATEY, V. S., *The United States and East-Central Europe 1914–1918*, Princeton, 1957.

—— 'The United States and Bulgaria in World War I', *The American Slavic and East European Review*, xii (1953), 236–57.

MARTIN, L. W., *Peace Without Victory*, New Haven, 1958.

MAY, ARTHUR J., *The Passing of the Hapsburg Monarchy*, Philadelphia, 1966.

—— 'Seton-Watson and the Treaty of London', *Journal of Modern History*, xxix (1957), 42–7.

MAY, ERNEST R., *The World War and American Isolation 1914–1917*, Cambridge, Massachusetts, 1959.

MAYER, A. J., *Political Origins of the New Diplomacy 1917–1918*, New Haven, 1959.

McGILL, BARRY, 'Asquith's Predicament 1914–1918', *Journal of Modern History*, xxxix, (1967) 283–303.

McKORMICK, D. G., *Pedlar of Death: Sir Basil Zaharoff and the Armaments Trade*, 1965.

MORGAN, KENNETH O., 'Lloyd George's Premiership: A Study in Prime Ministerial Government', *Historical Journal*, xiii (1970), 130–57.

NELSON, H. I., *Land and Power: British and Allied Policy on Germany's Frontiers 1916–1919*, 1963.

NEVIKIVI, JUKKA, 'Lord Kitchener and the Partition of the Ottoman Empire', *Studies in International History: Essays Presented to W. N. Medlicott*, K. Bourne and D. C. Watt, eds., 1967.

—— *Britain, France and the Arab Middle East 1914–1920*, 1969.

PELLING, H. M., *America and the British Left*, 1956.

PLATT, D. C. M., *Finance, Trade and Politics: British Foreign Policy 1815–1914*, 1968.

RENOUVIN, PIERRE, 'Le Gouvernement Français et les Tentatives de Paix en 1917', *La Revue des Deux Mondes*, 15 October 1964, pp. 492–513.

—— 'Les Buts de Guerre du Gouvernement Français 1914–1918', *Revue Historique*, ccxxv (1966), 1–38.

—— 'L'Opinion Publique et la Guerre en 1917', *Revue d'Histoire Moderne et Contemporaine*, xv (1968), 4 ff.

ROTHWELL, V. H., 'Mesopotamia in British War Aims 1914–1918', *Historical Journal*, xiii (1970), 273–94.

RUDIN, H. R., *A mistice 1918*, New Haven, 1944.

SAMRA, CHATTAR SINGH, *India and Anglo–Soviet Relations 1917–1947*, Bombay, 1959.

SMITH, C. JAY, *The Russian Struggle for Power*, New York, 1956.

—— 'Great Britain and the 1914–15 Straits Agreement with Russia: the British Promise of November 1914', *American Historical Review*, lxx (1965), 1015–34.

SMITH, DANIEL, M., *Robert Lansing and American Neutrality 1914–1917*, Berkeley and Los Angeles, 1958.

STEIN, LEONARD, *The Balfour Declaration*, 1961.

STEINER, ZARA, 'Grey, Hardinge and the Foreign Office 1906–1910', *Historical Journal*, x (1967), 415–40.
—— *The Foreign Office and Foreign Policy 1898–1914*, 1969.
TAYLOR, A. J. P., 'The War Aims of the Allies in the First World War' in *Essays to Namier*, A. J. P. Taylor and R. Pares, eds., 1956.
—— *The Troublemakers*, 1957.
—— Lloyd George centenary article, *Sunday Express*, 20 January 1963.
—— *Politics in Wartime*, 1964.
—— *English History 1914–1945*, 1965.
TRASK, D. F., *The United States in the Supreme War Council: American War Aims and Inter-Allied Strategy 1917–1918*, Middletown, Connecticut, 1961.
TRUMPENER, ULRICH, *Germany and the Ottoman Empire 1914–1918*, Princeton, 1968.
ULLMAN, R. H., *Intervention and War*, Princeton, 1961.
WAVELL, ARCHIBALD, *Allenby*, 1940.
WILSON, TREVOR, *The Downfall of the Liberal Party*, 1966.
WINKLER, H. R., *The League of Nations Movement in Great Britain 1914–1918*, New Brunswick, New Jersey, 1952.
WOLFF, LEON, *In Flanders Fields*, Corgi Books edition, 1966.
WOODWARD, E. L., *Great Britain and the War of 1914–1918*, 1967.
YALE, WILLIAM, 'Ambassador Henry Morgenthau's Special Mission of 1917', *World Politics*, i (1949), 308–20.

INDEX